USAF HISTORICAL STUDIES: NO. 175

THE RUSSIAN AIR FORCE IN THE EYES OF

GERMAN COMMANDERS

by

Generalleutnant a. D. Walter Schwabedissen

USAF HISTORICAL DIVISION
RESEARCH STUDIES INSTITUTE
AIR UNIVERSITY
JUNE 1960

Personal views or opinions expressed or implied in this publication are not to be construed as carrying official sanction of the Department of the Air Force or the Air University.

CONTENTS

		Page
FOREWORD		viii
PREFACE		xiii
ABOUT THE AUTHOR		xiv
AUTHOR'S INTRODUCTION		xv

1. DEVELOPMENT AND APPRAISAL OF RUSSIAN
   AIR POWER PRIOR TO THE RUSSIAN CAMPAIGN . . 1

   I. Development from 1918 to 1933 1

   II. The Period from 1933 to the Opening of the
   Russian Campaign in 1941 7

       A. German Procurement and Interpretation
   of Intelligence Information 8

       B. Soviet Command and Tactical Principles . 12

       C. Organization and Chain of Command . . . 14

       D. Strength and Strategic Concentration . . . 17

       E. Aircraft Types; Weapons; Equipment . . . 20

       F. Training 24

       G. Ground Services and Supplies 27

       H. Air Signal Services 31

   III. Antiaircraft Artillery 32

   IV. Paratroopers and Other Airborne Troops . . . 33

   V. The Air Armament Industry 36

			Page
	VI.	The Armament Industry in General	41
	VII.	Transportation	43
	VIII.	Soviet Air Forces in the Spanish Civil War	45
	IX.	Consolidated Luftwaffe High Command Estimate of the Soviet Air Forces at the Outset of the Russian Campaign	48
2.	THE SOVIET AIR FORCES FROM THE OPENING OF THE RUSSIAN CAMPAIGN TO THE END OF 1941		52
	I.	General Review	52
	II.	Reconnaissance Units	74
	III.	The Fighter Arm	81
	IV.	The Ground-Attack Arm in 1941	107
	V.	The Bomber Arm in 1941	124
	VI.	Special Air Operations	145
	VII.	Ground Service Organization; Air Force Technology; Supply System in 1941	148
	VIII.	Air Signal Services	153
	IX.	Training	155
	X.	Parachute and Other Airborne Troops	155
	XI.	Air Armament Industry; Military Economy; Transportation	157
	XII.	Support from the Western Allies	158
	XIII.	Summary	159
3.	THE RUSSIAN AIR FORCE IN 1942 AND 1943		162

		Page
I.	General	162
II.	Reconnaissance	182
III.	Fighter Aviation	190
IV.	The Ground-Attack Air Arm in 1942 and 1943	213
V.	Bombardment Aviation	229
VI.	Other Flying Operations	248
VII.	Air Force Ground Organization; Technological Development; and Supply Services	251
VIII.	Air Force Signal Communications	254
IX.	Training	256
X.	Paratroops and Airborne Forces	257
XI.	Aircraft Production, Armament Industry, and Communications Network	259
XII.	Allied Assistance	260
XIII.	Conclusions	261

4. THE RUSSIAN AIR FORCE ACHIEVES AIR SUPERIORITY 265

I.	The Course of the Air War in 1944-45	265
II.	Command and Operations	273
III.	Organization and Chain of Command	274
IV.	Strength and Distribution	275
V.	Aircraft Types, Weapons, Other Equipment	276
VI.	The Reconnaissance Arm	279
VII.	The Fighter Arm	298

		Page
VIII.	The Soviet Ground-Attack Air Arm in 1944-45.	332
IX.	Soviet Bomber Forces	348
X.	Special Air Missions	367
XI.	The Ground Service Organization of the Soviet Air Forces; Soviet Air Force Technology; the Supply Services	369
XII.	Air Signal Communications	374
XIII.	Training Activities	377
XIV.	Airborne Forces	379
XV.	Air Armament Industry, Military Economy, and Transportation	381
XVI.	Allied Support	383
XVII.	Summary	386
	Conclusion	389
FOOTNOTES		391
APPENDICES		431
1.	List of Equivalent Luftwaffe and USAF General Officer Ranks	431
2.	List of GAF Monograph Project Studies	432

Charts

		Facing Page
1.	Peacetime Control and Organization of Red Army Air Force Units in a Military Area Command	16
2.	Table of Organization, Air Division--Composite	18
3.	Presumed Wartime Organization of Soviet Army Air Forces	20
4.	Top-Level Organization of the Russian Air Force, Summer 1943	174
5.	Organization of a Russian Air Army, Summer 1943	176
6.	Soviet Fighter Regiment Headquarters Staff, 1 July 1944	304

Map

A German sketch showing the direction of the German air attacks in Russia and the operational areas assigned to the air fleets and the air corps 52

FOREWORD

<u>The Russian Air Force in the Eyes of German Commanders</u> by Generalleutnant a. D. Walter Schwabedissen, is one of a series of historical studies written by, or based on information supplied by, former key officers of the German Air Force for the United States Air Force Historical Division.

The overall purpose of the series is threefold: 1) To provide the United States Air Force with a comprehensive and, insofar as possible, authoritative history of a major air force which suffered defeat in World War II; 2) to provide a history of that air force as prepared by many of its principal and responsible leaders; 3) to provide a firsthand account of that air force's unique combat in a major war with the forces of the Soviet Union. This series of studies therefore covers in large part virtually all phases of the Luftwaffe's operations and organization, from its camouflaged origin in the Reichswehr, during the period of secret German rearmament following World War I, through its participation in the Spanish Civil War and its massive operations and final defeat in World War II.

The German Air Force Historical Project, (referred to hereinafter by its shorter and current title, "The GAF Monograph Project") has generated this and other especially prepared volumes which comprise, in one form or another, a total of nearly fifty separate studies, some of them in multi-volume form. The project, patterned, in part, after an Army program already in existence, was, upon recommendation of Headquarters Air University late in 1952, approved and funded by Headquarters USAF in early 1953. General supervision was assigned to the USAF Historical Division by Headquarters USAF, which continued principal funding of the project through 30 June 1958. Within the USAF Historical Division Dr. Albert F. Simpson and Mr. Joseph W. Angell, Jr., respectively, Chief and Assistant Chief of the Division, exercised over-all supervision of the project. The first steps towards its initiation were taken in the fall of 1952 following a staff visit by Mr. Angell to the Historical Division, Headquarters United States Army, Europe at Karlsruhe, Germany. There, the Army, as has been mentioned, was conducting a somewhat similar historical project covering matters and operations largely of primary interest to that service. Whereas the Army's project had produced or was producing a multiplicity of studies of varying length and significance (more than

2,000 have been prepared by the Army project thus far), it was early decided that the Air Force should request a radically smaller number (less than fifty) which should be very carefully planned initially and rather closely integrated. Thirteen narrative histories of GAF combat operations, by theater areas, and 27 monographic studies dealing with areas of particular interest to the United States Air Force were recommended to and approved by Headquarters USAF in the initial project proposal of late 1952. (A list of the histories and studies appears at the end of this volume.)

By early 1953 the actual work of preparing the studies was begun. Colonel Wendell A. Hammer was assigned as Project Officer, with duty station at the USAREUR Historical Division in Karlsruhe. General der Flieger a.D. Paul Deichmann was appointed and served continuously as Control Officer for the German phase of the project; he also had duty station at the USAREUR Historical Division. Generalleutnant a.D. Hermann Plocher served as Assistant Control Officer until his recall to duty with the new German Air Force in the spring of 1957. These two widely experienced and high-ranking officers of the former Luftwaffe secured as principal authors, or "topic leaders," former officers of the Luftwaffe, each of whom, by virtue of his experience in World War II, was especially qualified to write on one of the thirty-nine topics approved for study. These "topic leaders" were, in turn, assisted by "home workers"--for the most part former general and field-grade officers with either specialized operational or technical experience. The contributions of these "home workers," then, form the basic material of most of the studies. In writing his narrative, the "topic leader" has put these contributions into their proper perspective. The Project Editor, Mr. Edwin P. Kennedy, Jr., and Dr. Albert F. Simpson, Chief, USAF Historical Division, have, when necessary, indicated the relationship of the particular subject matter of each study to the other studies included in the project.

These studies find their principal authority in their authors' personal knowledge and experience. Thus, these studies are neither unbiased nor are they "histories" in the ordinary sense of that word. Instead, they constitute a vital part of the story without which the final history of Germany's role in World War II cannot be written.

In preparing these studies, however, the authors have not depended on their memories alone. Instead, they have supplemented their knowledge with a collection of Luftwaffe documents which has come to be known as the Karlsruhe Document Collection and which is now housed in the Archives Branch of the USAF Historical Division. This collection consists of directives, situation reports, war diaries, personal diaries, strength reports, minutes of meetings, aerial photographs, and various other materials derived, chiefly, from three sources: the Captured German Documents Section of The Adjutant General in Alexandria, Virginia; the Air Ministry in London; and private German collections donated to the project by its participating authors and contributors. In addition, the collection includes the contributions of the "home workers." Thus, the interested researcher can test the conclusions of the "topic leaders" against the basic documents or secure additional information on most of the subjects mentioned in the studies.

The authors have also made use of such materials as the records of the Nuremberg Trials, the manuscripts prepared by the Foreign Military Studies Branch of the USAREUR Historical Division, the official military histories of the United States and the United Kingdom, and the wealth of literature concerning World War II, both in German and English, which has appeared in book form or in military journals since 1945.

The complexity of the GAF Monograph Project and the variety of participation which it has required can easily be deduced from the acknowledgments which follow. On the German side: General der Flieger a.D. Paul Deichmann, who, as Chief Control Officer, became the moving force behind the entire project; Generalleutnant Josef Kammhuber, who heads the new German Air Force, and who has consistently supported the project; Generaloberst a.D. Franz Halder, Chief of the German Army General Staff from 1938 to 1942, whose sympathetic assistance to the Project Officer, the Project Editor, and the German Control Group is greatly appreciated; Generalfeldmarschall a.D. Albert Kesselring, who contributed to several of the studies and who also, because of his prestige and popularity in German military circles, was able to encourage many others to contribute to the project; and all of the German "topic leaders" and "home workers" who are too numerous to mention here, but whose names can be found in the prefaces and footnotes to the individual studies.

In Germany, Col. Wendell A. Hammer, USAF, served as Project Officer from early in 1953 until June, 1957. Colonel

Hammer's considerable diplomatic and administrative skills helped greatly towards assuring the project's success. Col. William S. Nye, USA, was Chief of the USAREUR Historical Division at the project's inception. His strong support provided an enviable example of interservice cooperation and set the pattern which his several successors followed.

In England, Mr. L. A. Jackets, formerly Chief of Air Historical Branch No. 6 of the British Air Ministry and now Librarian, Air Ministry, gave invaluable assistance with captured Luftwaffe documents.

At the Air University, Maxwell Air Force Base, Alabama, a number of people, both military and civilian, have given strong and expert support to the project. Lt. Gen. Idwal H. Edwards, a former Commander of the Air University, initiated correspondence with Maj. Gen. Orlando Ward, USA, which resulted in a Department of the Army letter outlining the respective USAF-Army responsibilities for the project's execution. General Edward's interest in the project and its goals was matched by the assistance given by his successors: General Laurence S. Kuter, Lt. Gen. Dean C. Strother and Lt. Gen. Walter E. Todd.

Other personnel at Headquarters Air University who have given freely of their time and experience include: Col. Garth C. Cobb, formerly Director of the Research Studies Institute; Dr. James C. Shelburne, Educational Advisor to the Commander; Mr. J. S. Vann, Chief of Special Projects Branch, DCS/Operations; and Mr. Arthur F. Irwin, Chief, Budget Division, DCS/Comptroller.

The project is grateful to Col. Fred W. Miller, USAF Air Attache to Germany, and the Assistant Air Attache, Lt. Col. Leonard C. Hoffmann, both of whom gave indispensable aid during the project's last year in Germany. Also in Germany, Mr. Joseph P. Tustin, the Historian of Headquarters, United States Air Forces in Europe, has ably assisted the project by solving a variety of logistical and administrative problems.

This study was translated by Mr. Helmut Heitman and Mr. George E. Blau, both of whom deserve special thanks for their skillful contribution.

The editors are especially conscious of their debt to Miss Sara E. Venable for her typing of the final draft.

Above all, the project is indebted to all of the members of the USAREUR Historical Division, the Office of the Chief of Military History, and the USAF Historical Division who, through direct assistance and advice, helped the project to achieve its goals.

Dr. Albert F. Simpson, Chief, USAF Historical Division, and Mr. Edwin P. Kennedy, Jr., the Project Editor, collaborated in the final editing of this study. To assure the technical accuracy of the translation, Mr. Kennedy compared the entire text with the original German manuscript. The stylistic peculiarities of the author, when they did not lend themselves to idiomatic English, were left in literal translation.

PREFACE

In World War II the Russian Air Force came of age. The men most vitally concerned with this, aside from the Russians themselves, were commanders in the German armed forces. The experience of these commanders, then, constitutes a unique source for information on an organization whose capabilities, both past and future, are of vital concern to the world.

German experience with the Russian Air Force has been both lengthy and intimate. It began in the early 1920's, when German flying officers, technicians, and engineers were sent to Russia to do work which the terms of the Versailles Treaty prevented their doing at home. From this early, rather uneasy association, the Russians gained valuable knowledge of German aircraft industrial techniques while the Germans acquired base facilities for tactical flying training of a select cadre of German officers.

The chief German experience with the Russian Air Force, however, derives from World War II. It was during this period that the Russians learned most from the Germans and the Germans learned most about the Russians. Although they almost ignored strategic air warfare, the Russians quickly followed the German example in other types of air operations and demonstrated a remarkable ability to adapt German tactics and procedures to the peculiar demands of their own circumstances. They also gave ample evidence of an ability to improvise and invent procedures and tactics of their own.

This study exploits this broad German experience. Compiled from the official records of the German Air Force and from reports written by German commanders who saw action in the Russian campaign, it documents many of the Russian Air Force's achievements as well as its failures. Although it is an abridgement of General Schwabedissen's original manuscript, every effort has been made to preserve what General Schwabedissen has to say and his way of saying it.

ABOUT THE AUTHOR

Both by training and experience Generalleutnant a. D. Walter Schwabedissen is well qualified to write the present study. Although he saw service in both World Wars as an air force officer, he is a member of that elite group of German Army General Staff officers which was transferred to the German Air Force in 1933, at the time the Air Force became an independent arm of the Armed Forces. Thus, General Schwabedissen is well schooled in the principles of both ground and air warfare, a necessity for anyone who writes about the Russian campaign where the latter was so dependent on the former.

Among his assignments prior to World War II were two years with the Training Branch of the Air Ministry, a year at the War Academy (Kriegsakademie) followed by two one-year assignments during which he successively commanded two different Luftwaffe Area Commands.

At the beginning of World War II General Schwabedissen commanded an antiaircraft artillery corps, after which he became Commander in Chief of all German Armed Forces in the Netherlands. Late in 1944 General Schwabedissen became Chief of the Activation Staff of the Hungarian Air Force, an assignment which gave him firsthand experience with the Russian Air Force during the closing phase of the war, when its strength had reached impressive proportions. He served in this capacity until the capitulation.

AUTHOR'S INTRODUCTION

For a proper understanding of the impression which German army, naval, and air force commanders had of the Russian air forces in the 1941-45 Russian campaign, it is first essential to obtain a clear picture of the status of the Russian air forces prior to World War II. An important part of this picture is the pre-war assessment of the Russian air forces by the German Command. It was this assessment which influenced the operational plans of the German Armed Forces, particularly of the Luftwaffe, and therefore governed the measures taken by German field commanders. An effort will be made in Chapter 1 to ascertain whether and to what extent the actual status of the Russian air forces deviated from the views held by the German Command.

The German Command, at the opening of the Russian Campaign, based its assessment of the Russian air forces primarily on the "Orientierungsheft Union der Sozialistischen Sowjetrepubliken (UdSSR)," which will be referred to in this study as the Intelligence Digest on Soviet Russia. This document was issued in February 1941 by Section IV of the Luftwaffe Intelligence Division. In preparing Chapter 1 the author has made use of this document and other military sources, of statements made by various German personalities who have occupied themselves with the problems involved, and of the writings of foreign observers. It must be borne in mind, however, that the latter sources are based in part on post-war information which was not available to the German Command at the opening of the campaign in 1941.

In the chapters which then follow an attempt is made to portray the Russian air forces as commanders in the three branches of the German armed forces saw them during the campaign. These chapters are based largely on numerous contributions by officers who served in the field. Their frequently diverging views are explained by the different time periods and front areas in which they gained their experience.

The author has also extended his research to after-action reports as well as documents of the Luftwaffe High Command, which represent a condensation of reports and information received at the time from field commanders. Here it must be borne in mind that from the moment German retrograde movements set in,

German field commanders were rarely able to obtain personal impressions of certain segments of Russian air power, such as the supply services, the ground service organization, and the air armament industry. Making allowances for these limitations, the present study can be considered a true presentation of the assessment by German commanders of Russian air power during the campaign.

Chapter 1

DEVELOPMENT AND APPRAISAL OF RUSSIAN AIR POWER PRIOR TO THE RUSSIAN CAMPAIGN

Section I: <u>Development from 1918 to 1933</u>[1]

As organic elements of the Army and Navy, Russian air units in World War I achieved no significant and independent development. Apart from their large 4-engine Sikorski model, constructed in 1914, and a remarkable achievement at that early date, the Russian air forces of 1914-18 were largely dependent on Allied support, their units being equipped primarily with French and British fighter aircraft. In the 1915-17 period the Russian aircraft industry produced approximately 1,500 to 2,000 aircraft annually.

At the commencement of the revolution in 1917 about 500 obsolete aircraft were available, most of them French models, and only two aircraft factories were in existence. No aircraft at all were produced in Russia from 1918 to 1920. The Bolshevist Revolution, civil war, and the war with Poland resulted in such complete destruction of the Russian air forces that it became necessary in the early twenties to create an entirely new air force.

Lenin, and later Stalin, clearly realized the necessity to create a strong air force and energetically tackled the difficult problem. Neither in the military nor in the technical or industrial fields was the Soviet Union in any position to develop a new air force with its own resources. Help had to be sought abroad, partly through purchasing foreign aircraft, but in a greater measure through engaging foreign military and technical experts.

In the military field the good Russo-German relations in the 1920's provided the essential conditions for this assistance.[2] Russian air officers were given careful training in the general staff courses conducted by the Reichs Ministry of Defense in Berlin, and in 1924 an aviation training school was established at the Russian airfield of Lipetsk--approximately 150 miles south of Moscow--for officers of the German Reichswehr,* as Germany's post-World War 100,000-man national defense establishment was called. The experience gained by

---

* Editor's note: The Reichswehr was the German national defense establishment under the terms of the Treaty of Versailles of 1919.

the German officers and the operational and training principles developed for the Luftwaffe were made available to the air forces of the Soviet Union.*

It is thus not surprising that most German views on the employment of air power were adopted by the Russians. The general view of the Reichswehr at that time was that air power must be auxiliary to the Army and the Navy. Although carefully studied, the theories of Douhet† and Rougeron†† had not yet been accepted. Consonant with German views, the new Russian Air Force was developed as an auxiliary of the Army and the Navy, so that main emphasis was placed on the establishment of fighter, reconnaissance, and light bomber units. Whereas the Luftwaffe later became an independent branch of the armed forces with far-reaching missions of its own, the Soviet air forces remained essentially an auxiliary of the Army and the Navy.

Foreign influences, however, were far more potent in the technical fields than in the military. Here again Germany initially took first place. In 1923, as a result of Russia's special interest in the construction of metal aircraft, the firm of Junkers, Dessau, established a branch factory** for

---
* The author was acquainted with Soviet AF officers Alksnis, Heinemann, and others while these officers were receiving training in the Reichs Ministry of Defense. He furthermore had the opportunity to acquaint himself with the training and experimental activities at Lipetsk during two extensive visits.

† Editor's Note: Giulio Douhet (1869-1930), Italian general and early exponent of strategic warfare.

†† Editor's Note: The author is possibly in error concerning Camille Rougeron, whose best known work, L'Aviation de Bombardement, Editions Berger-Levrault (Nancy-Paris-Strasbourg), echoes many of Douhet's ideas. This book was not published until circa 1936 and two years later appeared in a German translation (Das Bombenflugwesen, Rowohlt (Berlin, 1938)), thus much later than the period under consideration here.

** Editor's Note: This factory marked a turning point in the career of Hugo Junkers (1859-1935), the German aircraft manufacturer and inventor. With the secret assurance that he would be reimbursed from confidential Reichswehr funds, Junkers financed the construction of the Fili plant. According to the accounts cited below, he was never repaid. The ensuing financial loss was the first of a series, which saw Junkers slowly divested of all his holdings. For the details of this and other intrigues of which Junkers was the victim, see: Hauptmann Hermann, The Luftwaffe, Its Rise and Fall, G. P. Putnam & Sons (New York, 1943) and Curt Reiss, "Die Junkers Tragoedie," Muenchner Illustrierte, July and August, 1955 (copy in C/III/4, Karlsruhe Document Collection).

the construction of all-metal aircraft at Fili, on the outskirts of Moscow. There, fuselages and, on a smaller scale, Jumo-L-5 engines were manufactured. The factory was under German management and employed German engineers, designers, master craftsmen, and foremen, and it was here that Russian engineers and skilled workers received their training.[3] In addition to repairing existing Junkers aircraft of the F-13, W-33, and A-20 types, the factory engaged primarily in the construction of Junkers 21 aircraft, a high-wing cantilevered monoplane powered by a Jumo-L-5 engine. The plane, intended as a multi-purpose model, was placed in serial production and introduced as standard equipment for Soviet air units. Approximately 100 of these aircraft were produced by the end of 1925. Other types produced, but not in series, were the Ju-22, an all-metal high-wing single-seater fighter, and the K-30, a 3-engine bomber. When this stage was reached the Russians thought that they had learned enough and commenced producing independently, so that the 25-year contract with Junkers came to an early end in 1927. The factory at Fili was taken over by the Soviets as their twenty-second aircraft factory.

Through their collaboration with Junkers, the Russians acquired an exemplary system of metal construction and material testing, and an excellently equipped engine construction workshop. Furthermore, large numbers of Russian engineers, designers, technicians, draftsmen and other skilled workers received training under the contract.

In the field of practical science the Soviets also profited greatly from the close collaboration of German specialists with the Central Institute of the Soviet Air Forces which will be referred to in this study as the ZAGI.* The institute was under the direction of Professor Tupolev,† who later became famous for his aircraft designs. A special role was played in this collaboration by Professor of Aerodynamics Guenther Bock, who was taken by the Russians to the Soviet Union after World War II, has since returned to Germany and is presently on the staff of the Technische Hochschule at Darmstadt.

---

* Editor's Note: Sometimes called the "Central Aero Hydrodynamics Institute," the ZAGI was founded in 1918.
† Editor's Note: A.N. Tupolev (1888-   ), credited with having designed the Russian version of the B-29 as well as the famous Tu series of jet propelled transports which have been used by Russian civil aviation since 1956.

In retrospect there can thus be no doubt that the relatively quick progress made by the Russians, despite serious difficulties in the initial years, was due primarily to assistance from German military and technical personnel.

Compared with German influences on the development of Soviet air power, those of other foreign countries, during the first few years, were small. They remained more or less restricted to the purchase of Italian, French, British, and Dutch aircraft and later to the copying of foreign fuselages and engines. Italy and Britain played a not inconsiderable role, Italy with its Combat twin-engine /Komtal/ bomber--powered by Fiat engines, and Britain with its De Haviland 9a, and with Bristol, and Napier engines. It must be remembered that in these early years Soviet air units were equipped almost exclusively with foreign fuselages and, more particularly, with foreign aircraft engines.

While drawing extensively on foreign assistance in the development of its air force, the Soviet Union made strenuous efforts to make itself independent of this assistance. A number of steps were taken toward this goal. The first and most important of these was the creation of an efficient aircraft manufacturing industry. The program was logical and determined, particular stress being placed on the establishment of factories for the production of fuselages, aircraft engines, and accessories. In addition to the ZAGI previously referred to, a Central Directorate of the Soviet Air Forces was established in Moscow to direct the program. The ZAGI was assigned responsibility for all technological and construction measures adopted in connection with air armament.

The program was given added impetus by the First Five-Year Plan (1928-1932). In 1930 management of the air armament program was decentralized. Separate directorates were established for military and civil aviation and the overburdened ZAGI was relieved of some of its responsibilities through the establishment of a separate institute for aircraft engines (ZAMI), and another for conducting research on materials (VIAM). Most of the factories of the air armament industry at that time were established in European Russia west of the Urals, in the areas around Moscow, Leningrad, and in the Donets Basin. Besides Tupolev, other designers, including Ilyushin, Mikoyan, and Lavochkin* made

---

* Editor's Note: General Sergei V. Ilyushin (1894-   ), best known for the Il-2 (Stormovik) single-engine, low-wing, attack bomber; General Artem Mikoyan who, with General Mikhail Gurevich designed a series of famous planes designated by "Mig" (in WWII the well known Mig-3 single-engine, low-wing fighter); and Semyon A. Lavochkin (1900-   ) whose La-5 was a single-engine, low-wing fighter of WWII.

German personnel of the aircraft plant at Fili, near Moscow, 1925

Interior of the plant at Fili, summer, 1926

their appearance with models of their own, although these were frequently patterned on foreign prototypes.

In spite of all efforts the targets of the first Five Year Plan were not even approached. Thus, an annual output of 600 TB-1 and TB-2 bombers* had been projected, of which barely 50 percent was achieved. In the case of singleseater types--the main field of endeavor--the discrepancy between projected and actual output was almost if not quite as pronounced. The most serious difficulties encountered were the lack of machine tools, short supplies of aluminum and copper, and the lack of adequate numbers of skilled personnel.

In frequent cases quality was sacrificed for quantity and on the whole the manufacture and assembly of aircraft engines was so far in arrears that at the end of the first Five Year Program most of the first line aircraft were still powered by foreign engines. In addition, Russian fuselages were technically inferior to those of foreign make.

The program was also hampered by the purge of Trotzkyites, which began in 1928.

In spite of all defects and setbacks the Five Year Plan produced one important result: the Soviet air armament industry could be considered largely independent of foreign support. Other results included an increased output from Soviet aircraft factories which managed to produce approximately 2,000 planes annually; initiation of rationalized methods in the aircraft industry; and the discovery of a light metal--Kolchug aluminum--a Russian achievement. The progress thus made was also due in no small measure to the experience gained in the field of knock-proof fuels. In the manufacture of aircraft engines a logical course was being followed: concentration on the production of a small number of efficient types.

Another measure which furthered the development of the Soviet air forces was a program to expedite the training of aviators, ground service, and other specialized personnel. Here the Soviet Government succeeded, through a gigantic propaganda campaign, in arousing an enthusiastic national interest in aviation. A society, "Friends of the

---

* Editor's Note: The TB-1 (A.N.T. 4), a four to five seat medium bomber, was a monoplane powered with two German (B.M.W.) engines. Details on the TB-2 are lacking.

Russian Air Forces," was founded in 1923 and had as many as 1,000,000 enrolled members barely two years later. Generous measures to promote glider aviation on a large scale did much to arouse the enthusiasm of the younger generation and assisted materially in the pre-training of flying and technical personnel. Together with the (in some respects) ruthless methods of labor management of the totalitarian government, the inborn Russian characteristics of tenacity, endurance, frugality, and, particularly, obedience, promoted the speedy development of a solid foundation of suitable personnel. The widespread assumption that the average Russian has little, if indeed any, technical aptitude was soon proved a fallacy. The opposite was found to be true.

Although a long time was still to pass before the Soviet air forces and air armament industry would have an adequate reservoir of skilled labor to draw upon, the early results of the personnel training program certainly cannot be considered unsatisfactory since almost all personnel had to be trained from scratch.

While they were creating a military air force, the Russians took steps to promote civil aviation. The result was the development of a giant civil air transport service. Partly for propaganda purposes, the service used only aircraft of Russian manufacture. However, foreign aircraft were used on the route serviced by the Deruluft, a Russo-German airways company formed in 1921.* Military aviation and the aircraft industry profited to a certain extent from the use of installations of the civilian airlines and from the experience gained in civil aviation.

The stages in the development of Soviet military air power in the 1920-33 period were approximately as follows:

1923: The first squadrons were placed in service.

1928: The strength of the Russian air forces reached approximately 100 squadrons totalling roughly 1,000 aircraft. The units were stationed and trained almost exlusively in western Russia--in

---

* The Russo-German DERULUFT AIRWAYS was probably the first foreign air line in which the Soviets particpated. So far as can be remembered, the aircraft chiefly in use were Junkers F-13 and W-33 during the initial stages. Later these were replaced by the German standard model for air traffic, the Ju-52.

the Leningrad, Moscow, Smolensk, Rostov, Kiev, Sevastopol, and other areas.

1930: Reports showed the existence of 20 brigades with 1,000 first line aircraft and 25 aviation schools of various types.

1933: Strength estimated at 1,500 first line aircraft at the end of the first Five-Year Plan. Annual production approximately 2,000 aircraft.

Russian reticence and secrecy and the immense size of the Russian territories made it extremely difficult for foreigners to gain an adequate picture of the growth of Russian air power. It was properly understood that the development which had taken place was achieved in the face of serious difficulties in the personnel and materiel fields, and that it was achieved at the cost of considerable sacrifices. In addition, individual reports showed that the training standards of flying personnel had made considerable progress. In 1933, for example, a large bomber formation of approximately 80 to 100 aircraft was observed operating in Central Russia. The aircraft flew in good formation and then landed by flights. In the same year it was reported that during a night exercise over Moscow a group-sized bomber force flew over the city by flights without untoward incidents. [4]

An appraisal of the status of Soviet air power in 1933, shortly prior to commencement of the second Five-Year Plan, can thus be summed up generally as follows: thanks to foreign support and its own strenuous efforts, the Soviet Government had succeeded, despite numerous difficulties, in building up a new force from nothing; numerically, this air force already had to be considered a power factor although it had not yet achieved the standards of efficiency common to other major military powers; in addition, the need for outside assistance had been overcome in both the military and technological fields, and the road was open to complete independence.

Section II: <u>The Period from 1933 to the Opening of the Russian Campaign in 1941</u>[5]

Following the pattern of development which had led to the status of its air power in 1933, the Soviet Government, in the following years, continued logically and undeterred on the course it had adopted. Military and technological developments in foreign air forces were watched carefully and ideas were adopted without hesitation. Apparently suitable aircraft models, engines, and appliances were purchased or copied, and foreign consultants were even called in, particularly from the United

States of America. All these measures were, however, of secondary importance.

Main emphasis during this period was on promoting the development of the air forces and achieving the highest possible standards of performance with exclusively Russian ideas and resources. This purpose was served particularly by the second and third Five-Year Plans, in which the air force and the air armament industry were given high priorities. The determining factors here were the words of Stalin: ". . . what the Soviet Union needs for the protection of its economic development and the pursuit of the objectives of its foreign policies is an air force ready at all times for action."

Although numerous changes took place in the tactical principles, organization, and tactical and technological structure of the Soviet air forces in the years which followed--as was also the case in other countries--the fundamental principle, that air power should be auxiliary to the Army and the Navy, was retained almost unchanged. All measures influencing the development of Soviet air power must be considered in this light.

The information on German intelligence media which follows is offered in advance because an objective appraisal of the conclusions arrived at by the Luftwaffe High Command in its assessment of Soviet air power at the opening of the Russian campaign is only possible if the sources available to the Luftwaffe intelligence service and their limitations are first understood.

A. German Procurement and Interpretation of Intelligence Information

It has been mentioned previously that the means and possibilities available to the German Command for procuring intelligence information were seriously restricted because of the way in which Soviet Russia shut out the rest of the world. The situation was further complicated by the deficiencies of the German military intelligence and counterintelligence services. Up to 1935 the German intelligence service was still in its infancy and up to 1938 it had made no serious preparations against Russia.

After conclusion of the Russo-German Treaty of Friendship in the autumn of 1939, the Armed Forces High Command, under instructions from Hitler, issued a decree categorically prohibiting the procurement of intelligence information on the Soviet Union.[6] Since the Russian liaison officer attached to the Luftwaffe gave no replies whatever to inquiries concerning the Soviet air forces, a complete vacuum developed so far as intelligence on Soviet air power was concerned. Intelligence activities were only resumed in mid-1940 after much valuable time had been lost.

Under the German set-up, the procurement of intelligence information on Soviet air power was a responsibility of the Air Section, Counterintelligence Office, Wehrmacht High Command (OKW/Abwehr-Ost). Intelligence interpretation was handled for the Luftwaffe by the Foreign Air Forces Branch, Reichs Air Ministry (Reichsluftministerium/Abteilung Fremde Luftmaechte) and later by the Intelligence Division, Luftwaffe High Command (OKL/Ic). The interpreting agency tabulated its requirements in sequence of their urgency and forwarded them to the Counterintelligence Office, which was alone responsible for the procurement. Collaboration between the two agencies was not always methodical, practical, or without friction. Be that as it may, the Luftwaffe High Command remained essentially dependent upon the success achieved by the Counterintelligence Office, which in general was mediocre, producing only isolated items of information rather than a comprehensive picture.

The various sources of information and the results obtained from them up to the summer of 1941 can be evaluated roughly as follows:

<u>The Russian Press, Including the by no Means Numerous Publications on Aviation.</u>

Only generalizations and no details were published. The processing of press reports therefore produced no important information apart from a few not insignificant items concerning the Russian armament industry in general.

<u>Agents.</u>

Owing to the highly effective counterespionage system in force in Soviet Russia, the employment of agents was almost impossible, so that this source produced no material results.

Information from Russian Emigrants.

Usually the persons in this category completely lacked technical understanding. Their reports were meager and frequently tendentious, and therefore had to be accepted with considerable reservations.

The Attache Service.

The German air attache in Moscow, Lieutenant Colonel Aschenbrenner, had no opportunity to form a precise opinion on the Soviet air forces. Seriously restricted in his movements and under close surveillance at all times, he was generally not admitted to any installations of the Soviet air forces or to establishments of the air armament industry. Due to his efforts, however, in April 1941 members of the Luftwaffe Technical Office visited a number of Soviet air armament factories, including some in the Urals. This tour of inspection admittedly did not make a complete survey of the Soviet air armament industry possible, but it did permit a deep insight into the hitherto unknown and unsuspected capacity of that industry. (It will be necessary later in this study to return to this visit and the conclusions drawn from the information it provided.)

On the whole, the German air attache in Moscow was more impressed by Russian air power than the Luftwaffe High Command. The view held widely during and after the war that the air attache underestimated the efficiency of the Russian air forces and that shortly before the Russian campaign he fully concurred in the opinions expressed in the Intelligence Digest is erroneous. On the contrary, in a brief memorandum Aschenbrenner stated his opinion, which deviated from that contained in the Intelligence Digest. He was thereupon ordered to report personally at headquarters of the Luftwaffe High Command. There the Chief of the Luftwaffe General Staff and the Chief of the Intelligence Division endeavored to convince him of the rightness of their opinion but, as he writes on 3 November 1955, with negative results.

It must be stated here that the Luftwaffe General Staff did not share the opinion of the air attache and, furthermore, that the Commander in Chief of the Luftwaffe repeatedly refused to receive him when he called to make a personal report. In retrospect this must be considered particularly regrettable, since the air attache during his long stay in Soviet Russia had been able to form his own opinions on Soviet air power in spite of the restrictions to which he was subject there. His opinion deserved more attention by the Luftwaffe High Command than it received.

The German air attaches in Japan, Turkey and the other Balkan States, Sweden, Finland, and the United States were also called upon to procure information on Russian air power. The attache in Japan was able to furnish valuable information on the Soviet air forces in the Far East, but the other officers produced only meager results.

Air Photo Reconnaissance.

This was one of the most important mediums for the procurement of information on Soviet airpower. Operating from airfields in Rumania, Hungary, Poland, East Prussia, and Finland, the high altitude planes of the strategic reconnaissance group commanded by Lieutenant Colonel Theodor Rowehl were able to obtain almost complete air photo coverage of the ground service organization of the Russian Air Force and of the fortifications in western Russia. The group also obtained air photos of numerous factories, communication targets, and major cities. Because of the restricted range at which the aircraft could operate, however, it was not possible for them to obtain information either on airfields farther inside European Russia or on industrial installations in the Donets Basin, along the middle reaches of the Volga River, or in the Ural region.

The Radio Intercept Service.

This proved an extremely valuable and highly successful medium for the procurement of information. By painstakingly piecing together the numerous items of information gleaned from intercepted Russian messages, the service secured good results on the strategic concentration, strengths, chains of command, organization, and types of aircraft of the Soviet air forces in the western areas of European Russia. On many an occasion it was due to such information alone that the command was able to decide on the proper employment of air reconnaissance.

B. <u>Soviet Command and Tactical Principles.</u>

The political and military leaders of the Soviet Union adhered steadfastly to the basic concept that the main mission of air power was to render direct support to the Army and the Navy. Accordingly, the air force remained firmly integrated with the Army and the Navy until 1935. Even after 1936, when the air force was uniformly organized and withdrawn from direct control by the Army and Navy and required only to cooperate with these two services, this basic concept remained unchanged.

The creation of heavy bomber units and a strong parachute force led temporarily to the assumption that the Soviet air force would now be required to perform more far-reaching strategic missions, but it soon became evident that these elements of the Soviet air force would also be directed primarily against targets of importance in relation to ground and naval operations. However, this by no means implied a basically defensive policy. On the contrary, the tactical principles, organization, and strategic concentration provided irrefutable evidence of the offensive nature of the Soviet air force.

The knowledge available to the Luftwaffe High Command concerning Soviet tactical air doctrine up to the opening of the Russian campaign can be summarized roughly as follows:

In the light of events in the Russo-Finnish War, training standards seemed low in coordinated action with ground forces, particularly during mobile warfare.

The Luftwaffe High Command expected close cooperation between the Soviet Army and Air Force, with the latter supporting the Army in areas of main effort during combat and assisting the Army in the execution of its mission. Accordingly, the composite air divisions assigned to armies were committed within the clearly defined operational zones of the armies concerned. No development of areas of main effort in the sense of strategic air warfare were recognizable. The command was considered awkward, old-fashioned, and inclined toward stereotype methods in the conduct of operations. In addition, the command appeared to be hampered at times by political party control.

The primary mission of Soviet fighters was to protect their

ground forces and supply routes. Low-level attacks on German troop concentrations, marching columns, and airfields in the near front areas were also to be expected. It was not usual for Soviet fighters to penetrate deeply behind the front lines. According to Soviet regulations, the main mission of fighters was ". . . to keep the air above the Soviet front on the ground free of enemy air forces."[8] For these reasons the commitment of fighter units was largely dependent on ground operations. Fighter units under direct control of the Army High Command were assigned, as the situation required, to assume responsibility for air support in the areas most vulnerable to air attack.

Soviet ground-attack air units were, above all, to cooperate with units of the Army by attacking roads, rail routes, railhead depots, marching columns and troop concentrations. Of special importance were low-level attacks, under fighter escort, in support of armored and motorized ground forces in both attack and retrograde operations.

Also within the scope of army operations, bomber forces were to attack hostile supply movements and installations in the near front areas. The German command did not expect any sizable commitment by the Russians of bomber forces, including long-range bombers, in daylight missions far in the German rear. On the other hand, it was expected that single planes would carry out long-range harassing raids at night and during favorable weather. It was considered probable that such attacks might be extended occasionally into East Prussia and against sea routes to Stettin. The Luftwaffe High Command, however, did not anticipate the Russians employing their long-range bombers in a manner consonant with the principles of strategic air warfare.

Of the Soviet air transport services it was known that a large number of units existed and that they were to be used for carrying parachute and airborne infantry units as well as for other type transport missions. Plans were known to exist for the conversion of the civil air services to perform military supply and transport missions. In view of the defective standards of the civil air services, however, the German Command assumed that this would have only an insignificant effect.

The parachute and airborne infantry arm, organic to the Soviet air forces prior to the war, will be dealt with separately in Section IV.*

---

* See below, p. 33.

Experience in the Russo-Finnish War provided no indications of any properly preplanned employment of air power or of any concentration of effort in the operations of the Soviet air forces.

On the whole, the Luftwaffe High Command accurately assessed the tactical doctrines of the Soviet air force in spite of the difficulties encountered in the procurement of intelligence information. This overall impression is not disturbed by the fact that the German appraisal was inept and even positively faulty in some of its aspects, which will be dealt with later in this study. One factor must not be lost sight of: in estimating the Soviet Command's principles for the conduct of the war, the Luftwaffe High Command was dependent on the opinions of the supreme German command, namely, the Armed Forces High Command, and in the final essence on the personal opinions of Hitler. The Luftwaffe High Command, however, had no possibility of forming a general estimate, and to have done so would have exceeded its responsibilities.

C. Organization and Chain of Command.

The impression prevailing at the Luftwaffe High Command up to 1941 concerning the organization of the Soviet air force was more or less as follows: The Soviet Command held the view that the air force must be considered an auxiliary arm of the Army and the Navy and the organization of the forces was adapted to this view. This was thought to be particularly evident in the top levels of command and in the chains of command.

It would exceed the scope of this study to investigate the various changes made in the organization of the Soviet air force in the 1930's. Such an investigation would also hardly be worthwhile, since the basic concept, as stated above, was retained throughout in spite of modifications in the details.

Certain progressive developments occurred in 1936, however, when the air force was given a little more independence. Until then, the "Air Forces of the Red Worker and Peasant Army" remained integrated with the Army and the Navy. Air operations in coordination with operations of the Army were directed by the commanding officers of the army forces in the various military areas. In cooperation with the Navy, the arrangement was similar.

At higher levels of command, the air units--air divisions or brigades--were usually composite. Although these large units were no longer directly integrated into the Army or Navy after 1936, practically no change occurred in the actual tactical organization and doctrines. A real difference was that from then on most of the large units were organized to include only one specific aircraft type each. It also seemed that some stress was placed on the development of a long-range bomber force, as well as paratroop and airborne infantry units.

In detail, the Luftwaffe High Command had the following information on the organization of the Soviet air forces in the summer of 1941:

Peacetime Organization.

Air forces assigned to the Army were commanded by the "Commander of Air Forces of the Red Workers' and Peasants' Army," who was under the direct control of the Peoples' Commissar for Defense. Tactically, the air units with the Army were controlled by the commander of Army forces in each of the sixteen military areas and two military commissariats, and in the area of the Army of the Far East.

A "Chief of Air Forces," under the command of the Commander of Air Forces of the Red Workers' and Peasants' Army, was attached to each military area headquarters* in an advisory and executive capacity for all matters concerning the air forces. His responsibilities included the handling of administrative, training, personnel and materiel replacement, and ground service organization problems.

The Central Administration of Red Army Air Force units had a status equivalent to that of an air ministry in other countries. It was controlled by the Commander of the Air Forces of the Red Workers' and Peasants' Army and organized into ten branches: Air Forces Inspectorate; Aviation Research Commission; Science and Technology Commission; Administrative Branch; Equipment Branch; Replacement Branch; Supply Branch; Meteorological Branch; Training Branch; and Personnel Branch.

---

* See Figure 1.

The chain of command was similar in the Navy, where the air forces were under the Chief of Naval Air Forces who, in turn, was under the Peoples' Commissar for the Navy. An Administration of Soviet Naval Air Force Units had the same responsibilities as those described above for the Central Administration of Red Army Air Force Units within the Peoples' Commissariat for Defense. The Naval air units were tactically assigned to the individual Naval commands; for administration and training they were controlled by the Chief of Naval Air Units, a member of the staff of the Peoples' Commissar for the Navy.

Finally, the units responsible for border defenses and for the prevention of internal uprisings were organized as Air Forces of the Commissariat of the Interior. They were consolidated in a brigade, the squadrons of which were deployed throughout the Soviet territories.

According to German opinions, the reorganization initiated in April 1939 and still in progress in the summer of 1941 involved decisive changes in the organization and strengths of Soviet air units. One special feature was the apparently gradual disappearance of air corps and air brigades directly integrated with ground service units. Under the new system the air division, either single or composite type,* was the largest unit of the Soviet air forces. Each air division controlled from three to six air regiments and a number of air bases, the latter being units of the ground services. In 1941, thirty-eight air divisions had been identified and a total of 50 was assumed to exist. As a general rule each air regiment contained four squadrons; plans provided for a wartime increase to five squadrons. One hundred and sixty-two air regiments were reported in existence, the majority of them single-type units.

Wartime Organization and Chain of Command.⫲

It was assumed that in the event of war, the air forces would be directed by the Army High Command pursuant to directives from the Peoples' Commissariat for Defense. Presumably army groups would be assigned strategic bomber and fighter divisions, possibly

---

* See Figure 2.
⫲ See Figure 3.

SOVIET AIR FORCES

Peacetime Control and Organization of Red Army Air Force Units in a Military Area Command

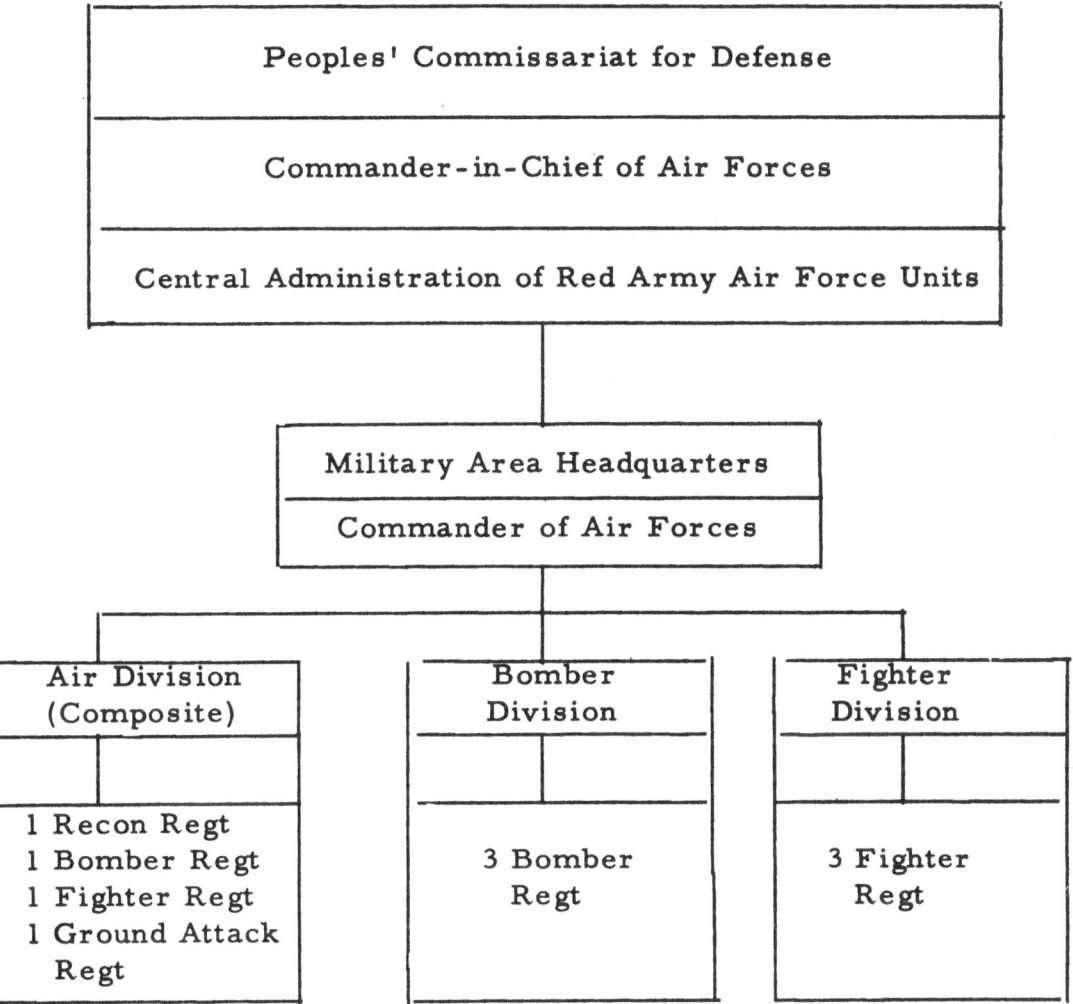

Figure 1

consolidated under air corps headquarters; armies would be assigned composite air divisions; and corps would be given temporary command of light bomber and ground attack air regiments. In addition it was assumed that all of these commands would have reconnaissance aircraft.

Circumstances in the Navy were assumed to be very much the same.

Strategic bomber divisions and one-third of the existing fighter divisions and strategic reconnaissance units were to be used to form a reserve under the Peoples' Commissariat for Defense.

In addition, fighter divisions would remain in rearward military areas, together with antiaircraft artillery forces, for home defense purposes.

D. <u>Strength and Strategic Concentration.</u>

The last estimates of the strengths of the Soviet air forces prior to the outbreak of hostilities were given in the Intelligence Digest on Soviet Russia in the spring of 1941. These were the source for the Luftwaffe High Command's estimate of the strengths of the Soviet air forces at the outset of hostilities.

According to that estimate, 10,500 military aircraft were in field units, 7,500 in European Russia and 3,000 in the Far East.* Approximately 50 percent of all aircraft were thought to be modern types.

---

* Editor's Note: By comparison, in 1939 the Operations Staff of the Luftwaffe High Command estimated the total strength of the Soviet air forces, including Army and Navy, at 5,000 front-line aircraft. Of these, 4,000 were assumed to be in European Russia and 1,000 in the Far East. (Auszug aus Chef des Generalstabes, Nr. 700/39 g.K. (5. Abt. I) 2. Mai 1939 (Extract from Chief of the General Staff No. 700/39, Secret (Branch 5, Operations) 2 May 1939)). Extract in G/VI/2a, Karlsruhe Document Collection.

In detail the figures were as follows:

European Russia	Modern	Outdated	Total
Reconnaissance aircraft	-	620	
Fighters	2,000 (I-16)*	980	
Bombers	2,100 (1,100 SB-2† & SB-3, 1,000 DB-3)††		
Transport & liaison planes		1,800	
	4,100	3,400	7,500
Far East	1,000	2,000	3,000
	5,100	5,400	10,500

Of the above strengths, the 1,800 transport and liaison planes were not considered military types, so that actually only 5,700 combat aircraft were estimated in European Russia. Owing to the high percentage of inoperable aircraft the probable actual effective strength of the Soviet air forces was estimated at only 50 percent of the above figures. It was also estimated that the fighter forces would be increased by about 700 in the first half of 1941, and that some of the existing units would be equipped with approximately 200 to 300 new aircraft of the I-18** type. No appreciable increase in the number of effective bombers was expected, but it was assumed that roughly 50 percent of the existing units would be reequipped with new types of aircraft.

The total number of fully trained aviators was estimated at 15,000, ground service personnel at approximately 150,000, and school and training aircraft at 10,000.

---

*Editor's Note: The I-16 was a single-engine monoplane equipped, like its predecessor, the I-15, with an M-25 (Wright-Cyclone) engine.

†Editor's Note: The SB-2 was a high-performance, twin-engine, mid-wing cantilever monoplane (see below, pp. 142-43).

††Editor's Note: The SB-3 was similar to the SB-2, but was equipped with more powerful engines. The DB-3 was a twin-engine, low-wing, cantiliver monoplane employed as a reconnaissance bomber (see below, pp. 142-43).

** The I-18 (Mig-3 or I-61) was a single-seater, low-wing, cantilever monoplane with a 1,200 horse power engine.

SOVIET AIR FORCES

Table of Organization:

Air Division--Composite

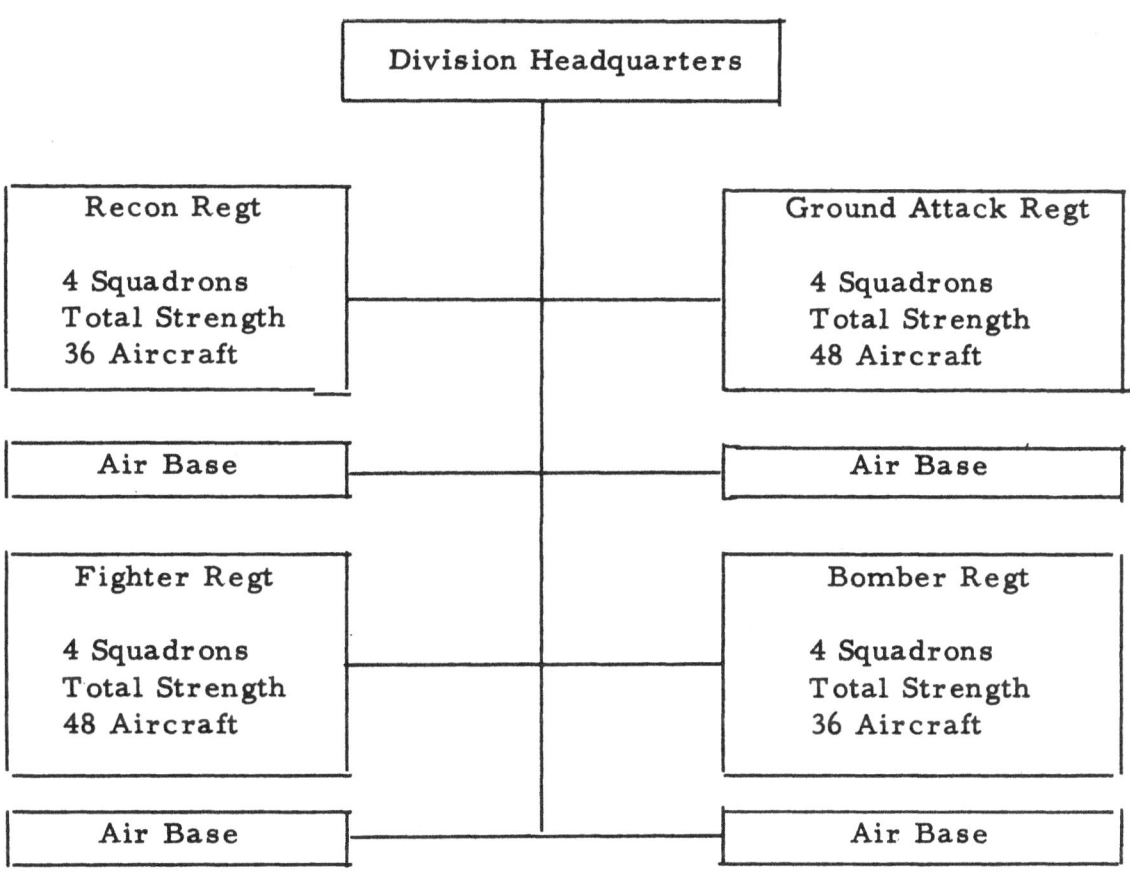

Figure 2

According to the Intelligence Digest, in February 1941 there were 570 bomber and reconnaissance aircraft and 585 fighters in Military Area Leningrad, 315 bombers and reconnaissance aircraft and 315 fighter aircraft in Special Baltic Military Area, 660 bombers and reconnaissance planes and 770 fighter aircraft in Special Military Area West, 460 bomber and reconnaissance aircraft and 625 fighters in Special Military Area Kiev, and altogether 395 bombers and reconnaissance aircraft and 445 fighters in Military Areas Odessa, Karkhov, and Transcaucasus. In addition 320 bombers and reconnaissance planes and 240 fighter aircraft were in the Moscow and Orel Military Areas as first line reserves. These figures correspond to the previously quoted total strength of 5,700 combat aircraft.*

In another study by the Luftwaffe General Staff in 1941[9] the following main concentrations of air power are reported: 1,296 aircraft in Military Area Kiev, 1,662 in Special Military Area West, and 1,428 in Military Area Leningrad. The disposition of Soviet air forces was considered to be a strategic concentration for offensive operations.

Other sources arrive at different figures. In accordance with opinions held by the Luftwaffe High Command, the figures published by Russia in 1936, giving a total of 4,700 combat aircraft corresponded approximately to the information obtained by the German counterintelligence service. The Handbuch der neuzeitlichen Wehrwissenschaften[10] quotes the strength in mid-March 1938 as 6,000 front line aircraft, 2,000 of them in Siberia and the Far East.

In contrast with the above estimates the German radio intercept service, from an analysis of intercepted messages, arrived at a figure of 13,000 to 14,000 Soviet combat aircraft,[11] a figure which Georg W. Feuchter[12] considers accurate.

The strategic concentration of Soviet air power in western Russia assumed by the German Command and the separate existence of the Far East forces is confirmed by other sources.

It thus emerges that the estimate formed by the Luftwaffe High Command--prior to the Russian campaign--of the main concentrations

---

* See above, p. 18.
╪ (Manual of Modern Military Sciences).

in the disposition of the Soviet air forces was approximately accurate. Concerning the strength of the air forces, however, opinions varied. It was to become evident later that the opinions of the Luftwaffe High Command were inaccurate on this point.

E. Aircraft Types; Weapons; Equipment.

In developing its air forces, the Soviet Command adhered steadfastly to its original policy of restricting itself to standardized construction, and to a small number of aircraft and engine types. For a long time the influences of German industry and American construction licenses remained predominant.

The Intelligence Digest gives the opinions of the Luftwaffe High Command on Soviet aircraft types, weapons, and equipment as follows:

Air regiments.

Previously mentioned these were always monotype--either fighter, or reconnaissance, or ground attack. In strength, the air regiment corresponded approximately to the German air group, and usually had four squadrons. The squadron was the smallest standard unit. The regiment had an authorized strength of 60 aircraft. However, in 1941 fighter and ground-attack regiments had an actual strength of only 48, and bomber and reconnaissance regiments of 36 aircraft. Correspondingly, the actual strength of a squadron was thus 12 or 9 aircraft.

The air reconnaissance forces.

These were organized in air reconnaissance regiments, independent air reconnaissance squadrons and independent long-range reconnaissance squadrons. Both regiments and independent squadrons were assigned to air divisions. They were equipped with types R-5, R-6, RZ, R-10,[*] and in some cases I-16 aircraft. All of these types

---

[*] The R-5 was a two-seat, single-engine biplane. The R-6 was a twin-engine, low-wing monoplane. The RZ was a single-engine biplane (also used as a ground-attack aircraft). The R-10 was the same as the Vultee V-11GB. Built under license by the Russians, this was a single-engine, two/three seat monoplane.

SOVIET AIR FORCES

Presumed Wartime Organization of Soviet Army Air Forces

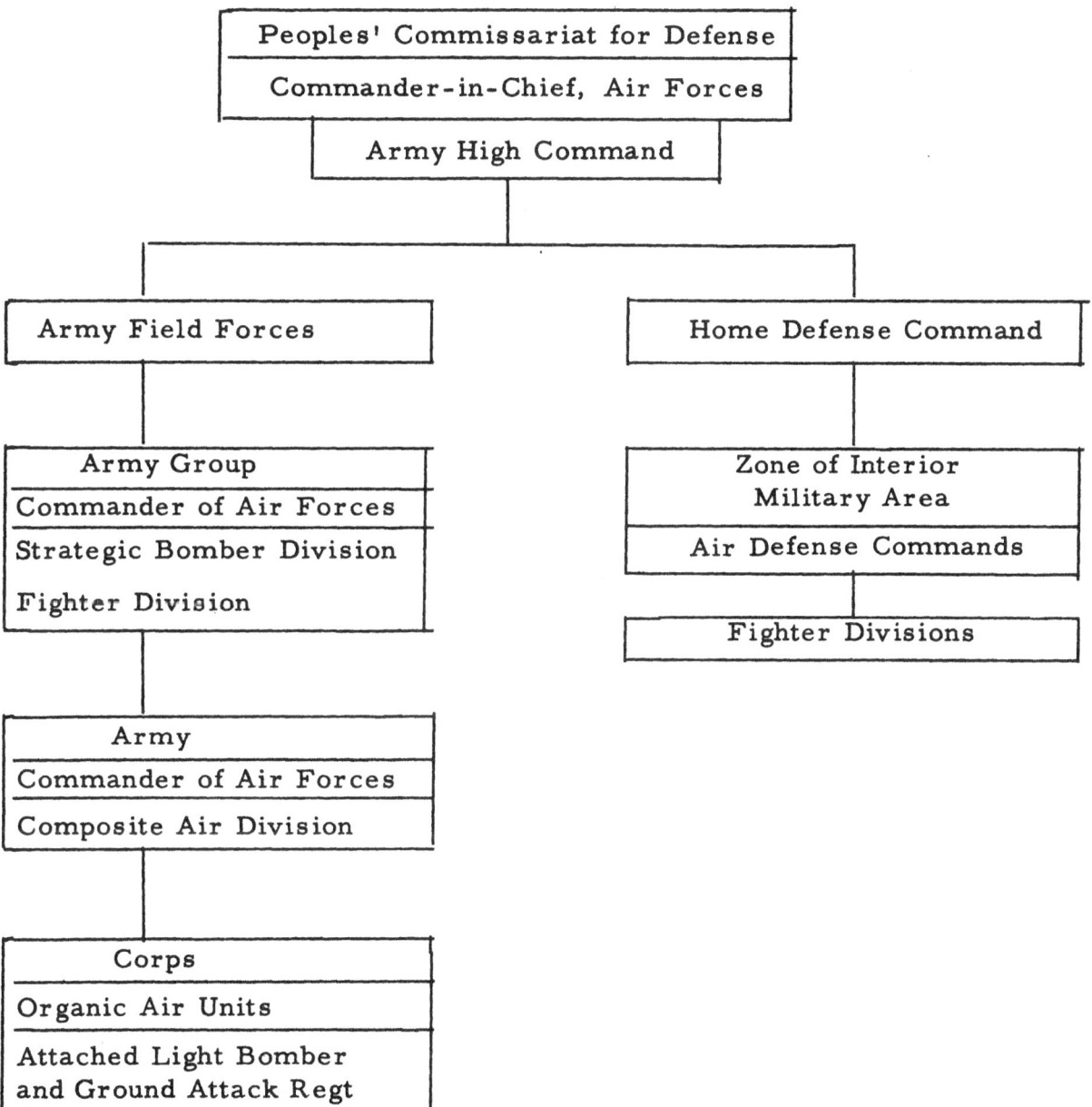

Figure 3

were outdated, with the exception of the R-10 and I-16, of which there were only a small number. In addition to the regiments and independent squadrons assigned to air divisions, there were independent air squadrons which, while they were assigned directly to army corps for close reconnaissance, artillery observation, or liaison missions, were administered, for logistical matters, by an air division.

The fighter forces.

These were organized in regiments, independent squadrons, and independent, long-range fighter squadrons, and as such were assigned to air divisions. The units were equipped generally with Type I-16 (Rata) aircraft and with types I-151 and 153 (modified versions of the I-16). The I-15[*] was considered obsolete. The I-16 was capable of good performance. Although slower than the German fighter aircraft, it was more maneuverable. It was a suitable weapon for attacking German bombers and was superior to them in air combat.

The older models in use, of primitive wooden construction, were inflammable and highly sensitive to gunfire. These disadvantages were less evident in later metal models. In these, the pilot was protected in front by the engine and in the rear by 8-mm armor plating. The planes had no cannon mounted in the engines, but they did have a cannon in each of the wings. The cannons fired normal explosive and solid core ammunition, the machine guns fired phosphorus steel core ammunition. The fire power of these weapons was inferior to those mounted by German planes. Most of the I-16 aircraft had four machine guns mounted in the fuselage, others had a cannon mounted in each wing and two machine guns mounted in the fuselage.

Very little was known of the modern Mig and Lagg types which were arriving at the front as part of a reequipment program, and practically nothing was known about a twin-engine fighter which presumably was still only available in test models.

Bombers.

Organized in fast bomber regiments and long-range bomber

---

[*] A single-seat, gull-winged biplane.

regiments, most of these were consolidated in appropriate air divisions. As a rule fast bomber regiments were equipped with types SB-2 and SB-3 aircraft, long-range bomber regiments with DB-3 aircraft. Some units still had the old TB model. SB-2 and SB-3 types were estimated to have a penetration range of 360 miles with a bomb load of 2,200 pounds; the estimated penetration range of DB-3 bombers was 660 to 720 miles. The SB models were copied from American Martin bombers. Their defensive power was rated low because the guns firing to the rear and upward and downward were served by one gunner who was simultaneously the radio operator. The defensive power of the DB-3 was rated higher. The older TB-3, 5, 6, and 7[*] were inferior to German models in every respect and were suitable as bombers only conditionally and only in night operations. No information was obtainable on a modern twin-engine bomber in serial production.

Ground-attack aircraft.

These were organized in ground-attack air regiments and were assigned to air divisions. The aircraft types in use were RZ, DI-6[†], I-15, and in some units the I-4,[††] all of which were considered obsolete. In addition it was assumed that between 100 and 200 SB-1[**] and Vultee V-11 aircraft, with modern equipment, were in service.

Transport aircraft.

These were organized in what were called heavy air regiments. Nothing definite was known concerning their control. They were used to carry paratroopers and airborne infantry and for transport missions of all types. In general the regiments were equipped with TB-3 aircraft, some with TB-5, 6, and 7, and in smaller numbers with DC-3, copied from the Douglas prototype. The TB-3 and 5 were completely obsolete.

Finally, a small number of ambulance aircraft existed which in wartime were assigned to armies, corps, and divisions. Nothing

---

[*] These were all four-engine, bomber-transports.
[†] A two-seat, single-engine biplane with a Wright (Cyclone) engine.
[††] Probably the same as the DI-4, a two-seat, single-engine biplane.
[**] A twin-engine, mid-wing, cantilever monoplane.

The TB-3, a Russian bomber and transport aircraft.

The TB-7, also a bomber and transport aircraft.

was mentioned as to the type of aircraft employed for this purpose.

The Naval air forces.

Organized in brigades and independent squadrons, these included the coastal patrol squadrons, some of which were equipped with land-based aircraft. Tactically, they were assigned to the various naval commands. In other respects they were controlled by the Chief of Naval Air Forces. The units were equipped with TB-1 /a twin-engine monoplane/ and TB-3 aircraft mounted on floats, seaplanes of the Savoia, Sikorski, Martin, and Consolidated types, and Russian RM-5, Ant-22, and MBR-2 and 5 seaplanes.* The majority of the seaplanes in use were below modern standards in their performances. The Soviet Navy had no aircraft carriers.

Weapons.

The standard weapon for aircraft was the Shkass machine gun with a caliber of 7.62 mm, on a fixed or swivel mount, and with a firing performance of 1,300 to 1,400 rounds per minute. It had been found satisfactory under battle conditions in Spain and China[13] and was known to be mounted in I-16, SB-2, SB-3, and DB-3 aircraft. Some planes also had double-barreled machine guns, but no details are available on aircraft cannon. The machine guns fired steel-core, armor-piercing, explosive, incendiary, smoke and tracer ammunition.

During the Russo-Finnish War a number of bombs used by the Soviet air forces were identified.† The demolition bombs were armed with fuzes that were too sensitive, so that their penetration performances were low. Duds, in contrast, penetrated deeply even in hard ground--110-pound bombs to a depth of approximately 20 feet and 220-pound

---

* The RM-5 was a three-seat, single-engine, reconnaissance flying-boat. The Ant-22 was a twin-hulled, six-engined, commercial flying-boat. The MBR-2 was a single-engine, short-range flying boat. The MBR-5 was probably another short-range, reconnaissance flying boat.

† 110-, 220-, 440-, 550-, and 1,100-pound demolition bombs; 5.5-, 25.3-, and 33-pound fragmentation bombs; 4.4-pound electron incendiaries (120-200 in each container), 5.5-pound thermite incendiaries, and 22- and 110-pound oil bombs with naptha and thermite fillings.

bombs to an approximate depth of 40 feet. The pressure effect varied widely. In bombing from an altitude of 3,000 to 6,000 feet the explosive pressure progressed horizontally, in bombing from altitudes of 16,000 to 20,000 feet the force travelled vertically. Incendiaries were armed with effective fuzes, but were easily extinguished unless coupled with an explosive charge.

Fuel Tank Protection.

This was provided only in I-16 and SB-3 aircraft. It was assumed that the pilot seat was armor protected in all models.

Other Items of Equipment.

These included bomb release devices, navigational, blind-flying, and other panel instruments, air photo, and automatic steering instruments, which were manufactured largely in Russian factories. In most cases they were manufactured under license from foreign firms and were not equal in quality to German instruments. Various types of radio transmitters and receivers were in use as well as radio aiming devices and radio beacon instruments. It was doubted, however, that bomber aircraft other than unit lead planes were equipped with radio transmitters and receivers. To what extent radio aiming devices were in use was unknown.

On the whole the Intelligence Division of the Luftwaffe High Command[14] arrived at the conclusion that most of the first line aircraft in use by the Soviet air forces were obsolete models, and that the Soviet Air Command was making strenuous efforts to reequip all front line units with modern types. It was assumed, however, that the reequipment would proceed slowly in consonance with the general circumstances in the Soviet Union.

Foreign views coincided largely with the German appraisal of the Soviet aircraft types, weapons, and equipment which would probably be encountered at the beginning of the Russian campaign. Thus, the views of the Luftwaffe High Command in these fields were fairly realistic.

F. Training.

The views of the Luftwaffe High Command concerning the

The Russian MBR-2 Flying Boat

Another flying boat, the MBR-5

training status of the Soviet air forces were as follows:

Pre-military training was given in the military association Ossoaviakim. Here, over a period of three years, flying and ground service personnel received their instruction, which included paratroop training. The graduation certificate entitled the holder to enrollment in the air forces. Inadequacy of the training thus received, however, was in evidence by 1941.

Military training was given during three years of active service in the air forces; the period of service was to be extended to four years in the autumn of 1941. The entire training program for aviation and ground service personnel was controlled by the Central Administration of Red Army Air Force Units.

Flight training and advanced training for personnel who had received preliminary training in the Ossoaviakim was given in military aviation schools. Some schools trained pilots exclusively, others also trained air gunners, air observers, and air radio operators. The aircraft types used in training were the U-2, UT-1, UT-2, and in some cases the I-5.*

Ground and technical personnel, apart from those who received training in the Ossoaviakim, were trained in "schools for Junior Avio Specialists," of which there was one in each air division. Special schools existed for the training of engineers and designers.

Training in units appeared to be hampered by fuel shortages and by the inadequate operability of aircraft. Pursuant to the requirements of the Soviet training manuals, special emphasis was placed on formation flight training. Training in formation flying for fighter and bomber pilots was out of proportion to their other training. They gave evidence of good flight discipline and could be employed in daylight missions in good weather. Fighter pilots were also proficient in attacking ground targets. All units exhibited great interest in high-altitude aviation. Although blind and night flying were formal requirements, they were not mastered by the majority of Soviet pilots. Whenever

---

* The U-2 was a single-engine, training and ambulance bi-plane. The UT-1 was a single-seat, low-wing, training monoplane. The UT-2 was a two-seat, low-wing, training monoplane. The I-5 was a single-seat biplane, originally intended as a fighter.

possible, the assignment of night and bad weather missions was avoided. The known results of bombing tests were not impressive, and apparently only some of the bomber units were trained in cooperation with fighter forces. In like manner, the standards achieved in cooperation with ground forces, a subject considered particularly important, left much to be desired.

Although in 1941 the training status of the Soviet air forces was estimated to be considerably lower than that of the Luftwaffe, it was still assessed as good. In addition to being inadequately skilled in night and blind flying, it was believed that individual aircraft crews could be employed only conditionally in independent missions, since they had lost the faculty for independent thought and action because of excessive training in formation flying. Training for daytime operations during fair weather, however, was considered adequate.

The views of foreign observers and later German experience serve to substantiate and complete the above picture. Asher Lee, writing after the war of the prewar training status of the Soviet air forces states that[15] the Soviet air command fully realized the importance of aviation training. This was why pre-military training commenced as early as in the colleges and continued in the Ossoaviakim, which established hundreds of aero clubs. After one year of theoretical instruction in night, week-end, and holiday courses, pilots received their initial practical training in type U-2 aircraft. The first solo flight took place after 25 to 30 hours of flight training. Then followed approximately 20 hours of flight at an airfield and one or two parachute jumps. By the end of 1940 the clubs had almost achieved their target of 100,000 trained pilots. Thereby they created the conditions which made possible the surprisingly rapid replacement of the heavy losses in pilots in 1941.

The training of pilots in the military aviation schools took two years. The first three months were taken up exclusively with infantry training and theoretical instruction in aviation. This phase was followed by practical training with U-2, later with UT-2 aircraft. After a total of 12-15 months of training the decision was made whether the candidate was to be enrolled as a fighter, bomber, or other pilot, or transferred to the ground services.

After two years of basic training, 50 percent of all pilot

Improvised transport of wounded with a U-2

UT-2 trainers in flight

trainees were transferred to fighter pilot schools, where they were trained in courses lasting 6-9 months with UT, I-5, I-7, and in some cases I-15 aircraft. Tactical flight and formation flight were the weak points of Soviet fighter pilots, whereas their general flying proficiency and their performances in air and air-ground combat were considered good. The training principles were judged sound, considered, and effective.

Bomber pilots, and particularly observers, were very carefully trained, and candidates were selected with meticulous care. The training course for bomber pilots lasted 12 months, during which time main emphasis was placed on smooth cooperation between crew members. Training for ground attack pilots was less thorough and lasted only three months.

The training of reconnaissance pilots was badly neglected. No special schools existed for training in this area. It is hard to find an explanation for this in view of the fact that the main mission of the Soviet air forces was to support the Army and the Navy.

Special schools existed, such as the Air Warfare Academy--where air force general staff officers received training--a chemical school, an air forces medical school, and an air transportation school. In addition institutions existed in which women received technical training and in some cases were trained as transport aircraft pilots.

Although the views of the Luftwaffe Command thus deviated very little from these postwar views of Asher Lee, it must be admitted that the German Command failed to realize and understand fully the scope and effectiveness of the pre-military training in aviation given in the Soviet Union.

G. Ground Services and Supplies.

The information available to the Luftwaffe High Command concerning the ground services and supply organization of the Soviet air forces at the outset of the Russian campaign in 1941 was approximately as follows:[16]

The ground services were controlled by the Central Administration of Red Army Air Force Units within the Peoples' Commissariat for Defense, at lower levels by air divisions. Ground service installations existed in each of the military areas, the number varying according to the importance of the military area. There was no recognizable pattern for the subdivision of the ground service organization in specific assembly regions for reconnaissance, fighter, bomber, or ground attack forces. A densely meshed system of ground service installations existed in the western areas of European Russia. The system was in a constant process of improvement and was particularly dense around Leningrad and Moscow. Information was available that numerous new airfields had been developed after 1939 in the Baltic areas and in Eastern Poland, and that others were under construction. The rapid construction of airfields was favored by terrain conditions in the Russian plains. The location of the majority of the airfields in Western Russia was corroborated by air photo reconnaissance results.

Airfields were classified as first, second, and third class airfields, and landing strips.

Airfields in the "First Class" category, usually located in the vicinity of large cities, were at least 1,100 yards square, frequently much larger, could accommodate at least one air regiment, and had reinforced concrete hangars, concrete runways, often rail and always road connections, surface and underground fuel tanks with a capacity of at least 1,100 tons, and bomb depots.

Second class airfields compared to first class airfields in size, and could accommodate units up to the size of a bomber regiment. The sheds were usually timber structures, and the fields had fuel tanks and bomb depots, and usually only road connections.

Third class airfields were equivalent to German tactical airfields but with longer runways. They had no permanent structures, no rail connections, and maintained a small supply of fuel in drums.

The landing strips could be compared with German advanced airfields. They had no service installations. They were available in large numbers, and new ones were constantly under construction.

To accommodate an air regiment a number of airfields could be consolidated into what was called an airfield system. In such cases, a first class airfield was usually designated as a base airfield for the regimental headquarters.

The supply services of the Soviet air forces were also controlled by the Central Administration of Red Army Air Force Units and administered in peacetime by the military areas. For this purpose each military area headquarters, in accordance with its size, controlled a number of main bases with supply facilities and assigned rear service units to perform approximately the functions of an air park of the Luftwaffe. Organizationally, supply procedures were at an extremely primitive level. One of the main defects was the inadequacy of the stocks of aircraft spare parts maintained. For maintenance or major repairs aircraft had to be sent to special workshops or to aircraft factories.

From the main bases supplies were channeled through mobile supply bases, which were the supply staffs of air divisions, to the troops. As a rule, each main base headquarters was at a first class airfield. This base airfield, together with the airfield system it controlled, was assigned to the base headquarters by an air division. If a flying unit moved into the airfield system, it also established its headquarters at the main airfield and assumed tactical control over the supply base headquarters already there. Mobile air supply bases had no permanent location but were transferred together with their divisions. The Soviet Air Command placed particular value on this mobility, which was practiced and tested in numerous maneuvers.

A mobile air base comprised the following:

One airfield company of three platoons, one of them an air force machine-gun platoon; one signal company of three platoons-- one of which was a radio platoon--and a weather service station (the signal company handled the communications for the airfield system and was tactically assigned to the flying unit stationed on the system); one motor transport company of three platoons (one truck and one tractor platoon, and one platoon with special vehicles such as fuel, water, and oil tank trucks, starter wagons, fire-fighting, and workshop trucks. The company had a total of approximately 70 vehicles, including trucks.); one headquarters platoon; one ration depot; weapons, ammunition, POL, equipment, clothing depots and a number of workshops.

The Luftwaffe High Command arrived at the following overall appraisal of the Soviet ground service and supply organization:

Apart from the first class and some of the second class airfields, the ground service organization was considered below modern standards. Of roughly 2,000 airfields in Western Russia, only approximately 200 could be considered suitable for operations by bomber units. The others were unsuitable because of defective construction and equipment. Furthermore, according to the season of the year, a large number of airfields were only conditionally usable because of the dust, water, snow, or cold.

The operability of flying units was reduced by the inadequate development of airfields, the inadequate stocks of fuel and ammunition, and the inadequacy of available signal facilities. The Soviet ground service organization could not be compared with that of the Luftwaffe and ". . . the numerous airfields in existence in European Russia can therefore be considered as only conditionally useful for wartime air operations."[17]

In German views, the supply organization was unsound, particularly in respect to the supplies and the storage of fuel and aircraft spare parts. The advantages accruing from the permanent cooperation of each mobile supply base with a particular air division were more than balanced by the detrimental effect this had on the natural high mobility of air units. The loss of main bases or mobile bases would, therefore, seriously harm the entire supply system. The disadvantageous supply situation was further accentuated by the enormous areas involved, inadequate rail routes and their condition, the shortage of railway rolling stock, and the generally difficult road conditions.

Very few other German sources of information are available on the ground service organization of the Soviet air forces prior to the war.[18] Those that are available present approximately the same picture as that just described. There were those, however, who warned against a too one-sided appraisal based exclusively on German views and underestimating the effects of the Russian ability to improvise and the natural Russian habit of frugality.

It was to become evident that the Soviets approached the problems of ground service and supply organization from a different and more primitive point of view than that of the western air powers, and that in Russian circumstances the methods chosen could also insure success. In this respect, and in respect to their gift for improvisation, the Russians were actually underrated by all concerned.

H. *Air Signal Services.*

At the outset of the campaign in 1941 the Luftwaffe High Command estimated that no separate organic air signal service existed in the Soviet air forces such as the Air Signal Corps of the Luftwaffe. According to the information then available, the signal services were directed by the Signal Inspectorate of the Red Army, to which the staff signal officers assigned to the air forces of the various military areas were responsible for signal communications within their respective command areas. These signal officers in turn controlled divisional, regimental, and mobile air base signal officers. From reports received it appeared that military area air commands and air division headquarters had signal battalions. The signal units assigned to a mobile air base were responsible for the establishment and operation of wire and radio communications on all airfields of their assigned airfield system, and were required to maintain a reserve of signal personnel and to maintain the weather reporting services. When a flying unit arrived, the commander of the air regiment assumed tactical command over the signal company stationed in the airfield system.

Flying units had no signal units assigned to them. Instead, radio operators and other radio personnel on aircraft were an organic part of the flying unit.

In wartime the military staff signal officers were transferred with their personnel to the headquarters of the air commands attached to army groups and armies.

The following signal equipment was in use: wireless telegraphy and radio as the main media of communication; wire communications; emergency means of communication, such as code and marking panels, message drop and reception facilities; visual signals, such as signal lamps, light signals, signal flares, and rockets.

About radio, the main means of communication, it was known that separate networks existed for ground-air-ground, ground-ground, air traffic control, and weather service. A radio directional service as part of the air traffic control system was still under development and could by no means be compared with the use made of radio direction techniques in the Luftwaffe. Only a few radio beacons existed and most of these were exclusively for civil aviation.

Radio traffic was governed by the "Regulations for the Radio Services of the Red Army," which stipulated among other requirements that all radio messages must be sent in code, including messages by voice radio. Experience in the Russo-Finnish War had shown, however, that in spite of the undoubted progress achieved in the training of radio personnel, messages were frequently sent in the clear during critical situations or under the pressure of time.

German authorities were unable to estimate the number of instruments available or in use.*

No important information was procurable concerning other communication media, which were insignificant in comparison with radio communications.

The Luftwaffe High Command, summarizing its evaluation of the signal communication services of the Soviet air forces found that they were poorly organized and that the Russian air signal network was unsuited to the flexible conduct of air warfare. It would appear that, on the whole, the Luftwaffe High Command estimate of the signal services of the Soviet air forces was sound.

Section III: <u>Antiaircraft Artillery</u>[19]

In the Soviet Union the antiaircraft artillery arm was an organic part of the Army. For this reason it will not be treated in detail in this study. Since, however, its activities were directed primarily against the Luftwaffe and since German aircraft personnel, thinking in terms of their own concepts, always regarded the Soviet antiaircraft artillery arm as a part of the Soviet air forces, a few remarks on the subject are necessary.

Soviet antiaircraft artillery units were assigned to all large Army units, down to division level, and to home defense commands. Home defense was organized in defense regions or locally defined

---

* The following radio instruments, however, were known to be in use: 800-Watt Stations, truck-mounted; 200-Watt stations, truck-mounted; 20-Watt stations, truck-mounted or on horse-drawn vehicles; 100-Watt aircraft radio instruments; 40-Watt aircraft radio instruments; 20-Watt aircraft radio instruments (two types); radio aiming devices; 500-Watt radio beacons, stationary or truck-mounted.

defense sectors. Within each of these regions or sectors all fighter, antiaircraft artillery, and aircraft reporting and air-raid warning units were assigned to one single air defense command. This insured uniform control. The equipment of the antiaircraft artillery units was considered obsolete.

The estimate[20] of the Soviet antiaircraft artillery arm by the Luftwaffe High Command in 1941 indicated that the arm was defectively equipped. The equipment was not uniform and only a small percentage was modern. The effectiveness of the arm was thought to be reduced particularly by the diversity of the weapons and other equipment in use and the resultant supply and training difficulties, and by the seriously inadequate number of automatic fire data computers. Serious resistance by antiaircraft artillery was expected only in the Moscow, Leningrad, Kiev, Odessa, Batum, and Baku areas.

On the whole it was considered that in view of the enormous size of the Soviet territories and the size of the Soviet Army, the antiaircraft artillery units in existence could not provide adequate protection.

No other sources are available to confirm the accuracy of the above Luftwaffe High Command estimate. It can be assumed, however, that the estimate was not far off the mark, although it was to be found later that the fire of Soviet antiaircraft units could be highly effective, and above all that Soviet training had reached astonishingly high standards in teaching the Soviet soldier to protect himself against air attack through active defense and camouflage.

Section IV. <u>Paratroopers and Other Airborne Troops</u>[21]

If the Soviet Union produced nothing else really new in the entire field of aviation, following foreign leads in many respects, it did pioneer the organization of paratrooper and airborne infantry units and for a long time was far ahead of other military powers in this field.

The origins of the Soviet paratrooper and airborne infantry arm, the units of which were assigned to the air forces, date back to 1930. In that year a Soviet military journal stated: "The parachute is no longer merely a lifebelt; in the future it will serve as a means of attack." The first paratrooper regiments and airborne infantry brigades made their appearance in 1933; in 1935 the interest of military circles throughout the world was aroused by the Russian developments. In that year a force of approximately 1,200 landed by parachute with all weapons and equipment during the maneuvers around Kiev. Later in the year a complete division, together with tanks, was transported by air without serious mishap from Moscow to Vladivostok, a distance of 4,200 miles.[22] Minister of War Kliment Voroshilov was therefore fully justified in stating at a congress in 1935:[23] "Parachuting is the field of aviation in which the Soviet Union has a monopoly. No nation on earth can even approximately compare with the Soviet Union in this field, far less could any nation dream of closing the existing gap by which we are leading. There can be no question at all of our being surpassed."

In the Caucasus maneuvers of 1936, the paratrooper arm still participated publicly, but from then on all exercises and maneuvers of the arm were carried out in strict secrecy. Without being able to give any definite reasons, foreign observers at the time arrived at the conclusion that in some way or other the results obtained with the new arm had been a disappointment. However, the maneuvers had served to demonstrate clearly that, as was the case with the Soviet air forces in general, paratrooper and airborne infantry units would be employed exclusively in very close cooperation with Army forces.

In 1938 it became known that the Soviet paratrooper forces were organized in four brigades, "Dessant brigades" as they were called, each approximately 1,200 strong.

The Luftwaffe High Command considered that the use of Soviet paratrooper forces in regimental size units during the occupation of Bessarabia* in 1940 provided no standards by which the value of these troops could be judged, since the operation encountered no resistance. The same applied to paratrooper operations in the Russo-Finnish War. In the large areas of Finland with their extensive forests the operations failed and the landed paratroopers either died of hunger and exposure

---

* Editor's Note: On 26 June 1940 Russia presented an ultimatum to Rumania demanding the return of Bessarabia and the cession of northern Bukovina. Two days later the Russians, using 1,000 paratroops, occupied the disputed territory, about 22,000 square miles extending west, northwest from Odessa, between the Ukraine and Rumania.

to the severe cold or were captured at their landing sites. (The Luftwaffe High Command rejected the widespread version current at the time that the failure of the Russian parachute operations in Finland was an intentional bluff by the Red Army.) Because of the reasons given above and the inadequate number of transport planes available in the Soviet air forces, the Luftwaffe arrived at the following views concerning the Soviet paratrooper and airborne infantry forces at the outset of the Russian campaign:[24]

Following the successful German airborne operations in Belgium and Holland, it was to be assumed that the Soviets had devoted special attention to their paratrooper forces, which were reputed to have considerable numerical strength. Sizable paratrooper forces appeared to be assembled in the Kiev area, where a considerable number of transport aircraft had been identified. No details were available on strengths and organization.

One airborne infantry division of three regiments was known to have been concentrated in Military Area Moscow. The execution of large-scale airborne operations would be hampered by the necessity to use large numbers of transport planes for the movement of supplies. Isolated airborne operations, however, were to be expected.

From later statements by German observers the picture given above can be completed by noting that all sources acknowledge the unique development of the Soviet paratrooper and airborne infantry forces, and confirm the special value attached to their development by the Soviet Command as well as the unrestricted propaganda launched in their support.

According to Russian directives issued in 1936 the primary mission of these forces was to deal annihilating blows to the enemy rear. All operations were to be based on cooperation with Army forces in attack and pursuit. Thus, a passage in the regulations reads: "The most important mission of the paratrooper and airborne infantry arm is to support the Army in operations to envelop and destroy enemy forces."

On the whole, it appears that the German estimate of the Soviet paratrooper and airborne infantry arm, and particularly of the probability of their use, was fairly accurate.

Section V: The Air Armament Industry[25]

It was common knowledge (and has been mentioned previously in this study) that Russia expended special efforts to promote its air armament industries and did everything possible to render its air forces independent of foreign sources.

In the spring of 1941 the Luftwaffe High Command estimated[26] that Russia had approximately 50 fuselage and 15 aircraft engine factories, 40 factories manufacturing equipment and appliances, and 100 auxiliary factories. The same source indicated that the annual output fell far short of the targets set for 1938 and 1939--8,000 and 12,000 aircraft respectively--and in 1939-40 averaged only 450 fuselages and 1,200 engines monthly, or between 5,500 and 6,000 fuselages and approximately 15,000 engines annually. It was thought that the industry could by no means dispense with the necessity to copy foreign models, particularly in the manufacture of engines. The output in engine parts, appliances and equipment, carburetors, spark plugs, and oil and fuel pumps was unsatisfactory. Flight safety was seriously reduced because of the poor quality of engines and engine parts. The existing weakness in the air armament industry had become more pronounced as a result of the introduction of light metal alloys which had proved unsatisfactory, and because of the purges of 1937, and it was evident that these weaknesses had not been overcome. Electrometals still had to be imported from Germany.

The number of personnel employed in aircraft and aircraft engine factories alone was estimated at 250,000, while the inclusion of personnel in all auxiliary factories increased the figure to over one million. It remained to be seen, however, how long it would take to develop an adequate cadre of skilled workers, engineers, and designers.

For these reasons it was considered unlikely that the output would rise appreciably in the near future or that any considerable technical progress was to be expected in the production of aircraft and aircraft engines. Although the aircraft industries had commenced manufacturing modern types of fighter and ground-attack aircraft, it was not possible to predict when air units could be re-equipped with more modern aircraft.

The air armament industries were concentrated locally around the centers of the metal manufacturing industries and thus in the Moscow, Leningrad, Central Russian, Ukrainian, and Ural regions, with the appliances, instrument, and equipment industries chiefly in the Leningrad and Moscow areas.

The Luftwaffe High Command estimated that, owing to slow rates of production, the introduction of new aircraft types would proceed more slowly than in other, more up-to-date industrial countries, so that the Soviet Union would only be able, under peacetime conditions, to maintain a nucleus of modern units; in the event of war, however, the industry would be unable to prevent a rapid decrease of front-line strengths. In this respect, engine production would prove to be a particularly serious bottleneck owing to the difficulties already being experienced by the Russians in trying to manufacture enough engines to meet their requirements.

In contrast with other subjects connected with Soviet air power, numerous German and other sources of information are available on the Soviet air armament industries. The following passages are quoted from the Handbuch der neuzeitlichen Wehrwissenschaften 1938:[27]

> The air armanent industry of the Soviet Union is shrouded in mystery. It is difficult to obtain a clear picture of the actual circumstances. The factories are closed to unauthorized investigators; only a small number of exhibits are shown; and the opinions of visitors are favorably or unfavorably biased according to their political views.

> Particularly favorable conditions exist for air armament because of the availability of all required raw materials-- including plentiful sources of oil--and because of the size of the Soviet territories, which make it possible to establish factories at great distances from the national borders.

> The air armament industry is organized for mass production and is constantly being expanded. In view of the overall industrial requirements, however, it is doubtful whether the essential materials and labor can be furnished for the air armament industries.

> It is estimated in 1938 that 50 fuselage and engine factories

and factories producing equipment and appliances are in existence, with an annual output of 6 to 7,000 aircraft fuselages and 70,000 aircraft engines.* It is estimated that the industry employs approximately 350,000 workers.

In spite of the indisputable progress thus revealed, it seems doubtful that the Soviet aircraft industry will be able to equip the large air forces which the Soviet Command is endeavoring to establish. A serious technological crisis has developed because of the outdated aircraft presently in use, and this applies particularly to heavy bombers.

Soviet air power can no longer be rated as high as it was two years ago.

Another German observer[28] comes to similar conclusions and draws particular attention to the strenuous efforts of the Soviet Government to develop an enormous air armament industry. He states that this industry was established either in large areas where the necessary raw materials were immediately available or in regions with good traffic channels to the raw material areas. Thus, as he points out, a western air armament industry region has been developed in proximity to the coal region of Rostov and the iron ore deposits of Krivoy Rog; a central region in proximity to the coal basin of Moscow, the iron ore deposits of Magnitogorsk (Magnetogorsk), and the non-ferrous metal deposits around Troitsk; and a third--Asiatic--region in the Far East, in the center of the coal and iron ore areas around Irkutsk and Chabarowsk (Khabarovsk).

Following a tour of the Soviet Union in 1936, French aircraft manufacturer, Louis Charles Breguet,[29] arrived at the following appraisal:

> The blast furnaces, foundries, and electric power works are remarkably well equipped, and the engineers are unquestionably capable. Summarized, the impression is that with ten times as many personnel employed as the French, the Soviet industry is producing twenty times as many aircraft.

---

* Editor's Note: This figure seems inordinately high.

The efforts of the Soviets in the field of serial production are beyond conception. The factories work with production belts as is the case with our automobile factories. Personnel are employed in three shifts.

French aviation industrialist Henry Potez comments similarly, while French authorities on the subject estimated that the Soviet air armament industry employed 370,000 personnel in 1937 and produced 7,000 aircraft and 40,000 engines in 1936.[30]

In April 1941 Lieutenant Colonel (now Generalleutnant a.D.) Heinrich Aschenbrenner,[31] the then German air attache in Moscow, arranged for a number of Luftwaffe engineers to tour Soviet aircraft factories. The reports turned in by these engineers provided the Luftwaffe High Command with a particularly clear insight into the Soviet air armament industry. Besides the air attache, ten Luftwaffe engineers participated in the tour, which lasted from 7 through 16 April and included visits to the Experimental Institute for Aeronautics in Moscow, a fighter aircraft factory and an engine factory in Moscow, two engine factories at Rybinsk (Shcherbakov), the Fili Aircraft Factory and an engine factory in Molotov, in the Urals. Each of the factories visited was a giant enterprise, employing up to 30,000 workers per shift and operating three shifts per day.

The consolidated report on the visit stressed among other things: (1) that the factories were almost completely independent of subsidiary part deliveries, (2) the excellently arranged methods of work--extending down to details, (3) the well maintained modern machinery, and (4) the technical and manual aptitude, devotion, and frugality of the Soviet workers. Other remarkable features were that up to 50 percent of the workers were women, who were employed at work performed in other countries exclusively by highly qualified personnel, and that the finished products were of excellent quality.

Even though it must be assumed that the German commission was shown the best factories in existence, the compelling conclusion was that the other factories of the air armament industry must also have been at usable standards.

At the end of the tour of inspection, Chief Engineer Artem Mikoyan, designed of the Mig fighter and a brother of Anastos Mikoyan, the Peoples' Commissar for Industry,* said to Aschenbrenner:[32] "We have now shown you all we have and all we can do; and we shall destroy anyone who attacks us." This was an unmistakable warning and was conveyed verbatim by the air attache to the appropriate German authorities.

It is not yet, or perhaps no longer, possible to ascertain whether the final report by the commission was shown in the original to Hitler and Goering. According to Aschenbrenner, Hitler's reaction when he heard of the results of the industrial tour was to exclaim: "Now one can see how far these people already are. We must start at once!" It is interesting in this connection to note that during the Nuremberg Trials Field Marshal Milch, after admitting knowledge of the reports by the German engineers on the Soviet aircraft production capabities,[33] stated that Goering refused to believe the reports. Milch gave no reply when questioned as to what Goering had done to have the report on the industrial tour submitted to Hitler.

It is thus clearly established that the leading authorities of the Luftwaffe were informed of the results of the tour. Unfortunately, it is just as clear that the Luftwaffe High Command failed to draw any significant conclusions from the information and did nothing to change its official estimate of the capacities of the Soviet air armament industry. Instead, they assumed that the Soviets had bluffed the German engineers.

A comparison of the Luftwaffe High Command's 1941 estimate of the capabilities of the Soviet air armament industry with other German and foreign views reveals clearly that the Luftwaffe underestimated the Soviet air armament industry. This is all the more surprising in view of the fact that the highly illuminating report of the German engineer commission of April 1941 was known to Luftwaffe command circles. That this report found so little credence and produced no effects is hard to understand. Some observers[34] incline to the view that the German Command did not want to draw conclusions from the report, because such conclusions would not have fitted into the general picture of the military potentials of the Soviet Union developed by the highest levels of command, i.e. Hitler and the

---

* Editor's Note: Now (1960) First Deputy Minister of the Council of Ministers and ostensibly number two man in the Soviet hierarchy.

Armed Forces High Command. It is difficult to establish to what degree these views are justified, but they cannot be entirely discounted.

Section VI. **The Armament Industry in General**[35]

It would exceed the scope of this study to go into details on the military economic condition of the Soviet Union prior to World War II. Since, however, the general state of the armament industry had an important impact on the development of Soviet air power, the 1941 views of the German Command on this subject are worthy of some study.[36] Its information indicated, for instance, that the rich mineral deposits within Soviet territories would secure adequate supplies of almost all mineral raw materials required for many years to come. In the armament and other heavy industries the pace was being forced at the expense of the production of consumer goods. In spite of this, however, the Soviet economy could not fully meet the requirements of the armament and other heavy industries. Other detrimental factors were the relatively high percentage of manufactured goods which failed to meet minimum standards, a serious shortage of skilled labor and management personnel, organizational deficiencies, and irregularities in the supply of raw materials; all of which resulted in frequent stoppages in production.

The fuel supply situation was unsatisfactory in spite of the existence of large petroleum deposits, of which 43 percent were in the Caucasus, approximately 30 percent in the Ural-Volga River regions and the Emba basin, and 27 percent in Central Asia and on Sakhalin Island. The principal reasons for fuel shortages were the increasing mechanization throughout the country, the heavy consumption of oil for heating and lighting purposes, heavy losses in transit and the wear and tear on drilling equipment and cracking and refinery installations. The latter even resulted in reduced outputs. The total output in oil was estimated at 34,000,000 tons in 1940 compared with a target production of 42,000,000 tons. This output included only 2,000,000 to 2,300,000 tons of aviation gasoline. Therefore, the output forecast for 1942--54,000,000 tons, of which 14 to 15 million were to be aviation gasoline--would be impossible to achieve. It was assumed that there would be a shortage of petroleum products, and particularly of aviation gasoline, for some time to come. Even the peacetime requirements of the air forces and the Army could be met only through restrictions on the consumption by industry and the civilian population.

The Armed Forces High Command believed that the main centers of armament and general military industry were still in European Russia west of the Urals, particularly in the Ukraine and the Donets Basin. The great industrial and economic importance of the Ural region (Ufa and Sverdlovsk), and the large-area projects of the Ural-Kuznetsk Combine were known to the Armed Forces High Command, but it was at the same time considered as certain that the Soviet Government would not be able to achieve its goal of transferring 40-50 percent of all industries to the Combine. Although a few highly informative reports existed concerning the development of large industries in Asiatic Russia, no conclusive information concerning what was really happening was available.

The Luftwaffe High Command considered that the wide distribution of industries and their location in well protected areas made it seem unlikely that the Soviet economy could be so badly disrupted as to cause any decisive interruption of the overall national supply systems.

According to another German source,[37] the German Command's estimate of the economic structure of the Soviet Union was based primarily on statistics published by the Soviet Government in 1938 and on unrelated items of information from German engineers and technicians, and was summarized in a voluminous study by the Armed Forces High Command Economics and Armaments Office. In the light of presently available information there can be no doubt that the study arrived at false conclusions both in respect to the capabilities of the Soviet armament industries and the transfer of industries to Asiatic Russia. This faulty estimate was one of the major factors influencing the German Government in its decision to wage war on the Soviet Union, since it was assumed that seizure of the most important economic and industrial centers in European Russia--the Donets Basin, the Ukraine, and the armament producing areas around Moscow and Leningrad, could bring about the end of the campaign.

What has been said previously in this study concerning the German estimate of the Soviet air armament industries thus applies in even greater measure to the German estimate of the entire Soviet armament industry.

Section VII: <u>Transportation</u>[38]

Soviet authorities admitted that their transportation system was the weakest link in their program for the development of the Soviet Union. The Luftwaffe High Command estimated[39] that railroads formed the major means of transportation, accounting for 90 percent of all freight and passenger traffic. All efforts to develop the widely meshed rail net, particularly in the Asiatic territories, so that it could meet the growing requirements of the country, had failed. Development of the Russian rail system had never kept pace with the goals set in the various Five-Year Plans. It was expected that during a war the junctions at which the overburdened north-south industrial rail routes in European Russia intersected the east-west routes, which were so highly important for the movement of troops and supplies, would develop into particularly critical bottlenecks. Stoppages or interference in any form at these points would necessarily have a most harmful effect on the westward movement of troops and supplies and on the militarily important north-south industrial traffic.

Inland waterways were estimated to carry only 8 percent of all freight traffic against 20 to 25 percent in former times. Current efforts to relieve the burden on the rail system by increased use of waterways were not expected to take effect for a few years since the development of important projected canals would take much time.

The road net was considered inadequate, with roads too far apart and in poor condition. Road traffic could therefore not contribute much to relieve the rail system. A few motor highways existed or were under construction. The motorization program was seriously hampered by the inadequate road net and by the poor condition of existing roads.

For the above reasons the German Command came to the conclusion that the rail system was the only transportation medium which could be considered of military importance.

At this point it is necessary to discuss civil aviation in Soviet Russia.[40] It was generally known that every possible measure was being taken to develop civil air transportation and that a network of air routes covered practically all areas of the Soviet Union. Apart from European Russia, with its traffic hub at Moscow, air routes were established primarily to those areas in which other means of traffic were underdeveloped, such as Siberia, the Far East, Central Asia, and Kazakhstan.

The following categories of air routes existed: main routes, called <u>Magistral</u>, which were of national importance and included the Moscow-Vladivostok, Moscow-Tiflis, and Moscow-Tashkent routes; routes of local importance, such as the Moscow-Astrakhan, and the Irkutsk-Yakutsk routes; periodic routes, which were only served periodically when the need existed; and the so-called Polar Sea routes. Numerous routes were operated exclusively for the transportation of freight. The aircraft types most often used were PS-35, PS-37, PS-40, PS-84, PS-89, Zig-1, and Stal-11.*

The Luftwaffe High Command realized the high significance of civil air traffic in the Soviet Union because of the poor road conditions, the inaccessibility of entire regions by any means other than air travel, and the enormous size of the Soviet territories. It was estimated, nevertheless, that the following deficiencies existed: the airways were equipped with outdated types of aircraft; the construction of airfields and their tanking facilities were, in general, primitive; the air traffic safety service was inadequately developed; and only 12 to 15 percent of all routes were equipped for night air traffic. The Luftwaffe High Command, therefore, considered that the outdated and inadequate development of the air routes and of the aircraft used seriously hampered the regular operations of civil aviation.

The Luftwaffe High Command also was aware of the plans to convert all civil aviation to military purposes in case of war. It decided, however, that this would have only insignificant results because of the defective condition of the civil air traffic system.

In contrast, other German observers[41] pointed out as far back as 1938 that the general public in the Soviet Union was practically

---

* Editor's Note: Both the PS-40 and the PS-84 were Douglas aircraft built in Russia, the latter being the DC-3. All of the others (PS-89, PS-35, PS-37, Stal-11 and Zig-1) were twin-engine transport-passenger aircraft of various types.

excluded from air transportation, the main reason being that the entire system was to be reserved for military purposes. All airways, it was pointed out, were serviced by a firmly controlled military ground service organization which made it possible, whenever desired, to convert all civil air transportation lines to serve military purposes. These observers also considered that the existence of a comprehensive network of airways would considerably facilitate large-scale transfer movements of military air forces. This applied particularly to the east-west Moscow-Vladivostok Magistral. The additional importance of the possibility of using the civil air traffic facilities for the movement of military supplies and vital industrial commodities and raw materials was not to be underestimated, particularly in wartime.

In contrast, the Luftwaffe High Command had failed to appreciate adequately the military significance of the civil air services in the Soviet Union.

Section VIII: Soviet Air Forces in the Spanish Civil War[42]

An extraordinary opportunity to estimate the quality of the Soviet air forces before World War II was afforded by the performances of Soviet air units in the Spanish Civil War of 1936-37. This was the first demonstration before the eyes of the world of the capabilities of Soviet air units. The views of a number of Germans who participated in the campaign are available on this subject and can be summarized more or less as follows:

Air support for the Reds in Spain was furnished almost exclusively by Soviet units under the command of Soviet officers. Aircraft, other materiel, and personnel replacements came primarily from Soviet Russia. In short, the Spanish Civil War was exploited by the Soviet Union as an opportunity to test its aircraft, weapons, other equipment, personnel, doctrines, and tactics under actual wartime conditions. It can be regarded as a unique dress rehearsal for a later war.

On frequent occasions the Soviet Command in the Spanish Civil War gave evidence that it was not capable of mastering the numerous difficulties in the fields of personnel, materiel, technology, and organization. There was evidence of awkwardness in operational thinking, and of inadequacies in general staff training. On the other hand, there was also unquestionable evidence of ability to master organizational and supply problems by improvisations, and of aptitude in camouflage, ground services, and cooperation in air-ground operations. Also, it was found that the methods of handling command matters were uncomplicated.

Operational methods were generally primitive and revealed the following defects: (1) inadequate flexibility in attack and defense; (2) lack of originality; (3) failure to concentrate power; and (4) a tendency to dissipate forces. For these reasons the losses incurred in the Spanish War were disproportionate to the results achieved or to the existing personnel and materiel situation.

Although Soviet flying personnel were remarkable courageous and aggressive and fought well over friendly terrain, they were timid and uncertain of themselves over hostile terrain, and rarely pursued enemy aircraft beyond their own lines. Technically, Soviet pilots were good individual performers. In contrast, their training and performance in unit formation were inadequate. There can be no doubt that the personnel sent to Spain were an elite body, who after their return to the Soviet Union were to serve as instructors and to teach what they had learned from the Spanish campaign.

In the initial stages of the Spanish Civil War Soviet fighters appeared only individually. Later, they operated in flights of four, and only rarely in large formations of twenty to thirty aircraft. Although good in single combat, the Soviet fighter pilots remained inferior to their German opponents owing to their inadequate tactics for formation operations and the inadequacy of their fighter commands. This situation remained unchanged even after the appearance of their I-16 (Rata) aircraft, which were excellent for those times. These aircraft were a great surprise; they were far superior to the German He-51 type in speed, maneuverability, weapons, and climbing ability, but hardly equal to the German Me-109 model introduced later in the campaign. In the initial stages the Soviets also employed I-15 (Curtiss) planes, as fighters. After the appearance of the German Me-109, however, the use of the I-15 was restricted to ground-attack missions.

Soviet bombers played only a minor role in the Spanish campaign. The few bombing missions carried out were usually by units of one to two flight size--never above squadron size--and produced no practical results. This was probably due to the inadequate preparation of the personnel for operations of this type and to the lack of training in such basic subjects as blind and normal navigation, and night operations. The SB-3, a twin-engine Martin bomber, was used in these missions. In speed, weapons, and other equipment it was inadequate to the requirements. These aircraft were also used more and more as ground attack aircraft as the campaign progressed.

The longer the campaign lasted, the more the Soviets used their aircraft as ground-attack units. Gradually, close support became the main mission of Soviet air power in Spain, although at that time the Russians had no specially developed model for ground attack. This mission had to be assumed by fighter and bomber units, which thus, in an ever increasing measure, had to be withdrawn from the missions for which they were best suited.

The number of reconnaissance planes used was so small that their operations were insignificant.

In the operation of their ground and supply services, the Soviets displayed remarkable gifts for improvisation, camouflage, and flexibility. Ruthless and unproblematical as they were by nature, they mastered many difficulties.

A relatively large number of Soviet antiaircraft units were engaged in Spain and showed signs of remarkable improvement in their firing methods and tactics during the campaign. The light and medium antiaircraft units were considered particularly effective.

No signs were noticed of the existence of a separate air signal service. From the operations of the Soviet air forces it was noticeable, however, that whatever signal system was employed must have been very faulty.

An extremely critical German observer[43] in Spain and later in the Russian campaign has the following to say of the Soviet air forces in the Spanish Civil War and of the lessons they apparently learned there:

    The Soviet air forces, which were the only air forces employed on the Red side in Spain, revealed fundamental weaknesses in their command, organization, training, and technical performances. These weaknesses they were unable to remedy in spite of their pronounced aggressiveness and flying ability, their aptitude at improvising, and the ruthlessness of their command methods.

The Soviets learned a lot in the Spanish campaign. That they had applied the lessons learned there to further develop their air forces became evident later in the Russian campaign. The lessons applied produced both positive and negative results. Those with a positive influence were the general experience gained by the command and troops--particularly in operations, formation flight, training, etc; the deductions drawn in the technological and organizational fields; and the importance of the ground attack arm, which they developed to remarkably high standards. False conclusions led them to forego the development of an effective bomber arm and thereby forfeit an opportunity for strategic air warfare. Another false conclusion was their application of experience gained in a limited campaign to the conditions of a general, major war.

It is certain that the Luftwaffe Command was able to develop, from the numerous reports received and from direct combat with Soviet air units in Spain, a fairly accurate picture of the status of the Soviet air forces at that time. The present writer has no information as to whether and in what measure this experience might have contributed toward a proper estimate of the later development of the Soviet air forces or whether this experience was properly used at all. No reference to the subject is to be found in any of the documents of the German Command presently available which deal with the last few years preceding World War II.

Section IX: Consolidated Luftwaffe High Command Estimate of the Soviet Air Forces at the Outset of the Russian Campaign

In closing this chapter, the overall Luftwaffe High Command estimate of the Soviet air forces at the outset of hostilities between Germany and the Soviet Union in 1941 can be summarized as follows:

In spite of the German numerical inferiority of 1:3 or 1:4, the striking power of the Soviet air forces and their chances of success were considered on the whole to be considerably smaller than those of the Luftwaffe.

Lack of combat experience and a defective command system, it was thought, would adversely affect Soviet air operations. In particular, it was thought that the clumsy command system would prevent the productive coordination of ground and air operations--above all during mobile warfare--and the concentration of air power to suit current situations and changes in the area of main effort.

Because of existing defects in the ground service and supply organization, and the low degree of technical aptitude of the average Russian, the Soviet air forces were considered inadequately prepared for combat action: the effective strength of front line units was only approximately 50 percent of their authorized strength. Out of a total of 5,700 first-line aircraft only approximately 1,300 bomber and 1,500 fighter aircraft were fully operable. It was also taken for granted that the effective strength of units would be rapidly reduced in combat against a highly developed military opponent with modern equipment.

The main concentration in the Soviet strategic assembly of air power, excluding the strategic bomber units, was in European Russia where numerous airfields had been constructed since 1939. Efforts to increase the number of airfields in these territories continued. The main concentrations were in Latvia, Lithuania, and Eastern Poland. While hoping to be able to destroy the Soviet air units on the ground by means of an annihilating surprise attack, the Luftwaffe High Command nevertheless assumed the possibility that the Soviets would employ its remaining units in efforts to repel German air attacks and halt the German advance on the ground, the latter to be achieved by means of ground-attack air operations.

In like manner, it was assumed that Soviet air units would bomb German airfields and Army targets within the operational zones. Whereas it was known that only weak defenses existed at Soviet airfields, it appeared that the Soviet home air defenses were remarkably strong in fighter and antiaircraft artillery units for the defense of major cities and industrial centers, particularly Moscow and Leningrad.

In respect to types of aircraft, weapons, and other equipment, the Soviet air forces were considered inferior to the Luftwaffe. The aircraft with which units were equipped were considered more or less obsolete, with the exception of a few modern fighter types, of which only small numbers were in front-line units. Another assumed weakness was that units of the Soviet air forces were in the process of re-equipping with different types of aircraft. This, it was thought, would be a lengthy process.

The ground services and supply organization were considered awkward in operation and far below modern requirements. The same applied to the air signal system.

For the above reasons, the Luftwaffe High Command arrived at the conclusion[44] that because of their poorly organized supply system and because of their dependence on seasonal conditions in the use of their airfields, the Soviet air forces were highly vulnerable and their operability could be seriously depleted, if not entirely paralyzed, by means of repeated, sudden, massed attacks against their airfields and supply installations.

The parachute and other airborne forces were considered a well trained and well equipped force. However, it was thought that they were hardly likely to carry out any large-scale operations because of the awkward command system and the lack of transportation.

The main concentration of armament industries was assumed to be still in European Russia. The Luftwaffe High Command underestimated the extent to which factories had already been transferred and were in process of transferring to the Ural region and farther east. Great importance was attached to the existing personnel and materiel difficulties hampering the Soviet air armament industry and to the results these difficulties were thought likely to produce during war. The same views were held to an even greater extent concerning the entire Soviet armament industry.

The transportation system was considered the weakest factor in the Soviet military potential and was known to have a low capacity. The most important means of transportation, the rail system, could by no means meet requirements and furthermore was highly vulnerable at certain critical points. Any serious interruption of rail traffic would have a considerable impact on the execution of military operations. It was thought that the use of civil aviation facilities to solve wartime problems of transportation and supply movement would produce only insignificant results.

Other German and foreign sources confirm the appropriateness of the above overall Luftwaffe High Command estimate of the Soviet air warfare strength and potential in all essential points, with the exception of the air armament industry, the armament industry in general, the transportation system, and in some respects the numerical strength of the Soviet air forces and their ground service and supply systems, all of which the Luftwaffe High Command had underestimated.

Chapter 2

THE SOVIET AIR FORCES FROM THE OPENING OF THE RUSSIAN CAMPAIGN TO THE END OF 1941

Section I: <u>General Review</u>[1]

    A. <u>The Course of the Air War and Russian Air Operations</u>.

When the German attack struck the Soviet Union in the early dawn on 22 June 1941, the German Command was hoping to bring its campaign to an early end through the employment of <u>blitzkrieg</u> tactics.

Although the Luftwaffe High Command possessed a fairly accurate appraisal, Russian air power was, in general, an unknown factor for field commanders in the German Air Force, Army, and Navy, who had only very vague and indefinite concepts concerning its capabilities. Nevertheless, Luftwaffe commanders, confident because of their past victories and wide combat experience, entered battle against the Russian Air Force with a secure feeling of superiority.

Before the campaign, German air commanders were briefed on Russian air power and its probable employment. In this orientation the Intelligence Digest on the Soviet Union,[2] mentioned at the opening of the previous chapter, played a large role. In view of the gigantic scope of the successes achieved against the Soviet air forces in the first months of the campaign, however, it is understandable that German commanders paid little further attention to the appraisal given them on Soviet air power at the beginning of the campaign, or to whether or not it had proved correct.

During the first year of the campaign three points evolved which conflicted with the briefing and caused a great and unpleasant surprise. These points were: 1) the numerical strength of the Soviet air forces at the opening of the campaign; 2) the strength of Soviet antiaircraft artillery forces; 3) the unexpectedly quick recovery of the Soviet air forces around the end of 1941 and the beginning of 1942 in spite of the annihilating blows it had received during the preceding summer.

Thus, Major a. D. Guenther Rall[3] writes that at the beginning

A German sketch showing the direction of the German air attacks in Russia and the operational areas assigned to the air fleets (Luftflotten) and the air corps (Fliegerkorps).

of the campaign the German estimate of Russian fighter forces was extremely vague and a precise knowledge of the types of aircraft involved or of numerical strengths was lacking. Therefore, the appearance of a Soviet fighter force with an incredible numerical superiority came as a surprise, although soon afterwards the technical superiority of the Luftwaffe was clearly demonstrated.

Major a. D. Manfred von Cossart[4] reports that German flying personnel were briefed on the basis of the Intelligence Digest, according to which Soviet antiaircraft artillery and fighter defenses were "hardly worthy of mention." Von Cossart's opinion is that the briefing under no circumstances did justice to the numerical strength of the Russian air forces. He leaves it open to question whether the intention existed at the briefing to depreciate the effectiveness of the Soviet defenses, and concludes that the German field forces entered the campaign carrying the burden of these preconceived notions.

It has been definitely established that the Luftwaffe Command had no intention whatever of misleading its forces by such means, but von Cossart's statements show what conclusions commanders at lower levels might draw from a false appraisal of the capabilities of an enemy.

It is not possible from the material available at this writing to determine in what form command personnel in the Army and Navy were briefed on the Soviet air forces, but it can probably be assumed that their briefing was even less thorough than that given to Luftwaffe personnel. Later statements by Army and Navy command personnel concerning the relatively weak air forces committed by the Soviets and the small results obtained by them in the first months of the campaign indicate that these two branches of the Armed Forces were not surprised as the Luftwaffe had been because, unlike the Luftwaffe, they did not encounter large numbers of Soviet aircraft. Their experience thus confirmed the briefing they had been given and they were, therefore, unaware of its inaccuracies.

The German air attack on 22 June took the Soviet air forces completely by surprise. Hundreds of Soviet aircraft of all types were destroyed on the first days of the attack. Many of them were destroyed on their airfields without any defensive action, others were shot down in air combat. The numbers destroyed on the ground were many times more than those shot down while airborne. One fact which should have been borne in mind, however, and which was not given enough attention by the German Command, was that in these circumstances Soviet losses in personnel were far smaller than in materiel. This explains in part the unexpectedly rapid recovery of the Soviet forces.

German commanders are unanimous in their views on the effects of the concentrated German air attacks during the first few days, which were well organized and soundly conducted. Thus, Captain a. D. Otto Kath,[5] who at the time was a pilot in the 54th Fighter Wing in the northern area, writes that on their first mission the units of his wing dealt annihilating blows to Soviet air units still on the ground on the Kovno /Kaunas/ airfield. The German bombs hailed into the SB-3 and DB-3 bomber aircraft closely packed along the runway and in front of the sheds. The German Me-109 escort fighters dived with the dive bombers or, after accomplishing their escort mission, searched out Soviet fighters in other areas of the airfield and destroyed most of them on the ground. Those that did manage to take off were destroyed in their take-off or immediately thereafter.

Major von Cossart, a flight leader in the 3d Group, Hindenburg Bomber Wing (committed in the northern area) writes[6] that in its first attack on 22 June 1941 his group dropped its bombs onto long rows of completely uncamouflaged aircraft standing in close formation as though on parade along the edges of the Libau /Liepaja/ airfield. The only defense was from one antiaircraft gun at the airfield and a few guns in the port area, which did no damage at all. Later attacks on the afternoon of the same day and on the next morning encountered just as ineffective defenses. The few Soviet fighters which were in the air flew around singly with no signs of unit integration, and flew off as soon as the German Ju-88s opened fire. Typical of the situation was an intercepted radio message from the Soviet air command at Libau to Riga: "Can give no support, my fighter regiment has been destroyed by bombs."

Lieutenant Colonel a. D. Horst von Riesen,[7] Commander of the 2d Group, 30th Bomber Wing, on the Polar Sea front, describes the Soviets' complete lack of awareness at the opening of the campaign as a pleasant surprise. The first German attack on Murmansk, 22 June 1941, encountered neither fighter nor ground defenses. Even aircraft making low-level attacks--after the dive-bombing was over--

Improved method of transporting wounded with a U-2

Russian aircraft destroyed on the ground by the German surprise attack (Kovno airfield, 1941)

were not taken under fire. German aircraft were able to operate completely unchecked over this hostile territory. Von Riesen describes the Soviets as having been "rolled over" and the overall air situation as a classical example of complete air supremacy. As he puts it: "Literally, no hostile air force was in existence."

Any number of such examples from the first days of attack could be quoted for the entire eastern theater to prove that the Soviet air forces were taken completely by surprise and to a large extent destroyed on their airfields. Thus, Captain H. Pabst, squadron leader in a dive-bomber group operating in the southern area, writes[8] that on 28 June 1941 he landed on a former Soviet airfield which was strewn with Soviet aircraft that had either been shot down or destroyed on the ground.

According to a report by Generalleutnant a. D. Hermann Plocher, the first attacks by units of the First Air Fleet found the Soviets completely unprepared.[9] The greater part of the Soviet air units was destroyed by these attacks and by the continued attacks on the days which followed. After the territory was occupied by German ground forces, checks carried out on the ground resulted in the same picture of inconceivable destruction as in the southern and central areas of the eastern front. Hundreds of wrecked aircraft were found burned out and shattered by bombs of all calibers on the ploughed-up airfields. The installations, mostly wooden structures, were burned or otherwise destroyed. The results achieved by units of the First Air Fleet in the 22 June to 13 July period are given at 1,698 Soviet aircraft destroyed--487 downed while airborne and 1,211 destroyed on the ground. In an outline report by the Luftwaffe, Soviet losses in aircraft for the period of 22-28 June 1941 are given at approximately 700 in the northern area, 1,570 in the central area, and 1,360 in the southern area of the eastern theater.

The result of this first devastating blow against the Soviet air forces was that for the time being the Germans had uncontested air superiority in the entire eastern theater, amounting in some parts to absolute air supremacy.

However, it was less from this surprise success during the first days of the campaign that German air commanders derived confidence in their own superiority than from their experience gained with Soviet flying personnel and aircraft in combat. It was soon found that the Soviet air forces in spite of their pronounced numerical superiority--both in personnel and materiel--were no match for the Luftwaffe. Soviet aircraft crews completely lacked combat experience, a deficiency which could not even be compensated for by their frequently evident aggressiveness and obstinacy. Their training had not kept pace with modern requirements, and their operational and tactical principles were outdated and inadequate. Soviet air force personnel were thus far inferior in combat efficiency to German aircraft crews with their extensive combat experience. Another factor was the largely obsolete aircraft of the Soviets, which were no match for German aircraft types.

The experience of German air commanders was also fairly uniform on this subject, as is borne out by the following German officers quoted. Lieutenant Colonel a. D. Helmut Mahlke,[10] commander of a dive-bomber group in the central area of the eastern theater, concludes that at the opening of the Russian campaign the Soviet air forces were equipped primarily with outdated materiel, which could meet the requirements of modern air warfare only conditionally or not at all. Thus equipped, Soviet air units found themselves opposed to an air force far superior in technical and tactical aspects. In addition, Luftwaffe personnel had gained wide combat experience in operations against Great Britain, whose Royal Air Force units were equipped with highly developed technical materiel.

Generalmajor a. D. Klaus Uebe,[11] described 1941 as the period in which the Soviets conducted air warfare with inexperienced personnel and inferior materiel almost to the point of complete annihilation of the entire Soviet potential for air warfare. Soviet airmen in general were found to be not only inferior, but vastly inferior, to their German opponents. This inferiority was not due alone to the shock effect of the first hammering German blows and inferior Russian aircraft. It was due rather to a lack of the feeling for aviation, the absence of uniform thought, and to mental inertia and inadequate training. Inadequate training also caused the generally evident and exaggerated caution, which often bordered on cowardice. In spite of their numerical superiority, the Soviet air forces were thus not a dangerous opponent.

Colonel a. D. Freiherr H. H. von Beust, commander of a bomber group in the southern area, gives a particularly lucid appraisal of the period under discussion, from which the following lines are quoted:[12]

> At the beginning of the campaign the Soviet air forces had a numerical superiority of approximately 6 or 8 to 1 over their opponents. However, they had failed to keep pace with the times in respect to their organization, training, and technological development. The entire Soviet air forces were thus nothing but a large and cumbersome instrument of small combat value, all elements of which the Luftwaffe was able to destroy within a few weeks so far as they were within striking range. Lacking the large territories of the Soviet Union, which made reorganization, training, and reinforcement possible in safe areas beyond the reach of the Luftwaffe, and without the large personnel and materiel reserves available, the Soviet air forces would probably not have recovered.

Colonel von Beust considered the average Russian as:

> . . . an opponent completely incapable of independent air attack operations and representing only a small threat in defensive action. In contrast to German airmen, the impression was often received that Soviet pilots were fatalists, fighting without any hope of success or confidence in their own abilities and driven only by their own fanaticism or by fear of their commissars.

The Russian airman's lack of aggressiveness seems understandable to von Beust, who asks:

> And how could one expect real enthusiasm in combat from airmen with aircraft, weapons, and other equipment so hopelessly inferior, who themselves were so vastly inferior in techniques, tactics, and training to their opponents, and who were aware of the terrific reverses the Soviet Union had just suffered? It is well known that Soviet units frequently had to follow their unit leader into action, suiting their actions to his, like machines, without any knowledge of their target, route, or the enemy situation.

While discussing the psychological aspect of aviation

performances, it remains to be said that over their own territory and in defensive action the performances of Soviet airmen were in general far better than in attack and over German-held territory. This was without doubt due primarily to the mentality of Russian airmen and soldiers in general, which differed very widely from that of the average German.

Von Beust's summation expresses essentially the views held by most German air commanders in the summer and autumn of 1941 on the Soviet air forces, although it was emphasized occasionally by some writers that, despite the inadequacies of their combat flying, Soviet airmen often evidenced extreme courage, adhered rigidly to what they had learned and to their orders, and were adept at improvising. It was also pointed out by some that Soviet resistance was steadily growing, and that the Russians of World War II were very different from those with which the German Army had had to reckon in World War I. [13]

The behavior of Soviet fighter, reconnaissance, ground-attack, and bomber pilots will be dealt with in detail in a later chapter.

In connection with the severe losses suffered by the Soviet Air Forces at the beginning of the campaign, the statement of Colonel Wanyushkin,[14] commander of the Russian Twentieth Air Army, Smolensk, who was captured on 2 November 1941 is of interest. He considered that the heavy losses of the Soviet air forces in the first days of the campaign were due to: 1) the very clever timing of the attack by the German Command; 2) the critical weakness of the Soviet air units at the time because of the re-equipment program then being carried out; 3) the fact that this re-equipment was carried out on front area airfields; 4) the fact that in their strategic assembly the Soviet air forces were based so close to the border; 5) the poor development of Soviet airfields; 6) the masses of aircraft sent into action by the Luftwaffe; 7) Russian negligence; 8) the failure of the Soviet Command.

First signs became evident near the end of 1941 that the Soviet air forces were beginning to recover from the severe defeats suffered in the past summer. The Luftwaffe still managed to maintain its air superiority during this period, but it realized that the desired complete annihilation of Soviet air power had not been achieved. In fact, strong Soviet air units, equipped with modern aircraft types, gradually began to appear. This slow recovery of Soviet air power did not take place uniformly in all areas, nor was it evident in all sectors simultaneously, so that German commanders only gradually realized that they were witnessing a general recovery. It was in areas of main effort, such as Moscow, Leningrad, and Demyansk, that Soviet resistance in the air became most evident.

This recovery of Soviet air power was favored primarily by three factors: 1) the fact that large numbers of personnel had escaped when their materiel was destroyed in the summer of 1941 plus the existence of fairly numerous personnel reserves deeper inside Russia and in the Far East; 2) the transfer (in spite of enormous difficulties) of air armament industries to eastern territories where they were beyond German air attack; 3) the early arrival of an exceptionally severe Russian winter, which hampered the Luftwaffe in the execution of its missions in a manner which could not have been predicted. This provided the Soviet Command with a long period of quiet for the reorganization of its air forces.

Major a. D. Heinz Joachim Jaehne,[15] air observer in a strategic reconnaissance squadron in the central area of the eastern theater, reports that during the initial stages of the campaign his unit suffered no losses whatever due to Soviet fighter defenses, but that from approximately August 1941 on the Soviet fighter airfields within his unit's reconnaissance area, particularly around Moscow, developed steadily into more and more difficult obstacles.

Dr. Karl Bartz[16] reports that during the battle of envelopment at Demyansk in the winter of 1941-1942, Soviet aircraft were once again beginning to appear in large numbers, and that the Soviet fighter defense at high altitudes was remarkable.

Finally, Colonel a. D. Hans-Ulrich Rudel* points out[17] that in the battles for Leningrad Soviet fighters attacked the approaching

---

* Editor's Note: Colonel Rudel, one of the most highly decorated German pilots in World War II, was credited with destroying 500 Russian tanks--enough to equip a tank corps--and countless vehicles of different types. On 22 September 1941 he achieved his greatest victory by sinking the battleship "Marat" in the harbor of Kronshtadt.

German air formations as far forward as the coast. He also states that in the battle for Moscow the German aircraft crews found it more difficult to fight the cold than to fight their Soviet opponents. Rudel expresses the opinion that the Soviets could not have hoped for a better ally than their winter, which, in his opinion, saved Moscow.

The above observations of German air commanders had not yet become common knowledge toward the end of 1941, but they indicate that a change was taking place in the behavior of the Soviet air forces.

Brief mention of Soviet antiaircraft artillery is also necessary. As already stated, Soviet antiaircraft artillery was organic to the Army and not to the air forces. It was only natural, however, that the arm was employed primarily against German aircraft.

German commanders differ in their opinions of the effectiveness of the Soviet antiaircraft artillery forces, which is understandable because their opinions are based on personal experience gained in different areas of the theater. On the whole, however, their views can be summarized more or less as follows: During the first surprise attacks by the Luftwaffe, the effectiveness of Soviet antiaircraft artillery was small. The arm recovered very quickly from the initial shock, however, and developed into a very serious opponent, particularly in areas of main effort along the front. On one point German commanders are fairly agreed: they were all the more surprised at the operations and effectiveness of the enemy's antiaircraft arm because the estimate given them by the German Command had presented Soviet antiaircraft artillery as obsolete and hardly effective. Opinions are also almost unanimous that defensive fire by light weapons, and particularly by the ground troops, was highly effective and disturbing and caused numerous German losses.

Major von Cossart[18] expresses the opinion that, contrary to information on the Soviet Union in the Intelligence Digest, the Soviet antiaircraft artillery arm must have been highly effective even prior to the campaign, since the antiaircraft artillery units were very successful in their fire against German air units flying in formation. It would have been impossible for the Soviets to develop such effective ground defenses within so short a time. Although Soviet antiaircraft artillery was also taken by surprise and heavily stricken at the outset of the campaign, well organized antiaircraft artillery centers soon reappeared.

Usually, the heavy antiaircraft units succeeded in placing their first salvos at the correct altitude; frequently the first shells fired struck into the middle of the German formation. From August 1941 on the ground defenses around Leningrad were exceptionally strong and included balloon barrages up to an altitude of 15,000 feet. During their approach to Leningrad, Ju-88 units encountered fire from heavy antiaircraft guns, and after their dive attack they ran into dense fire by medium and light guns. Owing to the well organized fire by machine guns and infantry weapons, low-level air attacks on ground targets were frequently exceedingly costly. Von Cossart gives the causes for German losses in aircraft in the following order of sequence: antiaircraft artillery fire, infantry fire, fighter attack.

Colonel Rudel[19] also considered the Soviet antiaircraft artillery exceedingly effective around Leningrad, where in one area of 38 square miles 1,000 antiaircraft guns were deployed. To quote his words: "... the zone of massed antiaircraft guns begins as soon as one flies over the coastal zone ... the antiaircraft artillery fire is murderous .... The smoke puffs from bursting antiaircraft shells form whole banks of clouds." He also thought the Soviet ground defense with infantry weapons and light antiaircraft guns highly effective.

Heavy antiaircraft artillery and other ground defenses are referred to repeatedly by Captain Herbert Pabst,[20] who states that the effects were often considerable and frequently damaged or destroyed aircraft.

Colonel von Riesen[21] reports that in the initial stages the antiaircraft artillery defenses at the Polar Sea front at Murmansk failed completely, but that the units were quick to adapt themselves and within a few weeks they constituted a serious hazard to attacking German aircraft. Their effectiveness could be compared in every respect with that of antiaircraft artillery in similar concentrations on the British Isles. To defend the important rail routes and roads in the rear areas, the use of light antiaircraft artillery and machine guns was stressed. These weapons proved particularly effective against low-level attacks on trains. The attackers rarely escaped damage, due in large measure to the determination of the Soviet machine-gun crews.

It is evident that Soviet antiaircraft artillery and other ground defenses made a quick recovery and proved a serious deterrent to attacking air units.

As for Army and Navy command personnel, they also acknowledge that in the early stages of the campaign the Luftwaffe had clearly established air superiority. German Army personnel state unanimously that the Soviet air forces played no role whatever in operations at the opening of the campaign in June 1941. It was a source of surprise and satisfaction that extremely worthwhile targets for Soviet air attacks, such as dense troop concentrations, long columns of troops on the march, bridges and other traffic bottlenecks, and supply installations, were rarely attacked and then only by small numbers of planes and with little effect. This was something inconceivable to the troops and unfortunately often resulted in a certain degree of carelessness in matters of unit air raid protection and camouflage measures.

This appraisal of Soviet air power by army command personnel remained practically unchanged in 1941, although it is admitted that with the progress of German operations Soviet air activities increased and revealed more careful planning. In certain sectors and during certain battles the effectiveness of Russian air power in fact increased quite considerably, mounting occasionally even to local superiority.

From the experience of German army command personnel in the southern area of the eastern theater,[22] and particularly in the Kiev battle of encirclement, it is obvious that Soviet air power, at times and in certain areas, was used effectively here and was only weakened when Moelder's* fighter wing commenced operating in the area.

It is interesting to note that Soviet air action in the south was restricted almost exclusively to attacks on the forward German

---

* Editor's Note: Colonel Werner Moelders, commander of the 51st Fighter Group, and unofficially credited with having shot down 115 planes (14 of these date from the Spanish Civil War), was one of the Luftwaffe's best-known aces (one of 29 high-scoring German aces, each of whom was credited with having shot down 100 planes or more-- the highest single number being 352 claimed by Major Erich Hartmann). Colonel Moelders was killed in an airplane crash on 22 November 1941.

panzer divisions. This was also the case in the northern area of the eastern front, where the infantry divisions following up the advance were not molested. A good example of this occurred at Kiev, where the panzer units forming the eastern prong of the envelopment were attacked repeatedly and fiercely by air units, while the infantry divisions forming the enveloping force in the west were not troubled at all from the air.

In their attacks, Soviet airmen gave evidence of willingness, aggressiveness, courage, and appreciable standards of training, as is emphasized by Colonel Pelsmueller. Pelsmueller summarizes his experience by stating that time and again the Soviet air forces hampered the German ground forces in their movements and inflicted heavy losses, particularly during critical situations. In his opinion, the Luftwaffe failed to achieve the destruction it had wrought in other campaigns. Moreover, he felt that a large number of Soviet airfields, owing to the nature of their construction, their location, and excellent camouflage, had escaped detection by German reconnaissance.

Generalleutnant a. D. Helmuth Huffmann, Commanding the V Corps Artillery Group, Army Group Center, states[23] that after the first devastating German attacks, the Soviet Command concentrated in the south larger numbers of the aircraft which had escaped destruction, and that although these forces at no time developed a real power concentration they did at times achieve absolute air superiority. However, after the arrival of Moelders and his fighter wing, Soviet air power was again completely eliminated in this area. The same appraisal is arrived at by Field Marshal Erich von Manstein,[24] at that time Commanding General, Eleventh Army.

Whereas Soviet air power in the southern area seriously hampered German ground operations--particularly so during the battles around Kiev and on the Crimean Peninsula--its effects in the central and northern areas were hardly noticeable. Huffmann[25] goes into great detail in evaluating the views expressed by army command personnel, and his findings show that the Soviet air forces were far inferior in these areas to the German air forces committed, and that the German ground forces fully realized this fact. Occasional Soviet air attacks--for example against German bridgeheads across the Dnieper, Seim (Seym), and Dvina Rivers and against marching columns and troop assemblies--cannot alter this overall impression, although they sometimes inflicted grievous losses on German ground forces. On the whole, German army commanders in the central and northern areas consider that the Luftwaffe maintained absolute superiority in their areas up to the end of 1941. Even the difficult retrograde movements at Kalinin and Moscow, though seriously vulnerable to air attack, were hardly interfered with by the Soviet air forces.

Huffmann[26] considers that this was due largely to: 1) the excellent cooperation between the Luftwaffe and German ground units, particularly in the quick seizure and destruction of Soviet air bases; 2) the large-scale destruction of Soviet aircraft by German fighter and antiaircraft artillery forces; 3) the failure of the Soviets to develop proper power concentrations; 4) their failure to penetrate deep behind the German lines; 5) their clumsy methods of reorganization after the loss of most of their airfields. He is not far wrong[27] in ascribing the greater successes secured by Soviet air power in the southern areas not only to the development of power concentrations, but probably in even larger measure to the entirely different characteristics of the terrain. In the wide, open plains of the south, the advancing German panzer and infantry columns found far less cover and protection than those operating in the forest terrain of the central and northern areas. This facilitated the operations of attacking Soviet air units.

Air support given to the Soviet Navy, particularly in the form of air action against German naval units, was so negligible throughout the war, and especially so in 1941, that German naval commanders found it hardly possible to form any opinions about the Soviet air forces on the basis of combat experience. A study by Captain (now Admiral a. D.) Wilhelm Moessel (Navy)[28] reveals that the Soviet Command apparently considered naval air reconnaissance, coastal air patrols, and air combat operations at sea of secondary importance. This applies equally, with only a few reservations, to the Polar regions, the Baltic, and the Black Sea. At no time did properly planned operations conducted by large air formations interfere with German naval operations during the German advance in the summer and autumn of 1941. The use of aircraft in coastal defense missions was more pronounced in the Black Sea than in other coastal areas. Broadly speaking, however, the onus of supporting ground operations was so heavy and the naval operations were so unimportant in comparison that the Soviets apparently considered it hardly worthwhile or necessary

Drawing of a Russian tank
erasing its tracks in the snow

Aircraft camouflage with a simulated dwelling

to conduct sizable air operations against the German Navy or German sea routes. Possibly this attitude is due in some measure to the Russian mentality, which is directed primarily to land warfare and its problems. Whatever the causes, it can be stated conclusively here that their negative experience, namely their lack of experience, necessarily influenced German naval commanders to infer that the Soviet air forces in 1941 were in no way a dangerous opponent for the German Navy. These views are supported by Admiral L. Buerkner.[29]

B. Command and Operations.

In appraising the command and operations of the Soviet air forces in 1941 the views expressed by almost all German commanders concur on two points: 1) that Soviet air power was employed exclusively to support ground operations and had no strategic air missions to perform; 2) that the activities of the Soviet air forces, whether bomber, ground attack, or fighter, during this period were primarily of a defensive nature.

In addition, various German commanders mention the lack of planning, the obstinacy, and the lack of versatility and flexibility in the Soviet conduct of air warfare.

Major Rall,[30] commander of a fighter squadron in the southern area, finds that the main emphasis in Soviet air activities in 1941 was on ground support, and that the operations of air units at any given time were directly connected with the tactical movements of ground units.

Thus, even roving fighter operations were intended primarily to support the operations of ground forces, with the fighters frequently participating in ground action through low-level attacks. Their technological inferiority, and the heavy losses they had suffered also caused the Soviets to restrict themselves chiefly to providing protection for their ground operations. In addition, they confined themselves to the defensive, never seeking battle with German aircraft. Continuous air attacks against ground targets from dawn to shortly before nightfall with large numbers of aircraft were a characteristic feature of Soviet air activities. No attempt was made, however, to form real concentrations of force defined in time or place.

The caution displayed by Soviet airmen when flying a mission is confirmed, among others by Major a. D. Egon Stoll-Berberich,[31] squadron leader in a dive-bomber group in the southern area. Quoting a downed Soviet pilot, Stoll-Berberich reports that an order existed for all Soviet ground-attack and bomber units to avoid any combat with German dive-bomber, ground-attack, and bomber units and to cease their own current attack mission if German units appeared in order to resume their attack after departure of the German aircraft. The reason given for the order was that German formations were always escorted by fighters, and the intention was to avoid the heavy Soviet aircraft losses resulting from German fighter action. In Stoll-Berberich's opinion, the lack of aggressiveness in Soviet airmen was due, in some measure, to this order.

Major von Cossart[32] supports this view, mentioning that the Soviet Command hampered the operations and the aggressiveness of Soviet fighters. He believes that this was due not solely to the initial heavy Soviet losses from the first German attacks, but also to the Soviet realization that the defensive power of their air units was no match for German fighters, that Soviet airmen were not good at independent air combat, and that the Soviet air forces, although they were numerically strong, could not measure up to the standards of modern air warfare.

Colonel von Beust,[33] however, arrives at somewhat different conclusions. According to his view, the operational doctrines of the Soviet air forces emphasized the performance of the mission above all else. The chances of success or the losses which might be incurred were, by comparison, of no importance. The main requirement was that Soviet airmen be in the air and achieve contact with the enemy, no matter what the circumstances or results. That the Soviet Command desired and endeavored to achieve more tangible results is, however, taken for granted. Von Beust also remarks that Soviet air operations were the result less of deliberate planning than of currently existing circumstances and the exigencies of current situations. Inadequate versatility and flexibility under these circumstances frequently resulted in the stereotype repetition of operations with the same tactics, at the same times of the day, and in the same areas, even when the necessity for such operations no longer existed. This was due to deficiencies in commanders at intermediate and higher levels, who had not been able to give the front units adequate training and an adequate knowledge of tactics.

Von Beust's view is supported by Generalmajor a. D. Fritz Morzik,[34] who remarks that the manner in which Soviet bomber, fighter, and ground-attack units executed their attack missions revealed inconsistent training.

Numerous commanders concur in the view that Soviet air operations in general were designed only to support the operations of the ground forces.[35] Many observers also state that the Soviets, both in the performance of assigned missions and when in pursuit of German aircraft, did not penetrate beyond the German front and the near-front areas.[36] The formation or unit leader was frequently the only one who possessed a map and had any knowledge of the target to be attacked, and if he were shot down it was often impossible for the rest of the attacking force to complete its mission.[37]

A brief resume of what Generalmajor Uebe has written on the command and operations of Soviet air forces during 1941 follows:[38]

Essentially, Uebe confirms the general views of German air commanders that the tactics of the Soviet air forces reflected Stalin's demand for harmonious cooperation between all arms and services, and Stalin's opinion that attacks on industrial targets far in the enemy interior could have no important effect on the outcome of a war. In view of the weakness of their infantry, the Russians employed an almost completely tactical use of air forces in support of the Army.

Russian air tactics, Uebe finds, were rigid and stereotyped; once a decision was made it was adhered to for a long time. Occasional variations in details and occasional diversionary maneuvers represented no real changes. Large formation operations were a rare occurrence, because the Soviets lacked the flying and command ability to conduct such operations.

The targets of attack were infantry and artillery positions, or troop concentrations and reserves, with penetrations of usually only six to nine miles and rarely over twelve to fourteen miles behind the German front lines. Such attacks were directed primarily against targets which could not be taken under artillery fire; in other cases they were intended to support artillery fire.

Daylight attacks usually commenced sixty or ninety minutes after full daylight and ceased well before dusk; night attacks usually lasted from early dusk until shortly after midnight.

The flying altitudes preferred were under 17,000 feet. Only a few reconnaissance aircraft operated at higher levels, bombers and fighters only very rarely.

In 1941 the Soviet air forces were still very dependent upon weather conditions, usually restricting their missions to fair weather.

Operational orders for the Soviet air forces were frequently transmitted by radio and, therefore, often intercepted. This enabled the German command to employ its fighter forces in concentration and inflict heavy losses.

Uebe's views are largely confirmed by the opinions of numerous German Army command personnel.[39] Time and again these sources state that the attack objectives of Soviet bomber and ground-attack units, and in part also of fighter units, included advancing columns, artillery positions, troop concentrations and assemblies, command posts, reserves, tank units, bridge sites, and supply installations. Mention is also made of the frequent repetition of attacks and the stereotyped and determined manner in which they were carried out. Army commanders, like Luftwaffe commanders, were rarely able to discern any development of real power concentrations.

The outstanding feature in the appraisals given by army command personnel, with very few exceptions, is their surprise at the relatively rare and ineffective operations of the Soviet air forces and the meager results they obtained in 1941.

None of the appraisals by German naval commanders contradict the views of Luftwaffe and Army commanders presented above. Furthermore, the activities of the Soviet air forces in cooperation with the Soviet Navy and against the German Navy were so insignificant in 1941 that it would hardly be possible to draw any worthwhile conclusions from them.

C. **Organization and Chains of Command.**

Generally speaking, German field commanders had no opportunity to develop any picture of the organization and chains of command in the Soviet air forces. Prisoner of war statements and the results of other intelligence activities reached them too late, or not at all. Thus, only a few Luftwaffe commanders have expressed themselves on this subject, and command personnel of the German Army and Navy have not commented at all.

The few reports available serve to confirm the ideas of the Luftwaffe High Command, as already set forth in Chapter 1. According to Major Jaehne,[40] several air units were organized into regiments consisting of approximately 20 aircraft.[41] Air regiments were often based alone on an airfield, and were controlled by air divisions, which received their directives from the appropriate army headquarters. Air corps and air armies were also known to exist and it was known that they were under the command of army command staffs. Furthermore, information was available on the employment of fighter units under the home defense commands.

Colonel a.D. R. von Heimann,[42] a former expert adviser in the Luftwaffe High Command, considers that in spite of frequent improvisations, the organization of the Soviet air forces was in general sound, and that the command techniques in use apparently caused no serious difficulties. The number of air units assigned to an army command depended on the size of its command zone, the existing or intended areas of main effort, the intended conduct of operations, and in part on intentions to deceive the enemy.

Generalleutnant a.D. Adolf Galland*[43] regarded the Soviet air forces not as a separate service but as an integral part of the Red Army. As such, he considers that they were perhaps more appropriately and more uniformly organized and employed than the units of the Luftwaffe.

Soviet Colonel Wanyushkin[44] generally confirms the views of the Luftwaffe High Command on the organization and chains of

---

* Editor's Note: In American military circles Galland is certainly the best known of all the German fighter Aces of World War II. Credited with having shot down 103 enemy planes, he eventually became Inspector of the Fighter Forces. After the war he worked for the United States Air Force on the Von Rohden Project, authored a widely read book (The First and the Last, Henry Holt & Co., New York, 1954), served as an adviser to the Argentine Air Force, and is now reportedly representing an American aircraft company in Germany.

command of the Soviet air forces. He also confirms the stated average authorized strength of the air regiment as 60 aircraft. The actual strengths, however, were far lower after the initial weeks of the campaign. Thus, Colonel Wanyushkin's division on 25 June 1941 actually had only 60-70 aircraft in the two bomber and three fighter regiments it controlled, and by the end of August the division's units had a total effective strength of only 20 aircraft.

D. Strength and Strategic Concentration.

German field commanders in all three branches of the Wehrmacht had no way of ascertaining the numerical strength of the Soviet air forces. Their knowledge was naturally restricted to their specific command areas. Nevertheless, all German field commanders agree unanimously that the Soviet air forces far outnumbered German air forces.

The number of Soviet aircraft shot down or destroyed on the ground also soon revealed that the Luftwaffe High Command was far below the mark with its estimate of 5,700 Soviet front line aircraft in European Russia. In an address before the Reichstag on 11 December 1941 Hitler placed the number of destroyed or captured Soviet aircraft at 17,322.[45] This figure appears inordinately high. Possibly the results achieved were intentionally exaggerated in the address for the purposes of propaganda. There can be no doubt that the figure included large numbers of other than combat aircraft. Nevertheless, the figure does serve to show clearly that the Luftwaffe High Command had considerably underestimated the numerical strength of the Soviet air forces.

Information is available from a small number of Luftwaffe unit commanders concerning the strategic concentration of the Soviet air forces. Colonel von Beust,[46] for example, considers the Soviet strategic concentration to have been primitive, describing it as follows:

> Almost parallel with and at a distance of not more than 30 miles from the border, all fighters, ground-attack, and tactical reconnaissance units were in position on airfields in an almost linear disposition, without any organization in depth, without outposts, without defined areas of main effort, and with their sub-units loosely distributed. The disposition of the heavier air forces was very similar, in areas between

60 and 120 miles farther back. Even the services farther in the rear, the reserve and training units, and the industrial air services, showed clear signs of rigid schematism. The results of this defective plan of concentration are generally known: within the first two weeks of war they were to cost the Soviet air forces more than 50 percent of their total front-line strength and were to lead later to almost complete annihilation.

The Luftwaffe High Command and Luftwaffe commanders, with one exception,* confirm the reports that Russian air units were massed on airfields close to the border. This fact and the resultant destruction of a large percentage of the units of the Soviet air forces on their airfields at the beginning of the Russian campaign were major factors which contributed to the superiority of the numerically weaker Luftwaffe in the eastern theater in 1941.

E. Aircraft Types, Weapons, Equipment.

Field commanders of the Luftwaffe are unanimous concerning the quality of Soviet aircraft, their weapons and other equipment. They considered the Soviet air forces, with their largely obsolete materiel, to be definitely inferior to the Luftwaffe.

This advantage was soon discovered by German aircraft crews in battle. The knowledge increased their feeling of superiority considerably and must also be considered as one of the important factors which contributed to the almost complete ineffectiveness of the Soviet air forces during the first months of the campaign.

Numerous German commanders admit, however, that the modernization program of the Soviet air forces, which began to take shape in some areas as early as the autumn of 1941, came as a sharp surprise to the Luftwaffe after the important German successes of

---

* The exception is Major Jaehne, who operated in the central area. In his opinion the Soviet air concentration was of a defensive pattern, without noticeable massing, and--on the whole--with the air units widely dispersed.

the summer months.

The serious inferiority of Soviet aircraft types in technical development, in the materials used in the construction of fuselages and engines, in their general flight performances, and in their weapons and equipment, is emphasized time and again by a large number of Luftwaffe field commanders.[47]

The disadvantages of Soviet models and their hopeless inferiority in combat against German aircraft are very clearly illustrated by Captain Kath.[48] Kath goes on, however, to emphasize the astonishment on the German side as the first modern Soviet aircraft models made their appearance in the late summer of 1941, when I-18 fighters and P-2* bombers were first encountered, and in the autumn when IL-2† ground-attack aircraft first entered combat.

Similar conclusions are drawn by Generalmajor Uebe,[49] who notes the early introduction of considerably improved Soviet models and of large numbers of aircraft received under the Lend-Lease Agreement. Uebe also gives first place to the IL-2, which, after its first appearance at the front in the autumn of 1941, was soon available in large numbers and proved an ideal plane for ground-attack operations.

Colonel Wanyushkin,[50] stated under interrogation that Mig fighters were introduced in field units in early 1941, and Lagg fighters in September of the same year. P-2 bombers and IL-2 ground-attack aircraft were introduced in Military Area Orel in May and April 1941, respectively. Judging by the appearance of these types of aircraft in front areas, however, the dates given by Wanyushkin can refer only to initial and isolated deliveries, since the aircraft were not encountered at the front in noticeable numbers before the autumn and winter of 1941.

F. <u>Consolidated Appraisal.</u>

In an attempt to summarize the general impressions of German

---

* The P-2 (or YAK-4) was a twin-engined, monoplane, bomber, employed as a dive bomber, light bomber or reconnaissance plane.

† The IL-2 was the well-known Ilyushin "Stormovik," a ground-attack aircraft. This single-engine, low-wing, cantilever monoplane was armed with 2 cannon, 2 machine guns and equipped with bomb racks.

Luftwaffe, Army, and Navy command personnel concerning the Soviet air forces in 1941, the following picture evolves:

1) Soviet air power was used exclusively to support the operations of the Soviet ground forces, and the air units thus employed demonstrated commendable aggressiveness and frequently considerable energy in attempting to fulfill this mission. Their partial failure was due, primarily, to the fact that the Luftwaffe achieved air superiority.

2) The Soviet air forces during this phase of the campaign were inferior and were forced to restrict themselves to defensive operations. Nevertheless, Russian air superiority did exist in specific areas and during specific periods, a fact which naturally was felt more severely by the German Army commanders concerned than its significance merited within the overall situation.

3) The inferiority of the Soviet air forces was due primarily to: a) the destruction of innumerable Soviet aircraft on the ground and in air combat during the first surprise German air attacks; b) the tactical, flying, and general training inferiority of Soviet aircraft crews and their lack of combat experience; c) the stereotype methods of the Soviet conduct of air operations and rigid operational doctrines; d) obsolete aircraft models, weapons, and other equipment at the outset of the campaign; e) the destruction of the Soviet ground service organization through German air attacks and the loss of airfields through the rapid advance of the German armies.

4) That the Soviet air forces proved several times superior in numbers to the Luftwaffe came as a complete and unpleasant surprise to German commanders. In this respect the Luftwaffe High Command had gravely underestimated the situation. The numerical superiority of the Soviet air forces, however, did not produce the logical results because of the factors listed under item 3, above.

5) Toward the end of 1941 signs that the Soviet air forces were gradually recovering from the losses suffered in the past summer increased. The early arrival of a severe winter greatly helped their recovery.

6) The Soviet antiaircraft artillery arm, together with all other branches of ground defense, was frequently exceptionally effective, and recovered quickly from the first surprise. It proved

far more capable of performing its missions than the Luftwaffe High Command had assumed.

Section II: <u>Reconnaissance Units</u>[51]

    A. <u>General</u>.

To assess the performances of Soviet air reconnaissance forces was no simple matter for German field commanders, for they came into contact with these units far less frequently than with fighter or ground-attack units, so that the results of Soviet air reconnaissance, or, in other words, the success or failure of Soviet air reconnaissance units, frequently remained obscure to German eyes. Nevertheless, the number of opinions by German commanders on Soviet air reconnaissance units in 1941 is adequate to form a probably accurate picture of this arm of the Soviet air forces.

A characteristic feature of all reports on the subject is the opinion that the air reconnaissance arm was seriously neglected by the Soviets in all respects, including methods of operations, performance, training, and equipment. This is all the more surprising in view of the fact that the exclusive use of Soviet air power in support of the Army would have made it seem logical that the reconnaissance arm would merit particular attention. For this neglect no satisfactory reasons have been found. Occasionally the view has been expressed that the Soviets could afford to dispense largely with air reconnaissance because of their excellently functioning system of espionage and general intelligence, but this can hardly be considered a sufficient cause. Two possible explanations are that: 1) in building up their air forces, the Soviets could not devote equal efforts to the development of all branches of air power; 2) the fact that reconnaissance aviation requires particularly thorough and careful training. Another reason of primary importance might be that the nature of the duties of a reconnaissance pilot at that time, who had to rely largely on his own initiative in operations, was not consonant with the innate characteristics of the average Russian.

    B. <u>Organization and Chain of Command.</u>

German commanders were able to obtain only a very general but fairly accurate impression of the organization and chain of command of the Soviet air reconnaissance arm.

Colonel von Beust[52] admits that the operational controls governing the Soviet reconnaissance arm were not known in detail, but that the Soviets had found a solution favorable for the Army. Colonel von Heimann[53] points out that actual air reconnaissance units in the German sense existed only in isolated cases, an opinion which is shared by other German commanders.

Major Jaehne[54] mentions that Soviet reconnaissance units were consolidated in regiments, but not in divisions. The strength of twenty aircraft per regiment quoted by him is understandable in view of the low effective strengths of Soviet air units in general after the initial German attacks.

The finding that air reconnaissance units were assigned to higher air command headquarters and were governed in their operations by the controlling surface forces headquarters is correct. In Jaehne's opinion the organization of the Soviet air reconnaissance arm, seen from the Soviet side, was probably a practical solution.

C. Air Reconnaissance Operations.

1) General. The opinions of German commanders concerning Soviet air reconnaissance operations in 1941 coincide, particularly in the following points: a) the conduct of air reconnaissance was irregular, unsystematic, inadequately adaptable, and did not extend deeply enough into the German rear areas; b) generally speaking, cooperation with the ground forces on the field of battle was awkward, and reconnaissance results were not translated into action speedily enough; c) owing to inadequate tactical and aviation training, inferior types of aircraft, and the lack of individual self-reliance, Soviet reconnaissance pilots ceased operations prematurely or carried out their missions incompletely when they encountered German air units, unfavorable weather conditions, or any other difficulties; d) air reconnaissance was conducted sometimes by single aircraft--particularly strategic air reconnaissance--sometimes by a number of aircraft simultaneously--particularly in the case of battle reconnaissance (in operations over the battlefield reconnaissance aircraft were frequently given strong fighter escorts); e) particularly in the case of tactical and battle reconnaissance, specific reconnaissance aircraft types were replaced largely by fighter and ground-attack aircraft types. This occurred at an early stage in the campaign.

2) <u>Long-range</u>. The long-range reconnaissance arm of the Soviet air forces is considered to have been generally poor. According to Uebe[55] the personnel lacked resiliency. Thus, if unfavorable weather conditions or German defenses were encountered en route, or if even minor technical difficulties occurred, the crews would discontinue their flight and return to their bases; if they encountered defenses in the target area, they would carry out their reconnaissance mission too hastily and with too little precision.

Visual observation was not thorough enough, and the processing of air photos was too cumbersome. In neither case were the results obtained properly interpreted. It can be stated definitely that important German operational movements were recognized too late or not at all by Soviet long-range air reconnaissance.

Colonel von Beust[56] also arrives at the conclusion that the Soviet long-range air reconnaissance arm was in no way equal to its task, and regards inadequate training in aviation and in tactical and operational subjects as the causes. Obviously lacking the ability to conduct real strategic reconnaissance, the units restricted their activities to the front areas and other target areas within the tactical reconnaissance zones. For this reason the higher levels of the Soviet Command remained ignorant of German preparations and were unable to recognize German assembly movements, or, at a later stage, to keep track of the German advance and envelopment movements. The method of assigning reconnaissance missions was tactically inappropriate. Planes were dispatched on a direct course to their reconnaissance areas, and the timing of operations and the routes to be followed were never changed. This resulted in disproportionately heavy losses. Employing these methods there was no possibility of conducting systematic and promising reconnaissance operations.

Major Jaehne[57] supplements what has been said above by the statement that the operations of Soviet long-range air reconnaissance units were restricted principally to reconnaissance missions flown for the Army and did not serve the purpose of determining strategic targets, since the Soviets rarely employed long-range bomber units. To countercheck the results obtained in air reconnaissance, the mission was apparently frequently assigned to two aircraft separately. Single-plane missions were, in any case, not popular with the Soviets.

3) <u>Short-range</u>. German air commanders comment more

favorably on the performance of the Soviet short-range air reconnaissance arm than on the long-range reconnaissance arm. Contributors repeatedly emphasize the efforts of Soviet aircraft crews to cooperate very closely with the Army. A number of sources confirm that fighter and ground-attack air units, at an early stage during the war, were required to assume major responsibility for battlefield and other short-range reconnaissance.[58]

Captain a. D. von Reschke,[59] observer in a short-range reconnaissance squadron operating in the southern area, reports that already on the fifth day of the campaign a modern (Mig-1 ?) plane was observed on reconnaissance missions, and that in the period approximately four to six weeks after the opening of the campaign two I-16's (Rata) flew early morning reconnaissance missions daily in addition to frequent surprise battle reconnaissance missions. These planes operated at low levels, took clever advantage of terrain conditions, and also carried out strafing attacks along the roads if favorable opportunities arose. The Soviets lost relatively few fighter aircraft in reconnaissance missions, and from the attacks flown by their bomber and ground-attack units it appears that the units employed in reconnaissance activities produced useful results.

Generalmajor Uebe[60] reports that obsolete aircraft models were withdrawn from battlefield reconnaissance missions during 1941, and that from then on this type of reconnaissance was conducted principally by fighter and ground-attack aircraft. These aircraft operated singly at middle altitudes and were protected by strong fighter escorts, or they operated in flights of two or three IL-2 aircraft at low or tree-top altitudes without fighter protection. It was only on exceptional occasions that artillery spotter planes were employed, or that other reconnaissance planes operated at high altitudes.

Tactical reconnaissance extended to a depth of ten or fifteen miles behind the German lines, and the areas were frequently only very incompletely covered. In a steadily increasing measure P-2 aircraft were employed on this type of mission, flying at altitudes of 26,000 feet and higher, and often following the same course day after day at the same time of the day. On the approach of German fighters, aircraft usually endeavored to escape attack by diving down toward their own front lines. In exceptional cases the Soviets employed IL-2 units for tactical air reconnaissance. These units operated at medium altitudes and were usually shot down easily by German fighters.

Little experience was gathered in 1941 on the subject of Soviet night air reconnaissance. It was generally known that type U-2 aircraft were primarily employed for the purpose, but the results obtained must have been extremely meager, since they were at no time translated into tactical action.

4) <u>Views of German Army and Navy Command Personnel</u>. The views of German Army command personnel on Soviet air reconnaissance operations coincide with the views of German air commanders on the subject: they consider that the effects of Soviet air reconnaissance activities on German army operations in 1941 were small.

The only area in which some views differ is the south. Thus, Generalleutnant Huffmann[61] writes of lively Soviet reconnaissance activities in the southern areas whenever German fighter units were absent. In most cases missions were flown here by from one to three aircraft, which usually returned to their own lines quickly on the appearance of German fighters.

The bombing activities of Soviet reconnaissance units had a particularly harassing influence on German troops. Although the material damage which these bombings inflicted was small, the influence on troop morale was frequently serious. In these raids, the reconnaissance planes usually made their bombing run from the rear of the marching German column.

Air reconnaissance was a simple matter in the southern areas of the eastern theater; the terrain was level and almost completely devoid of cover so that no movements could remain concealed. In spite of this, it was rarely noticed that the Soviets made good use of the reconnaissance results obtained or that they translated this information into tactical action.

During the battles along the Dnieper River and on the Crimean Peninsula, however, it became obvious that the Soviet Command was interpreting air reconnaissance results quickly and accurately and applying the information thus obtained to plan and conduct attacks by bombers and ground-attack aircraft. It is clearly discernible that close and sound cooperation existed in these areas between the

Soviet ground and air forces.

In contrast with the above observations concerning the southern area, Generalleutnant Huffmann[62] reports that Soviet air reconnaissance activities were rare in the northern and central areas, where there were no indications that the Soviet Command made any use of the information obtained through this medium. Even on the first day of the campaign there were complete sectors in which not a single Soviet reconnaissance plane was sighted.

In a similar manner Generalleutnant a. D. B. Frankewitz, who commanded an artillery regiment in the northern area,[63] comes to the conclusion that the Soviets lost the battle on 22 June because they had no air reconnaissance. During the further course of the campaign he remarks with astonishment and satisfaction--in common with other German Army commanders--that the Soviets had practically no artillery observation aircraft. According to Huffmann, it was not until late November 1941 that Soviet air reconnaissance activities increased in the northern area.

It is thus obvious that from the viewpoint of German army command personnel the Soviet air reconnaissance arm on the whole was not considered a serious threat in 1941.

Concerning the experience of German naval personnel on Soviet air reconnaissance activities in 1941, the following is summarized from a report by Admiral a. D. Wilhelm Moessel:[64] generally speaking, Soviet strategic reconnaissance against the German coastal areas and sea routes was not very lively and was not conducted systematically. It was only during periods of increased German supply movements and during the periods of approach and departure of Allied convoys in Polar waters that Soviet air reconnaissance activities increased. The same applied to the Rumanian coastal areas in the Black Sea prior to occupation of the Crimean Peninsula by German forces.

On the whole, no remarkable operations by Soviet air reconnaissance units in 1941 are on records.

D. Aircraft Types, Weapons, Equipment.

The almost unanimous opinion of German commanders is that

at the outset of the Russian campaign the aircraft, weapons, and equipment of the Soviet air reconnaissance arm were on the whole obsolete, so that the force as such was inferior to the Luftwaffe. After the loss of their old types of reconnaissance aircraft, the Soviets brought about a gradual improvement of the situation by an increasing use of P-2 aircraft for long-range air reconnaissance, and fighter and ground-attack aircraft for tactical reconnaissance.

Major Jaehne,[65] on this subject, expresses himself somewhat as follows: Battlefield and other tactical reconnaissance was conducted primarily by IL-2 aircraft, produced as a two-seater for the purpose. The IL-2 had good armor plating, its technical and flight performances were good, and it was suitable for employment in reconnaissance missions over the front. For long-range reconnaissance the Soviets employed P-2 aircraft, the two-seater version of which can be considered useful in respect to its technical and general flight performances. Types R-5 and U-2 aircraft were used for night reconnaissance; both were slow and of primitive construction, but highly maneuverable and easy to handle. For photo reconnaissance the Soviets had too few appropriately equipped planes available, and those available had photographic equipment far below the standards of German equipment. This may have been due to production difficulties.

It was noted that during this phase of the campaign Soviet reconnaissance aircraft were armed exclusively with machine guns.

Jaehne concludes that, with the exception of the IL-2 and P-2 aircraft, the aircraft, weapons and general equipment of the Soviet air reconnaissance forces were below standard.

E. Consolidated Appraisal of Soviet Air Reconnaissance Activities.

Appraisal of the Soviet air reconnaissance services in 1941, based on the experience of Luftwaffe, Army, and Navy command personnel would read somewhat as follows: 1) Soviet air reconnaissance served the purposes of the Army almost exclusively. It was restricted to the near front areas, was incomplete and unsystematic. No reconnaissance was carried out to identify strategic targets for attack by long-range bomber units; 2) The Soviet long-range air reconnaissance arm was unable to perform its appropriate mission because of operational, training, and technological weaknesses. The large initial successes of the German armed forces and the catastrophic conditions which resulted for the Soviets during the first months of the campaign were partly due to the failure of the Soviet's long-range air reconnaissance arm, which produced no intelligence data for the Soviet Command concerning the movements of the German armies. 3) After recovering from the initial heavy reverses suffered, the Soviet tactical air reconnaissance arm gave a better performance, particularly after the introduction of modern types of aircraft for battlefield and other tactical reconnaissance. Apart from exceptional cases, however, the Soviet tactical air reconnaissance arm failed to achieve any really major and decisive results in spite of serious efforts in cooperation with the army. The reasons for this failure must probably be sought to a large extent in the inadequate training of both air force and army personnel for the purpose. 4) Naval air reconnaissance was incomplete in its coverage and generally unsatisfactory. Apart from the lack of suitable long-range aircraft, the failure here was probably due to a general underestimation of the importance of naval warfare and a consequent neglect of coastal air reconnaissance activities in favor of reconnaissance for the Army. 5) The organization and chain of command for the Soviet air reconnaissance arm and the dependence of its units on the Army were suited to the existing circumstances. 6) The aircraft types, the weapons, and the general equipment--including air photo and radio equipment--were not suited to the requirements of modern warfare. The situation improved only gradually through the introduction of more modern types of aircraft.

In summary, Soviet air reconnaissance in 1941 was little in evidence. With the exception of German troops in the southern areas, the advancing Germans paid no attention to Soviet air reconnaissance activities.

The Luftwaffe High Command prewar appraisal of the small value of the Soviet air reconnaissance services was confirmed by the course of events.

Section III: <u>The Fighter Arm</u>[66]

A. <u>General.</u>

In contrast with reconnaissance units, Soviet fighter units were well known to Luftwaffe commanders because they came into contact with them frequently. Consequently, numerous statements concerning

Russian fighters are available. These reports vary according to the time, place, and circumstances under which the fighters were encountered, but in all essential points, they are in agreement. Thus, all Luftwaffe commanders consulted agree that the Soviet Command had given particular attention to the development of its fighter arm. The fighter arm was therefore far ahead of the other arms, not only in numerical strength but also tactically and technologically, so that it played the most important role in the struggle against the Luftwaffe. Personnel for the fighter arm were specially selected and trained, and represented an elite body within the Soviet air forces.[67]

In spite of their privileged position and their numerical superiority, however, Soviet fighters in 1941 did not succeed in seriously challenging German air superiority. On the contrary, in the autumn of 1941 the Soviet fighter arm suffered such terrific losses that its units were hardly ever encountered in strengths which could have constituted a serious threat.

The battle against the Soviet fighter arm in 1941 was characterized by the effects of the devastating German attacks against the Soviet airfields, by the superior combat experience of German fighter personnel, and by the superior quality of German fighter aircraft. As a result of these factors German fighters, during the initial stages of the campaign, had no difficulty in shooting down their Soviet opponents by the hundreds. Together with the general inadequacies and faultiness of the entire Soviet fighter arm, which will be described later, these circumstances soon produced uncontested German air superiority, which in parts amounted to absolute air supremacy.

Nonetheless, German hopes that the Luftwaffe would succeed in completely eliminating Soviet fighter activities for a considerable time and thereby secure complete air supremacy failed to materialize. On the contrary, as early as the end of 1941 the Soviet fighter arm had passed through its worst stage and was beginning to recover. An effort will be made in the present section to uncover the reasons for these developments.

B. Organization, Chain of Command, Strength, and Strategic Concentration.

Only a few comments by German commanders are available concerning the organization and chain of command of the Soviet fighter arm. What information is available from these sources confirms the views of the Luftwaffe High Command according to which fighters were organized in regiments and divisions,[68] although some of the officers come to the conclusion that the organization of Soviet fighter units was very similar to the German organization.[69] In arriving at this latter conclusion the German officers in question do not appear to have grasped fully the fundamental difference between the German and the Soviet organizational structure, namely, that in spite of all apparent similarities between the two organizations, the Soviet fighter forces, in contrast with their German counterparts, were controlled by the Army and not by an air force high command. For the persons involved this basic problem of organization was also of minor importance. What was of more importance to them was the organization of Soviet fighter forces for combat and other operations. Owing to the rapid German advance in the summer and autumn of 1941 German command personnel had little time to devote to such subjects, and owing to the existing German air superiority they were only conditionally interested.

All German commanders realized the numerical superiority of the Soviet air arm, which undoubtedly was an unpleasant surprise to many of them. Later factual evidence confirmed that Soviet fighter aircraft had outnumbered German fighters many times over in 1941. A Luftwaffe High Command report of 1945,[70] for example, places the overall Soviet output in fighter planes for 1941 at 7,300, in addition to which 500 fighters were imported from the USA and Britain. In comparison, the German output in fighters for the same year was only 2,992. However, at the front in 1941 the numerical ratio in fighters was undoubtedly considerably more favorable for the Soviets than the above production ratio. On this subject the Luftwaffe High Command's prewar appraisal was, therefore, very much in error.

German commanders confirm the strategic concentration of the Soviet fighter forces with main concentrations in the near front areas. Colonel von Beust[71] considers such a disposition of forces to have been unwise. Stationed near to the front and without any disposition in depth, the Soviet fighter forces were extremely vulnerable to German air attack and were also constantly exposed to observation by German fighters. Quite apart from the fact that the close proximity of the Soviet fighter airfields to the front made it extremely difficult to intercept German units penetrating at high altitudes, this disposition of the fighter forces placed an exceptionally heavy strain on the Soviet supply and signal systems. It even happened occasionally that Soviet fighter airfields were so close to the front that they were exposed to direct action by German ground forces and were simply overrun by German troops.

C. Fighter Operations.

1) Fighter Pilots. According to their varying experience the opinions of German commanders differ concerning the behaviour of Soviet fighter pilots in combat. Some German commanders describe them as lacking in aggressiveness,[72] and consider their morale in attack and general combat low even when they had clear superiority.[73] Others considered the average Soviet fighter pilot as the toughest opponent hitherto encountered and describe him as aggressive and courageous.[74]

This apparent disparity of opinions can probably be explained by the circumstance that, conscious of their own inferiority and influenced by the German surprise attack and the retreat of their own forces, Soviet fighters in general fought a defensive battle, but fought with desperate and self-sacrificing determination once they became involved in battle. The characteristic features of the average Soviet fighter pilot were a tendency toward caution and reluctance instead of toughness and stamina, brute strength instead of genuine combat efficiency, abysmal hatred instead of fairness and chivalry. These features can be explained by the mentality of the average Russian.[75]

If the innate sluggishness and lack of initiative of the average Russian, and the inclination towards collectivism induced by his training--all characteristics which logically reduce the value of a man as an individual fighter--be taken into account, a careful evaluation of all factors would probably produce the overall impression that the Soviet fighter pilot was an opponent who had to be taken seriously even though he was no match, as an individual fighter, for his German counterpart.

2) General Operational Principles. From the opinions offered by German Luftwaffe command personnel the general principles governing the operations of Soviet fighter forces in 1941 can be outlined roughly as follows:

a) Basically, all Soviet fighter operations were geared to defensive action. This applied not only to operations against German bomber and dive-bomber units, but also to operations against German fighter units. Possibly because it realized within the first few days of the campaign that its forces were inferior in tactics, technical performances, and training standards, the Soviet Command appears to have issued fairly unequivocal directives restricting fighter activities to defensive action.

b) The primary purpose of fighter operations was to serve the requirements of the army directly or indirectly. In this connection direct support in the form of low-level attacks, in which fighters were employed as fighter-bombers, still played a subordinate role in 1941. Far more importance was attached to the mission of indirect support through establishing air superiority over the front areas and through escorting ground-attack and bomber units.

c) It was in consonance with this doctrinal concept that Soviet fighters rarely penetrated beyond the front areas into the German rear and that they always endeavored during air combat to draw their opponents to Russian territory or to escape German attack and withdraw to their own lines.

d) From the viewpoint of assigned numerical strengths, tactics employed, and technical quality, the fighter defenses for important targets in the home defense system were inadequate.

The above and similar thoughts recur time and again in reports from Luftwaffe commanders. Major von Cossart,[76] for example, expresses the opinion that operational doctrines and tactical considerations, or in other words the Soviet Command, intentionally restricted the activities of the Soviet fighter arm. The reasons are to be sought not only in the annihilating reverses of the initial stages of the campaign but even more so in the fact that the Soviet fighter arm was not yet capable of meeting the requirements of offensive warfare.

In a similar sense Captain von Reschke[77] suggests that the Soviet Fighter Command undoubtedly realized the weaknesses of its forces and therefore endeavored to conduct a defensive war. Even within the scope of its essentially defensive missions, however, the Soviet fighter arm secured hardly any successes.

Major Rall[78] elaborates on this subject:

> Air activities took the form of continuous operations, with very strong numerical superiority, which lasted from earliest dawn until shortly before dark. No indications were observed of any special system in the form of efforts to develop points of main effort. Broadly speaking the intention was evident to maintain aircraft in the air at all times on "constant roving missions over the field of battle." In addition, special areas for purely protective fighter missions existed at focal points of ground combat, such as Kiev (battle of encirclement),* bridges (Kremenchug, Dnepropetrovsk) and the Tatar Ditch† in the Crimea. In these areas fighter forces flew continuous protective missions at altitudes between approximately 3,300 and 13,000 feet.
>
> Independent fighter sorties into the German rear for the purpose of attacking and challenging German fighter units were a rare occurrence. From the heavy losses suffered in combat against German fighters, the Soviets had probably realized the futility of such action.
>
> The Soviets did little to develop fighter defenses systematically for protection of targets in their homeland, because the bulk of all fighter forces were employed in the near front areas for combat missions over the field of battle on the ground, leaving

---

* See note, p. 118.

† Editor's Note: The Tatar Ditch, originally constructed in the 15th century by the Tatar khan of the Crimea, is now a thirty-foot high rampart running from west to east across the Perekop Isthmus. The latter is a land bridge, from two (at Ishun) to twelve miles wide, which connects the Crimea to the Ukranian mainland. Since, in the fall of 1941, General von Manstein's 11th Army which invaded the Crimea had to pass this way, the Russians incorporated the Tatar Ditch into their extensive fortifications on this flat, treeless, step-like isthmus, in an effort to stem the German advance. In spite of the fortifications, the difficult terrain and the stubborn Russian ground and air defense, the German forces were able, after ten days of hard fighting, to break through the isthmus and secure this gateway to the Crimea. See note, p. 133.

only unsuitable and numerically weak forces for home defense. Owing to their poorly developed reporting system, the Soviets had to depend in their operations almost exclusively on visual observation. It was therefore possible to fly over long distances in the Russian rear and take the defenders by surprise in the target area.

The behavior of Soviet fighters in air combat, in operations against German fighter, reconnaissance, bomber, and dive-bomber units, in air defense of fixed installations, and in roving missions reflected the fundamental concepts of the Soviet Fighter Command discussed above.

3) <u>In Combat with German Fighters</u>. Numerous opinions are available on the behavior of Soviet fighters while airborne, particularly on the subject of their action in combat against German fighters. The more important of these opinions now follow.

According to the experience of the 54th Fighter Wing,[79] operating in the northern area under Major Trautloff, Soviet fighters restricted themselves primarily to defensive action, usually operating in small units over various sectors and without developing special areas of main effort in time or space. Under threat of attack by German fighters, the Soviets immediately attempted to form a defensive circle, which was hard to break up because of the excellent maneuverability of their aircraft. As a rule they maintained this formation and flew back to their own lines, where they usually first curved at low altitudes over their own antiaircraft positions and then slowly returned to their bases, always maintaining their circle formation. The heavy losses inflicted by German fighters on Soviet fighter units over their own territory seriously affected the combat morale of the fighter pilots: almost 90 percent of all Soviet fighters downed were shot down over Soviet-held territory. If German fighters succeeded in breaking up the Soviet defensive circle or in taking them by surprise, the first losses frequently resulted in confusion. Most of the Soviet pilots were then helpless in air combat and were easily shot down by their German opponents with their superior Me-109 aircraft.

From the same source,[80] particularly with reference to the area around Leningrad, we learn that during the German advance, German-Soviet fighter battles were a rare occurrence. When these did take place, the Soviets were usually surprised and shot down; if they recognized the intention of German fighters to attack, they immediately tried to avoid battle and escape. When they outnumbered the Germans, however, they usually accepted battle. German commanders in this area were therefore able to form a valid appraisal of the operations and behavior of Soviet fighters, particularly since all types of Soviet fighter aircraft were encountered.

Soviet fighters usually operated in small formations tightly organized in flights (3 aircraft) or pairs. Toward the end of 1941, however, they were frequently encountered in swarms (usually five aircraft--not a standard organization). Similarly to German units, the swarms, usually I-18 and I-26* planes, maintained proper battle spacing between the individual aircraft during operations, a sign that the Soviets were attempting to adopt German combat methods.

In the Leningrad area Soviet fighters usually operated in units of three to five aircraft and only rarely in squadrons of eight, ten, or twelve. These squadrons usually flew wedge formation. Whereas the units included various types during the first months of the campaign, mono-type units were encountered later.

When engaged in combat, Soviet fighter units immediately formed a defensive circle, with the occasional exception of I-18 and I-26 units. Owing to the inferior climbing ability and speed of the Soviet aircraft and the inadequate combat experience and modest flying skill of the Soviet pilots, German fighters frequently managed to break up the circle in curving maneuvers and then shoot down the Soviets individually. Broadly speaking, this was the case not only with the older types of Soviet aircraft but also, although in a somewhat lesser degree, with modern types.

Most engagements with Soviet fighters were fought at altitudes between 3,300 and 10,000 feet. Engagements at higher altitudes were rare; usually Soviet fighters avoided combat at higher levels by diving away.

In general, the Soviets only accepted battle when they

---

* The I-26 was a low-wing, cantilever monoplane with retractable landing gear.

outnumbered their German opponents. However, even then they almost always flew in a defensive circle, which frequently deteriorated into what might be called a merry-go-round. This was the stage at which it was easiest to separate individual planes from the circling unit and shoot them down, since the rest of the unit rarely came to the assistance of a plane thus separated.

The only units which attempted offensive action in air combat--for example through maneuvering for height--were those equipped with I-16 or I-26 aircraft. In such cases the aircraft would exploit the momentum of a dive to then approach the opposing plane at a steep climbing angle. However, they opened fire at extremely long ranges.

Major Rall,[81] who commanded a fighter squadron in the southern area, adds that although Soviet fighters in the early stages of the campaign approached, fought, and departed in close formation, they soon changed their tactics and adapted their formations to the German pattern of quadruple organization with each squadron divided into two swarms, and each swarm divided into attack and defensive planes. If at all possible, the Soviet fighter pilot avoided offensive air battle. In 1941 the Soviets had apparently not yet established a system to control their fighters by radio from the ground. It is also probable that while airborne the unit leader controlled his unit by means of visual signals, since air to air radio traffic was at no time observed. Because of their excessive losses, Soviet fighter units soon ceased operating in flights of three and changed to a four-plane formation, with the entire unit flying in close order in which no clear-cut organization was discernible. Owing to the peculiarly irregular manner in which they flew, Soviet units were easily identifiable at a great distance. At an early stage in the engagement the Soviets would form their defensive circle, from which they would make brief and unsystematic attacks, exploiting their better maneuverability and ability to curve sharply. In close formation the fighters usually flew at staggered altitudes. The return flight was carried out in the same irregular and constantly curving formation as the approach. Aircraft separated from the circle frequently attempted to escape the German attack by curving away at low altitudes.

Generalmajor Uebe[82] supplements the above observations with the remark that in dogfights the Soviets frequently neglected even the most primitive basic rules, lost their heads after a brief period of combat and then reacted so unwisely that they were easy to shoot down. However, they preferred to dive down to ground level and effect a timely escape over their own territory.

The above experiences of German fighters concerning their encounters with Russian fighters in 1941 are confirmed by other sources.[83]

4) <u>Operations against German Bombers</u>. All reports by the commanders of German bomber units confirm that in 1941 Soviet fighters constituted no danger to German bomber formations. In fact, Soviet fighters frequently avoided battle with German bomber units.

Major von Cossart,[84] flight leader in a bomber wing operating in the northern area, reports that members of his unit never considered Soviet fighters to be a serious hazard for German bombers flying in formation. His opinion is that the reasons were not so much the annihilating German successes of the first few days or the inadequate aggressiveness or training of the Soviet fighter pilots, but the defensive nature of the Soviet operational doctrines and the fact that the Soviet defense preparations were not completed. Because the Soviet air reporting system was extremely primitive and functioned very slowly, air battles with Soviet fighters usually only developed after the German bombers had released their loads, sometimes even when the target was a Soviet fighter base. When battle did develop German crews had the impression that the Soviet fighters had orders to keep their losses as small as possible when attacking. The only tactic observed in attack was the approach from above and rear, usually by single planes and less frequently by a small number of planes simultaneously. Sizable Soviet fighter formations remained at a safe distance from German bombers flying in formation. Even when they did attack, they frequently ceased action before reaching favorable positions close to the German bombers.

In sixty missions in which von Cossart participated up to 9 September 1941 his unit encountered Soviet fighters on only ten occasions. Soviet fighter defenses were encountered over Soviet airfields or over especially important target areas, such as Leningrad, or over major rail junctions, but not over the Soviet withdrawal routes and even less so over areas farther in the rear. At the opening of the campaign, von Cossart was assigned the mission, with his unit, of attacking the Libau /Liepaja, Latvia/ airfield twice on 22 June and a third time on the next day. Although a large number of fighters were stationed on the airfield, the first and third attacks encountered no fighter defenses. In the case of the first attack this was probably due to surprise, in the third attack to the destruction done to the field and to the large number of fighters destroyed on the ground. In the second attack, the Soviet Rata fighters were apparently only alerted by visual observers. There were no signs at all that they were operating in formations, not even in such small units as pairs or flights. In the few cases where the Soviets actually attacked the German bomber unit, they opened fire when still 550 yards distant and attempted to escape in a dive immediately their fire was returned. On another occasion, on 11 August, von Cossart's unit had dispersed in thunder clouds after accomplishing its mission; flying alone he encountered eight Rata fighters. At irregular intervals each of these attacked him in succession. Each plane flew in to the attack only once, diving downward to escape counterfire while still at a safe distance. As a result, von Cossart's plane received only a few harmless hits. This almost inconceivably passive behavior von Cossart also attributes primarily to the defensive nature of Soviet operational doctrines.

In a description differing somewhat from the above, Colonel von Beust,[85] group commander in a bomber wing in the southern area, reports that owing to the inadequacy of the Soviet warning and reporting system it was hardly necessary to reckon with any serious opposition by Soviet fighters in the Soviet rear, and that it was only on exceptional occasions that defenses were encountered in the target areas. Consequently, it was primarily in bombing missions against targets in the near front areas that air battles developed. Owing to their poorly developed combat tactics, Soviet fighters were unable to achieve any results against German bomber units, even when they had numerical superiority. Soviet fighters were even less of a threat, of course, if German fighters were assigned to escort the bombers or to patrol the area concerned. There was not only a lack of any logical and firm direction of the attacking units, but in general Soviet fighter pilots frequently lacked the necessary flying ability and firing precision. This situation was aggravated by the heavy initial losses, which had resulted in a large number of pilots with completely inadequate training being employed in fighter missions. Far from being capable of shooting down German aircraft, these men served merely as easy kills for the German fighters, which was one of the main reasons for the rapid increase in the number of aircraft shot down by the German Air Force.

Under these circumstances Soviet fighters had to restrict themselves to attacks against German planes which had been damaged or separated from their units, and the small number of successes scored here was dearly bought at the cost of numerous Soviet losses. It was only after the bad autumn weather set in that the situation gradually changed in favor of the Soviet fighters. Their operations and the results achieved remained restricted because of their past heavy losses, but they now presented a more serious hazard for German bombers, which during this phase were compelled to fly their missions singly or in very small units, or at low altitudes.

Colonel von Riesen,[86] group commander in a bomber wing on the Arctic front, considers that the Soviet fighters were a considerably smaller menace than, for example, British or French fighters. Soviet fighters made no effort to adapt themselves to the German bomber tactics of diving at a steep angle from altitudes between 13,000 and 17,000 feet to release their bombs and then making their getaway at very low levels. As a rule, the moment an impending German bombing attack was recognized Soviet fighters on all fields in the area would take to the air, assemble at a low altitude, and remain close to their bases awaiting the attack. Although this placed them in a favorable position to intercept the individual Ju-88 bombers close to the ground, the fighters at no time attacked. Von Riesen reports that he himself on several occasions almost collided with Soviet fighters when flying through their formation in such situations, but was not even fired at. Of the twenty aircraft lost by his unit in 1941 only three or four were not accounted for, and these were the only cases in which the loss may have been due to Soviet fighter action. In all other cases the losses were proved to be due to other causes. Soviet fighters were rarely sighted at high altitudes and never sighted over German-held territory. At no time did they penetrate into the German rear to attack, although German bombers at the time usually operated only in pairs or at the most in flights.

Major a.D. J. Joedicke,[87] in 1941 a squadron captain in a bomber wing which operated in the northern and central areas, reports of the missions on which he was employed that up to the autumn of 1941 his unit either encountered no Soviet fighters or was not attacked. According to him the activities of Soviet interceptor fighters first increased during the German attacks on Leningrad and Moscow. Lone German planes in these areas were exposed to persistent attacks and a number of them were shot down.

Major Rall,[88] then a squadron captain in a fighter wing operating in the southern area, reports that Soviet fighter attacks against German bomber units were not systematically directed and did not provide for protection against German fighters while attacking the German bomber formation. As a result, the German escort fighters usually succeeded in repelling attacks. Although the Soviets had adequate numerical superiority to offset these tactical weaknesses, they did not succeed in their effort to prevent German formations from accomplishing their missions. Attacks by closed swarms or squadrons to disperse the German defensive fire were unsystematic and deteriorated into single-plane action. Their obstinate determination and their indifference to losses also led the Soviets to attack from unfavorable positions. German units were never subjected to continuous attacks during their approach, while over their targets, or during their return flight. Even in attacks far in the Soviet rear, German bombers encountered Soviet fighters only at the target.

The views expressed above are shared and supplemented by other Luftwaffe command personnel.[89] It was general knowledge that Soviet fighters were reluctant to attack bombers flying in formation, particularly if they were accompanied by fighter escorts. Even single straggler bombers were usually safe from attack by Soviet fighters if German fighters were in the area. Usually, the Soviet fighter units would take off in a scramble start when a German bomber formation was approaching. At some distance from their airfields they would gain altitude and then some elements endeavored to contain the escorting German fighters while other elements attempted to attack the bombers. In pursuit the Soviets often displayed tenacity and endurance.

According to Soviet fighter pilot First Lieutenant Peter Kulakoff,[90] the heavy repelling fire of German bomber units in formation was feared, but no order existed to avoid such units. As a rule the attack was flown from the rear and below, without regard for the enemy strength. In the first attack all planes followed the unit leader on a given visual signal; from then on each fighter pilot attacked on his own initiative. On encountering a German bomber unit under fighter escort the mission was divided into one of containing the German fighters and a simultaneous one of attacking the bomber unit.

In summary, however, Soviet fighter operations against German bombers in 1941 were chiefly defensive and ineffective.

5) <u>Operations against German Dive-Bombers</u>. As was the case with normal bomber units, the commanders of dive-bomber units conclude that Soviet fighters presented no serious hazard for German dive-bombers. Entries in the diary of Captain H. Pabst,[91] deceased, who commanded a squadron in a dive-bomber group in the central and northern areas, reveal that he flew 100 missions in the 22 June-10 August 1941 period and encountered Soviet fighters on only five occasions; no serious air combat developed on any of these occasions.

Major a. D. A. Blasig,[92] in 1941 a group commander in a ground-attack wing operating in the Polar and Finnish areas, reports that when dive-bombers encountered Soviet fighters this was merely a matter of chance, and that Soviet interceptor fighters were rarely met during attacks on targets near the front lines. An exception, however, was Murmansk where numerous Soviet fighters were encountered during dive-bomber attacks. The German dive-bombers were always accompanied by fighter escorts on these missions and the Soviet fighters at no time succeeded in penetrating to attack the dive-bomber squadrons. The bulk of the Soviet fighters would wait at the altitude at which the dive-bombers flattened out after dive-bombing. The fighters did not press their attack resolutely enough, however, and failed to approach to close enough ranges, opening fire too soon and then curving away. For the most part, they restricted their operations to attacks on planes on lone missions and to planes which had become separated from or were lagging behind their formation; the fighters rarely left the vicinity of their bases.

According to Major Blasig, Soviet fighters also showed no persistence in pursuit operations. Thus, he was on one occasion attacked at a low level by two Soviet fighters while returning alone from a mission. After flying in twice to the attack the Soviet fighters ceased their attack although the gun manned by Blasig's radio operator was jammed. After performing their bombing missions the dive-bomber squadrons invariably managed to shake off the Soviet fighters after five minutes of maneuvering in a defensive circle and then set off on their home route at a low altitude. Even the arrival of American and British (Curtiss and Hurricane) aircraft toward the end of the year brought no change in the Soviet tactics against dive-bombers or in the results achieved by them.

The Soviets realized that the critical moment for a dive-bomber was from right after the dive until it rejoined its unit. This is confirmed by the experience of the 54th Fighter Wing[93] in the northern area. In frequently attacked areas, therefore, Soviet fighter units would wait at the altitude at which the dive-bombers flattened out after their dive in order to attack and shoot them down individually.

From the same area Major Rall[94] reports that during the German advance in 1941 the Soviets constantly had to defend themselves against dive-bombers, and therefore gained considerable experience with this type of attack. During continuous German raids, the Soviet defense fighters restricted their activities to the target areas. German bombers were rarely attacked during their approach or return flight, but air activity was intense over the field of battle. During the first few weeks of the war the Soviets usually employed modern (Yak) aircraft to intercept the German bombers at their approach altitude, and stationed older aircraft types (I-153* and I-16) at the leveling out altitude to pursue and attack the dive-bombers as they came out of their dive. In spite of their massed fighter tactics, however, the Soviets failed to prevent German dive-bomber attacks, particularly if the dive-bomber unit was escorted by fighters.

6) **Operations against Reconnaissance Units.** The reports of German tactical and strategic reconnaissance pilots and observers reveal that on the whole the operations of Soviet fighters against German reconnaissance aircraft were not very effective and that serious resistance was encountered only in particularly vital combat or protective areas, such as Leningrad and Moscow.

Major a. D. H. E. Schlage,[95] in 1941 an observer in a strategic air reconnaissance group operating in the northern and

---

* Editor's Note: The I-153 was a further development of the I-15 (see note, p. 21). Like its predecessor, it was a biplane with gull wings. It differed from the I-15 in being a little faster and having a retractable landing gear.

central areas, reports that fighter defenses were hardly noticeable at the outset of the campaign, even in the far interior of the Baltic areas. The Soviets possessed no suitable aircraft to employ against the high-quality German Ju-88, which attained an altitude of 16,500 to 20,000 feet by the time it crossed over the front areas. In addition, the Soviet aircraft reporting system was incapable of getting fighters off the ground in time to intercept German reconnaissance planes during their approach. Thus, Major Schlage flew twenty-one strategic reconnaissance missions far into Russian rear areas up to the end of 1941, and encountered Soviet fighters only once. On that occasion a squadron of I-16 (Rata) fighters were unable to attack at the altitude of 20,000 feet. All they could do was follow the reconnaissance plane 660 to 1,000 feet lower down and about 500 yards to the side, while showing a serious tail drag. The only remarkable feature in this incident was the astonishingly short time the fighter unit, which the reconnaissance crew saw taking off, required to get this close to the German reconnaissance plane.

Major Jaehne,[96] air observer in a strategic reconnaissance group in the central area, reports that on missions over Soviet airfields, German reconnaissance units had to expect Soviet alert fighters to attack either in pairs or singly during the return flight. German reconnaissance planes usually flew in along the rail routes, and the impression existed that the Soviet aircraft reporting service reported their approach quickly, since the reconnaissance planes on reaching the airfield involved found the Soviet fighters either already in the air or just taking off. Fighter defenses were particularly strong around Moscow, where the Soviets apparently had their best reporting and control system. The Soviet fighters operated singly or in units of three or four aircraft and endeavored to achieve surprise by attacking from the direction of the sun from below or above. The pilots of modern fighter aircraft attacked from above and the rear in an effort to force German planes down. These aircraft had superior maneuverability and could easily follow German planes in a dive.

Captain von Reschke,[97] who served in the southern area as air observer in a tactical reconnaissance squadron and as an air liaison officer, supplements the above presentations with his report that no Russian fighters were encountered at altitudes above 13,000 feet, and that the Rata fighters usually employed in escort missions did not attack single German tactical reconnaissance planes, even when sighting them at close range. It was only during the battles for the Dnepropetrovsk bridgehead* that the Soviets for the first time became more active in air patrols and in attacks on German tactical reconnaissance units; these attacks caused heavy losses in reconnaissance aircraft and periodically prevented German air reconnaissance on the battlefield.

7) <u>Night Fighter Operations.</u> Up to the end of 1941 Soviet night fighter operations were rare and, according to Colonel von Beust[98] no Soviet night fighters were reported shot down. Major Jaehne gives an even more negative report,[99] in which he states that up to the end of 1941 Soviet night fighter operations were completely unknown and only developed later.

Of all the Luftwaffe command personnel interrogated only one officer personally experienced a night attack by Soviet fighters, which he describes essentially as follows:[100] During an attack against the Riga airfield on a fairly light night the aircraft crew was surprised at suddenly seeing green tracers passing nearby, followed by the unmistakable sound of projectiles striking their plane. The attacking plane, recognized as a Rata fighter, disappeared after its one pass. The crew members would have thought themselves the victims of a hallucination if a subsequent examination had not clearly proved the reality of their experience.

The assumption seems justified that in 1941 no plans for the systematic employment of night fighters existed and that they were committed only in isolated cases.

8) <u>Cooperation with Other Arms of the Air Forces.</u> Soviet fighter cooperation with bombers, dive-bombers, and fighter-bombers in escort and other protective missions proved inadequate to the task. Generalmajor Uebe,[101] for example, reports that when on direct or indirect escort missions, the latter in the form of operations ahead of the escorted unit, Soviet fighter units remained in the same area as the escorted unit, but maintained no real contact with it and frequently abandoned it. A report of the 54th Fighter Wing[102] similarly

---

* Editor's Note: This was one of the last of the battles fought for control of the great bend of the Dnieper River in 1941. As soon as they had won control of the bend the Germans were able to begin their two-pronged offensive in the South, towards the Crimea and Rostov.

concludes that when Soviet fighters on escort missions were engaged by German fighters they frequently left the unit they were to protect and endeavored to reach Soviet territory flying in a defensive circle.

Captain von Reschke[103] reports that Soviet Rata fighters cooperated with ground-attack units from the outset of the campaign, but rarely with bomber units. I-15 ground-attack units with attack missions over the field of battle were assigned Rata (I-16) fighter escorts, which frequently participated in the ground action. It was only after four weeks of warfare that Rata fighter escorts were observed with Soviet bomber formations. As a rule the fighters flew approximately 1600 feet above the escorted unit in formations of 15 to 25 aircraft. If German fighters attacked the bombers the Soviet fighters rarely dived down, were themselves engaged in combat, and proved of little use in attempting to execute their mission. It was generally observed that the escort fighters were not very flexible and adhered rigidly to their assigned mission.

Major Rall[104] reports that Soviet ground-attack aircraft with fighter escorts were frequently in evidence over the battle area. The fighters on such missions flew in an echeloned formation. Owing to their inferior speed, however, they were not very effective. In the Battle of Kharkov massed missions of this type were flown two to three times daily. In concentrated attacks German fighters succeeded in penetrating the fighter screen, shooting down the ground-attack aircraft before they could reach their target areas, and then destroying the Soviet fighters in their headlong flight. When escorting bomber units the behavior of the Soviet fighters was similar and they were unable to protect the clumsy and inadequately armed bombers against heavy losses.

The above statements reveal the following defects in the operations of Soviet fighters supporting other units of the air forces in direct escort, patrol, or interception missions at the front: 1) Soviet fighter operations were not flexible enough to master the difficulties encountered on escort missions; 2) the technical inferiority of Soviet fighter aircraft made it impossible for the pilots to take effective action against attacking German fighters; 3) well-directed German fighter attacks inflicted extraordinarily heavy losses on the Soviet fighters as well as on the bomber or ground-attack forces they were escorting.

9) As Fighter-Bombers in Direct Support of Army Operations.

The impact of Soviet fighter direct-support operations was felt more by Army than by Luftwaffe command personnel. The reports of German Army commanders reveal that Soviet fighters were rarely in evidence during the initial phase of the campaign, but that they became increasingly active in later months, particularly in focal areas of combat. Still, they had no important influence on the German ground troops in 1941.

Thus, Lieutenant Colonel a. D. F. Wolff,[105] commander of an artillery battalion in the central area, reports that no Soviet fighters were seen in the early stages, and that the first Rata fighters were sighted, usually in groups of two to three, during the crossing operations at the Dnieper River on 10-11 July. Apart from repeated fighter attacks on marching columns on 13 July, which caused numerous delays, the next air attacks were by single fighter-bombers in mid-August and mid-September and the last attack recorded was on 30 November 1941. The losses inflicted on the German forces in these attacks were insignificant.

Generalleutnant Frankewitz,[106] commander of an artillery regiment in the northern area, reports the first Soviet fighter activities on 17 July. Later, fighter strikes increased in intensity in the Reval /Talinn, Estonia/ region. There, attacks by I-16 fighter-bombers were a daily occurrence. German losses in these attacks varied. Thus, a light artillery battalion lost almost 50 percent of its horses--dead or injured--in a single low-level attack by two flights of Rata fighters, while in a heavy battery only a few horses were slightly injured in three repeat attacks by seven Rata fighters. In general, however, the fighter-bombers achieved no major successes and were not taken very seriously by the troops. In later operations of 1941, including the battles for the Baltic Islands, for Narva, and for Tikhvin,* no sizable Soviet fighter actions occurred.

In 1941, during his assignment in command of an artillery unit in the central area, Generalleutnant Huffmann had no personal experience with Soviet fighters.[107] From his contribution to the present study, in which he consolidates the reports of five Army

---

* Editor's Note: These were all objectives along the route of the northern offensive, which was aimed at Leningrad. The final goal of the northern offensive was to stop the flow of Allied supplies coming from Murmansk.

commanders from all areas of the eastern theater, it can be gathered, however, that Soviet fighters operating as fighter-bombers or in fighter missions over the combat areas had no real influence on the advance of the German Army. He remarks quite pertinently that Generaloberst a.D. Heinz Guderian (C.G., Second Panzer Group) only twice makes mention of Soviet fighters in 1941, and considers this a sign that the Soviet fighter arm made no impression whatever on the German troops or Army commands.

Thus, in 1941, fighter operations, particularly in the form of fighter-bomber missions in support of the Soviet Army, were on a very small scale and had practically no effect on the Germans.

10) <u>Operations under Special Weather Conditions</u>. German commanders are not in full agreement on the subject of Soviet fighter operations under special weather conditions. While some express the view that Soviet fighters were able to continue operating in bad weather, others deny this. Possibly this disagreement stems from the circumstance that all-weather aviation is largely a matter of training, and training varied widely in the Soviet fighter arm. On one point, however, all German commanders agree: Soviet fighter personnel were better able than their German counterparts to master the difficulties of Russian weather conditions and the Russians exploited this ability in their efforts to recuperate.

Whereas Major Jaehne[108] finds that Soviet fighters displayed little zest for action in bad weather--which he considers quite natural because of their inadequate instruments--and that therefore cloudy weather provided good cover for German air reconnaissance, Majors Rall and Blasig[109] express the view that the technical characteristics of Soviet aircraft enabled them to carry out fighter missions in the battle area during weather conditions which made it almost impossible for German fighter units to operate.

The experience of the 54th Fighter Wing[110] indicates that Soviet fighters operated when there was a solid cloud cover and that they cleverly flew in the lower cloud fringes, emerging for surprise attacks. Special caution therefore had to be exercised during such weather.

Colonel von Beust[111] maintains that the bad weather which commenced in the autumn of 1941, and even more so the difficult conditions of winter--snow, ice, intense cold, poor visibility, and fogs, for instance--produced certain advantages for Soviet fighters. They were accustomed to these conditions and were better able to cope with them--both in respect to aviation and their ground services--than German fighters who were experiencing their first Russian winter.

Rall[112] reaches similar conclusions. With a certain measure of surprise he finds that Soviet fighters were extremely active over the battle area even during extreme cold, while German fighter units were still busy trying to start their engines. There is no doubt that the Soviets had wider technical experience in starting their engines during severe cold, and they soon recognized this weak point of the German fighters. It was thus by no means rare that while a German fighter group could hardly ready three of its aircraft for action by 1100 hours, Soviet fighter-bombers were able to attack the unit airfield at 0900.

D. Aircraft Types, Weapons, and Other Equipment.

Luftwaffe command personnel declare unanimously that Soviet fighter aircraft (particularly with respect to their climbing ability and speed), their weapons, and other equipment were inferior to German fighters at the beginning of the campaign; and that they represented no serious hazard for German bomber or dive-bomber units flying in formation. Even lone German aircraft, if expertly handled, could defend themselves against Soviet fighter attack. With the appearance of the newly introduced more modern Mig, Lagg, and Yak aircraft in the autumn of 1941, the performances of Soviet fighters admittedly improved, but the German BF 109-F* aircraft then in use were superior even to these modern models.

In detail, the various types of Soviet fighter aircraft were evaluated as follows:

1) <u>Rata (I-16) Aircraft</u>. Initially, this was the standard

---

* Editor's Note: This is an early designation of the Me 109. "BF" stands for Bayerische Flugzeugwerke (Bavarian Aircraft Industries) which later became Messerschmitt A.G. The plane was a single-seat fighter, designed by Messerschmitt and put into production during the second half of 1938.

fighter of the Soviet air forces. In a Luftwaffe study,[113] the superior maneuverability of the Rata as compared with that of the BF 109 is emphasized, with the qualification, however, that in combat the Rata was soon forced over to the defensive because of its inferior speed and climbing and diving performances. Only very experienced airmen were able in combat to take full advantage of the I-16's superior maneuverability. This maneuverability was seriously reduced at high speeds, and the plane easily caught fire if struck from above or from the sides. According to Captain Kath[114] the Rata was 60 miles per hour slower than the German BF 109, and trapped itself in the narrow circle of its own sharp curves. The moment it went into a straight course, German fighters were in position above its tail. Major Rall[115] comes to very much the same conclusions, and mentions that from the outset of the campaign to the end of 1941 the majority of all Soviet fighter units were equipped with I-16 (Rata) and I-153 (Rata biplane), both powered with air cooled radial engines, and that the re-equipment of the units with Lagg 3, La 5, and Yak 3* aircraft from the autumn of 1941 on was very noticeable. The opinions of other commanders on the Rata are similar,[116] one of whom, Generalinginieur a. D. Otto R. Thomsen,[117] adds that the equipment of the plane and the arrangement of the pilot's seat were extremely primitive. The open cockpit was completely obsolete and the windscreen met neither technical nor tactical requirements.

2) <u>I-15 and I-153 Aircraft</u>. The slowness of these models, according to a report of the 54th Fighter Wing,[118] put them at a serious disadvantage in air combat. Their high maneuverability, however, did much to compensate for this weakness. Both models could be downed by fire directed at the center from the rear, while a few rounds fired into the sides were often enough to set them on fire. These outdated models gradually disappeared during the winter months. Captain Kath[119] describes the I-15, with its slow speed of 150 to 168 miles, as inferior from the outset to German fighter models and also considers its fire power, with only two machine guns, to have been inadequate. Nevertheless, aircraft of this type were mounted on skids for winter operations in 1941. Other German commanders

---

* Editor's Note: The Lagg 3, the La 5 and the Yak 3 were all single-seat, low-wing, cantilever monoplanes. Whereas the Lagg 3 was employed both as a fighter and a fighter-bomber, the other two were essentially fighters.

The Lagg-3, a one-place Russian fighter

A Russian Yak-3 fighter

give very much the same appraisal of these types.[120]

3) <u>Mig 1-3 (also known as I-200, I-61, I-18), Yak 1 (I-26), and Lagg 3 (I-301) Aircraft.</u> These more modern aircraft, which appeared in steadily increasing numbers from autumn 1941 on, are more favorably evaluated in a report of the 54th Fighter Wing,[121] although the German BF 109F was considered superior to them.

The Mig aircraft (I-18) showed better climbing and speed performances than the Rata, but it was not as maneuverable as the BF 109F. It is to be presumed that rudder pressures were heavy in these aircraft at high speeds, since they were then very maneuverable. The planes easily caught fire if hit from any direction.

The Yak model was considered the best Soviet fighter plane. It had even better climbing performance and was faster than the I-18, and approached the performances of the BF 109F although it was not as fast. It was more difficult to set on fire in attack from the rear than was the Mig 3. Up to 19,100 feet it still climbed well but showed poor maneuverability. For this reason, pilots encountered at these altitudes dived down to avoid combat.

Major Rall[122] confirms the above statements on the properties of the more modern Soviet fighter aircraft and also mentions their water-cooled engines and their closed cockpits. He also considers the German fighter models superior. Major Jaehne,[123] however, admits that the new Soviet models were superior to the German Ju-88, and Colonel von Heimann[124] supplements the picture with the statement that the new Soviet fighter models were of simple construction, fast, and maneuverable, and on the whole not much inferior to the German BF 109F.

4) <u>American and British Aircraft.</u> Finally, a number of Luftwaffe commanders[125] mention that American and British fighter aircraft (Curtiss and Hurricane) supplied under the Lend-Lease Agreement entered the scene toward the end of 1941--which made things more difficult for the German fighters--but that Soviet pilots were unable to obtain better performances from these models than from their own. In appraising the American P-40 model, the report of the 54th Fighter Wing[126] states that it was equal to the German BF 109F in turning, but that its climbing and speed performances were inferior to those of the German plane. According to prisoner

of war statements it was unpopular with Soviet fighter pilots.

    5) <u>Weapons</u>. Reports by German commanders[127] concerning the weapons of Soviet fighter aircraft are fairly uniform. In 1941 they were as a rule armed with a number of machine guns, and a few had cannon mounted in the wings. Although the fire power appeared weak, the weapons are described as good, with the qualification that their effectiveness was reduced considerably by factors such as the Soviets' tendency to spray their fire, to commence firing at too long range, and their reluctance to approach closely enough to their German target. Occasionally Soviet fighter aircraft, particularly the more modern types, were also armed with rockets with which they attempted to repel German fighters attacking them from the rear.

    6) <u>Other Equipment</u>. Apart from those previously mentioned, no opinions by German commanders are available on other items of Soviet fighter aircraft equipment. The only item which is mentioned specifically is the excellent armor plating which protected the pilot against weapons fire from the rear.[128] Otherwise, general mention is made time and again of the technical inferiority of the Soviet fighter aircraft to German fighters, which may have been due in part to the limited technical facilities available to the Soviets to maintain operability.

    On this subject the statements of captured Soviet fighter pilot 1st Lieutenant Kulakoff[129] are of interest. Among other things, Kulakoff ascribes the poor technical condition of Soviet aircraft partly to the circumstance that the aircraft had been in operation too long, and states that numerous failures occurred in operation even without the effects of enemy action. Important causes of mechanical failure were the frequent stoppage of the oil vents in the crank-shafts, and the seizure and burning out of bearings. In general, Kulakoff comments favorably on the weapons of the Soviet aircraft types just dealt with, particularly the wing-mounted cannon of the I-16. In contrast with the machine guns, these cannon rarely jammed. He finds that the rockets, of which each plane carried four and which shattered into innumerable fragments after covering a distance of 2,000 feet, were of little use in air combat but highly effective against ground targets.

E. **Overall Evaluation of the Soviet Fighter Arm in 1941.**

An analysis of the most important features of Soviet fighters as revealed by the above numerous and varying opinions of German Army and Luftwaffe command personnel produces approximately the following picture:

1) As a result of the initial surprise action and the following continuous air attacks against Soviet airfields at the outset of the campaign, the loss of forward ground service installations, and the large number of aircraft shot down by German fighters, the Soviet fighter arm was seriously crippled and remained so until the autumn of 1941. From then on the arm made a gradual recovery, in which it was favored considerably by the early arrival of the Russian winter.

2) Soviet fighter pilots showed little adaptability, but were courageous to the verge of stupidity, which at times even led them to carry out ramming attacks. As an individual fighter, the average Soviet fighter pilot often lacked self-confidence and was frightened; fighting in formation, in contrast, he was a tough opponent. The personal inferiority of the average Soviet fighter pilot was perhaps less due to traits of character than to a lack of combat experience and adequate training, which lack produced a feeling of uncertainty. Really high grade performers were rare but those who did exist were almost equal to the best German fighter pilots.

3) The basic feature in the conduct of fighter operations by the Soviet Command was one of defensive combat. The reasons for this were to be found in the previously mentioned heavy losses in aircraft and personnel incurred in the first weeks and months of the campaign, technical inferiority, inadequate training, inherent Russian traits of caution and reserve, and occasional cases of inferiority complex.

4) The fighter aircraft used by the Soviets at the outset of the campaign were hopelessly inferior. Although this condition improved through the increasing introduction of more modern aircraft from the autumn of 1941 on, the new types were still no full match for the standard German fighter, the BF 109F. The situation was somewhat relieved in this respect by the numerical superiority which the Soviet fighter units almost always had.

5) In operating against German fighter forces, Soviet fighters

did their utmost to avoid air combat. If engaged in combat by German fighters, they as a rule formed a defensive circle and endeavored to withdraw to their own territory.

6) In operating against German bombers, Soviet fighters showed a reluctance to attack, particularly if the bombers were escorted by fighters. They also failed to take advantage of the weak moment of dive-bombers, namely the moment when they pulled out of their bombing dive. In general, the defensive fire from German bombers flying in formation deterred Soviet fighters from attacking.

7) Over the battle area, German reconnaissance planes from autumn 1941 on encountered increasing, and at times highly effective, fighter defenses. In contrast, German strategic reconnaissance operations, which were conducted at great altitudes, encountered almost no interference from Soviet fighters.

8) Soviet fighters showed little ability to cooperate with other arms of the air forces. When on escort missions they were unable to repel attacking German fighters.

9) Soviet fighters were not very active in operations in direct support of ground forces or in fighter-bomber missions in 1941; no direct support operations in cooperation with naval forces are on record.

The Soviet fighter forces suffered exceptionally heavy initial losses and until the arrival of winter conditions were unable to prevent German air superiority. Nevertheless, the Soviet Command successfully preserved its facilities for the manufacture of fighter aircraft, the training of fighter pilots, and the functioning of the replacement and supply services. It thereby created the necessary conditions for the rehabilitation of its fighter arm. At the same time the Soviet fighter pilots gained combat experience and through their personal efforts contributed to the achievement of the same goal.

Colonel von Beust[130] summarizes his opinion on the Soviet fighter forces in the period up to the end of 1941 in words which reflect the findings of almost all German command personnel:

Concerning the Soviet fighter forces in this period it can

be said that they suffered unprecedented reverses. Through their tenacious determination and their almost inconceivable personal sacrifices--the reader is reminded here of their efforts to ram German bombers--they nevertheless succeeded in preventing a total collapse and in creating conditions which made a later recovery possible.

Section IV: The Ground-Attack Arm in 1941[131]

A. General.

The general opinion of German Army and Luftwaffe command personnel is that the ground-attack forces were the most logically developed and employed arm of the Soviet air forces. Also, the ground-attack arm came closest to conforming with Soviet air doctrine, according to which the major mission of air power was to support the operations of the Army.

Although the arm as it existed in 1941 had not yet achieved its later high tactical and technical standards of performance--certain missions of the ground-attack arm at that time were performed by fighter or similar units--its strong development was already beginning to take shape.[132]

In reports on the first weeks and months of the Russian campaign German Army and Luftwaffe commanders make little mention of Soviet ground-attack operations and consider that the ground attacks carried out with obsolete aircraft models had little effect. The situation changed radically, from approximately August 1941 on, after the appearance of the IL-2 (Stormovik) model.

The entire first year of warfare in the east was dominated by German air superiority, and German Army commanders have emphasized repeatedly that Soviet ground-attack units were closely restricted in their operations, the effects of which were correspondingly small. Nevertheless, in spite of extremely heavy losses, the Soviet ground-attack arm improved in technical performances, grew in numerical strength, and toward the end of the war was employed logically in close cooperation with ground forces. Beginning with the winter of 1941-1942 it was capable of affecting German troop morale and destroying materiel. The Soviet ground-attack arm thus grew steadily in importance and eventually became the "backbone of

Soviet air power."[133]

B. Organization, Chain of Command, Strength, and Strategic Concentration

German field commanders had no opportunity to gain an insight into such matters, because they were rarely directly affected by them. They learned very little from prisoner of war interrogations, since captured Soviet aircraft crews usually were immediately evacuated to the rear without previous interrogation. Furthermore, what they could have learned would have been of little importance to them in the performance of their missions.

Major Jaehne,[134] one of the few contributors to mention this subject, states that ground-attack units were organized in regiments of thirty aircraft and were assigned to ground-attack divisions, which were primarily responsible for the conduct of ground-attack operations. He also assumes that they were controlled occasionally by corps, which, however, were composed of mixed units.

According to Generalmajor Uebe,[135] the smallest standard ground-attack unit was the squadron of 10 aircraft, organized in regiments of approximately 25 aircraft.

C. Ground-Attack Operations

1) *Personnel.* German field commanders[136] describe Soviet ground-attack aircraft personnel as aggressive, courageous, and determined.

Uebe[137] is one of the few who endeavor to examine the causes for the behavior of Soviet ground-attack airmen. He reaches the conclusion that they also were not quite free of the characteristic Russian weaknesses--inadequate initiative, stamina, and versatility; and evidence of inferiority complexes and inferior training--, but that these weaknesses were somewhat modified by unit cohesion. Since these units were as a rule employed collectively and within direct view of the ground forces, the personal defects and weaknesses of the airmen did not have their full effect. The airmen carried out their clearly defined missions stolidly and with determination. Thus, as an example, rear gunners of damaged and burning aircraft continued firing until their planes crashed. Generally speaking, Uebe describes

Soviet ground attack units as "unpleasant opponents."

It is evident that the average Soviet ground-attack airman was a courageous and utterly fearless opponent.

2) <u>Basic Principles</u>. The doctrines governing the control and operations of Soviet ground-attack units during the first year of the campaign are generally described by German Army and Luftwaffe command personnel as follows: a) employment chiefly in operations over the battlefield and against targets in the battle area within range of approximately six miles; operations in German rear areas primarily directed against German airfields; b) exploitation of the element of surprise; c) continuous attack missions over centers of main effort on the field of battle, frequently with direct of indirect protection by fighters; d) integrated action with bomber units in attacks on particularly important and lucrative targets; e) avoidance of air to air combat during the performance of assigned missions.

There was evidence that the Soviet commands actually endeavored to employ ground-attack units in consonance with the doctrines stated above. However, existing conditions were vastly different in 1941 than those anticipated, and the inadequate capabilities of airmen and their lack of experience often made it impracticable to carry out the attacks for which the arm was designed. The essential concentration of effort was also often lacking.

Summarizing his experience with Soviet ground-attack operations, Major Stoll-Berberich[138] reports that up to the winter of 1941-42 the Soviet commands frequently made unwise use of the arm and therefore hardly achieved appreciable results. Instead of concentrating on a restricted number of defined areas of main effort and carrying out continuous attacks there, the commands dissipated the power available to them in ground-attack air units. They thus not only achieved no favorable results, but incurred heavy losses, which were increased by the wrong tactics employed in attack operations.

Furthermore, Stoll-Berberich mentions that a downed Russian ground-attack pilot confirmed the existence of a Soviet order, according to which all bomber and ground-attack units were to avoid all combat action with German dive-bomber, bomber, or ground-attack units. On encountering German air units, the Soviets were to cease their attack mission in order to resume it after departure of the German units. The Soviet pilot stated that the reason for this order was that when German bombing units of any type were encountered in an area, strong German fighter forces could also be expected in the vicinity. By returning to their bases the Soviet units would avoid the losses they would have incurred in combat under these conditions. However, the order allegedly applied only to Soviet units operating against targets within the main line of resistance. Stoll-Berberich thinks that this explains in part the lack of aggressiveness frequently observed in Soviet airmen and concludes with the statement that he personally noticed no change in the tactics of Soviet ground-attack forces up to the end of 1941.

Generalleutnant Frankewitz,[139] an army commander, also observed that Soviets failed to mass their ground-attack units adequately and employ them in tight formations. His impression was that they were experimenting, still feeling their way without experience or firmly established principles for the conduct of operations, and that this explained the small effects of their operations.

Generalleutnant Huffmann,[140] another army commander, states that the frequent Soviet combined employment of ground-attack and bomber units usually occurred when the Soviets had detected German preparations for offensive ground operations. Combined ground-attack and bomber forces then attacked German troop assemblies, troop movements, concentrations within the battle area, artillery positions, bottlenecks, and supply movements and installations. In brief, they were directed against all targets whose destruction might interfere with or even prevent the German attack. These Russian air attacks never penetrated farther than sixteen miles behind the foremost German positions, and it was often found that the panzer divisions in the forward areas were affected, but that the infantry divisions following farther in the rear escaped attention. The Soviets usually repeated their attack after two or three hours.

Huffmann also finds that Soviet ground-attack units only accepted battle with German fighters when they had numerical superiority; in such cases they proved remarkably trigger-happy, firing far too soon and too heavily. They usually avoided battle with German fighters, however, and endeavored to escape to their own lines at ground altitudes.

In 1941, according to Huffmann, the ground-attack units did everything possible to avoid areas protected by German antiaircraft artillery, and rarely attacked antiaircraft positions as such.

Major Jaehne[142] amplifies the above with the information that Soviet ground-attack units showed a marked preference for surprise attacks, securing surprise through approaching at ground altitudes or by the timing of their attacks. Very early morning and late dusk attacks were the rule. Thus, he reports that Soviet ground-attack aircraft were frequently still over the German front in the evening hours, when German fighters were already on the way to their bases. However, his opinion that the Soviet command of ground attack forces "was at that time sound both from higher to lower levels and vice versa," is probably too favorable.

In general, the Soviet ground-attack air arm, in 1941, failed to accomplish the primary missions for which it was intended. These missions were: 1) by employing strong units, to render direct support to the ground forces during combat; hold down the enemy ground forces; create breaches for the attack by friendly ground forces; and eliminate hostile centers of resistance; and 2) as long-range artillery to prevent the approach of hostile troops and the concentration of reserves in the far rear of the main battle area.

3) <u>Flying Conduct of Soviet Ground-Attack Air Units</u>. German Army and Luftwaffe command personnel dealt in close detail with the tactics and general behavior of Soviet ground-attack air units during operations. Generalleutnant Huffmann,[143] for example, writes that the attacking Soviet units varied in strength between three and twelve aircraft, that they usually approached at altitudes between 300 and 1,000 feet, attacked with bombs and weapons fire, and frequently flew in to repeat attacks, sometimes diving at an oblique angle.

Generalmajor Uebe,[144] in contrast, states that Soviet ground-attack units usually approached at medium altitudes, around 10,000 feet and higher, and whenever possible with the sun behind them. In attacking targets not directly within the main defense area, they approached in a flat curve, ending in a head-on attack. Line and circle formations were the most favored forms for attack. Units did not change their formation during the target approach or within the target area. In executing the attack, the planes descended to low levels, and at times to ground levels. Bombing and strafing were done while in horizontal flight. Light bombs were usually used, including phosphorus incendiaries, and at times the attacking planes fired rockets. Occasionally, the attacking unit would fly in attack circle formation over the target area without evasive maneuvers of any type. From the circle, the aircraft would dive down to repeat their attacks until their ammunition was exhausted. However, repeat attacks remained the exception rather than the rule. When attacking in waves, units flew in line formation, the individual squadrons spaced approximately one minute's flight apart. On leaving the target area, the units usually dispersed, each plane immediately flying at top speed toward its base. Less frequently the aircraft would assemble at a medium altitude, rarely above 1,600 feet, immediately after the attack, and then fly at top speed across the front.

A certain measure of reluctance was noticeable just prior to low-level attacks. It was also clearly evident that the pilots desired to remain at an altitude which would enable them to reach their own line if they were forced to make a crash landing or bail out. On encountering German fighters or antiaircraft fire, Russian ground-attack pilots frequently released their bomb loads prematurely. Whether their escorting fighters waited for them or not, ground-attack air units made no change in the execution of their mission. Employing the above tactics they were able to achieve successes but they also suffered heavy losses. IL-2 units maintained good flight formation but lacked flexibility and carried out no evasive maneuvers even when under extremely heavy antiaircraft fire. This led to exceptionally high losses. Occasionally, units were observed moving into closer formation when under fighter attack.

A German army officer, General der Infanterie a. D. Hans von der Groeben[145] mentions that Soviet ground-attack air units suffered severe losses in battle with German fighters but nevertheless tenaciously continued their attacks, that they continued doggedly on their course when under antiaircraft fire, that when threatened by German aircraft they would descend to ground levels, and that as a rule they were escorted by fighters.

According to the experience of the 54th Fighter Wing,[146] IL-2 units frequently dispersed for their attack, each plane seeking out its individual target. The moment at which they dispersed was the most favorable moment for German fighters to attack.

The various tactics of R-10* and IL-2 units are described by

---

* A single-engine, 2-3 seat monoplane.

Captain von Reschke.[147] As a rule, he writes, R-10 aircraft attacked in units of eight to ten, usually at very low levels with clever exploitation of existing cover, so that the German ground defenses could only go into action at a relatively late stage during the approach. Under antiaircraft artillery fire R-10 units generally continued obstinately on their course. Operating at such low levels and in such close formation they had little opportunity to carry out evasive movements. IL-2 aircraft, generally in units of 15-20, usually approached at around 1,300 feet and then dived down to the attack, releasing their bombs in sticks while firing simultaneously with their mounted weapons. They were nearly always escorted by fighters. However, the escort fighters failed to follow down low enough.

Major Stoll-Berberich[148] and Captain Pabst[149] describe attacks by Soviet ground-attack units from their own experience. Their illuminating and stirring accounts of the inexplicable and suicidal behavior of the units when attacked by German fighters or when exposed to German antiaircraft artillery fire relate how the Russians would continue stolidly on their way without changing their course, without any form of evasive action or defensive maneuver, in some cases until the entire unit was destroyed.

4) <u>Ground-Attack Air Operations over the Field of Battle.</u> In 1941 the main mission of the ground-attack arm of the Soviet air forces was to operate over the field of battle and support the operations of the ground forces. Numerous reports are available from German Army and Luftwaffe field commanders on the methods adopted by Soviet ground-attack units to accomplish this. Since Army commanders were most effected by these Soviet operations, their views will be given first.

Writing of the northern area, Generalleutnant Frankewitz[150] states that attacks by Soviet ground-attack units were first noticeable in the Reval /Tallinn, Estonia/ area, where their use of weapons fire and demolition and fragmentation bombs were a daily occurrence. The usual targets were marching columns, resting units, vehicle concentrations, and command posts. The attacks were carried out by single planes or by units up to squadron size. On the whole, the damage done was small. As operations progressed during the seizing of the Baltic Isles and during later battles around Narva and Tikhvin, ground-attack aircraft were rarely encountered.

Lieutenant Colonel Wolff[151] reports that in the central area Soviet ground-attack air units were not encountered before August 1941. The Soviets always attacked at low levels, single planes usually flying in to bomb and then strafe the attacked area with machine-gun fire, later also with aircraft cannon. Soviet ground-attack air operations, however, remained on a small scale in 1941 and inflicted little damage. From 25 August to 4 December 1941 Wolff experienced a total of eleven attacks by Soviet ground-attack aircraft. The largest number of aircraft mentioned by him in any single attack is three and he makes mention on only three occasions of a few German personnel wounded and small damage done. In most cases the attacks had no effect whatever.

According to Generalleutnant Huffmann,[152] Soviet ground-attack air operations were generally only on a small scale and not very effective in the northern and central areas but were very active and effective in the south. Frequently, for example, the lead aircraft of an attacking unit would first carry out careful reconnaissance and then lead the actual attack, with the rest of the unit following. The approach was habitually flown at altitudes between 1,000 and 2,200 feet, and the targets attacked were always in the near front area and within the combat zones. The Soviets often employed IL-2 units as what might be called airborne artillery. Thus, a case is mentioned in which approximately twenty ground-attack aircraft operated against a German column moving along a highway in the south area. Flying in from the rear, the aircraft repeated their attack four or five times with fragmentation bombs and cannon fire, inflicting twenty casualties and killing or injuring sixty horses. Another case worthy of mention is that of the commander of an artillery battalion in the south area, who reports an attack by forty ground-attack aircraft in 1941. Quite apart from the casualties, attacks of this type in the bare flat terrain of the Ukraine undoubtedly imposed a severe strain on the morale of the troops.

In many cases bridges over the numerous rivers were also heavily attacked. It is reported, for example, that the Dnieper River bridges were attacked daily at daybreak, and that these attacks repeatedly caused grave ammunition and other supply crises. In contrast, Soviet attacks against the Dvina River bridges are mentioned in which squadron after squadron flew in at low altitudes with astonishing obstinacy, only to be shot down. In these attacks 64 Soviet aircraft were downed on a single day.

Army circles also confirm the sensitivity of Soviet ground-attack airmen to attack by German fighters and to German antiaircraft fire. Whenever possible, it is reported, Soviet ground-attack units avoided areas strongly protected by antiaircraft artillery. Nevertheless, German fighters and antiaircraft artillery took a heavy toll of ground-attack aircraft, particularly over the main line of resistance, owing to the stubbornness of Soviet airmen's flight tactics and their lack of flexibility during antiaircraft fire.

General der Infanterie von der Groeben[153] confirms the view that the Soviets employed their ground-attack aircraft in heavier concentrations against those areas of the battlefield which their artillery could not reach, and thus particularly against the areas behind the main German defense area.

Both von der Groeben and Luftwaffe General F. Kless reject the views expressed by certain circles that the Soviets employed their artillery and their ground-attack aircraft simultaneously against the same targets. General der Flakartillerie a. D. Walther von Axthelm[154] agrees, but notes that it did happen that after an artillery fire concentration the Soviet IL-2 units would follow up with bombing and strafing attacks on the same target, as happened in the Yel'nya salient* in 1941.

The views of German army commanders concerning the operations of Soviet ground-attack aircraft over the field of battle are substantiated and supplemented by Luftwaffe reports on the subject. Thus, Generalmajor Uebe[155] writes that the attacks of Soviet ground-attack aircraft were directed primarily against targets within the main defense area: troop concentrations and movements, firing guns, heavy infantry weapons, and settlements close to the front. In their

---

* Editor's Note: The Yel'nya salient (named after the city of Yel'nya 45 miles East-Southeast of Smolensk) was a bulge in the German lines and the scene of very heavy fighting in late summer of 1941. This Russian wedge in the lines of German Army Group Center was aimed at the recapture of Smolensk, which had just fallen to the Germans in the second of the seven great battles of encirclement executed by the Germans in Russia in 1941. Total Russian losses in these battles (2,256,000 POW's, 9,336 tanks and 16,179 artillery pieces) give some insight into the magnitude of operations in this first year of the campaign in the East.

firing plan the Soviets utilized their ground-attack aircraft as a long-range, high-trajectory arm of the artillery.

Major Stoll-Berberich[156] reports that in attacking German columns on the march, the Soviets usually only employed flights of about five aircraft, and at the most squadron sized units. The tactics employed were primitive. Instead of flying lengthwise over the highway under attack, the planes usually attacked at right angles to the moving column so that the results achieved were small. Individual targets were usually attacked from altitudes between 2,000 to 2,600 feet by planes spaced between 600 and 1,000 feet apart. Usually all planes attacked from one direction and not with the sun in their rear, and the attacks were very costly for the Soviets. The inadequate maneuverability of the IL-2 aircraft proved a serious handicap in attacks on the main line of resistance or targets in the rear, since the planes were unable to quickly change their direction to attack a more profitable target. It was observed as early as 1941 that Soviet ground-attack air units were directed by radio and air directing teams on the ground, but it was not possible to determine whether these teams were organic to the Army or the air forces.

Both Army and Luftwaffe command personnel concur in the following summary appraisal of Soviet ground-attack air operations over the battlefield and in cooperation with army forces: a) the main mission of the Soviet ground-attack air arm in 1941 was to operate over the field of battle and to support the operations of the Army; b) this mission the Soviet ground-attack air forces attempted to perform with commendable courage and aggressiveness; c) the personnel lacked adequate combat experience, however, and their equipment was technically too inferior to secure telling and decisive results, although the effects secured in local instances cannot be denied; d) the targets for attack were situated primarily within or in the immediate vicinity of the main defense area. The Soviet ground-attack air arm represented the long-range artillery of the Army; e) attacks were executed from low altitudes, and lacked variety and flexibility, so that the attacking units suffered unnecessarily heavy losses. Power concentrations were not developed; f) whereas ground-attack air operations in the northern and central areas were relatively insignificant, they were on a considerably larger scale in the south, where they occasionally produced a feeling of inferiority in the German troops.

    5) <u>Soviet Ground-Attack Air Operations in the Communications</u>

Zone. The operations of Soviet ground-attack air units in the communications zone were directed primarily against settlements in which German troops were quartered, supply installations, and airfields. Attacks of this type were experienced and are described by almost all Luftwaffe commanders.

Among others, Captain von Reschke[157] reports that the airfield on which his unit was stationed in the Ukraine was attacked by R-10 and IL-2 units. R-10 units usually attacked in strengths of eight to ten aircraft, which approached at ground levels from the direction of the front. The approach flights were cleverly carried out and every advantage was taken of available cover. As a result, the German fighter interceptors usually only took off when the attacking unit was over the field, which seriously complicated the operations of the ground defenses. The attacks habitually took the form of stick bombing with 22-pound bombs, which were poorly aimed and only inflicted minor damage. When they encountered fire from light antiaircraft guns the Soviet ground-attack pilots showed little initiative, due probably to the difficulty of carrying out evasive maneuvers at low altitudes and while flying in close formation.

The first attacks against von Reschke's airfield by IL-2 ground-attack units in strengths up to fifteen and twenty aircraft occurred in mid-July 1941. The Soviets glided down from altitudes of approximately 1,300 feet to attack simultaneously with machine guns and light bombs up to 110 pounds. The attacks were almost always directed at German aircraft on the ground; the results achieved were insignificant. Even when under fire by antiaircraft guns the IL-2 units continued obstinately on their course and therefore suffered considerable losses. In most missions of this type the ground-attack units were escorted by fighters. The fighters remained too high up, however, with the result that heavy losses were inflicted by attacking German fighters.

The obstinacy and lack of flexibility described above are also mentioned by Major Stoll-Berberich[158] as the particularly characteristic feature observed during a Soviet ground-attack strike against the Orel-West airfield, in which all attacking aircraft were downed by German antiaircraft fire and fighters. The attack also revealed the limited combat experience of Soviet ground-attack airmen and their lack of adaptability. They could easily have approached unobserved from the direction of the sun and could have achieved complete surprise by attacking directly from their approach flight. Instead, they skirted the airfield on the south at an altitude of 2,500 to 3,300 feet and then attacked from the west. It is only natural that by the time they flew in to the attack the German anti-aircraft batteries and interceptor fighters were alerted and ready to give them a hot reception.

This seemingly inexplicable behavior is easily understood when one realizes that the Russians, when attacking German airfields, almost always approached in such a way that they could fly back over the front by the shortest route immediately after their attack. Such tenacious adherence to established patterns, even when they are out of place, illustrates clearly the Soviet unit leaders' lack of versatility and initiative.

Captain Pabst,[159] in his diary, gives a highly graphic description of a far more cleverly executed attack repeated by successive waves of aircraft. Exploiting the cloud cover, the ground-attack aircraft flew in on their target, the Kiev* airfield, at close to ground level. Although almost 50 percent of the attacking aircraft were shot down and the light Russian bombs dropped in sticks did relatively little damage and caused comparatively few casualties, some parked German planes which were hit were exploded by their own bombs. It must be admitted that the entire pattern of the attack was by no means inept or careless.

Generalingenieur Thomsen,[160] in describing a Soviet attack against the Pleskau (Pskov) airfield, and Colonel Rudel,[161] both confirm that Soviet attacks against airfields were only of short duration, that the Russians very often released their bombs without aiming, and then immediately dived down to a ground level getaway.

Reporting on Soviet ground-attack air operations against the Smolensk-North airfield, Major Jaehne[162] states that on the whole the Soviets rarely attacked, approximately once per month, and then

---

* Editor's Note: The city of Kiev was the center of the German Army's fifth and largest battle of envelopment (16 Sept 1941) in the Russian campaign.

usually in the late evening. One of these strikes in September 1941, was directed against aircraft parked along the edge of the airfield. Instead of flying over the city area, which was protected by antiaircraft batteries, the attacking force of ten IL-2 aircraft cleverly approached across a wooded area. In a number of repeat low-altitude attacks, the force finally succeeded in exploding an ammunition depot.

In the light of what the above Luftwaffe commanders have to say the most prominent features of Soviet ground-attack forces in the German communications zones can thus be considered to have been as follows: a) operations in the German rear were directed primarily against airfields; b) in attacking German airfields, the approach and actual attack were so arranged that the planes could immediately fly to their base at a downward angle and by the shortest route; c) the approach was always carried out at low or middle altitudes; if the whole attack action was not carried out at ground level, the planes always attacked in a sloping dive; d) as a rule the attacking unit only flew in for a single attack; repeat attacks were a rare occurrence; e) owing to lack of experience, the Soviets displayed little flexibility in the conduct of operations and as a result suffered heavy losses when they encountered antiaircraft fire or were attacked by fighters; f) for the above reasons the results achieved by Soviet ground-attack units in missions against targets in the German rear, which were flown with commendable vigor, were usually entirely disproportionate to the losses incurred.

6) <u>Night Ground-Attack Air Operations</u>. Most probably Soviet ground-attack air units did not operate at night in 1941. According to Generalleutnant Huffmann[163] it appears from the statements of the majority of Army commanders interrogated on the subject that no night attacks by Soviet ground-attack aircraft were reported up to the end of 1941. The same conclusion can be drawn from reports by Luftwaffe command personnel.

In 1941 there were no specific night ground-attack air units in existence. The numerous and constantly repeated harassing raids at the time were carried out by outdated models (U-2) and will be dealt with in Section V: The Bomber Arm.

7) <u>Operations under Special Weather Conditions</u>. According to available reports by German Army and Luftwaffe commanders Soviet ground-attack aircraft were relatively independent of weather

conditions in their operations. In view of the general training standards of Soviet airmen and their lack of adequate instruments, this is surprising. German commanders have little to say on this subject, but not a single statement is available that the Soviet units at any time failed to fly their missions because of weather conditions. On the contrary, Major Jaehne,[164] for example, states that IL-2 units were frequently observed attacking at times when German aircraft were grounded because of weather conditions, and that in this respect the training of Soviet ground-attack airmen was so surprisingly high that they could even be assigned missions during unfavorable weather.

Generalleutnant Huffmann[165] writes that Soviet ground-attack aircraft flew in all weather, including rain and snowstorms, and that neither wind nor storm, rain nor temperatures as low as -22° F. prevented their operations. In this connection Huffmann mentions an episode from the battles for Kerch* in November 1941: the city of Kerch was already under German control, but the Soviets were still loading ships in the port. In this situation, in which they had no possibilities for observation, and in spite of heavy snow flurries and the extreme cold, the Soviets employed ground-attack aircraft in an effort to slow down the German pursuit, a mission which the air units valiantly endeavored to accomplish.

8) <u>Integrated Action with Other Arms of the Air Forces.</u> Cooperation was almost always evident between ground-attack and fighter units in missions flown by ground-attack units. As a rule, ground-attack units, when they attacked targets in the German rear, were accompanied by a fighter escort. Sometimes, however, the assigned fighters would patrol within the area in which the ground-attack aircraft were operating rather than fly close escort. This latter form of fighter protection was practiced only in the immediate

---

* Editor's Note: Kerch is a port on the Kerch Peninsula which stretches out east from the Crimea (between the Sea of Azov to the north and the Black Sea to the south) toward the Taman Peninsula and the Caucasus beyond. Kerch's strategic importance, as the eastern gateway to the Crimea (see note, p. 86), as a stepping stone to the Caucasus and because it controls the entrance (Kerch Strait) to the Sea of Azov and access to several important ports, was recognized by both the Germans and the Russians. In 1941 it changed hands twice.

front areas.

German commanders criticize this type of cooperation because the escorting fighters flew too high while the ground-attack aircraft were carrying out their actual strike. In consequence, the ground-attack aircraft were exposed to attack by German fighters at the most critical moment, namely, the moment after they had completed their attack. Occasional mention is also made of the mistake Soviet fighters made by accepting battle with German fighters, thereby neglecting their protective mission.

Cooperation with bomber units was frequently observed in 1941, although it was not as pronounced as later in the campaign.

Captain von Reschke[166] reports that in his command area the first combined ground-attack, bomber, and fighter attacks were carried out by the Soviets in July 1941. In these operations the ground-attack aircraft approached their targets while gliding down from an altitude of between 350 and 1,300 feet, with the bombers releasing their bombloads from an altitude of 2,000 to 2,700 feet, and the fighters providing cover at altitudes between 3,600 and 3,900 feet. Although these tactics resulted in a dispersal of the German defensive fire, the losses, particularly in bomber aircraft, were considerable. Attacks of this type were repeated frequently and were directed chiefly at the heavily occupied Belaya Tserkov airfield. The results achieved were meager.

Generalleutnant Huffmann[167] finds that cooperation between Soviet ground-attack and bomber units was good, that these two types of aircraft were frequently employed in integrated action in the southern area, and that massed operations of this type dispersed the German defensive effort. It was considered normal practice for ground-attack air units to operate with escort fighters.

The foregoing observation is also confirmed by Generalmajor Uebe,[168] who reports that Soviet ground-attack units were usually assigned strong fighter escorts, but that the fighters were on the whole considered incompetent and therefore ineffective. Soviet fighters were unable to master the difficulties encountered in escorting units of widely varying speeds at altitudes of approximately 5,000 feet and in providing overhead protection for a unit flying at a lower altitude.

9) **Ground-Attack Aircraft, Weapons and Equipment.** In the early stages of the campaign Soviet ground-attack units were equipped with Type R-10 and occasionally I-16 (Rata) aircraft. Neither type was very suitable for the purpose. German Army and Luftwaffe commanders considered the R-10, a plane of mixed construction, to be primitive, slow and not very maneuverable. It carried only 22-pound bombs and was armed with one rear swivel-mount machine gun and rigidly mounted forward machine guns of an unknown number. It was an obsolete model and could not meet requirements as a ground-attack plane. The I-16 (Rata) aircraft, employed as ground-attack aircraft, was considered hardly suitable for the purpose and vastly inferior to German fighters in the performance of its missions.[169]

In contrast, almost all German commanders describe the IL-2 as a highly useful airplane for ground-attack missions. In spite of a number of weak points this type proved highly useful and up to the end of the war rendered good service as the standard type for ground-attack air units. Major Jaehne[170] reports that German troops feared the IL-2 aircraft, which were flown recklessly and tirelessly. Owing to its good armor plating, the plane could only be brought down by very well directed ground fire. It had a speed of 210 miles, and could carry a bombload of 180 to 290 pounds. It was produced as a single-seater with two rigidly mounted machine guns and two cannon, and as a two-seater--which later became the standard model--with two rigidly mounted machine guns and two cannon forward and one machine gun on a swivel mount in the rear. Both models had rocket attachments.

General der Flakartillerie a. D. Wolfgang Pickert[171] adds that the IL-2 was impervious to light 20-mm armor-piercing or 37-mm shells. The same views are expressed by General der Infanterie von der Groeben,[172] who emphasizes the nose armor and remarks that direct hits with 20-mm shells frequently had no effects on the plane. The wings, where the fuel tanks were mounted, were considered the most vulnerable parts.

The experience of the 54th Fighter Wing[173] also shows that it was hardly possible to shoot down an IL-2 aircraft in an attack from the rear, because of its excellent armor protection. The best chance was to take its top surface under fire in a steep dive, or to fire into its sides.

Major Stoll-Berberich[174] is more critical in his appraisal of the IL-2 and lists the following disadvantages of the plane: it was sluggish, unstable, lacked maneuverability, its power reserve was small--a handicap in climbing--its construction was primitive, and since it could only carry light bombs up to 110 pounds its carrying capacity was inadequate. Stoll-Berberich considers that the plane had only one advantage: its strong armor plating.

E. General Summary of the Soviet Ground-Attack Air Arm in 1941:

1) Badly battered and hardly in evidence during the early stages of the campaign, the Soviet ground-attack air arm made a relatively quick recovery and gained visibly in importance and effectiveness. This was due in no small measure to the introduction of the IL-2, a modern aircraft suited to the purpose of ground-attack missions.

2) Soviet ground-attack airmen were personally courageous and aggressive. The characteristic weaknesses of the Russian mentality were less evident in these personnel than in Soviet fighter pilots.

3) The specific mission of the ground-attack air arm was to support the operations of the army. It was thus in every respect consonant with the basic concepts of the Soviet Command. All other missions were considered of secondary importance. There can be no doubt that the activities of the ground-attack air arm provided a steadily mounting measure of support for the Soviet army in 1941, even though the operations of the arm remained relatively restricted in comparison with the overall war effort. The material results achieved were admittedly small, but the support to Army morale was unmistakable.

4) In consonance with their main mission, Soviet ground-attack units were employed primarily over the main defense areas, where they sought out their targets. Owing to lack of experience, and technical inadequacies, however, the tactics employed were not always suited to the purpose. This resulted in disproportionately heavy losses and small achievements.

5) Attacks on targets in the German rear played only a secondary role and were directed mainly against airfields. Here,

also, the German fighter and antiaircraft artillery defenses inflicted heavy losses because the Soviet attack tactics were inappropriate.

6) In the execution of their attacks the Soviets frequently showed a lack of flexibility and experience. Escort fighters were usually assigned but were not proficient enough for their protective mission. Cooperation with bomber units increased during the year 1941 but failed to produce appreciable results.

7) Whereas the ground-attack aircraft employed by the Soviets at the beginning of the campaign were of inferior quality and by no means suitable, the Soviet air forces from the summer of 1941 on had in their steadily increasing numbers of IL-2 aircraft a machine which was tactically and technically suitable for the performance of ground-attack missions both in the immediate battle area and in the rear areas.

The progress made by the arm is appropriately expressed by Major Jaehne:[175]

> The Soviet ground-attack air arm was considerably more capable than had been assumed prior to the campaign. In spite of their excessively heavy losses at the beginning of the campaign, the regiments were able to recuperate and build up their strength in an astonishingly short time. As early as by the end of 1941 training reached commendably high standards.
>
> The aggressiveness of ground-attack personnel also deserves special mention. The dogged calmness with which they flew their attacks, also when in unit formation, was surprising. As a result, these units strongly supported the morale of the Soviet ground forces and contributed largely to the successes achieved by them in their winter offensive.

Section V: The Bomber Arm in 1941[176]

A. General.

The opinions of Luftwaffe and German Army command personnel vary widely concerning some aspects of Soviet bomber arm operations and effectiveness. Whereas Army commanders report that Soviet bombers were remarkably effective, at least in some front areas and during certain periods,[177] Luftwaffe commanders declare almost unanimously that the results achieved by Soviet bombers in 1941 were very small.[178] Probably this disparity between the views of Army and Luftwaffe commanders is due to the Soviets employing their bomber forces preponderantly in support of the operations of their ground forces. As a result, bombers operated almost exclusively in the vicinity of combat areas or against advancing German troops. Bombing attacks in the German rear were a rare occurrence and the Soviets made no strategic use whatever of their bomber arm. The effects of Soviet bomber activities were thus felt primarily by the German Army and not by the Luftwaffe.

For the above reasons Colonel von Beust is basically correct in remarking[179] that an air force which fails to apprehend, or misapprehends, or rejects the concepts of strategic air warfare gives the lowest priority to the development of its bomber arm. This was true of the Soviet bomber arm: at the outset of the campaign the bomber types in use were obsolete, and the command and operational doctrines of the arm, its training standards, and its equipment were faulty.

Another reason the Soviet bomber arm made such a poor impression was that it suffered extraordinarily heavy losses in aircraft destroyed in air combat and on the ground in the first few days and weeks of the campaign. The basic attitude of the Soviet Command toward bombing operations and the increased emphasis placed on the development and re-equipment of the fighter and ground-attack air forces in the autumn of 1941 combined to prevent the Soviet bomber arm from achieving any appreciable combat effectiveness by the end of the year.

The fact must nevertheless be borne in mind that within its limited capabilities, and in cooperation with the ground forces, the bomber arm did achieve remarkable local successes.

B. <u>Organization, Chain of Command, Strength, and Strategic Assembly</u>

Little was known to German commanders concerning the organization, chain of command, strength, and strategic assembly of the Soviet bomber arm. Apart from very general information to the effect that at the outset of the campaign the Soviets had a large number of bombers ready for action,[180] and that a strategic air regiment--the Stalin Regiment--was stationed on an airfield near Moscow with a mission which was only surmised,[181] the notes of German commanders contain no details on these subjects.

Concerning the strategic assembly of the Soviet bomber units, Colonel von Beust states[182] that, so far as any appraisal can be formed, the units were stationed in areas from 60 to 180 miles behind the frontier. Light and heavy units were echeloned successively to the rear, some of them on airfields of the peacetime ground service organization and some on tactical airfields of better construction than the forward airfields.

C. The Soviet Bomber Arm in Combat.

1) **Behavior of Personnel.** The conduct of Soviet bomber crews, according to German commanders,[183] was similar to that of Soviet ground-attack airmen: they were aggressive, courageous, and frequently rashly determined and obstinate. In many cases special mention is made of the rear gunners, many of whom continued firing fearlessly even while their plane was burning and crashing.

Generalmajor Uebe,[184] who subjects the behavior of Soviet bomber crews to a particularly critical examination, places the above favorable points in juxtaposition to a number of weaknesses: a) inadequate adaptability in reactions to changing weather conditions on long-distance flights and to defensive action and other conditions in the target area; b) inadequate powers of endurance, which became evident in the cessation of flight under unfavorable meteorological conditions, if enemy defenses were encountered during the approach, or if even minor mechanical defects developed; and c) indecision and nervousness when defensive action was encountered at the target, which resulted in the premature and inaccurate release of bombloads.

Uebe finds that the behavior of Soviet bomber airmen was essentially influenced by collective action, both within the individual aircraft crews and within entire units. Each individual crew member lived and flew in fear of the other crew members. Even the reestablishment of officer responsibility brought no basic change in this situation, because officers were also subject to the same weaknesses and influences as their crew members. This "lukewarm" behavior was at least condoned by responsible officers in all ranks.

Uebe's partial explanation does not alter the fact that these airmen, although they realized their hopeless inferiority, usually flew their missions courageously and fearlessly.

3) <u>General Operational Doctrine</u>. The view of the Soviet air command that bomber units support the operations of the Army first, and that operations against strategic targets in the rear or industrial targets be considered secondary is confirmed by all German commanders. According to them, the essential features in the operations of Soviet bomber forces were approximately as follows: a) attacks within or in the immediate vicinity of the battlefield and against marching enemy columns, always in direct support of the Army; b) isolated attacks in the rear areas, particularly against German airfields; c) attacks executed without fighter escort in the first weeks of the campaign, later with fighter escort; d) bomber units committed together with ground-attack units against particularly important targets and against German forces and installations in areas of main effort; e) during daylight, attacks flown in closed unit formation, at night by single aircraft; f) as far as possible bombers avoided combat with German fighters and also endeavored to avoid areas with particularly strong antiaircraft defenses.

Consonant with these operational principles, the activities of Soviet bomber forces were seriously curtailed from the very outset and were restricted mainly to attacks on tactical targets. Even within this restricted scope, however, the Soviet bomber forces secured no major successes because of existing flaws in their tactics, their technical equipment, and their training.

Captain von Reschke[185] reports from the southern area that even in the first few days of the campaign the Soviets flew large-scale bombing attacks against German columns in the German rear areas, against the Southern Bug River bridges, and--with special concentration--against the advancing German panzer divisions. The attacks were flown frequently and at regular intervals, initially without, but after four weeks with fighter escorts, which, however, hardly proved effective. It was only after a few weeks that operations were extended to include German airfields in intensified attacks lasting through the day and flown in successive waves. Soviet bomber units suffered heavy losses in their operations, particularly in the first few weeks of the campaign when they operated in very small units, without fighter escorts, and always employing the same tactics.

Von Reschke reports further--and his statement is corroborated by other sources--[186] that only the Soviet unit leaders were furnished maps and informed concerning the unit mission. Consequently, the execution of a mission frequently became impossible if the lead plane was shot down or if the unit was scattered.

Lieutenant Colonel Mahlke[187] reports from the central area that in the first few days of the campaign Soviet bombers sustained such heavy losses in attacks against such targets as airfields, rail junctions, and supply installations in the German rear, that from then on attacks were flown only by a few twin-engine bomber units with tactical missions and only limited penetration depths. Primarily because of poor bomb aiming, these attacks produced only small results and at no time had any decisive effects. This observation is also confirmed by Major Jaehne.[188]

Soviet bombers rarely flew strategic missions. The main reason for this was the attitude of the Soviet Command. Other contributing causes were the defective training of aircraft crews and their aversion to incursions far into the German rear areas. Soviet bomber operations of a strategic nature could therefore be disregarded. This finding is corroborated by Lieutenant Colonel von Riesen,[189] who, on the Polar Sea front in July 1941, experienced a high-altitude attack against the German base at Banak* by nine Soviet bombers,

---

* Editor's Note: Banak, Norway, located about 300 miles north of the Arctic Circle at the head of the Porsang Fjord. Two German airfields were located in northern Norway: one at Banak and the other approximately 175 miles to the east at Kirkenes, near the Finish-Norwegian border. German and Finish operations on this northern front had three purposes: 1) to defend the Finish town of Petsamo (now Russian - Pechenga) near the Russian border and important because of its strategic nickel mines; 2) to protect the northern Norwegian coast and interdict Allied shipping en route to the Russian port of Murmansk; and 3) to invade Russia and seize Murmansk.

the only attack against this tactically important German operational base in 1941.

On the strength of the above experience of German commanders it can be stated that: a) in consonance with the views of the Supreme Soviet Command, Soviet bomber forces were employed almost entirely on the field of battle to support Army operations; b) employment in strategic missions was the exception rather than the rule; c) no systematic pattern was noticeable in the execution of attacks; and d) for these reasons the results achieved by the Soviet bomber forces, tactically and technically inferior as they essentially were, were disproportionate to the losses they incurred.

3) <u>Flying Characteristics of Bombing Missions.</u> Numerous statements by German commanders are available concerning Soviet methods of approach, attack, and home flight. Although they vary according to the tactical areas, the type of targets, the time periods, and other details, these statements taken as a whole present a very clear picture.

Certain fundamental differences existed between the execution of bombing attacks on the field of battle and attacks on rearward targets. These differences were particularly noticeable in respect to the altitudes at which the various missions were executed, and the numbers of aircraft employed. Von Reschke,[190] for example, reports that on tactical missions, Soviet bombers usually approached and left the target area at altitudes of between 2,000 and 2,700 feet, and that the attacks were usually flown by forces of six to eight and rarely more than ten aircraft. In almost all cases the units flew and attacked in flight formation. Although they operated in tight unit formation, and in spite of attempted evasive maneuvers, the units were quickly scattered by German fighters. On encountering antiaircraft fire, a unit would continue doggedly on its course without increasing the distances between individual aircraft. Particularly heavy losses resulted from the slowness and inadequate maneuverability of aircraft, and from the lack of flexibility in aircraft crews and unit leaders. An Army source, Generalleutnant Huffmann,[191] fully confirms these findings.

Captain Kath[192] reports similar behavior of Soviet bombers attacking the bridges over the Dvina River on 27 June 1941. Throughout the day the Soviets attacked in flight-sized units from various directions, operating without fighter escorts at altitudes up to 7,000 feet. Because of the overhasty plotting of bombing runs, the bombs were widely scattered around the bridges and caused no damage. On this one day and within this area 69 Soviet bombers were downed without the loss of a single German plane.

Captain Pabst[193] records a similar situation. On one of the first days of the campaign he witnessed Soviet bombers attacking the German approach area throughout the day in small units of two to four aircraft. Not one of the attacking bombers escaped destruction by German fighters. Pabst describes the execution of these operations as inconceivably stupid and primitive by German standards.

That Soviet bombers usually operated in units of three to nine aircraft in the front areas but in larger units when attacking the German rear is mentioned by Colonel von Heimann,[194] who states that as a rule the bombers attacked during daylight, flying in for the bombing run from the direction of the sun. He adds that the Soviet habit of adhering obstinately to a course without regard for German defensive action resulted in losses which could have been avoided.

According to von Heimann, attacks on airfields and other targets in the German rear were usually flown at altitudes of between 10,000 and 13,000 feet by units varying in size between 3 and 25 aircraft. The usual formation was the flight, frequently widely spaced, with the aircraft flying at slightly different altitudes--a most unfavorable formation when the unit was attacked from the rear by German fighters. Bombing, usually with medium caliber bombs, was carried out while the plane was in horizontal flight, and the units sometimes left the target area at low altitudes.

Von Heimann mentions two remarkably good features observed in the conduct of Soviet bomber personnel. These were their firm maintenance of formation order and their efforts not to desert a crippled plane of their unit. If a damaged plane could maintain a reasonable cruising speed, every effort was made to keep it in the middle. Except in the first few weeks of the campaign, attacking Soviet bombers were always protected by escort fighters.

These observations on the operations of Soviet bomber aircraft are confirmed by a number of German commanders who served assignments in all areas of the eastern theater.[195]

The experience of the 54th Fighter Wing[196] indicates that in the first days of the campaign Soviet bombers usually operated in flight sized units at altitudes of approximately 6,500 feet and without fighter protection, and that the attacking units were, as a rule, completely destroyed by German fighters and antiaircraft fire. In the weeks and months that followed, attacks in the German rear were usually flown at altitudes of around 10,000 feet, by small units of up to six aircraft but sometimes by larger units, and always with fighter escort. P-2 units in particular maintained excellent flight discipline and supported each other with well directed fire. During the initial stages Soviet bombers, when under attack by German fighters, would move into close line or wedge formation to obtain maximum rearward fire power. Toward the end of 1941 the Soviets had adopted the German method of flying in flights with each successive flight slightly higher than the preceding one. The general rule, however, seems to have been for bombing units under attack by German fighters either to continue doggedly on their set course without any evasive maneuvers or immediately to cease their approach flight and endeavor to slope down toward the Soviet lines, if possible at ground altitude.

According to Generalmajor Uebe[197] bombers attacking targets in the near front areas released their bombs--usually medium calibers or small fragmentation--in horizontal flight, and then departed at an increased speed toward the front. Aiming was poor and a large percentage of the bombs frequently fell within the Soviet lines.

Admiral Moessel[198] reports that the Soviets carried out no systematically planned bombing operations at sea during the period under discussion, but restricted their activities to occasional, small-unit daylight attacks during fair weather. Owing to the loose manner in which these attacks were executed, poor flight discipline, and defective navigation, the results achieved were nil.

Colonel von Beust[199] places the strength of Soviet bomber units at an average of 10 to 20 aircraft. According to him the maintenance of unit flight formation by Soviet bomber pilots was their best accomplishment. This was an essential feature of Soviet bomber operations because of the activities of German fighters and because in many cases only the Soviet unit leader and his deputy were furnished the necessary data for the performance of the mission. All other planes in the unit merely followed the leader, releasing their bombs when the target was sighted or on a signal given by the lead plane. The sole tasks of these aircraft crews were, therefore, to maintain unit formation and to repel German fighters. The reasons for this may have been inadequate training and the desire of the Soviet Command to insure unconditional execution of the assigned mission.

Von Beust adds that the system adopted to repel German fighters was for all planes to fly in as close formation as possible. This enabled the unit to deliver heavy fire from all guns but also complicated the systematic direction of fire. On encountering anti-aircraft fire the units flew stolidly through the fire area without any attempt at evasive maneuvers. Once the German defenses succeeded in scattering a bomber formation or in shooting down the lead plane, the result was usually the loss of the entire unit.

4) <u>Bombing Operations in the Battle Area in Support of the Army or Navy</u>. Whereas it was consonant with the nature of the ground-attack air arm to consider attack operations in the battle area as its primary mission, the Soviets' use of their bomber forces in similar missions was undoubtedly out of keeping with the specific nature of bomber units. That the Soviets employed their bomber forces, similarly to their ground-attack air forces, primarily in the near front areas in support of army operations is authenticated by the unanimous statements of German command personnel. Since the army was most affected by these operations, army command personnel will be quoted first on the subject.

Concerning the northern area Generalleutnant Frankewitz[200] reports that in the initial stages of the campaign the Soviets only carried out frequent night harassing attacks, particularly in the Narva region and against the Narva River bridges. These attacks had a considerable nuisance effect but did no real damage. It was only at the beginning of December that the Soviets became more active in bombing and strafing attacks by single planes or flight-sized units against the main highways in the German rear. Although these attacks had no decisive influence on the tactical or supply situation, they did inflict casualties and they did affect troop morale. Frankewitz states that German troops took notice of them but did not allow them to interfere with their duties.

Writing on the central area, Lieutenant Colonel Wolff[201] reports that Soviet bomber units were encountered in strengths of six to twelve aircraft in the first days of the war, but that they were unable to operate against German fighter and antiaircraft artillery defenses. In the days which followed no Soviet bombers appeared. It was not before 7 July that Soviet bombers again were sighted. From then on they repeatedly attacked the advancing German troops but at irregular intervals in units of up to ten aircraft. The attacks were directed against main highways and other advance routes, troop concentrations and assemblies, river crossing points, occupied villages, etc. Between 7 July and 11 December, Wolff continues, he experienced 24 attacks of this type.

From the voluminous supporting study submitted by Generalleutnant Huffmann,[202] it appears that the Soviet bombers attacked in strengths of three to twelve aircraft during daylight at altitudes of between 1,300 and 2,600 feet. As a rule only medium caliber bombs were used. The attacks occurred at various times of the day. In critical situations they were repeated at intervals of from two to three hours. When weather conditions permitted, the attacking planes approached above the cloud cover over areas with strong ground defenses. The attacks, which were very disturbing for the German troops, were directed at all types of ground targets, but particularly at areas in which German troops were advancing and at crossing sites. In many cases good and useful integration of bomber and ground operations was observed, although the Soviets rarely developed a clearly defined area of main effort.

It has been mentioned repeatedly that Soviet air power was particularly effective in the zone of Army Group South, and this also applies to the Soviet bomber arm. Soviet bombers cleverly exploited the open terrain and the congestions which necessarily developed at crossing points over the Dniester, Dnieper, and Southern Bug Rivers, at the Perekop and Ishun isthmuses,* and during operations on the

---

* Editor's Note: The Ishun Isthmus is, in reality, a part of the Perekop Isthmus. Named after the town of Ishun (45° 57' N, 33° 49' E), it is located at the southernmost extremity of the Perekop Isthmus, where the latter joins the Crimea. Bordered by the Black Sea to the west and the Sea of Azov to the east, the Ishun Isthmus is further constricted by a series of lakes, making it the narrowest part (2 miles wide) of the Perekop Isthmus and the last obstacle to the German 11th Army's battle to gain entrance into the Crimea. See note, p. 86, also Field Marshal Erich von Manstein, Lost Victories, Henry Regnery (Chicago, 1958), pp. 217-20.

Crimean Peninsula. At times they inflicted telling losses on the German troops.

Soviet bomber operations increased considerably after the end of August 1941, when the German advance was approaching the Dnieper River, and continued with almost unchanged intensity throughout operations on the Crimean Peninsula. Army commanders, whose troops were constantly exposed to these air attacks, were therefore not entirely unjustified in their view that the Soviets had air superiority in these areas of the eastern theater.

Field Marshall Erich von Manstein gives expression to this view when he states[203] that the Soviet air forces had command of the air over the Perekop Isthmus,* their bombers and fighters continuously attacking every visible target. According to von Manstein, shelters had to be dug not only for the front-line infantry, but also for vehicles and horses, even in the rear areas, and antiaircraft batteries risked immediate destruction when they opened fire and thus disclosed their location to the Soviet aircraft. Moelders⸸ appearance in this area, however, caused an abrupt change as he succeeded in ridding the skies of Russian aircraft during the daylight hours.

Thus, the commander in chief of the Eleventh Army /von Manstein/ and his unit commanders agree that Soviet bomber operations very adversely influenced the German Army operations. In a final appraisal of the Soviet bomber forces in the southern area it must be admitted that their tactical operations, which were properly coordinated with army operations, resulted in heavy German losses in personnel and materiel and that a large percentage of these losses must be ascribed directly to action by Soviet bombers.

The situation in the southern area has been treated so exhaustively because it actually constitutes an exception in the campaign in the eastern theater. Conditions were entirely different in the northern and central areas. The nature of the missions assigned Soviet bomber forces there and the manner in which bombing attacks were executed were admittedly the same as in the southern area.

---

* See notes above, pp. 86 and 133.
⸸ See note above, p. 62.

However, the general consensus of opinion of all German command personnel, from battalion commanders to the army group commanders in chief, is that attacks in their areas were not very frequent, had only small effects, and did nothing to delay the German advance. Thus, it is reported that the seven corps controlled by the Second Army, each of which was assigned only one road for its two or three divisions, executed their march movements during daylight without any interference by Soviet air forces. Even during crossing operations at the Western Dvina River, during the Smolensk battle of encirclement and the double battle of Vyazma - Bryansk,* and during fighting in the Baltic areas Soviet bombers at no time appeared in such strength that they could have exercised any important influence on the decisions of the German commands or the operations of the German troops.

These impressions of German army command personnel concerning the tactical activities of Soviet bombers are confirmed by Luftwaffe command personnel.[204] Their reports mention attacks against panzer spearheads and asemblies, river crossings, and other bottlenecks on the German routes of advance. The results of these attacks, they agree, were meager because of inaccurate bombing and the effective operations of German fighters and antiaircraft artillery which, together, inflicted heavy losses on the Soviet bomber forces.

Generalmajor Uebe[205] points out that the tactical targets of Soviet bomber forces were the same as those selected for ground-attack aircraft, and that air attacks on these targets were often part

---

* Editor's Note: The Western Dvina River, Smolensk, Vyasma and Bryansk were all successive objectives in the 1941 offensive of Army Group Center, whose ultimate objective was Moscow. After breaking through Russian defenses on the Dnieper-Dvina line in July, Army Group Center launched a large-scale enveloping maneuver, which it successfully closed (6 August 1941) to the east of Smolensk. This was the second of the great battles of encirclement in 1941 (see note, p. 115). The double battle of Vyazma-Bryansk (18 October 1941), which is usually counted as the seventh and last of the battles of encirclement during the 1941 offensive, was the opening phase of the final drive on Moscow. During the course of the Vyazma-Bryansk encirclements Army Group Center purportedly took over a half million prisoners. See Kurt von Tippelskirch, Geschichte des Zweiten Weltkriegs, Athenaeum (Bonn, 1951), pp. 218-42 passim.

of the Soviet artillery fire plan, so that Soviet bomber forces frequently were nothing but an extended or long-range arm of the artillery.

Whereas operations by Soviet ground-attack and fighter forces against the German Navy were not even noticed in 1941, Soviet bomber forces did undertake such operations, although only on a small scale.

Admiral Moessel[206] reports that there was no evidence of any systematic employment of sizable Soviet bomber forces against German seaborne traffic or German naval operations in the Baltic or in the Black Sea. Only a few insignificant attacks by units not larger than ten bombers are reported. These were carried out in favorable weather and produced no important results. The use of aerial mines or air torpedoes was not observed in 1941. Moessel's opinion is that the Soviets were too heavily engaged in the conduct of land warfare to make sizable air forces available for naval operations.

5) <u>Soviet Bombing Operations in the German Rear.</u> Only a few Soviet bombing attacks in the German rear were directed against strategic targets. The large majority of attacks was directed against tactical targets located near the front, such as railroad junctions, bridges, supply installations, troop concentrations of all types, and particularly German airfields.[207]

Captain Kath and General Plocher report similarly on the complete failure of a Soviet bombing attack against the railhead and loading installations at Gumbinnen (Gusev)* on 23 June.[208] The Soviet force of 30 SB-3 bombers attacked without fighter protection, approaching at an altitude of approximately 10,000 feet in loose flight formation at echeloned altitudes. Whereas some of the bombers were downed during the approach, the unit leader and a few of the flights reached the target area, where they scattered their bombs

---

* Editor's Note: Called Gumbinnen by the Germans while it was in East Prussia. The city was renamed Gusev by the Russians in 1945. At the time of the Russian bombing attack mentioned above, the combat headquarters of 1st Air Corps, First Air Fleet was located in Gumbinnen.

without aim over Gumbinnen. The unit then broke up into individual flights, pairs, and single aircraft attempting to escape at ground levels. All were shot down over German-held territory.

A number of Luftwaffe command personnel describe Soviet bombing attacks against German airfields. Captain Pabst[209] experienced six Soviet bombings of his airfield at Kiev during the 21-26 July 1941 period. The attacking forces varied in strength between three and ten aircraft, some of which cleverly exploited the existing cloud cover. The attacks were carried out at various altitudes, without fighter escorts, and with inconceivable doggedness, no attempt being made at evasive maneuvers. German casualties and damage at the airfield were insignificant, but in most of the attacks all of the attacking planes were shot down by German fighters or antiaircraft artillery.

Writing also of the July 1941 period, Lieutenant Colonel von Riesen[210] described an attack by nine SB-3 bombers against the Banak* airfield in the Polar area. This attack also was flown without fighter escort and took the Germans completely by surprise because the attacking force approached from the sea. From an altitude of approximately 13,000 feet the bombers released small caliber bombs at brief intervals. The bombs injured a few of the servicing personnel and caused minor damage to some of the parked aircraft. Although the attacking force encountered no defensive action whatever and could therefore carry out its attack without interference, most of the bombs landed outside of the airfield area. On its return flight the bomber force was intercepted and almost completely destroyed by German fighters.

Major von Cossart[211] describes a well executed surprise attack by a flight of SB-2 bombers at an altitude of 10,000-13,000 feet against the Pskov (Pleskau) airfield in the summer of 1941. After an undisturbed approach, the Soviets destroyed three German planes and damaged a few others with well-aimed, small-caliber bombs. The bombers, flying without fighter escort, were then all downed by German fighters. Under interrogation one of the captured crew members stated that the flight had become separated from its

---

* See note above, p. 128.

parent unit and had no knowledge concerning the assigned unit target or any other flight or target data. All this information had been furnished only to the unit leader.

Finally, Generalinginieur Thomsen[212] reports on an attack against the Soltsy airfield, northern area, in early September 1941 approximately as follows: The surprise attack was flown by twenty twin-engine bombers, escorted by six to ten fighters, at an altitude of around 5,000 feet and carried out in two bombing runs. During the second run the escort fighters attacked aircraft on the field and the defending antiaircraft battery with weapons fire from an altitude of 300 feet. The bombs were well placed among the parked German aircraft, but the damage done was small. The bombs penetrated deeply into the ground, which reduced their fragmentation effect. The attacking unit departed at the same altitude as that at which it had approached. The attackers displayed no imagination, carrying out no evasive maneuvers even within the antiaircraft fire zone. In this attack the Soviets suffered no losses.

In other operations in the German rear Soviet bomber forces frequently suffered exceedingly heavy losses when attacking targets protected by antiaircraft artillery. This was due to excellent teamwork between the German antiaircraft and fighter forces. Antiaircraft fire broke up the attacking units because of the Soviets' habit of continuing doggedly on their set course. Once scattered, single planes, flights, or pairs of bombers were then downed without difficulty by the German fighters. Thus, whenever possible, Soviet bombers avoided targets with strong ground defenses.[213]

6) <u>Night Bombing Operations</u>. Whereas Soviet ground-attack aircraft carried out no night attacks in 1941, bombers frequently attacked at night. In these attacks a fundamental difference was noticeable between the permanent harassing night attacks on the front lines--as a rule by single U-2 aircraft--and night attacks against tactical targets in the near front areas or in the German rear.

Luftwaffe command personnel give approximately the following description of harassing night attacks:[214] Attacks by U-2 aircraft occurred during moonlit or starry nights, occasionally also when the sky was covered and when there was a low cloud ceiling. They were carried out by single aircraft at intervals of five, ten or fifteen minutes at altitudes of between 700 and 5,000 feet, the aircraft using the same routes for their approach and return flight. By these methods the Soviets succeeded in maintaining incessant harassing operations in the entire front area, to a depth of approximately six miles, from evening dusk until after midnight and sometimes even until early morning.

The regularity of the approach flight and the clearly visible exhaust flames facilitated the defensive employment of searchlights and antiaircraft guns, and the U-2 aircraft disappeared immediately when these went into action. The extreme maneuverability of the U-2 and the great difference between its speed and that of the fast German fighters complicated the defense by night fighters.

The tactics employed in these attacks were primitive--frequently the planes glided in to the attack with stopped engines. Only the wind whistling through their stays could be heard. Bombing, sometimes by hand, was inaccurate.

It would nevertheless be wrong to underestimate the effects of the attacks, since they were so unpredictable and therefore were extremely disturbing. The pilots dropped their bombs on any light or other target sighted, and the constant disturbance reduced the already short rest of the troops and had an adverse effect on supply operations, although the actual physical damage done in the raids was small.

The above observations of Luftwaffe command personnel are confirmed in all respects by their counterparts in the army. Thus, Generalleutnant Huffmann[215] reports that the Soviet night harassing plane--nicknamed "sewing machine" or "duty sergeant" by the troops--was known to every soldier who served anywhere in the eastern theater. In every divisional sector these planes made their appearance after dusk, to continue their operations in a shuttle service frequently until dawn. The raids were generally restricted to the immediate areas of the front, but occasionally extended as far as 16 miles in the German rear. On the whole the fragmentation bombs used, which were sometimes preceded by flare bombs to light up the target, did little real damage; and frequently they were dropped in open terrain. Because of them, however, it was necessary to be extremely cautious with lights, to construct shelter trenches, and take other measures which seriously curtailed the already short night rest period, particularly during the German advance. The troops thus found the Soviet night bombers quite disturbing, although the bombers hardly ever inflicted any actual losses.

No night bombing attacks at sea in 1941 are on record.[216]

In addition to the night harassing raids just described, the Soviets also carried out night bombing attacks against tactical targets in the near front or rearward areas. Such attacks, however, were far less frequent and, as was the case with daylight attacks, were directed primarily against German airfields.

Captain von Reschke[217] describes Soviet air attacks on the Sea of Azov port of Mariupol /now Zhdanov/, which were repeated on several successive nights. The raids were carried out by individual, 4-engine bombers at altitudes of between 1,300 and 2,000 feet. The planes approached from the land side between 2300 and 2400 hours each night and departed across the sea after stick bombing with heavy calibers, which, however, caused very few casualties and very little damage.

Captain Pabst[218] in 1941 experienced only one night attack against the airfield on which his unit was based. This attack took place on a very light, moonlit night, and was flown by a single plane which dropped a number of demolition and incendiary bombs without doing much damage.

Generalinginieur Thomsen,[219] in contrast, reports that the base airfield of his group in Smolensk-North was attacked approximately three times in 1941, each time before midnight. In each case three or four bombers, operating singly, attacked during fairweather at an altitude of approximately 5,000 feet. Some of the planes dropped a few bombs. Because of the large size of the airfield and the large number of planes stationed on it the results were satisfactory from the Soviet point of view. The high-explosive fragmentation bombs caused, in some cases, serious damage to parked aircraft, and a hangar containing aircraft burned down. No casualties occurred. No hits by the defending light and medium antiaircraft guns were observed.

Colonel von Beust[220] comments favorably on the manner in which Soviet night harassing raiders carried out their missions and on the effects these raids had on the German troops in the front lines, on supply and general traffic movements, and on German airfields, although the tangible results achieved in 1941 were small. The Russian talent for improvising and their thorough exploitation of all available means and possibilities is illustrated by the way they used otherwise obsolete aircraft in night attacks in order at least to achieve a nuisance effect, which they were decidedly successful in doing.

In evaluating Soviet night bombing attacks against tactical targets von Beust concludes that such air operations were more successful than daylight raids, although they were only carried out occasionally and in isolated cases and at best caused only a certain degree of unrest and delay. Attacks aimed at German night-bomber units failed to prevent or in any serious degree impair German operations. In 1941 the Soviets carried out no large-scale night attacks.

The quick decision of the Soviet Command to employ its obsolete aircraft--which were useless for daylight operations--in night operations, and the way in which the bomber crews adapted themselves to night operations merit acknowledgement.

7) <u>Operations during Special Weather Conditions</u>. Surprisingly enough, practically no comments by German command personnel are available on this subject. Generalleutnant Huffmann[221] states that unfavorable weather had no influence on the operations of Soviet bombers, and adds that bomber units continued to fly their missions in winter when temperatures were as low a -22° F. and during snow flurries.

Such a statement, however, might be misleading. In accomplishing their tactical missions, Soviet bombers had no opportunity to show whether they could carry out long distance combat missions under really difficult weather conditions, and the few operations in which bombers penetrated deep behind the German lines were not carried out under such conditions.

In a careful evaluation the proper conclusion would probably be that Soviet bomber crews were unable to execute bad weather missions. Their training in such subjects as all-weather and instrument flying was inadequate to the requirements of such missions, as were the instruments installed in their planes. Furthermore, the accomplishment of such missions was not required of them in 1941.

8) <u>Bombing Missions in Cooperation with Other Arms of the</u>

Air Forces. As already mentioned, it was only during the last months of 1941 that bomber units were always escorted by fighters.

According to the experience of the 54th Fighter Wing,[222] its units occasionally encountered sizable Soviet bomber forces with strong fighter escorts. On such occasions the assigned I-153 and I-16 fighters maneuvered and remained in the immediate vicinity of the bomber formation, while the faster I-18 or I-26 fighters flew at a higher altitude, sometimes completely out of sight and sometimes above an irregular cloud cover, to render indirect escort support.

On the whole, German commanders[223] reported that during an approach flight the direct escort planes maintained their proper positions in the immediate vicinity of the escorted bomber formation, but that the situation usually changed when German fighters attacked. As a rule, German fighters experienced little difficulty in luring away escorting Soviet fighters, who showed little sense of responsibility for the escorted unit and were anxious only to protect themselves. The bomber units, meanwhile, made the mistake when under attack of executing their bombing mission at top speed and then diving away. In many cases this reduced the effectiveness of the escort, since the speed of Soviet bombers and fighters was about equal.

Integrated Soviet bomber and fighter-bomber action has been described in Section IV of the present chapter, so that there is no necessity to treat this subject here. Although they achieved no major successes, Soviet combined fighter-bomber and bomber operations had a disturbing effect on the German troops.

D. Aircraft Types, Weapons, Other Equipment.

At the outset of the campaign Soviet bomber units were equipped with obsolete TB-2, TB-3, and TB-4* four-engine aircraft and more up-to-date SB-2, SB-3, and DB-3 models. During the summer months they also received P-2 twin-engine planes.

Luftwaffe commanders considered the four-engine models unsuitable for daylight operations.[224] They were sluggish, extremely

---

* Details on this aircraft are lacking.

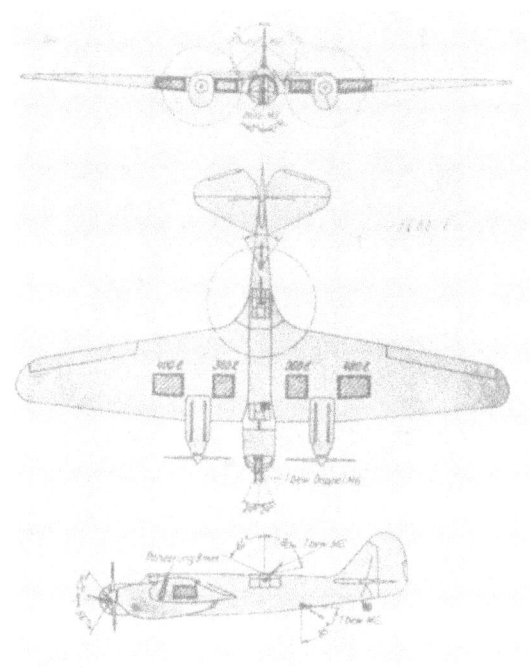

The Soviet SB-2, employed for both bombing and reconnaissance

The DB-3, a Soviet bomber

vulnerable to gunfire, and inadequately armed, and were thus completely obsolete, and unable to cope with German fighter and ground defenses. Soviet bomber units equipped with these types of aircraft suffered such annihilating losses in the first weeks of the campaign that they were withdrawn from use in daylight missions and employed only in night attacks and transport missions.

German commanders[225] were more favorably impressed by the SB-2, SB-3, and DB-3 twin-engine models. These aircraft were also by no means perfect, but could nevertheless be employed with some chance of success. In speed and at high altitudes they were about equal to the German Ju-88 and He-111, but had a smaller operating range, carried a smaller payload, and had less fire power.

SB-2 and SB-3 planes had a speed of approximately 240 miles per hour, carried a crew of three, and were armed with three swivel-mounted machine guns. Their fire power was inadequate against fighters, in spite of the fact that their bottom gondola, a feature unknown to the German Luftwaffe prior to the war, made it possible for them to fire downwards to the rear and sidewards to the rear. They could carry a bombload of 2,200 pounds and are not known to have delivered heavier calibers than 550 pounds. The main weakness of these aircraft was their high inflammability. Their fuel tanks were unprotected, and the drop-feed fuel tanks over the engines were easily ignited by weapons fire, thus causing the engines to burn.

DB-3 aircraft were more difficult to shoot down. The pilot was well protected by armor-plating, the fuel tanks were protected, and on the whole these planes were more ruggedly constructed and therefore less vulnerable to weapons fire. Their speed was about equal to that of the SB-2 and SB-3 models, but they could carry a bigger payload.

The best Soviet bomber type was the P-2, used increasingly from the summer of 1941 on. It was fast and highly maneuverable, had very effective fire power upward and downward, including rocket projectiles, and was difficult to shoot down, particularly since the entire plane, including the engine, was hard to set on fire.

The effectiveness of Soviet bombs was considered small, and it is stated repeatedly that only small losses in personnel and materiel were caused by Soviet bombs. This was due in part to the inadequate training and experience of personnel in bombing and in part to deficiencies in the bombs, detonators, and aiming instruments.

E. Appraisal of the Soviet Bomber Arm.

On the basis of the observations and experience of German command personnel the strong and weak points of the Soviet bomber arm in 1941 can be summed up approximately as follows:

1) From the outset the significance of the Soviet bomber arm was smaller than that of the fighter and ground-attack arms. This situation did not change in 1941, particularly because it was consonant with the concepts of the Soviet Command. At the end of 1941 performances gradually improved, simultaneously with a reorganization and general improvement of the arm.

2) In spite of weaknesses due to the inherent features of the Russian mentality, Soviet bomber aircraft crews flew their missions courageously. Since they were fully aware of their inferiority their behavior is particularly praiseworthy.

3) In accordance with Soviet operational doctrines, Soviet bombers were not employed on strategic missions but exclusively in the performance of tactical missions designed to support army operations. No development of power concentrations was noticed.

4) Accordingly, bombing attacks were directed primarily at targets on the field of battle or in the near front areas. In the southern area these attacks had a considerable impact on the German troops, in the northern and central areas the effects were small.

5) Bombing attacks in the German rear were also directed against tactical targets. In comparison with the effort expended and the losses incurred the results achieved were insignificant.

6) Operations by Soviet bomber forces against German naval forces and other bombing operations against seaborne targets were hardly worth mention.

7) Harassing night attacks by Soviet bombers against German troops had a considerably disturbing effect, tactical bombing attacks

at night against other targets produced only negligible results.

8) The conduct of bombing attacks was stereotyped and displayed little versatility. After their initial heavy losses during the first few weeks of the campaign Soviet bombers were assigned fighter escorts. Cooperation was not always satisfactory between the bombers and their escorts. Combined attacks together with ground-attack aircraft increased in scope but produced no significant results.

9) The four-engine aircraft with which Soviet bomber units were equipped were completely obsolete and useless in daylight operations. Even the newer types of twin-engine aircraft in some units were only conditionally capable of meeting modern requirements and were markedly inferior to German fighters. The only Soviet bomber really capable of performing the missions of a bomber plane was the P-2, of which only a few were available at the time. At the end of 1941 the technical standards reached by the Soviet bomber arm were not much higher than at the beginning of the campaign.

At the outset of the campaign the bomber arm was the stepchild of the Soviet air forces. In 1941 the arm made little technical or tactical progress. Nevertheless, Soviet bombers did not fail to achieve some measure of success--particularly in missions over the battlefield--within the narrow scope prescribed by these circumstances, although these successes were entirely disproportionate to the costs.

The status of the Soviet bomber arm is succinctly stated by Generalmajor Uebe:[226] "The Soviet bomber arm was the oldest but at the same time the weakest member of the Soviet air forces family."

Section VI: <u>Special Air Operations</u>[227]

A. <u>General.</u>

Little information is available from German commanders on the employment of Soviet aircraft for such special purposes as air transport, courier, liaison, command, and supply missions. Army commanders obtained no personal information at all on the subject and Luftwaffe commanders obtained what little information they had from observations made on the ground at captured Soviet airfields.

No Luftwaffe commander reports having sighted Soviet aircraft on transport, courier, or liaison missions during 1941. It can thus be assumed that the Soviets made small use of aircraft for these purposes during this period.

B. Transport Aircraft

According to German commanders the Soviets employed four-engine aircraft of the TB-3, 4, 5, and 6 types, the PS-84 (the Soviet version of the Douglas),* and the U-2 single-engine aircraft for air transport purposes. German commanders also noted a gradual increase in air transport activities.

In September 1941 Generalinginieur Thomsen[228] examined a number of three-engine transport planes of the Ant type found standing on the Soltsy airfield in the northern area. His findings were as follows: clumsy fuselage; corrugated metal outer covering; wings of the customary Junkers construction of the time; water-cooled Russian vertical engines; rough and defective worksmanship; primitive panel instruments; uncomfortable pilot's seat with poor visibility. Apparently the planes were intended for general transportation purposes and for the movement of paratroopers, but in Thomsen's opinion they could not be taken seriously.

C. Courier, Liaison, and Command Planes

According to Luftwaffe commanders[229] the Soviets employed types R-5 and U-2 aircraft for courier and liaison purposes. Although not a modern aircraft, the R-5, which was fabric covered, was just as suitable for these purposes as the U-2. It was known that the Soviet Command used aircraft in its communication services but the scope of this use was unknown. It cannot have been great in 1941, however, since such aircraft were rarely encountered airborne.

An unusual air mission is reported by Major Blasig[230] from the Polar Sea front. A German pilot shot down and captured during an attack on Murmansk was treated well by his Soviet captors. After promising that he would fly a German Ju-87 aircraft to the Soviet lines and land it on a precisely specified airfield, where he was then to train

---

* In the original draft of this study the author calls the PS-84 a "three-engine" plane. No evidence of such a type has been found, and it is believed that the plane had two engines. It is reported to have been armed with five machine guns.

Soviet pilots in dive-bombing, he was parachuted through the bombshaft of a Martin bomber near the Polar coast. From there he returned to his unit. Similar cases were reported at the time by the Finnish air forces.

D. Airborne Partisan Supply Missions.

According to Lieutenant Colonel Mahlke,[231] Soviet air units played an important role in their cooperation with partisan units operating in the extensive forest and swamp areas in the German rear. Weapons, equipment, medical supplies, and on a small scale personnel, were flown in to the partisans at night.

Although four-engine transport aircraft, which had to land on makeshift airfields, were sometimes used for this purpose, the usual plane employed was the U-2, which could land in a small area and in winter could land on skiis. In order to increase carrying capacities, a long ply-wood container was mounted under each wing of the U-2. Each of these containers could carry one man and was useful to fly in replacements or to evacuate casualties.

Navigation was by ground orientation, for which purpose directional signals were placed close to, and on the Russian side of, the front line. Light beacons or other light signals were used in the partisan area. Lanterns or straw fires identified the landing or air-drop points. These markings were changed daily in accordance with a pattern of irregular sequences and repeated after a period of several days. This pattern was determined beforehand by radio orders or by a predetermined code signal. German efforts to trap the supply aircraft and lure them to German airfields were frequently successful. Thus six planes of a U-2 squadron were trapped in one night.

If night landings were impossible, particularly during winter, because of the nature of the terrain, or for other reasons, the supplies were dropped, sometimes without parachutes, while the plane flew low and slowly over the supply point. In many cases even personnel were required to jump, without parachutes, into the deep snow from low-flying aircraft. Reports state that only slight injuries were sustained in such cases.

The circumstance that Soviet night attacks were flown by individual planes, the existing gaps of the aircraft reporting network in the German rear, and the lively Soviet night-harassing air operations made it practically impossible to keep track of penetrating aircraft. It can be assumed, however, that the majority of Soviet aircraft entering the German rear, apart from those on missions against tactical targets, were on partisan supply missions.

It must be admitted that with improvised means the Soviets maintained an excellent supply service for their partisans, a system that can almost be considered ingenious in its simplicity.

In summary, the Soviets made no significant use of aircraft for transportation, courier, command, and supply purposes in 1941. At least, no such use was observed on any large scale. For this reason no opinion can be ventured on the success or failure of such operations. In the matter of airlifted supplies for partisans the performances of Soviet airmen with their primitive and extemporized means were exemplary, and the aircraft employed on these missions were in every respect suitable for the purpose.

Section VII: <u>Ground Service Organization; Air Force Technology; Supply System in 1941</u>[232]

These were subjects with which German army command personnel had no contact whatever and in which Luftwaffe command personnel had little and varying experience. On one point, however, all opinions are unanimous: the Soviet ground service organization, air force technology, and supply system were inadequate and primitive by western standards, with the partially justifiable reservation that this very primitiveness was in many cases better adapted to the conditions in the eastern theater, particularly in winter, than the so-called technological perfection of the west.

A. <u>Ground Service Organization.</u>

1) <u>General.</u> In the opinion of Luftwaffe commanders[233] most Soviet airfields were primitive, but the ground service organization was flexible, met Soviet requirements, and was under constant expansion. Numerous landing strips existed, but there were few properly developed airfields with permanent-type installations.

During their retrograde movements in the first year of the

The U-2, equipped with plywood containers for carrying partisan agents behind the German lines

A close-up of the U-2's plywood container

campaign, the Soviets as a rule succeeded in evacuating important materiel and equipment. This was due in part to their ruthless exploitation of the civilian population for transportation purposes, and in part to the fact that no large stocks of materiel, equipment, and spare parts were stored at their airfields. It was only natural that aircraft and other equipment were frequently left behind when an airfield had to be abandoned in a hurry, but usually what was left behind consisted of aircraft destroyed on the ground and other items of useless materiel. Captain Kath[234] reports that during the German advance in the northern area fourteen airfields of various sizes, which were subsequently occupied by his units, were found to have been completely stripped by the Soviets before they withdrew.

2) <u>Operational Doctrines; Organization; Chains of Command.</u> These were subjects on which Luftwaffe commanders had little or no information.

Colonel von Heimann and Major Jaehne[235] express the view that ground personnel were not permanently located at specific airfields, but moved with the air unit to which they were organically assigned. When new ground personnel arrived in an area they were identified as such by the German radio intercept service. When a large number of newly arrived ground service units were thus identified, this was taken as an indication that the Soviets were massing air power in the area.

It is known that the above assumption was at least correct so far as the mobile air bases were concerned, so that the prewar Luftwaffe High Command estimate in this field can be considered as confirmed.

It must be emphasized, however, that what is said here is based on only a very few opinions by persons who had no detailed information on the subject. German command personnel were unable to obtain any deep insight into the organization and operating procedures of the Soviet ground services.

3) <u>Airfields and Airfield Installations.</u> Luftwaffe commanders became acquainted with numerous Soviet airfields during the German advance in 1941, and a large number of opinions are available.[236] Although these differ in details, the overall picture they present is as follows:

The outlay of Soviet airfields was simple and primitive by German concepts. Large airfields with all installations considered essential, such as concrete runways, repair hangars, halls, permanent-type billets, fueling and munitioning facilities, and repair shops, were relatively rare. The large majority of fields resembled German advance airfields, and had only a few widely distributed structures, such as small and medium prefabricated and wooden sheds. As a rule they were properly adapted to the local terrain and were also well camouflaged.

Most runways had only a firm grass surface and were not properly maintained. Permanent runways with a concrete or timber surface were a rare occurrence. Large airfields frequently had runways with a surface of octagonal concrete paving stones two yards square in size. The stones were set in a honeycomb pattern without mortice. Besides the time saved in construction--the paving stones could be set as soon as the top surface of the ground was leveled--the advantages of this type of surface were that it was very stable, was better adapted to the difficult conditions of the mud seasons, and because paving stones damaged by air attack could easily be replaced.

It is reported that airfields of this type were constructed in an inconceivably short time. Thus, fields were constructed in forest clearings measuring 2,000 by 500 yards, and the runways were completed in the manner described within one day for use by fighter aircraft. It must be emphasized, however, that ruthless use was made of the civilian population for such purposes. Frequently, women constituted as much as 90 percent of the labor force employed. The completed job was ugly and sometimes slipshod, and the construction equipment used was primitive.

Larger airfields had one repair hangar, storage sheds, an armory, a photographic shop, and some additional shed space, but lacked garages and permanent-type fueling facilities. Buildings on airfields were poorly maintained.

All structures and roads were extremely simple and often in poor condition, with unnecessarily long distances between buildings. The location of the various buildings in relation to each other showed no understanding of the requirements of air operations.

Airfields in this category usually had facilities for a radio locating service, airfield lighting, weather services and local defense. No detailed information is available on the operation and effectiveness of these facilities.

If Soviet airfields were far below western standards, it must be borne in mind that their very simplicity was an advantage, particularly in view of wartime conditions in the eastern theater. Also, there was the factor of Russian frugality. The Soviets made far more modest requirements in personnel and materiel than their German opponents. At any rate it is irrefutable that the Soviets with their primitive ground service organization frequently were able to adapt themselves to the requirements of war in their vast territories more readily and thoroughly than the German air units with their highly developed technical equipment. Other factors favoring the Soviets were their ability to improvise and the fact that their withdrawal in 1941 shortened their supply lines, while the German air forces were constantly moving farther and farther away from their home sources of supply.

German commanders fully realized that in spite of its inadequacies the Soviet ground service organization had some important advantages.

B. Air Force Technology.

Little is to be found in the reports of Luftwaffe command personnel concerning the technical aspects of the Soviet air forces. What they have to report on the subjects of aircraft, engines, weapons, ammunition, bombs, and general aircraft equipment has been dealt with elsewhere.

In other technological respects, the general trend evident in the reports[237] is that the Soviet air forces were considerably inferior to the Luftwaffe, without being definitely bad. Their aircraft were of simple and robust construction, the engines were copies of foreign prototypes but on the whole were usable and in some cases good. The only trouble was that both fuselages and engines were overworked, which resulted in numerous losses. Whereas small repairs and first echelon maintenance were carried out in mobile workshops near the front, aircraft or engines requiring major repairs had to be sent to rearward permanent workshops or to factories. In major engagements the technical operability of the units decreased rapidly and required a long time to recover.

No special types of equipment or installations permitting other than the usual means of fueling, munitioning, or bomb-loading became known in 1941. Thus, as a rule no fuel, no fixed fueling facilities, and hardly any fuel-tank trucks were found at captured airfields, so that it was often hard to imagine how the Soviets had been able to execute their missions at all.

On the other hand the Soviets proved inventive and dexterous in implementing measures to facilitate winter operations. Thus, at times when the highly technical heating wagons of the German units failed almost completely, the Soviets still succeeded in preheating and starting their engines with primitive means in a short time in spite of extreme temperatures. In some cases, a hand-driven ventilator was used to blow the hot smoke from a wood or gasoline fire through a strainer directly on to the engine. In other cases they poured oil heated over a primitive gasoline stove into the engines.

C. Supply System.

German commanders obtained no insight into the organization and operation of the Soviet air forces supply system. For this reason the few statements available on the subject[238] are of a general nature and give no details. According to the little information offered, the replacement of personnel, aircraft, and other materiel functioned with relative smoothness after initial difficulties had been mastered.

The means of transportation used were inconceivably primitive and not liable to disturbance. The Soviet withdrawal and the resultant shortening of supply lines from main supply bases produced definite advantages. Furthermore, the supply bases and routes were only temporarily exposed to German air attack, so that no serious and lasting disturbance of the supply services was achieved. Apart from the usual difficulties and disturbances, supply movements proceeded regularly and according to plan, in which the ruthless employment of forced civilian labor frequently played a large role. This latter circumstance is the only possible explanation for the fact that, in spite of the quick German seizure of airfields and supply depots, the Soviets as a rule succeeded in evacuating everything that was still useful in the way of aircraft, equipment, and installations, leaving only practically useless materiel behind.

The Soviets made large use of their traditional modes of

transportation in their supply movements. With the aid of their hardy peasant horses and simple peasant wagons and sleds they managed to cope with all difficulties much better than their motorized opponents, particularly in the autumn mud season and in winter. In one case it was established that the inhabitants of the surrounding villages were required to roll hundreds of gasoline barrels from the railhead depot to an airfield.

The general statements which German commanders have made on this subject do not reveal any details concerning the manner in which the Soviet supply services operated or whether the Luftwaffe High Command views on the supply organization of the Soviet air forces were correct or not. They do reveal, however, that the supply problem for the air forces was solved, even though various difficulties arose and many improvisations had to be made.

Section VIII: Air Signal Services[239]

German commanders gained only a vague impression of the ramifications of the signal services of the Soviet air forces. Without any detailed knowledge on the subject, they estimated the Soviet air signal services more or less as follows:[240]

In comparison with the German Air Signal Corps, the Soviet air signal services were extremely backward and not very efficient. This applied to the aircraft reporting and air raid warning services, and even more to the internal signal communication services within the air forces.

Radio was the most important medium of communication. This became evident, for example, from the fact that information gained through the interception of practically all Soviet radio traffic in the first few days of the campaign clearly revealed the shock effect of the German surprise attack, while increasing radio traffic later revealed the initial consolidation of the Soviet fronts.

Both Army and Luftwaffe commanders comment frequently on the lack of radio discipline and on the transmission of messages in the clear. The interception of Soviet operations orders transmitted by radio frequently made it possible for the German commands to take timely countermeasures.

The defectiveness of ground-to-air and air-to-air radio communication and the generally insufficient number of radio instruments issued to the units have been dealt with previously. As early as in October 1941, however, lively ground-to-air radio traffic from air control teams in the main line of resistance was heard during the battles in the Yesna /sic/* bend. The air directing teams not only transmitted instructions and directions to Soviet air units, particularly to airborne fighter and ground-attack units, but also through messages transmitted in German attempted to divert German dive-bombers to false targets. These observations were made at various points in the eastern theater. It was not possible to establish whether the air directing teams were army or air force units.

Another feature of Soviet radio communications in 1941[241] was that specific wave lengths were not assigned to specific units of the air forces, but that a complete wave band was allocated to one army group area. On this wave band the frequencies, and sometimes the call signals and codes, were changed arbitrarily, frequently as often as twice daily. Intercepted messages were thus often difficult to decipher; only the simpler codes were easily decipherable.

In comparison with the volume of radio traffic, wire communications played no significant role in the Soviet air forces and were inadequate. No trunk lines existed.

In the field of organization it was confirmed that the Soviet air forces had no organic signal service in 1941, in contrast with the Luftwaffe. The air signal service was part of the signal service system of the Red Army. It was also confirmed that signal staff officers at army, air division, and air regiment headquarters controlled the signal services and that signal channels, also in radio communications, were established from higher to lower levels of command.

The information obtained by German commanders concerning the signal communications of the Soviet air forces are too meager to permit a sound estimate of this service, particularly since no details are available on the organization and operational procedures or on the personnel and signal equipment and their capabilities.

---

* Editor's Note: Probably Yel'nya; see note above, p. 115.

However, from what is known concerning the operations of the Soviet air forces, radio traffic on the ground, ground-to-air and air-to-air traffic, and concerning such subjects as the inadequate provision of radio instruments for Soviet aircraft, the low status of training, and the frequently undisciplined behavior of personnel in radio traffic, the conclusion can be drawn that in 1941 the signal services of the Soviet air forces had achieved only low standards and could in no way meet the requirements of modern warfare.

Section IX: Training

Whereas German commanders, particularly Luftwaffe personnel, were able to form an opinion on the training standards achieved by Soviet airmen, a subject dealt with in the appropriate parts of this study, their reports and other available documents contain no information on actual training activities of the Soviet air forces, and particularly not on the methods and conduct of aviation training in 1941. Therefore, nothing can be said here on further developments in this field. However, it is probably safe to assume, and was actually substantiated by reports in later years, that no basic changes were introduced in the training system of the Soviet air forces in 1941 apart from a reduction of the time spent in training.

Section X: Parachute and Other Airborne Troops[242]

Although the Soviet Command had devoted special efforts to the establishment of strong parachute and other airborne troops, and although these troops were generally considered as an elite force, they were not employed on any appreciable scale in 1941. German Army and Luftwaffe command personnel could therefore form no opinion on Soviet parachute and other airborne forces, so that they hardly mention them in their reports.

The main reason why these units were not employed in operations similar to those carried out by German airborne troops is probably that in the general confusion caused by the German offensive the Soviet Command saw no opportunity to commit them. It is also possible that sufficient air transportation was lacking for large-scale airborne operations.

Because it did not appear possible to transfer the airborne

units to air bases far in the interior, and because of the succession of severe reverses suffered by the Soviet armies, the Soviet Command committed these excellently trained and equipped troops as infantry without proper planning. Through this precipitant employment, the forces suffered exceedingly heavy losses.

The only case in which airborne units were employed in a mission approximating that for which they were intended is that of the 214th Airborne Infantry Brigade. In July 1941 this brigade was moved through the German lines south of Smolensk to carry out partisan operations behind the German front for a period of three months pursuant to direct radio orders from the Soviet Army High Command. But even in this case the units were not air-carried to the operational area.

Otherwise, the only use made of these troops was as air-carried replacements for partisan battalions. These missions were only on a small scale and cannot be considered of major importance because personnel replacements could easily have been moved on the ground through the loosely connected fronts.

Untrained recruits drafted soon after the outset of the campaign and intended for employment in civilian clothing as partisans were captured together with paratroopers committed in combat as infantry.

Concerning the organization of Soviet parachute and airborne infantry in 1941, a later study[243] reveals that they were separated from the air forces in the autumn of 1941 and assigned directly to the Peoples' Commissariat for Defense. In the process a separate high command was established. Under direct orders from Stalin ten airborne infantry corps, each with three brigades, were newly activated after October 1941 in the territories of the German Volga Republic.* Serious difficulties were encountered here because of the lack of jump towers. Training was restricted largely to infantry and ski training.

---

* Editor's Note: Located north and northeast of Stalingrad, the German Volga Republic was an area inhabited largely by Germans whose ancestors had, in 1760-61, been invited to settle there by Empress Catherine II of Russia. The district was organized as an autonomous republic in 1924 and abolished on 24 September 1941.

Section XI: **Air Armament Industry; Military Economy; Transportation**

It is understandable that practically no information is offered by German commanders on the subjects of the Soviet air armament industry, military economy, or transportation system, since these were subjects with which they had no contact. From the few statements made and views offered the following picture evolves:

A. **Armament Industry.**

In spite of the time and materiel lost in evacuating factories from the near front areas to the eastern territories, the Soviet air armament industry succeeded on the whole in meeting re-supply requirements in aircraft and equipment. A serious bottleneck did develop in this field in 1941, but together with the evacuated and re-established factories the enormous air armament industries along the Volga River and in Western Siberia managed to avert the threatening catastrophe of a complete collapse of the aircraft replacement system. This may have been due in part to the fact that no really effective attacks were carried out by the Luftwaffe against Soviet air armament installations.

B. **General Military Economy.**

So far as the general Soviet military economy was concerned, the use of the skilled specialists and installations evacuated from the western industrial areas made it possible within a relatively short time to increase the output of factories along the Volga River, in the Ural region, and in Western Siberia.

The Soviets, in spite of the early loss of all industrial plants in the western territories of European Russia, succeeded in evacuating all important machinery and other important industrial facilities. This was an astonishing and unexpected feat of their military economy.

C. **The Transportation System.**

Contrary to all expectations, the Soviet transportation system, and particularly the railroad system, proved capable of coping with all requirements in spite of the enormous difficulties which developed. At any rate the expected collapse of the Soviet transportation system did not materialize. The destruction caused by German bombing attacks against railroad installations and rail depots was not lasting enough. Thus, it was established that after a direct hit with a 550-pound bomb on a rail track, traffic was resumed in full volume within forty-eight hours. The two-track rail route to Archangel made it possible to use this vital port for deliveries of military materiel, particularly aircraft and other air force equipment, from the Western Allies.

D. Conclusion.

Although future research may produce new information on the above subjects and thus modify some details of the picture presented here, it is hardly likely that the conclusion will be affected. That conclusion is that, in spite of the heavy losses suffered in 1941, the Soviet air armament industry, military economy, and communications system did not collapse but on the contrary continued to fulfill their missions and even helped to create conditions which made the later recovery of the Soviet military forces possible.

Section XII: Support from the Western Allies[245]

German commanders were unable to judge to what extent Allied support produced effective results for the Soviet air forces. Only those committed in the Polar Sea areas could obtain a limited impression, since part of the Anglo-American deliveries were imported into the Soviet Union through Archangel. Deliveries through Vladivostok and the Persian Gulf were beyond German observation and attack.

As early as October 1941 Soviet airmen flying American and British aircraft were encountered on the Finland front. However, even when flying these models, with which they first had to familiarize themselves, their performances did not improve. Allegedly, five or six squadrons of Hurricanes were identified in the Murmansk and Moscow regions. Allied airmen were observed in action only on very rare occasions.

The supplies shipped in through Archangel* included primarily

---

*Editor's Note: For an interesting British account of one of these early deliveries see: Denis Richards and Hilary St. G. Saunders, The Fight Avails, Royal Air Force 1939-1945, Vol. II, Her Majesty's Stationery Office (London, 1954), pp. 78-80.

aircraft (Airacobra, Tomahawk, Hurricane, and Spitfire), aircraft engines, weapons, ammunition, signal equipment, motor vehicles, high-octane aviation gasoline, and lubrication oil. In some cases terrific losses were inflicted on the convoys, but the Western Allies accepted these losses as a calculated risk.

A special case of Western Allied support was that of a low-level attack carried out on 1 August 1941 against the ports of Kirkenes and Linakhamari /Liinahamari/ (in the Bay of Pechenga /Petsamo/) by British Swordfish torpedo aircraft operating from the carrier Glorious 120 miles off shore.* The attack was planned to coincide with a high-altitude attack by Soviet bombers. However, the Soviet aircraft were detected in time and German fighters took to the air. Owing to this circumstance the British failed in their attack and lost approximately twenty aircraft. ╪

The opinions of German commanders are that the support from the Western Allies in 1941 contributed materially to the maintenance of the striking power of the Soviet air forces and to the ability of the Soviet military forces in general to continue their resistance. Lacking Allied support, German commanders consider that the Soviet economy might have been unable to supply adequate materiel to sustain the Soviet forces in the field.

In the light of later knowledge concerning the extent of Allied assistance to the Soviet Union the above opinions are probably correct.

Section XIII: Summary

In a final review of the Soviet air forces in 1941 the fact

---

* Editor's Note: See Captain S. W. Roskill, R.N., The War at Sea, History of the Second World War, Vol. I, Her Majesty's Stationery Office (London, 1954), pp. 485-86. Roskill mentions raids conducted by torpedo-bombers from the carriers Victorious and Furious against Kirkenes and Petsamo on the same approximate date. He, however, makes no mention of the Glorious as a participant in this operation.

╪ Editor's Note: Roskill mentions only ten aircraft being lost, all of them from the Victorious.

must be emphasized that German commanders, particularly Luftwaffe personnel, had the opportunity to gain extensive experience concerning the Soviet air forces, their operations, their performances, and their development. It is only natural that they gained more experience on certain subjects, for example, on the Soviet fighter, ground-attack, and bomber arms, than on others, such as the supply and replacement, air signal, and communications systems, or the air armament industry. Consequently, the comments offered by German commanders are better founded in some subjects than in others.

The picture of the Soviet air forces in 1941 presented in this chapter as an outcome of the evaluation of the material offered in a large number of contributions can nevertheless probably be considered appropriate. Furthermore, by comparison with the Luftwaffe High Command prewar estimate of Soviet air power, it permits the development of an opinion on how far the prewar views of the Luftwaffe High Command were confirmed by the experience of German command personnel and by the later course of events.

In brief, the estimate by German command personnel of the Soviet air forces in 1941 can be summed up approximately as follows:

The Soviet air forces as they existed at the outset of the Russian campaign were considerably inferior to the Luftwaffe in respect to tactical, technical, and aviation performances, command and combat experience, training standards, and materiel.

To this initial inferiority were added the destruction of the Soviet ground service organization, the disruption of the Russian Air Force's strategic assembly, heavy losses in personnel and even greater losses in materiel. During the first days of the German surprise attack the Luftwaffe shot down many Russian aircraft and destroyed an even larger number on the ground. Thus, during those first days of the campaign the Russian Air Force saw itself forced over to the defensive and German air superiority was established for the duration of 1941. Even the numerical superiority of the Soviet air forces did nothing to change this fact.

In 1941 Soviet air activities were restricted almost exclusively to support of Army operations. Although these activities were conducted without any recognizable development of areas of main effort and produced no significant or lasting results, local successes were occasionally achieved, particularly in the southern area. Furthermore, the operations served to support the morale of the Soviet ground forces, which were fighting under almost insurmountable difficulties. The influence of Soviet air operations on the German Army in 1941 was negligible.

In their combat behavior Soviet aircraft crews proved, in general, aggressive, courageous, frequently rashly determined, but seriously lacking flexibility. As an individual fighter the average Soviet airman lacked confidence and personal initiative; operating in a formation he proved a tough opponent who was not to be underrated.

Measured by the experience of German command personnel the Luftwaffe High Command prewar estimate of the probable capabilities, effectiveness, and status of the Soviet air forces and behavior of Soviet air personnel was fairly accurate; however, the strength of the Soviet air forces was considerably underestimated.

The inability of the German Command to destroy the rearward sources of power of the Soviet air forces, the energetic measures employed by the Soviet command to reconstruct its forces, the determined efforts of the remaining Soviet air units, the early winter (which gave the Soviets a breathing space toward the end of the year) all of these factors combined to enable the Russians to initiate a slow recovery of their air power.

Chapter 3

THE RUSSIAN AIR FORCE IN 1942 AND 1943

Section I: General

    A. The Course of Air Operations; Over-all Developments in the Russian Air Force.

During 1942 and 1943 the course of air operations and thus also the employment of the Russian as well as the German Air Force became more and more dependent on the vicissitudes of the ground fighting. Strategic air force missions gradually assumed a secondary role even for the Germans; the support of the Army in offensive operations became the primary and almost exclusive task. For this reason, one can understand the aspects of air warfare in Russia during that period and the evaluation of the Russian Air Force by German field commanders only if one is aware of the salient features of the ground fighting. The following decisive combat actions make up the most important military operations:

1942

January - March	Defensive fighting along the entire German front in Russia
May - September	German offensive, primarily in the south (Crimea, Caucasus, and Stalingrad)
November - December	Russian counteroffensive on both sides of Stalingrad and along the Don

1943

January	The Russians capture Stalingrad and its German garrison
January - February	The Germans are engaged in serious defensive fighting, particularly in the south
March	German counterattack near Kharkov

July	German attack near Kursk and Russian offensive in the Kharkov-Orel sector
August	Withdrawal of Army Group South toward and beyond the Dnieper
October - December	Heavy defensive fighting continues in the Army Group Center and South areas

This brief chronology indicates that the decisive combat actions took place almost exclusively in the Army Group South area, while the fighting in the Army Group Center and North sectors was relatively slow by comparison. For this reason the Russian Air Force made its main effort in the southern part of the theater; it was therefore in this area that German field commanders both of the Army and Air Force gathered most of their essential experiences pertaining to the Russian air forces; moreover, it was there that Russian air operations, developments, and performances made themselves particularly felt.

As shown in the preceding chapter, the Russian Air Force had overcome its worst crisis at the turn of 1941-42, after which it gradually began to recover from the serious losses of 1941. Despite many new reverses this strength-gathering trend continued during the following two years and led to a certain equalization of air strength in the Russian theater. Quite apart from the Russian factors contributing to this situation, which will be analyzed in detail in this chapter, there also were a great number of German factors which aided this shift of balance. The most significant of these were the great demands and stress placed on the German Air Force in other theaters of war, leading to the withdrawal of sizable air forces from the Russian theater; the heavy losses of the German Air Force in the fighting for Stalingrad--especially of bomber and transport aircraft--where irreplaceable crews and training personnel vanished forever; and the resultant weakening of the Luftwaffe in Russia because of these and other causes, together with the concomitant strengthening of the Russian Air Force. In evaluating the Soviet Air Force during the years 1942 and 1943 these factors must not be left out of consideration since they are essential for the understanding of this period.

The numerous evaluations of German Air Force field commanders[1] on the course of air operations, the over-all developments, and the conduct of the Russian Air Force in 1942-43 agree almost unanimously on the following points:

1) As of spring 1942 the growing strength of Soviet air power made itself felt. This recovery was only slightly impeded by the new Russian losses suffered during the German summer offensive of 1942. Progress in 1943 was even greater. In the same ratio in which the Russian Air Force grew stronger, especially numerically, the Germans lost their air superiority. As of autumn 1943 equality in the air was solely achieved by balancing the great Russian numerical superiority against German quality. The Germans were at that time capable of achieving only local air superiority, if they concentrated air forces at certain points for a limited period.

2) With certain exceptions the Russian air force units were committed en masse at points of main effort of the ground battle. Their task was almost exclusively to support the ground forces. For this reason, the air battle during this period took place in the southern sector of the theater.

3) In accordance with the concepts of the Russian command concerning the mission of air forces, the buildup and technical development of ground-attack and fighter units was given maximum priority, whereas bomber and reconnaissance units were neglected.

4) Training and combat effectiveness of the /Soviet/ crews did not keep pace with tactical and technical developments. Because of this, the Luftwaffe was able to hold its own, despite growing numerical disparity, and was even capable of achieving temporary and local air superiority by concentrating its forces.

The following observations from German Air Force field commanders substantiate the above conclusions:

Major Jaehne reports that in the winter of 1942 the German Air Force units suffered their first serious reverses in front of Moscow, where the Russian fliers were able to hold their own. Although the Soviet Air Force had by no means fully recovered at the beginning of 1942, the situation had definitely changed in favor of the Russians. There followed a concentrated buildup of Russian close-combat aviation, particularly ground-attack and fighter units. The offensive tactics of the air units improved as better trained and more spirited crews made their appearance. In 1943 the Russian aviation improved even more and benefited from its production, supply, and training facilities being situated in undisturbed rear areas, and from Allied assistance. Even though morale and fighting spirit were far from perfect, the Russians successfully equalized these deficiencies by mass commitment. The Germans thus gradually lost the air superiority they had achieved during the first year of the Russian campaign; they regained it occasionally, however, during individual operations.[2]

According to Major Schlage, the German Air Force enjoyed air superiority in the Finnish Theater during 1942, and near Leningrad even in the summer 1943. But in August 1943 the situation in the Army Group Center area was quite different, with the Russian Air Force becoming stronger and more effective until equality was achieved by the end of 1943.[3]

While Russian fighter strength in the north and central sectors was inferior in 1942, Major von Cossart and Major Stoll-Berberich state that it grew stronger in 1943; an increase in strength was especially noticeable in the south near Stalingrad, in the Caucasus, and in the Kharkov area.[4]

In the summer of 1943, in the central sector of the Russian front, a reconnaissance flier, Captain a. D. K. H. Wilke, encountered aerial combat on 6.5 percent of his missions. This figure increased to 19 percent during the German offensive in the Kursk salient and 31 percent during the defensive fighting in the autumn of that year. At the beginning of this same period, Captain Wilke encountered anti-aircraft fire on 48 percent of his missions. This figure later rose to 90 percent of his missions.[5]

According to Generalleutnant a. D. H. J. Rieckhoff,[6] the reconstruction of Soviet air power proceeded slowly because of constant attrition and sizable losses in defensive battles and counter-offensives. But the priority given to ground-attack and fighter aircraft benefited the Red Army which was no longer threatened by German air superiority and was able to attack after 1943 under the protection of Russian air power.

All German commentators[7] agree that the manpower reorganization did not keep pace with the production effort. This personnel buildup required more time. Moreover, it was psychologically difficult to instill confidence in the Russian crew members who had, during the first year of the war, acquired inferiority complexes. In this connection one must not forget that the Russian mentality, personality traits, and education did not particularly develop individual combat spirit. The primitive and often dull Russian remained inferior in individual combat because his basic concepts of life made him a less tough and stubborn fighter than his German adversary. The suppression of individuality led to failure as an individual fighter, which does not imply any general lack of courage or toughness. But a person who thinks and acts collectively lacks the mental flexibility essential to a good individual fighter. For this reason the Russian fliers performed much better as members of a collective unit than as individuals. Added to these personality traits were considerable training deficiences, above all the impossibility of coordinating training with production. This delay in the personnel buildup enabled the Luftwaffe to hold its own with the numerically far superior Russian Air Force even through 1943. But ever increasing signs indicated that Russian pilots were becoming more ruthless, confident, and self-assured. During 1943 the Germans encountered individual Russian pilots and units whose performance almost equalled their own. Although this was still exceptional, it indicated the coming trend.

In concluding these evaluations, Colonel von Beust's[8] summary of the 1942-43 period is paraphrased as follows:

When the German advance was stopped in November 1941, this also meant the end of a period of hopeless inferiority for the Russian Air Force and the beginning of a recovery which at first was hardly noticeable. The factors that had hiterto determined German air superiority, such as the systematic methods of conducting air operations, the concentration of forces at points of main effort, as well as the precision and frequency of attack operations, were of minor importance in winter fighting. With the over-all pressure relenting, the Russians were able to recover. Their air force was able to equalize the situation so that morale improved; at the same time, the Russian command tried to remove the tactical, operational, organizational, and technical deficiencies. This development, however, was at that initial stage difficult to discern since the Germans still enjoyed superiority of air personnel and materiel. As a result, the Germans failed to correctly evaluate their Russian adversaries or the existing ratio of strength.

An I-16 (Rata) one-place Russian fighter.
See description, pp. 101-02.

Captured Russian flying officers

The winter-imposed calm in the ground and air activities*
created the prerequisites for the buildup of Russian air power, for
intensifying training, and for accelerating technological progress.
The effects of this recovery made themselves felt in the summer
of 1942. The Russian air units were employed more systematically
and with more prior planning. This in turn showed that the intermediate level of command and the unit commanders themselves had
learned much and that the training of fighter and ground-attack pilots

---

* Editor's Note: While the characterization, "the winter-imposed calm," is essentially correct as far as any large-scale German offensive air operations were concerned, it is also a little misleading. After the rapid advances of 1941 which brought the German forces to the east of Leningrad in the north (the city itself remained in Russian hands), to the outskirts of Moscow in the center section of the front, and saw the short-lived capture of Rostov in the south, the Russians, at the turn of the year, unleashed powerful counteroffensives all along the front. Thus, they retook Rostov, relieved the pressure on Leningrad, and pushed the Germans back from Moscow. In the center section of the front Russian operations precipitated a serious crisis for all of the German forces in Russia. Since Hitler, for reasons of prestige and morale, refused to allow any of his commanders to retreat and thus shorten the length of the front, large German forces were surrounded at several points, but principally at Kholm and Demyansk where approximately 100,000 troops had to be maintained by air supply until the spring. Although the Germans were able to stem the winter offensive and the threatened rout did not take place, the winter offensive had serious and far-reaching consequences. The German armies in the East temporarily lost their initiative to the Russians and permanently lost their operational freedom to Hitler, who assumed direct command over the Army. From his strategy of "no retreat," which proved successful at that time, Hitler drew all the wrong conclusions. Thus, the success of Kholm and Demyansk was but a prelude to the failure at Stalingrad. And the idea of holding ground--instead of using retreats to create strategic and tactical advantages--became an obsession which was to cost the German Army heavy losses as the campaign wore on. See Richard Suchenwirth, Historical Turning Points in the German Air Force War Effort, USAF Historical Division (Research Studies Institute, Air University, 1959), p. 103; Tippelskirch, Geschichte des Zweiten Weltkriegs, pp. 242-50.

and crews had improved. In contrast to the events of 1941 that had brought Soviet aviation to the brink of disaster, the summer of 1942--with its territorial and combat strength losses of hardly lesser dimensions--did not diminish the recovery of the Russian air power. This difference was the significant indication for a positive change in the Russian Air Force potential. Thus, in the autumn of 1942 when the German offensives at Stalingrad and in the Caucasus ground to a halt, the Russian Air Force was unimpaired and ready for impending winter operations with better equipment and greater confidence than ever before.

The Battle of Stalingrad with its extremely high personnel and materiel losses* decisively affected all future German air operations in the Russian theater. At the same time, this battle proved clearly that Russian aviation matched that of the Germans who had lost their earlier superiority. Even the prowess of the German individual flier, who retained his superiority and continued to retain it, did not change the facts of the situation.

After the beginning of 1943 the Luftwaffe was mostly on the defensive, also because of the course of the ground fighting; the Russian Air Force, however, was on the offensive and was able to take the initiative. The German efforts to regain air superiority during the summer 1943 offensive had no continued or full success. After the last German attacks in the Kursk salient had failed in the autumn of 1943, the Russians definitely ruled in the air. Only quality, individual bravery, and greater experience enabled the German airmen to prevent their numerically much weaker units from being wiped out by the Russians.

In concluding, this author states again that the Russians purposely neglected strategic air operations and all problems connected with their development, giving top priority to fighter and ground-attack strength. The Russian strategic air force units thus remained outside the above-mentioned progressive development.

This generally accurate Luftwaffe picture of the Russian Air

---

* Editor's Note: Luftwaffe losses at Stalingrad amounted to 488 aircraft and about 1,000 flying personnel. Figures from the diary of Generalfeldmarschall Milch (Milch - Tagebuch), p. 87, G/VI/4d, Karlsruhe Document Collection. See also, Suchenwirth, Historical Turning Points in the German Air Force War Effort, pp. 100-107.

Force in 1942 and 1943 is essentially substantiated by Army commanders.

One of them, Generalleutnant Huffmann,[9] states that the Russian Air Force was committed mainly in support of the ground forces and concentrated at the focal point of the ground fighting. Occasionally the points of main effort for ground and air fighting did not coincide. Even the German Army units, which had improved and increased their ground defenses, felt a gradual increase of Russian air power during intensive battles, although the Russian fliers still showed their appreciation of German fighter prowess. Increasing Russian ground-attack aircraft intervention brought about such German reactions as the sending of more antiaircraft artillery to the front and improving its equipment and organization. Soviet air-ground coordination was generally effective.

The increased strength of Russian air power was felt primarily by German Army commanders in the southern part of the theater. New and better types of aircraft, stronger armor, reduced vulnerability of the ground-attack airplanes, and more effective bombs were observed, quite apart from growing over-all strength. The development of fighters seemed to be slower than that of the ground-attack aircraft. The Army commanders joined the Luftwaffe commanders in criticizing the training weaknesses of Soviet crews in 1943. Russian flying units did not seem to receive adequate replacements and the units' performances varied between good and bad; the same pertained to the performances of individual fighter pilots. In general, the Army commanders did not consider the Russian Air Force to be a well-balanced and uniform element of power at that time.

During the period 1942-43, the Russian Air Force concentrated its effort in the southern part of the theater: the Crimea, the Kuban Bridgehead,* and Stalingrad. As of December 1942 it struck hard against the German forces in the Stalingrad pocket, against transport aircraft approaching the encircled forces, and against the supply

---

* Editor's Note: The Kuban Bridgehead was a holding action in the Caucasus, begun during the Stalingrad crisis. By leaving a force of 400,000 men on the Caucasus' side of the Kerch Strait, Hitler hoped to tie down large Russian forces in the region and keep open a path to the Caucasus' oil fields. In addition, he hoped to deny the Russians the use of Novorossisk, an important port on the Black Sea. The holding action continued until 15 September 1943, when the Germans were forced to retreat to the Crimea.

airfields so that the already inadequate supply system of the Germans at Stalingrad, for this and a number of other reasons, collapsed. On the other hand, the Russian Air Force, in conjunction with the Russian ground forces, was incapable of bringing the entire German southern sector to a definite collapse, or of preventing German recovery and reorganization in this area. Perhaps the Russians did not have sufficient forces, or perhaps their leadership was lacking.

Compared to the south, the situation in the central and northern part of the theater was far more stable and the air force far less active. In these areas interest focused around the Rzhev-Orel (Central front) and the Leningrad areas. In the summer of 1942 the Russian Air Force was growing noticeably stronger in those areas. The Germans no longer enjoyed absolute air superiority, and during the defensive fighting of 1942-43 the German ground forces noticed greater equality in air combat. Russian superiority in numbers, however, did not influence the course of fighting decisively; strength was dissipated by local attacks without depth which were hardly more effective than during the German advance in 1941. This was probably caused, at least in part, by the concentration of forces in the south.

In summarizing, one Army general evaluates the course of operations and the conduct of Soviet air units during this period as a slow recovery from the heavy losses of 1941, with the Air Force giving a very uneven performance. Along some extended sectors Russian air power was almost non-existent. While 1942 was still a year of German air superiority, 1943 reversed this trend: the Russians enjoyed local and temporary superiority because of their great numerical strength, but they did not yet demonstrate their capability to fully exploit local successes.

A similar conclusion was reached by Generalleutnant Frankewitz,[10] who stated that the Russian Air Force gradually outgrew its infantile weaknesses. Its ability to concentrate its forces and select targets indicated better control and proper use of command principles. By summer of 1943 Russian bombing attacks in the Leningrad area proved very effective. There, the Russians had air superiority; wherever the Luftwaffe operated in strength, it was still superior but its forces were insufficient to guarantee constant superiority.

<u>Joint Russian Air Force-Navy Operations Against German Sea Traffic and Naval Installations.</u> Operations of this type remained

insignificant throughout 1942-43, in comparison with the other air activities of the Russians. German commanders found, however, that the Soviets flew more missions over the Arctic Ocean and the Black Sea, whereas there were no significant engagements in the Baltic area. When Soviet fighter-bomber and light-bomber aircraft intensified their attacks on coastal shipping in the Arctic in 1943, the Germans, according to Generaloberst a. D. Hans Juergen Stumpff,[11] had to build airfields for fighter aircraft in northern Norwegian coastal areas. Russian losses, however, were out of proportion to the damage inflicted on German shipping.

According to German officers[12] Russian air operations in the Black Sea area also increased in mid-1943, especially after the German withdrawal to Sevastopol. While, previously, outdated aircraft or single-engine naval planes had been used in this area, these were replaced by more modern types of aircraft. These engaged in bombing and torpedo attacks directed mainly against German naval convoys from Constanta or Odessa to Sevastopol. Although such missions were fairly frequent, they caused little damage. Repeated high-altitude bombing attacks against German-held port installations in the Crimea were equally ineffective. The Russian air units in the Black Sea were at that time rather primitive and exercised only a very insignificant influence on military operations.

Antiaircraft Artillery. Both Luftwaffe and Army officers agree[13] that Russian antiaircraft artillery became increasingly effective during the period under review. The Russian flak grew numerically stronger, developed its command technique and materiel, and improved its overall performance. Antiaircraft fire above the Russian ground forces constantly increased in intensity. During Russian ground attacks, light and medium flak were integrated into the advance parties and armored spearheads.

B. Command and Conduct of Operations

In evaluating the command and conduct of Russian air operations during 1942-43, German Air Force officers agree on the following points.[14]

1) The Soviet Air Force was even more exclusively committed for ground support than in 1941. This opinion is substantiated by the Russian directive on air-ground cooperation, dated 21 December

1943,[15] which indicates the dependence of air force missions on ground operations and their requirements.

2) Russian conduct of operations increasingly conformed to the concept of concentration of forces.

3) The conduct of operations gradually showed signs of more thorough preparation, greater flexibility, and better adaptability; here, the Russians partly imitated German doctrine of command and operations. Such improvements were noticeable especially at the intermediate level of command, whereas the lower level still lacked self-reliance and flexibility.

4) In contrast to the first year of the campaign, the Russians began to stress the offensive. This was particularly noticeable in the ground-attack units, while the fighter units continued to adhere to their basic defensive concepts. Concurrent with these changes, the Russians began to fly more close formations in larger units.

As of 1943 Russian aviation, according to Major Schlage,[16] concentrated all its efforts on direct front-line support of ground forces at points of main effort. Fighter and ground-attack aircraft were predominant, while long-range missions with fighter escorts were unknown until the autumn of 1943. The attacking aircraft flew in close formation up to group strength; only rarely did they fly deep into German-held territory, and their methods were generally primitive and inflexible.

Major Stoll-Berberich[17] states that the Russians changed their attack tactics as early as the spring of 1942, when the ground-attack aircraft in particular began to fly in major formations and refused to break formation even under German fighter attack. Especially during the winter months the German ground forces in the Leningrad area suffered heavy losses from this type of air attack.

Reporting on the Orel area, Captain Wilke[18] remarks that up to the start of the German offensive on Kursk--5 July 1943--there was little activity in the air and ground fighting, but then the situation changed very abruptly. Russian fighter, ground-attack, and bomber aircraft were committed in great numbers and almost exclusively in support of the ground forces. This still predominantly defensive conduct of operations became an offensive in October 1943, when Russian aviation directed incessant attacks on German ground forces and also on airfields near the front, in support of the Army's attack.

The gradual improvement in Russian Air Force command methods and conduct of operations was most impressively demonstrated by the evolution of the Battle of Stalingrad.[19] While the Luftwaffe was at first able to match the Russian Air Force, the ratio of strength soon changed in favor of the Russians because of the growing distance between the encircled forces and the German Army Group South bases. By mid-December 1942 the Russians were flying more and more missions in squadron and group formations. By mid-November 1942 German air transports could no longer approach in close formation, and by the beginning of January 1943 even individual transport airplanes were intercepted by Soviet fighters in daytime. By mid-December 1942 the Russians intensified their bombing attacks on German air supply bases to such a degree that the airlift was disrupted and the personnel and materiel losses became very serious.

Generalmajor Uebe[20] states that, in general, the Soviet Air Force selected its operational areas judiciously in accordance with the principles of concentration of effort. During Russian offensives the targets of the ground-attack and bombing aircraft were tactical and were integrated into the artillery fire plan. Immediately after a penetration the air units, with the armor, became the primary weapons of attack. The beginning of an attack was usually heralded by combat air reconnaissance; the point of main effort along a wide zone of attack often became manifest by the employment of ground-attack units, with attempts at deception being only rarely observed by the Germans. As of 1943 ground-attack and bomber units no longer attacked without fighter escorts. Although flying by instruments alone was unpopular, the Russian fliers became increasingly accustomed to less favorable and even bad weather, and flew night missions in any weather.

During this period, according to Colonel von Beust,[21] the Soviet command made every effort to change its conduct of operations and to introduce the principle of economy of forces. There were no more unplanned attacks or mass sacrifices. Even though the command wanted to disregard personal danger, missions were ordered only if the success promised to be in proportion to the effort, and procedures were improved accordingly. The advantages of forming points of main effort had been recognized and the conduct of operations was made more flexible.

This evaluation of the Russian command and its conduct of operations in 1942-43 is in agreement with the opinion of Army officers who obviously had less insight into these matters than did the Luftwaffe field commanders.

C. <u>Order of Battle and Chain of Command</u>

There is almost no direct information from German field commanders concerning the Russian Air Force's chain of command and order of battle in 1942-43. Major Jaehne[22] is of the opinion that the organization, top-level command structure, authorized strength figures, and chain of command had changed little since 1941.

A comprehensive publication of the German Air Force High Command, however, gives a clear picture of the Soviet Air Force's order of battle as of June 1943. This document provides the following general information on this subject:[23]

Using foreign organizational and operational principles as models, the Russian Air Force command had, without any show of prejudice, adapted valuable foreign methodology to Russian conditions. In so doing, the Russians indicated their extremely high esteem for technical matters by appointing expert technicians to all key positions in the technical service.

<u>Top-level organization</u>* remained basically unchanged: the Soviet Air Force was still not an independent third service; instead, it was split up into the <u>Red Army Air Force Units</u> and the <u>Soviet Naval Air Force Units</u>. These two air force elements were controlled by the Peoples' Commissariats for Defense and for the Navy, respectively. Both commissariats were controlled by a "Headquarters" which in turn was subordinate to the State Committee for Defense--the top-level political and military organization. The <u>Peoples' Commissariat for Defense</u> controlled, within the framework of the Red Army, the following air force elements: The Red Army Air Force Units; the Long-Range Bomber Command; the Air Defense Command with subordinate flying units; the Commander of Airborne Troops of the Red Army, including

---

* See Figure 4.

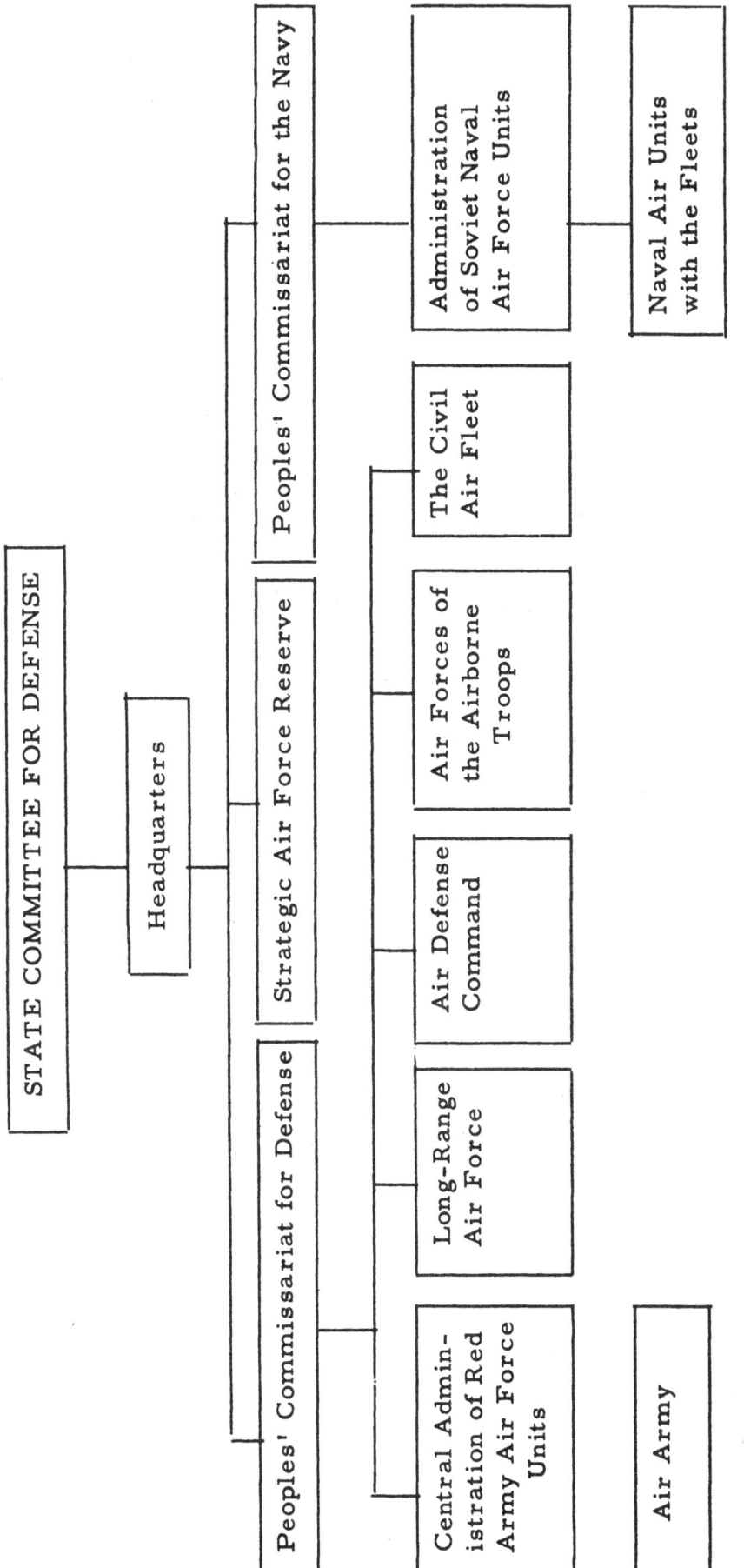

Figure 4

subordinate flying units; and the Civil Air Fleet (when used for military missions). The Peoples' Commissariat for the Navy controlled all naval air force units.

The Red Army Air Force Units were commanded and administered by the Central Administration of Red Army Air Force Units, which was part of the Peoples' Commissariat for Defense and which actually fulfilled the functions of an air force department.

The Central Administration of Red Army Air Force Units was, then, the top-level command and administrative agency of Red Army aviation. It combined two functional spheres--command and administration--thus assuring smooth cooperation. Under it came ten different divisions: The War Council, Staff, Central Administration for Rear Area Services, Central Administration for Technical Services, Inspector General, Economics Division, Personnel Administration, Navigational Administration, Administration of Military Schools, and The Administrator of Air Gunnery Training. Operational command was held by the Staff of the Red Army Air Force Units, which was really the general staff of the air force, controlling the air armies and replacement units for tactical employment.

An air army,* in its turn, was responsible for air force matters within an army group (front) area. The air army was under the operational command of the army group staff to which it was assigned, but was subordinate to the Central Administration of Red Army Air Force Units for all other matters. The establishment of air army commands was supposed to grant more freedom of action and decision to the air forces.† The commander of an air army was a member of the war council of his respective army group, over which presided the army group commander, and as such he took an active part in all operational planning and decisions. The air armies--there were 13 in European Russia--were committed exclusively in the theater of operations and not in the zone of interior. According to the needs of the respective army group sectors, they were composed of a varying number of uniform or composite air divisions and separate air force units. Air armies were

---

* See Figure 5.

† Author's Note: The Luftwaffe High Command concluded that this development indicated a progressive separation of the air force units from the ground forces. This conclusion eventually proved to be incorrect.

reinforced at points of main effort by employing air corps.

The air corps were merely tactical staff organizations, within the framework of an air army, which directed the employment of subordinate air divisions through air corps headquarters. The air corps supported Army operations in cooperation with the respective army, armored corps, or integrated combat group headquarters. The air corps headquarters were usually tactically subordinate to air armies, having no administrative, supply, and service functions and no organic ground organization. The number of air divisions subordinate to corps headquarters for tactical missions varied, but never exceeded three divisions. By the summer of 1943 the Germans had identified 25 air corps in Russia.

The air division, which occupied the next echelon, was a tactical unit of the air army--to which it was directly subordinate--but usually operated under the control of an air corps headquarters. The air division was to cooperate closely with Army headquarters in carrying out the orders it received from air army or corps headquarters. Its equipment could consist of fighter, bomber or ground-attack, aircraft or it could be a composite air division. With the exception of the latter, all air divisions were composed of only one type of aircraft. One exception were those ground-attack divisions which occasionally included escort fighter regiments. Fighter and ground-attack divisions usually were equipped with the same model aircraft within each regiment; this was not so with the bomber divisions. The composite air divisions, whose versatility in employment was their main feature, were preferably committed in quiet sectors. The Russian Air Force had no reconnaissance divisions. The average division was composed of three air regiments.

The air regiment was the smallest tactical unit of the Russian Air Force. Organizationally, it formed either part of an air division or was directly subordinate to an air army. There were fighter, bomber, ground-attack, long-range reconnaissance, reconnaissance, composite, and training air regiments. The composition of an air regiment was fixed at three squadrons, whose strength varied according to the type of aircraft. At the beginning of the war the Russians had planned to have five squadrons in each regiment, but this plan was abandoned.

As of 1942, the Long-Range Air Force (ADD) /Aviatsia Dalneyo Dyetsviya/ was composed of all long-range bomber and transport units

ORGANIZATION OF A RUSSIAN AIR ARMY, SUMMER 1943

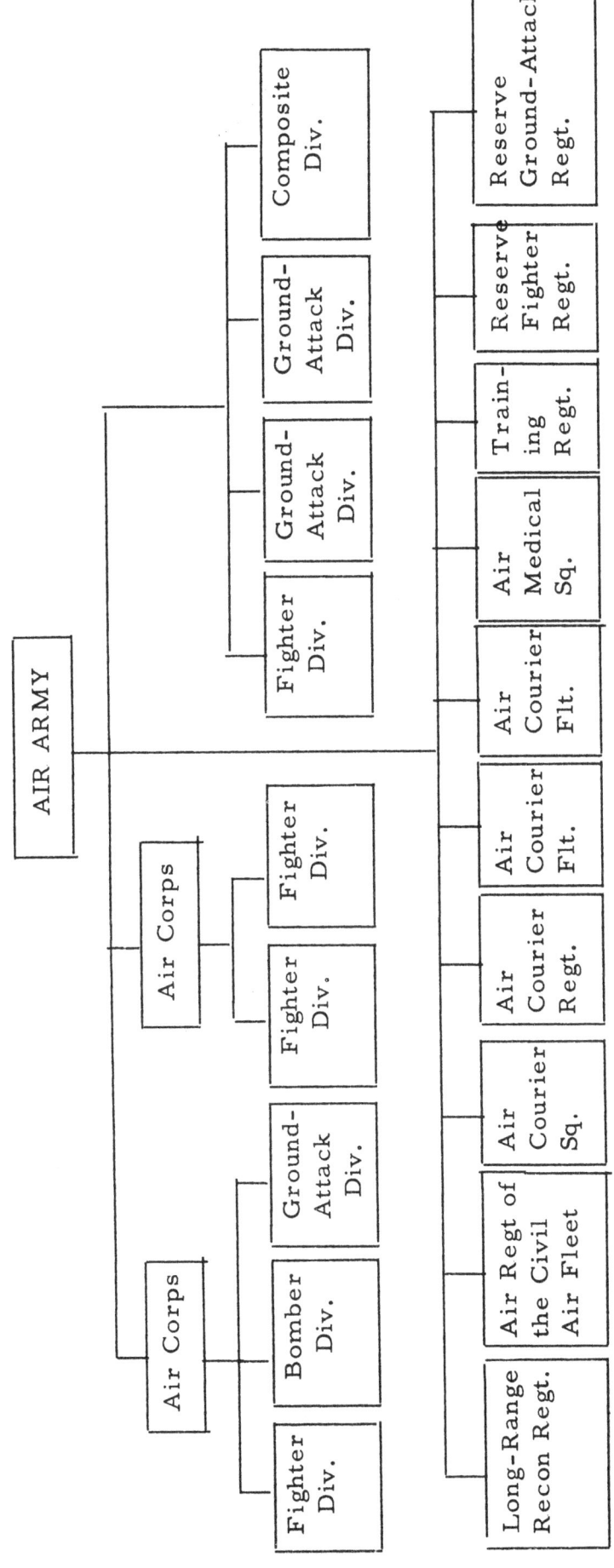

Figure 5

NOTE: Air divisions are operationally subordinate to the air corps; for all other purposes they are directly subordinate to the air army.

with the exception of the units stationed in the Far East. It was under the control of the Peoples' Commissariat for Defense and received its orders from the Long-Range Air Staff, not from the air army headquarters where its units were stationed. This type of commitment and chain of command was used, for instance, near Stalingrad. Since this force also had its own ground organization, replacement regiment, and aviation schools, and, furthermore, had selected personnel, the Russian command seemed to be specially interested in its development.*
The long-range air force was composed of divisions with two or three regiments each. Plans called for the organization of air corps as tactical command staffs and of long-range bomber divisions with two regiments of two or three squadrons each.

The air defense units of the Red Army were subordinate to the territorial military headquarters in the zone of interior. An air defense commander assigned to each headquarters was responsible for the organization and commitment of the fighter and antiaircraft artillery units in his military district. Air replacement elements were also utilized for air defense purposes in rear areas.

The Air Forces of the Airborne Troops of the Red Army were activated in October 1942 and put under the direct control of the Commander of Airborne Forces of the Red Army. They consisted of glider and transport units and were apparently being reorganized.

The Soviet Armed Forces also had a Strategic Air Force Reserve at its disposal, which consisted of a number of composite air corps, air divisions, and air regiments. These were committed in accordance with orders from Red Army headquarters issued by the Red Army General Staff and used at the points of main effort. By 1943 this entire organization was still in flux, the trend being to organize all strategic reserves within the framework of air corps. The Strategic Air Force Reserve, the size of which varied considerably, was composed of all types of aircraft.

The Soviet Naval Air Force, which was directly subordinate to the Peoples' Commissariat for the Navy, was commanded by the Naval

---

* Author's Note: The Luftwaffe High Command concluded from this fact that there would be more long-range bombing attacks on strategic targets in the near future. This hypothesis also proved to be wrong.

Air Force Commander, who was also its administrator.

The various fleets of the Soviet Navy--the Baltic, Black Sea, and Arctic Fleets, for instance--each had naval air force elements generally consisting of air brigades with three or four regiments, each composed of three or four squadrons. Aside from these brigades there were a few separate regiments and squadrons which were directly subordinate to the Naval Air Force Commander. The naval air elements of a fleet were controlled by a fleet air force commander who was under the operational command of the fleet commander, but for all other matters directly responsible to the Naval Air Force Commander. Shipborne aircraft were controlled by the ship's captain. Air defense of naval bases by fighter and flak units was the responsibility of the local air defense director.

The aviation outside of Red Army control consisted of the <u>Civil Air Fleet</u>, the NKVD* air forces, the air units of the executive councils, and the air forces of the Peoples' Commissariat for Economics. Of these forces only the Civil Air Fleet was subordinate to the air force staff of the Red Army for operational purposes at the beginning of the war; the Civil Air Fleet remained otherwise independent. In 1943 plans for integrating the Civil Air Fleet into the Red Army air forces were under way. Thus, for instance, the "air groups" of the Civil Air Fleet were transformed into air regiments and partly assigned to air armies; they remained subordinate to the central administration of the Civil Air Fleet for administrative and logistical matters, while receiving ground organization support from the Red Army air force units at their respective bases.

The other non-Red Army air forces mentioned above maintained their independence.

A comparison of the organization and chain of command of the Soviet Air Force of summer 1943 with conditions existing at the beginning of the war shows the following essential characteristics:

1) The fundamental principle of subordinating the Russian

---

* Editor's Note: The NKVD (Narodnyi komissariat vnutrennikh del = Peoples' Commissariat for Internal Affairs) was the Russian secret police organization from 1923 to 1946 when it was reorganized as the MVD (Ministerstvo vnutrennikh del.).

air forces to the Red Army and Navy, respectively, continued to be adhered to throughout 1943.

2) Within this framework, the establishment of air armies and their assignment to army groups (fronts) led to closer cooperation between ground and air force staffs, above all at the lower echelons of command. This new relationship increasingly replaced formal command and staff procedures. In accordance with the wishes and requirements of the ground forces and in close cooperation with them, the air force units conducted their operations with relative independence under the over-all direction of air army headquarters. This more flexible command relationship allowed the air forces more initiative in their conduct of operations than they had enjoyed in 1941.

3) The commitment of air units and the shifting of forces was facilitated by the formation of air corps as purely operational command headquarters.

4) The progressive transition to air divisions equipped with only one aircraft type (i.e. bomber, fighter, ground-attack, etc.) simplified command, operational, supply, and service procedures.

5) By detaching the long-range bomber units (1942) and the airborne forces (1941) from direct Red Army air force control, the Russians seemed to indicate the scope of their strategic planning for the future.

One may add, in conclusion, that both the organization and chain of command of the Russian Air Force corresponded to the Russian command and operational doctrines and were thus generally effective.

D. Strength Figures and Methods of Assembly

The German field commanders had no first-hand information on actual Soviet air strength in 1942-43. There were, simply, no important or detailed sources available. In general, the Germans felt that the numerical superiority of the Russian Air Force was steadily growing despite the heavy losses inflicted by the German fighter units. The air regiments, whose actual strength had been reduced to an average of 10-12 aircraft by the beginning of 1942, received a constant flow of reinforcements so that they were at

80-90 percent of their authorized strength in the summer of 1943. In addition, newly activated units strengthened the Russian air forces. The different estimates during that period--thus, for instance, the one made at the end of 1942 when the Luftwaffe High Command believed the Russians had 5,000 planes--were naturally inexact and rather too low than too high.

In the summer of 1943 the authorized strength of the Russian air regiment--the basic tactical unit--was 3 squadrons, with a total of 30 aircraft, regardless of whether the regiment was fighter, ground-attack, bomber, long-range reconnaissance, reconnaissance, or composite. In addition, most regiments were also assigned a liaison aircraft.[24]

This uniformity in the composition of air regiments existed only for Red Army air force units. The Long-Range Air Force had bomber air regiments composed of 3 squadrons with 15 aircraft each or 45 bomber aircraft plus a command echelon consisting of one bomber, one liaison, and one transport aircraft. Guard (elite) bomber air regiments consisted of four squadrons.

No details on the methods of assembly used by the Russian air forces during 1942-43 are available in German field commanders' records. There are only some general observations indicating that the assembly of air forces usually coincided with the concentration of ground forces and that the arrival of new units at airfields, when recognized by German air reconnaissance or radio intercept, often was indicative of impending operations.

The Long-Range Air Force units were usually concentrated at airfields in the vicinity of Moscow, from which they were transferred to operational points of main effort as the need arose, as for instance in the winter of 1942-43 when they were moved to the Stalingrad area.[25]

E. Types, Armament, and Equipment of Russian Aircraft

The impression of German officers at the turn of 1941-42, namely that technological innovations had begun to manifest themselves in the Russian air forces--particularly in types of aircraft-- was increasingly confirmed in 1942-43. The German Air Force officers agree[26] that technological progress after 1942 was undeniable and that it became particularly obvious in the development and standardization of new types of aircraft as well as in their equipment and armament. While the PE-2* was the principal reconnaissance aircraft, fulfilling all essential requirements, the well-known Mig, Lagg, and Yak types of fighter aircraft were further developed so that they became remarkably effective within a short time. Their capability was frequently considered higher than that of lend-lease fighters. In the sphere of ground-attack aircraft development, the Russians continued to adhere to their principle of sacrificing speed and maneuverability for stronger armor. In so doing, they used a diametrically opposite approach to that of the Luftwaffe which preferred a ground-attack aircraft without armor whose protection was its speed. The improved model IL-2 fulfilled all ground-attack aircraft requirements in 1942-43 and--according to competent Army and Luftwaffe officers--it was often considered ideal for that purpose. Aside from the DB-3 and PE-2, the bomber aircraft made the least technological progress; even these two types showed no outstanding features. The reason for stagnation in this field was probably the orientation of the Russian military command which intentionally gave preference to fighter and ground-attack aircraft over bombers. Allied bombers that might have brought about a certain equalization did not arrive in sufficient numbers. By the summer of 1943 there was only one Russian bomber division of three regiments composed of two squadrons each and equipped with American B-25's.

F. Summary and Conclusions

The impressions and data of German Air Force, Army, and Navy officers on the development and conduct of operations of the Russian Air Force in 1942-43 may be summarized as follows:

1) The Russian command adhered to the principle of subordinating air force units to the Army and Navy. The top-level command structure and employment of forces corresponded to this basic principle. For this reason, Russian air force units operated almost exclusively in support of the ground forces and as a rule were concentrated at the focal points of the ground battle. By this method the Russian ground forces were relieved from the pressure of German air superiority. The employment of air forces in support of naval

---

* Editor's Note: The PE-2 was a twin-engine bomber, dive-bomber, long-range fighter and reconnaissance monoplane (not to be confused with the shorter range P-2).

operations was of secondary importance.

2) During the period under review the over-all situation with regard to air operations gradually changed in favor of the Russians. An increasing strength of Soviet air power contrasted with a weakening of Luftwaffe capability. By the end of 1943 equality in the air could be restored spasmodically by the Germans because of the quality of their equipment and above all by the excellence of their personnel. Numerically, the Russian Air Force was far superior.

3) The reasons for this shift in air power--aside from over-commitment of the Luftwaffe in other theaters of war--were: the accelerated development, buildup, modernization and standardization of the Russian fighter and ground-attack forces with simultaneous de-emphasis of bomber and reconnaissance aircraft development; the rapid increase in the actual strength of Russian air units and the activation of many new units; the considerable progress made in command and operational procedures, with resulting improvement in tactics, planning and operations; the improved organizational structure and command relationships in accordance with the realities of the situation; and the gradually increasing combat experience of Russian pilots and crews.

4) The reasons Russian air superiority did not make itself felt more strongly by the end of 1943 are to be found in the greater ability of the German crews, the time lag between Russian technological progress and manpower organization, and the delays in improving the combat efficiency of Russian crews by intensified training. A contributing factor was still the Russian pilot's shortcomings as an individual fighter.

5) The Soviet Air Force flew almost no strategic missions during this period.

6) Russian antiaircraft artillery continued to improve and often was very effective in combating Luftwaffe attacks.

Section II: Reconnaissance

A. General

In 1942-43 German officers did not encounter much Russian

reconnaissance activity so that they arrived at the conclusion that there were few changes and little progress in this field. Only on rare occasions did they recognize a planned and systematic employment of Russian reconnaissance aircraft. On the other hand, the intensive Russian air activity, primarily above the battlefield, and the frequent use of fighter, ground-attack, and bomber aircraft for reconnaissance missions made it very difficult to obtain an adequate idea of the actual capability of the Russian reconnaissance units.[27]

In any event, the Russian military leaders seemed increasingly to have recognized the importance of reconnaissance on the course of operations. Thus, for instance, two reconnaissance units were assigned to guard air regiments in February 1942 for the first time. The same tendency was expressed through such measures as using only officers as flight personnel of reconnaissance units, selecting as replacements personnel from experienced bomber crews, paying higher salaries, granting special incentives and giving priority leaves to reconnaissance fliers. Finally, the production of reconnaissance aircraft was increased by improvements in procurement and supply procedures. However, a shortage of sufficiently trained observers continued. Since the Russians did not use the expedient of retraining suitable Army officers as air observers and since flying personnel lacked any close acquaintance with ground combat methods and above all with hostile organizational, tactical, and operational peculiarities, and since furthermore there existed no specialized training for air observers at observer schools, the reports of Russian observers were usually limited to registering the obviously visible on the ground. Visual reconnaissance was therefore primitive and correspondingly depreciated; the main emphasis was placed on photographic reconnaissance which provided satisfactory results, occasionally even good ones.[28]

B. Organizational Structure, Chain of Command, and Strength Figures

The information available to the Luftwaffe on the organizational structure, chain of command, and strength figures of Russian reconnaissance units was summarized in the Wartime Structure of the Soviet Air Forces, Status of June 1943 approximately as follows:[29]

The basic tactical and organizational unit of the Russian reconnaissance arm was still the air regiment or less frequently the independent squadron. The regiment was composed of three, sometimes only two, squadrons with a basic authorized strength of ten aircraft each. One differentiated among long-range reconnaissance regiments for strategic reconnaissance, independent regiments for short-range reconnaissance, composite air regiments for short-range reconnaissance missions and other assignments, and independent reconnaissance squadrons.

Every air army had one long-range reconnaissance regiment, several reconnaissance regiments, composite air regiments, and independent reconnaissance squadrons.

The long-range reconnaissance regiments were assigned their missions according to available information. Such assignments were often made directly by the Red Army air staff through the chief of the reconnaissance branch, (Intelligence officer). The individual long-range air reconnaissance regiments were under the operational control of the air armies or directly under the Red Army High Command in carrying out these missions. The long-range reconnaissance squadrons were usually equipped with only one type of aircraft, while the air regiments had squadrons equipped with different models; for example: two squadrons of PE-2's for daytime missions and one squadron of IL-4's for night flights.

The organizational structure of the independent reconnaissance air regiments for short-range reconnaissance corresponded to their mission; in general, these units were subordinate to air army headquarters.

The composite air regiments, committed at quiet frontal sectors as multiple purpose units to support the ground forces, were responsible for air support of an army. They were generally composed of individual fighter, ground-attack, and U-2 squadrons. For example, one composite air regiment, with one Yak-1[*] and one U-2 squadron, conducted daytime reconnaissance and fighter missions with its Yak-1 squadron, while the U-2 squadron transported ammunition to the front during daytime and flew reconnaissance and interference missions by night.

---

* Editor's Note: The Yak-1 was a single-seat, low-wing, cantilever monoplane, the forerunner of the Yak-9.

Russian PE-2 bombers in flight

The Russian Yak-1 fighter aircraft

C. Air Reconnaissance Operations

1) *General*. Russian reconnaissance operations were predominantly local, i.e. tactical and combat air reconnaissance missions flown by single PE-2's or pairs of fighter or ground-attack aircraft in good or bad weather. This type of reconnaissance gradually increased, as did night reconnaissance. The Russians usually flew armed reconnaissance missions that were often combined with nuisance raids, especially at night. The aircraft most used were the IL-2 for short-range reconnaissance, and the PE-2 for long-range missions. The pilots, however, were still afraid of German fighters and flak, and often failed to complete their missions when they encountered antiaircraft fire or were intercepted by fighters. In such instances they dropped altitude and turned eastward. In carrying out their missions they avoided aerial combat, even against inferior or damaged German aircraft. [30]

The reconnaissance missions were issued by the ground forces; the army group (front) headquarters assigned general missions to the air army, which in turn spelled out individual tasks in detail to the air reconnaissance units and prescribed the number of flights in some instances. Fighter, ground-attack, and bomber units also received reconnaissance missions, which were often the same ones issued to the reconnaissance units. Combat reconnaissance was mostly accomplished by composite air regiments; tactical reconnaissance by independent air reconnaissance regiments; and strategic air reconnaissance by long-range air reconnaissance regiments. The latter had better qualified personnel and special equipment for long-distance flights.

2) *Long-Range Reconaissance*. At the end of 1942 each air army had one long-range air reconnaissance regiment composed of three squadrons for the sector held by an army group (front). [31] The principal reconnaissance objectives that were to be systematically and daily observed were troop and supply movements along main roads, moving and stationary trains, and airfields. The air army staff maintained a traffic chart. The airplanes did not penetrate beyond 350 to 450 miles in depth, and for such missions only the most experienced crews were selected. In general, the two PE-2 squadrons flew daylight missions on alternate days; they flew an average of 8 to 12 missions per day in summer, and in winter proportionately less.

The Russian procedures of assigning missions and reporting

differed from the German. The "reconnaissance branch" of the army group headquarters, which corresponded to the intelligence branch of a German army group, received requests for information from the operations branch and transmitted these requests and missions to the reconnaissance branch of the subordinate air army headquarters. These requests were transmitted to the chief of staff or directly to the chief of the reconnaissance branch (Intelligence officer) of the long-range air reconnaissance regiment. He prepared the plan of operations after reporting to the regimental commander, and together with the squadron commanders he selected the crews for each individual mission. The mission assignment was therefore an intelligence, and not an operations, function. After returning from a mission, the aircraft pilot reported verbally to the chief of the reconnaissance branch. Important observations were immediately transmitted to air army headquarters. All reports were collected and transmitted to the reconnaissance branch of the air army by liaison aircraft at the end of the day, together with all photographs. Air army headquarters forwarded reports and photographs to army group. To maintain secrecy, reporting via radio was avoided, if possible. Photographic reconnaissance results were considered as important operational planning data, while visual reconnaissance was used only to supplement available information.

Thus, while the Russian command attributed more significance to long-range reconnaissance than hitherto and a certain degree of methodology in assigning and executing missions was recognizable, such progress was still considered as relatively minor and ineffective during 1942-43 by German Air Force experts.[32] There were many reasons given: insufficiently trained crews; long and complicated training of long-range reconnaissance fliers; the assignment of missions was not extensive enough nor was it properly planned--a criticism that touches upon the basic principles of Russian conduct of operations; and finally, the fact that reports from agents and partisan units as well as other sources of information provided sufficient data on airfields, troop movements, transportation, supply, and military installations in rear areas to make long-range air reconnaissance largely unnecessary.

3) <u>Short-Range Reconnaissance.</u> According to German Air Force officers,[33] Russian short-range reconnaissance had become more effective in fulfilling its principal tasks of front reconnaissance and ground support. The tactical and operational procedures were

exclusively and successfully geared to the closest possible cooperation with the ground forces. By 1942 the Germans gradually felt the impact of this improvement at their expense, since the Russian command was no longer ignorant of what happened at the German front line and in the rear areas, as had been the case in 1941. The tactical and combat reconnaissance objectives remained generally the same. Tactical reconnaissance missions were rarely flown at altitudes below 13,000 feet; they consisted of taking photographs individually or in series. Area photographic reconnaissance--by photographing reconnaissance strips from parallel flight lines--was not noticed; nor, in 1943, was reconnaissance of airfield targets with follow-up attacks. In view of the intensive Russian air activity, Luftwaffe officers found it difficult to determine the intensity and effectiveness of combat air reconnaissance at the points of main effort. Nevertheless, higher frequency of tactical and combat reconnaissance missions usually indicated the imminence of attacks. The Russians rarely used aerial observers for artillery fire.

In good weather single PE-2's carried out short-range reconnaissance missions, in bad weather they were conducted by pairs of fighter or ground-attack aircraft.

In proportion with the daylight tactical reconnaissance, the night reconnaissance missions also assumed increasing importance. The missions flown during the hours of darkness stressed information on approach routes and assembly areas; they were carried out as armed reconnaissance, often with the use of flares.

No information is available on Russian procedures for assigning short-range reconnaissance missions and reporting after their execution. But it may be assumed that they were the same as for long-range reconnaissance.

4) <u>Evaluation by German Army and Naval Officers</u>. German Army officers[34] generally agree with the evaluation of their Luftwaffe counterparts. Obviously, they were more impressed by combat air reconnaissance than by Russian long-range reconnaissance. They stress that during the period under review the Russians made considerable progress in air-ground cooperation and that the effect of Russian air reconnaissance was much more noticeable than in 1941. This was particularly so in the southern sector of the Russian theater during 1943 at the focal points of the struggle. While reconnaissance activity in the air had been intensive in the Crimea as early as 1942,

the Russians flew few reconnaissance missions at other crucial points in the Army Group South area. This was true even during the Battle of Stalingrad and the withdrawal movement of the German army group in 1943. In the central and northern part of the theater, Russian air reconnaissance was restricted to minor missions in 1942, but grew constantly more intensive in 1943. Only rarely did air reconnaissance information affect top-level planning, but there was evidence of reconnaissance data obtained by Russian fliers having been used for immediate tactical decisions or for directing fire. These were additional indications for the smooth cooperation between air and ground forces. Artillery spotting by air was almost non-existent in 1942 and extremely rare in 1943. Nor was fire for effect, after adjustment fire with air observation, reported by German army officers. On the other hand, they agree that night reconnaissance activities increased considerably, and that these missions were used extensively to maintain contact with partisan units.

The little information on Russian Air Force activities in cooperation with the Navy[35] indicates that air reconnaissance played a very secondary part in naval planning and operations, as was the case in 1941. Even so, there was some progress: both in the Black Sea and the Lake Ladoga-Leningrad areas high-altitude reconnaissance aircraft flying daytime missions for Russian naval units warned of approaching German naval or air forces. Russian air reconnaissance flew regular missions in the Black Sea area to identify German naval convoys. But the reconnaissance aircraft did not maintain contact with the convoys; instead, they sent radio reports while on their return flights. By taking cross-bearings, German radio intercept stations were regularly able to ascertain the approach of Russian bomber and torpedo aircraft in time for German fighters to protect the naval convoys. This was another proof of Russian lack of flexibility. Moreover, for a long time Russian air reconnaissance did not fly any missions south of the 44th parallel. The Germans took advantage of this when plotting the course of naval convoys.

    D. <u>Types, Armament, and Equipment of Russian Reconnaissance Aircraft</u>

All sources agree[36] that the outdated types of aircraft used for air reconnaissance in 1941 had disappeared, except for the U-2 that was still suitable for night reconnaissance. The others had been replaced by more recent models like the PE-2 for short-range reconnaissance and the PE-3--a special modification derived from the PE-2--for long-range missions. These aircraft fulfilled all requirements regarding speed, climbing ability, maneuverability, armament, and depth of penetration. By eliminating a third crew member, the PE-3 was faster and had longer range than the PE-2. Elimination of the third crew member, however, also reduced the PE-2's firepower and made it more vulnerable to fighter attacks. At the end of 1943 the TU-2* was used as a multi-purpose aircraft for armed reconnaissance. Occasionally, the American Boston III (Douglas A-20) airplane was also reported as having been used on reconnaissance missions. Long-range night reconnaissance missions were flown by DB-3F (IL-4)/ airplanes, while night reconnaissance was otherwise accomplished by U-2's. Combat air reconnaissance continued to be flown by such fighter aircraft as the Lagg-3, La-5, and Yak-7// and by IL-2 ground-attack planes, which were also used for other tactical air reconnaissance.

The armament of reconnaissance aircraft was the machine gun, except for types of airplanes--such as fighter or ground-attack aircraft--that were equipped with cannon.

There is little information on special equipment provided for reconnaissance aircraft. The Germans established that the Russians had produced imitations of the German automatic aerial cameras, such, for example, as the 30 by 30 centimeter aerial camera that had a focal distance of 50 centimeters. This item of equipment was an exact copy of the German model; however, the lense was greatly inferior so that the photograph was less clear, which considerably affected the interpretation value of the photographs.

In summary, during 1942 and 1943 Russian air reconnaissance had made up for most of its backwardness of 1941. Short-range reconnaissance, in particular, made good progress, as did night

---

* Editor's Note: The TU-2 was a twin-engine, 3 to 4 seat attack bomber intended to replace the PE-2.

/ Editor's Note: The DB-3F, or IL-4 which it was called after the spring of 1942, was a further development of the DB-3. A twin-engine transport aircraft, it was also used for towing freight gliders and for reconnaissance.

// Editor's Note: The Yak-7, a single-engine, two-seat, cantilever monoplane, was an advanced training aircraft.

reconnaissance and, to a lesser extent, air reconnaissance at sea. Reconnaissance aircraft and their armament and equipment improved considerably during this period. Replacement personnel, training, and long-range reconnaissance remained weak and kept the Russian air reconnaissance performance below that of the Germans.

Section III: Fighter Aviation

A. General

German Air Force officers in the field[37] had ample opportunity in 1942-43 to acquaint themselves with Russian fighter aviation. This was equally true for German reconnaissance, fighter, bomber, and dive-bomber crews. Their evaluation of the Russian fighter arm during that period is essentially in agreement. They describe the operations and developments of this hostile air arm approximately as follows:

When the Russian command reorganized the Air Force after the disastrous defeat suffered in 1941, it made a special effort to make fighter aviation the elite arm. Because of the wartime pressures and the suffering of new losses, such an effort could obviously only be gradual. It was equally understandable that the units with the most modern equipment and the best trained and led personnel were committed at the points of main effort of the ground battle, while the weak fighter units equipped with old types of aircraft were employed along less active sectors. This meant that the Russians made their main fighter effort in the southern part of the theater.

Along the Leningrad sector, for instance, the Russian fighter command remained very reserved even through the first months of 1943, showing scarcely more aggressiveness than earlier when opposed by German fighter units. By contrast, however, the Russian fighter pilots committed in the Kuban bridgehead and on the Crimea were quite aggressive as early as 1942. There the Russians had employed their best units. Among these was a naval fighter brigade which excelled because of its good staff work, tenacity in attacking, outstanding ability, and wealth of experience. Thus, it was in the southern part of the Russian theater that Soviet fighters achieved tremendous numerical superiority for the first time. There, apparently up to two-thirds of the entire Russian Air Force was temporarily

Soviet TU-2 light bombers in flight

The Russian La-5 fighter

committed.

The real turning point, after which Russian fighter strength clearly was on the ascendancy, was the Battle for Stalingrad where the Luftwaffe suffered such heavy losses that the Russian fighter arm achieved absolute air superiority for the first time, especially after the German fighters could no longer provide air cover above the pocket because of excessive distances from their air bases. Stalingrad gave Russian fighter pilots the confidence they had lost in 1941, providing them with the inner strength necessary for rebuilding their disorganized arm; the technical prerequisites for such a rehabilitation had already been provided by modern types of aircraft and improved command and staff procedures.

Like magnets, the centers of ground fighting attracted all forces of both opponents, and the fighter forces were concentrated above the important attack, defense, and breakthrough points at the front. The Russian fighter arm grew steadily through 1943 in numerical strength and in command, staff, and operational capability as well as in flying techniques and aircraft. Improved and up-to-date Russian aircraft were reinforced by sizeable numbers of Allied fighter airplanes, whose presence was particularly noticeable around Leningrad. By the end of 1943 the Russian fighter arm had become an adversary whose strength was not to be underestimated. Russian numerical superiority, however,--they had several times as many planes as the Germans--did not affect the over-all situation in the air more strongly because most of the Russian fighter pilots lacked the training and experience of their German opponents. Even though the Russians had some very good units--the guards fighter regiments in particular--and outstanding individual pilots, the average unit or pilot was inferior to its or his counterpart on the German side. The Russian performance was geared too much to the ability and courage of the unit commander, whose qualities or deficiencies determined the performance of the entire unit.

The correctness of this evaluation was proved with particular clarity during Operation Citadel,* which started on 5 July 1943.

---

* Editor's Note: In comparison with the ambitious objectives of the summer offensives of 1942 (Stalingrad and the Caucasus), Operation Citadel had a more modest goal--the achievement of a stalemate in Russia. See Field Marshal Erich von Manstein, Lost Victories, Henry Regnery (Chicago, 1958), pp. 443-49.

During this last major German offensive in Russia, the Germans committed strong air force units in the Kursk salient. In the subsequent air battles numerous Russian aircraft were shot down by the Germans, who suffered few losses. Although the Russians employed far more fighter aircraft than the Germans, they were unable to achieve air superiority, which the Germans held undisputedly for the following weeks in that sector. The uninterrupted fighting, however, eventually lowered German combat readiness so that the Russian numerical superiority was able to achieve limited effects.

Colonel von Beust, in a very graphic and exact description of the over-all development of Russian fighter aviation in 1942-43[38] mentions that the severe winter of 1941-42 permitted the Russian command to rehabilitate and train its fighter units. By the spring of 1942 a fighter arm numerically superior to the German opponents supported the Russian war effort. Even though the Russians had not been able to compensate for German experience, training, and technical know-how, their greatest deficiencies in flying ability, operational procedures, organization, and command and staff methods had been eliminated. Russian fighter aviation had therefore become more effective and its losses had dropped proportionately. These developments naturally took time so that the German air superiority was still uncontested in the summer of 1942. Since the Russian fighter arm carried the brunt of the air war during the major German offensives, it suffered the relatively highest losses and its reorganization could not be but gradual and time-consuming.

According to von Beust, the Russians developed into remarkable adversaries in the struggle for air superiority. The slow but continuous deterioration of German air power was, to a considerable degree, attributable to Russian fighter aviation. In general, though, the Russians shot down relatively few German aircraft, not only because the Germans used better combat tactics and had more experience but also because of the previously mentioned personal deficiencies of the average Russian fighter pilot. The effectiveness of the Russian fighter aviation was essentially its ability to force the Luftwaffe, and above all the German bombers, to take measures and adopt dispositions that reduced the effect of German air operations and increased the German air effort without bringing compensating results. Thus, for example, considerably stronger fighter escorts had to accompany the bomber units on their missions.

Insofar as they are capable of evaluating the general development of Russian fighter aviation in 1942-43, German Army officers endorse the above opinion of the Luftwaffe officers.[39] They note a considerable and steady increase in Russian fighters in 1943 with the fighter strength concentrated at the points of main effort, such as the Crimea, the Kuban bridgehead, near Stalingrad, Orel, Rzhev, and Leningrad. The Army officers also observed, however, that the Germans had air superiority during their attacks on Kerch and Sevastopol.

Nevertheless, the growing confidence of Russian pilots is dramatically illustrated by the remark[40] of 1st Lieutenant Peter Kulakoff, a Russian fighter pilot who had shot down nine German planes in severe battles during which he had frequently had to bail out. On 24 February 1942 he landed voluntarily on a German airfield. Much as he admired the performances of the Luftwaffe, when asked what chances he thought Germany had in the war he replied succinctly: "None."

B. Organizational Structure, Chain of Command, Strength Figures, and Methods of Assembly

The obviously not very comprehensive or pertinent information[41] available from German officers regarding this subject can be summarized as follows: existing Russian fighter units were reorganized and decentralized and thus strengthened, while many new ones were activated. At the same time they were echeloned in depth from the main line of resistance /MLR/ to rear areas. Only occasionally, at points of main effort in the ground fighting, were strong concentrations formed, and there they were almost unavoidable.

The fighter divisions were almost solely composed of fighter units to the exclusion of all other types. Internal cohesion within the division was, however, relatively loose.

The division was generally composed of three air regiments, each of which might be equipped with different types of aircraft so long as the intra-regimental equipment was uniform. The fighter regiment, in turn, was composed of 3 squadrons of 30 fighter aircraft and one liaison airplane (U-2) each. The personnel consisted of 34 flying officers, 130 technicians in officer and NCO grades who formed the organic regimental technical ground organization, and 15 men acting in various functions, for a total of 179. There was often a certain percentage of women, who were employed as weapons and engine mechanics and in similar technical capacities, exceptionally also as pilots. The air regiment had no organic trucks or signal equipment, relying completely on the air-ground organization for this type of support. Supplies and personal baggage were kept to a minimum so that the air unit would be as flexible as possible and ready to move at short notice. The transport aircraft needed for such moves were requisitioned from the respective air army headquarters.

Night fighter units, whose activation was accelerated in the summer of 1943, also formed part of the air defense forces and as such were subordinate to the fighter divisions. There were night fighter regiments and separate night fighter squadrons as well as alert night fighter units forming part of air replacement and training regiments. In cases of emergency, these night fighter units could be employed by the air defense commander of a military district in the zone of interior.

C. Fighter Operations

1) Personal Conduct. In the 1942-43 period German Air Force officers continued to differ greatly in their opinions concerning the personal conduct and aggressiveness of the Russian fighter pilots. Some mention lack of combativeness, low morale, respect for their German opponents, little courage, even cowardice and lack of will power,[42] while others emphasize pugnacity, confidence, self-assurance, tenacity in conducting operations, and even self-sacrifice and disregard of danger.[43] These apparent contradictions can be explained by differences in time and location, but even better by the fact that the Soviet fighter units varied greatly in quality during that period. There were individual pilots and units, such as the naval fighter brigade committed in the Kuban bridgehead fighting or the guards fighter regiments, which, especially when they had the benefit of numerical superority, were equal to their German opponents in aggressiveness, courage, and tenacity. At the same time, there were units--until the autumn of 1943 they were probably still in the majority--lacking the above qualities. Characteristics based on the Russian mentality, personality, and education, which favored collective operations to the disadvantage of individual combat ability, were also recognizable in 1942-43 among Russian pilots. The German fighter pilot therefore continued to be a superior fighter in the air. But there was little doubt that, in general, the Russian fighter pilot had more self-assurance than in the past, and that confidence in his

modern aircraft and knowledge of his numerical superiority had strengthened his morale. The personal conduct of the Russian fighter pilot in the autumn of 1943 indicated that he had overcome the shock of 1941.

   2) <u>General Principles of Conducting Operations</u>. Luftwaffe officers agree that Russian control of fighter operations from the ground and in the air improved considerably during 1942-43. To achieve such progress, the Russians adopted many of the German principles of conducting operations. The main characteristics of Russian fighter operations during that period were as follows:

   a) There was a gradual transition from a basically defensive to a more offensive conduct of operations.

   b) Fighter operations were focused upon the main line of resistance and the contiguous area; up to summer 1943 there were relatively few missions flown into the German rear areas, but thereafter such penetrations increased.

   c) The principal mission was pursuit in formation or fighter sweeps against German aircraft, while escort flights were secondary missions. Employment of fighters as fighter-bombers was infrequent.

   d) The commitment of fighters was no longer carried out without planning and in a piece-meal manner; instead, forces were concentrated at the points of main effort. While previously fighters were committed in pairs or in flights of four, they now began to appear in squadron strength and in even larger units. The units in the air were well directed from fighter control centers on the ground.

   e) When the Russians started their major offensives in 1943, they weakened the fighter protection covering their rear areas. The German Air Force officers[44] add, however, that important objectives, such as Moscow, continued to be protected by the most up-to-date Russian and Allied aircraft.

   In endorsing these comments, one author[45] states that Russian fighter operations became more systematic and straightforward, the division of units into attack and cover elements more effective. This was particularly striking in the case of elite units which confronted the numerically inferior German fighters with increasingly dangerous situations. Ground control methods, which were limited to observing the air space and conducting air operations against identified targets, also gained in effectiveness. The Russian conduct of operations was similar to the methods used in the West, even more so after the increasing arrivals of Allied aircraft in 1943. While low-level attacks by fighters in the zone of combat decreased, fighter thrusts into German rear areas with attacks on airfields were on the increase. The protection of Russian rear area objectives was gradually neglected; for instance, in the summer of 1943 the German surprise air attack on Grozny* achieved complete surprise and was not interfered with by Russian fighters.

A special method of fighter operations was observed in the Kuban bridgehead in 1943.[46] This method was designated "Kuban escalator" by the Germans; it consisted of Russian fighter units being committed in large formations at different altitudes. No outstanding success was scored by this method, which had the disadvantage that the simultaneous commitment of almost all fighter units resulted in the absence of fighter cover at other times.

3) <u>Flying Technique</u>. Except for the outstanding units, the flying technique[47] employed to the end of 1943 was still the tightly closed, uneven, and easily recognizable formation. Compared to 1941, the flight formation was better controlled. The approach flight altitude varied from 13,200 to 16,500 feet so that the pilots had sufficient space for maneuvering during aerial combat. This tactical grouping was quite effective under the conditions and with the type of aircraft of the first years. The conduct of Soviet fighter attacks depended on the hostile objective and will be dealt with in detail in the following sub-sections. The circular formation for defense was still of major importance to the majority of Russian fighter units, and the transition to other combat formations based on flying in pairs and on a division of responsibilities between attack and cover aircraft was slow. Surprise assaults were stopped prematurely as soon as the element of surprise had been lost.

In contrast to these units, the Russian fighter elite, such as

---

* Editor's Note: Grozny (sometimes spelled Groznyy), at the northern foot of the central Greater Caucasus, was an important German objective in the 1942 drive to capture the Caucasus' oil fields. The German forces were stopped 50 miles west of the city.

guards fighter regiments, units equipped with Allied aircraft, and a few other units, flew their approach in well organized, steady, and properly extended formation. These units were difficult to identify from a distance, had ample opportunity for observation from distinctly formed echelons of altitude, and thus almost completely eliminated the danger of being surprised. Their combat methods were based on the principle of attack and cover, they reassembled after attacking in a quicker and more effective manner than the other units, and their return flight was governed by the same principles as those governing the approach.

4) <u>Combat with German Fighters</u>. According to Major Rall,[48] modern-type aircraft and increased self-assurance gradually led to a change in Russian fighter tactics after the spring of 1942. Although the Russian fighters became more aggressive, their units were still not being effectively led in combat with German fighters. The circle formation was still standard. After the autumn of 1942 Russian fighter aircraft began to accept individual challenges on an increasing scale without immediately trying to get back to their unit. Pilots of guards regiments in particular were experts in individual fighting and flew their attacks on German fighter units in well-organized formations, divided systematically, the attack and cover elements alternating adroitly.

The Soviet pilots were not sufficiently familiar with the British and American types of aircraft to be able to get optimum performance from them. Nevertheless, the Airacobra (P-39) units, for instance, were serious adversaries, whereas the Spitfire units were quickly destroyed and never seen again.* Free French units that were mainly committed in defensive missions in rear areas were considered inferior to the Russian fighter units and quickly annihilated.

During 1943 the Russian fighter pilots not only accepted the challenges of German fighters but sought them out. This meant a considerable change from 1941. The Soviet elite air units, in particular, were masters in individual fights, having adopted Western

---

* Editor's Note: This is a somewhat puzzling statement, for the Spitfire was a far superior plane to the P-39. Perhaps the Spitfires in question were the earliest models, with inadequate armament; or perhaps the P-39's were flown by the best Russian pilots.

fighter tactics. Dog fights became more and more common, and even in the smallest unit--a pair--the pilots alternately flew attack and cover positions. When German fighters attacked by surprise, the Russian fighters would still form a defensive circle, a formation they mastered fully and one which gave them the opportunity to develop attacks under favorable circumstances. After combat, the Russian commanders showed better control than previously, since they reassembled their units much faster. Whereas the less skillful Soviet fighter pilots still tried to escape whenever their aircraft were in a position of inferiority, the experienced Russian pilots reacted differently. They took advantage of the maneuverability of their aircraft which excelled when flying steady horizontal curves. But despite these generally recognizable progressive developments, the Russian fighter pilots remained tactically inferior to their German adversaries through 1943, mainly because of training deficiencies, lack of experience, and certain technical handicaps.

Other officers[49] generally agree with the above opinion. Although some of them still emphasize, on the basis of their personal experience, that the Russian pilots continued to feel inferior to their German opponents and that they accepted aerial combat only under compulsion or fled when they observed German fighters and felt threatened by German cannon fire, these authors agree that aerial combat between fighters grew increasingly tough. The Russians frequently still used their old circular defense tactics, and thrusting into the defensive circle and breaking it up was a costly operation, leading to the sacrifice of the best German pilots, with the unit commanders from the lowest echelon to the wing level losing their lives first. Such losses could not be replaced simply by moving up the next ranking man.

5) <u>Combat with German Bombers</u>. In contrast with the previous year, German bomber units were increasingly and almost regularly attacked by Russian fighters during 1942-43. The basically defensive attitude adopted by Soviet pilots on encountering German bombers no longer existed. Only Lieutenant Colonel von Riesen[50] indicates that in 1943 in the Leningrad area strong Russian fighter units, observed in the vicinity of the target areas of German bomber units, did not attack. But the same author also remarks that Russian fighters launched frequent and disturbing attacks on German bomber pairs or flights whose target was the railroad traffic between Leningrad and Moscow. Since these Soviet fighter attacks were often carried out as early as during the German approach flight and since some 6 to 10 fighter aircraft suddenly appeared above the target area by the

time the German bombers arrived, the Germans arrived at the conclusion that the Russian aircraft warning service functioned well, even though at that time it was probably still primarily based on optical and acoustic observation. Equal efficiency could be attributed to the fighter control agencies. However, German bombers were often able to escape Russian fighters by flying into the clouds and by frequently changing their course.

Other Luftwaffe officers[51] point out that the German bomber pilots gradually had to adjust their conduct of attack operations to the Russian fighter capability, with the result that their missions became more complicated. Thus, for instance, Russian fighter operations forced the German bomber units to increase the strength of their formations and to maintain them at such increased strength. In selecting flight routes and altitudes, for instance, they had to take the Soviet fighter defenses into account. Because of the advanced types of fighter aircraft used by the Russians, some of the German bomber operations had to be scheduled for the hours of darkness. Also, it became necessary to employ more and more German fighters as escorts. The Soviet fighters usually attacked above the combat zone and pressed home their assault with tenacity. If these attacks had been more systematized and launched from superior positions, they would have proved more effective. As it was, the Russian fighter defenses failed also in 1942-43 to divert the German bomber units from their targets or to stop their attacks.

Writing about his experiences on the Russian conduct of fighter attacks on German bombers, Major a. D. R. Brunner[52] states that the Russians often attacked simultaneously from all sides to dissipate the German escort aircraft and open avenues of attack to the bombers which they usually assaulted from the rear by clever exploitation of the dead space of the Heinkel 111's. Oblique attacks from the rear and higher altitudes proved ineffective because they were easy to repel so long as the attacked bomber unit remained properly staggered and close together. The far more effective assaults from the rear conducted simultaneously from both sides of the bomber units were exceptional. Because of the well-directed fire of the bomber aircraft, the Russian fighters rarely downed German planes. Surprised by sudden bursts of accurately placed defensive fire, the Russians frequently veered off, returning only rarely for a second sweep. In many instances the Russian fighters committed their earlier mistake of opening fire much too soon and thus wasting ammunition. Whenever the number of aircraft shot down by the Russian fighters was on the increase, this was to be attributed to deficient coordination and fire direction of the German bomber unit. In the German experience the Soviet fighter attacks rarely occurred just before or during the dropping of bombs, but usually at the moment just after they had dropped their bombs and were changing their course. It was then that the bombers' defenses were weakest. German bomber units often suffered considerable losses from attacks so timed. Finally, Major Brunner mentions that in view of their numerical strength the Russian fighter units could have prevented almost completely the daytime operations of He-111 and Ju-88 aircraft as early as 1943, if they had been better led, had demonstrated more aggressiveness, and had been better trained. But despite remarkable progress over the past, the Russians' 1943 performance was not sufficient to achieve such results.

Russian fighter operations against German bombers in 1942-43 can be summarized as follows: a) Russian fighter aircraft switched from defensive to offensive tactics in their operations against bombers and increased their attacks which forced the Germans to strengthen their defensive measures; b) whenever German defensive fire was effective, the Russians were reluctant to press home the attack and, in these circumstances, their success was usually out of proportion to their effort; c) Russian fighters generally were still opening fire at too great a distance; and d) their aircraft warning service and their methods of leading the fighters toward the approaching German bombers had improved considerably over the past.

6) <u>Combat with German Dive-Bombers</u>. By the spring of 1942 Soviet fighter pilots were no longer hesitant and defensive in their attitude toward German dive-bombers. As in the case of encounters with German fighter and bomber units, the Russian fighters became steadily more aggressive. Frequently, they attacked German dive-bombers as they came out of their dive, so that the Germans had to dive in closed formations to cover one another. All German commentators agree on this point. Captain Pabst,[53] states that at the beginning of 1942, during dive-bomber attacks on Black Sea ports, Russian fighters intervened rarely and then mostly too late so that the German escort fliers were able to disperse them. During the early stages of the Battle for Stalingrad the Russian fighters were still very reluctant in their attacks, often turning away when German escort aircraft made their appearance.

This situation, however, soon changed. The strong Soviet fighter defenses obstructed dive-bomber assaults very effectively by surprise attacks from below and by committing fighters armed with cannon. Sometimes, dive-bomber squadrons were attacked during their approach flight toward Stalingrad by 20 to 30 Russian fighters, which by engaging the Germans in aerial combat prevented them from carrying out their mission and forced them to reassemble farther to the rear. When the dive-bombers attacked objectives in the vicinity of Stalingrad, they became involved in stubborn dogfights with Russians attacking from all directions as well as from above and below until the Germans returned to their own lines. In such sorties the Russian pilots demonstrated courage that bordered on stubborn silliness. In this connection, Pabst relates how he was flying straight toward a Russian fighter, with both of them firing at each other at maximum rate, until Pabst turned off at the last moment. He concludes by saying: "The Russian was even sillier and more stubborn than I, and would have rammed me."

Major a. D. B. Meyer,[54] telling of his experiences near Orel in 1943, writes that his ground-attack unit was opposed by Russian fighters belonging to an elite unit, who were brave daredevils, well trained and excellent fliers with a sure flair for German weaknesses. Their aircraft--Yak-9's*--had powerful engines and were capable of climbing at a steep angle and attacking German aircraft from below. They attacked in a superior manner with short bursts of fire from all guns at short distances, directing their fire mainly at the lead aircraft of the German squadron or flight, eight of which were shot down in one week. On one occasion, when Major Meyer was engaged in aerial combat, his aircraft suddenly caught fire, with his Russian opponent returning to make another pass. He jettisoned his cabin roof, which flew straight into his opponent's propeller; this coincidence saved his life, since he was able to make an emergency landing close to the point where his opponent's aircraft had crashed. The dead pilot turned out to be a woman, without rank insignia, identification or parachute.

The elite unit, of which Major Meyer writes, was undoubtedly composed of outstanding Russian pilots. His study also reveals the type of performance of which Soviet fighters were capable even

---

* Editor's Note: The Yak-9, a single-seat fighter, was the all-metal, modified version of the Yak-1. With a top speed of 370 m.p.h., the Yak-9 was 35 m.p.h. faster than the Yak-1.

at that time.

Major Rall[55] also emphasizes the progress made by Russian fighter aviation in combat with German dive-bombers. German dive-bomber units, according to him, were exposed to continuous fighter attacks during their approach and return flights. If they were escorted, they could usually defend themselves against such attacks without suffering major losses. Russian fighter operations were obviously benefiting from the tremendously improved air warning system and the fighter control stations set up at the front, which provided the Russian fighters with precise and clear information. Even though the aerial combat technique of the Russian fighters engaged with German dive-bomber and ground-attack aircraft showed no particular change, the effectiveness of Russian fighter operations was increased by Russian numerical superiority, more systematic conduct, and the technical improvement of their aircraft.

7) <u>Russian Fighter Attacks on German Reconnaissance Aircraft.</u> The strategic as well as the tactical and combat reconnaissance sorties flown by the Germans in 1942-43 almost invariably encountered Russian fighter resistance, at least at the points of main effort. The German reconnaissance activities were thus greatly hampered.[56]

German Ju-88 long-range reconnaissance aircraft, for instance, were picked up by Russian radar sets above the eastern Black Sea ports of Poti and Batum, whereupon they were caught by superior Soviet fighter forces. As a result, reconnaissance missions in that area could be flown only under cover of low clouds. Since low clouds were rare in summer and autumn in the eastern Black Sea area, no reconnaissance missions could be flown over these important ports for many weeks at a time.

In describing the tactics employed by Soviet fighter aircraft in their encounters with German reconnaissance planes, Captain Wilke states[57] that the Russians often attacked by surprise, mostly from a higher altitude in the rear or from whatever their position was at the time of encounter, without attempting to assume a more favorable attack position. The Bf-109-G's, used by the Germans as reconnaissance aircraft in the beginning, were capable of evading by climbing at a flat angle and outrunning the Russian fighters. Although the fighters attempted to follow, they would eventually fall behind because of lack of speed. When a pair of Bf-109 reconnaissance aircraft would turn to counterattack, the Russian fighters often would dive down to a level where they were protected by antiaircraft fire.

Later, however, these attack methods changed. The Airacobra fighters, committed by the Russians near Smolensk in the autumn of 1943, were armed with cannon and had a superior rate of climb. Thus, their pilots gained a certain feeling of superiority so that they persevered in their attacks and often forced the German reconnaissance aircraft to turn back.

In the winter of 1943 Russian fighters flew defensive patrols above the main line of resistance near Orsha, thus preventing German reconnaissance aircraft from gaining access to the combat zone. These patrols were flown by four flights of four aircraft each. Two of these flights flew at higher altitudes but at different levels, one flight following a north-south course and the other flying in the opposite direction. The other two flights followed, respectively, east-west and west-east courses at a lower altitude and on two different levels. Whenever the lower flights passed each other the upper flights were reaching the end of their courses and about to turn, and vice versa. This system provided mutual protection and secured the air space.

These observations are supplemented by Major Schlage, who reports[58] that the Russian fighters dreaded the rear guns of the twin-fuselage Focke-Wulf-189's and therefore preferred to attack them in favorable weather by oblique surprise passes launched from clouds in the rear. Since these tactics were unsuccessful, the Russians formed several attack groupings, launching simultaneous attacks from the right, left, and rear. Even these tactics did not inflict any losses on Major Schlage's reconnaissance squadron, although his squadron was attacked almost daily. In many cases, effective defensive fire and good escort protection given by German fighters kept the Russian fighters at a respectful distance. In other instances, Russian flak and fighter barrages interdicted access to reconnaissance objectives to the Germans at points of main effort. In one case a Russian fighter intentionally rammed a German reconnaissance aircraft.

In summary, long and short-range German reconnaissance aircraft encountered strong fighter resistance in 1942-43, especially at the focal points of battle, and this resistance partly hampered

German reconnaissance activities. While this resistance was at first stereotyped and unsure, the Russians later used proper operational procedures and launched stubborn attacks. At particularly important sectors Soviet fighters flew defensive patrols, interdicting occasionally all German reconnaissance activity.

8) <u>Russian Fighter Attacks on German Transport Aircraft.</u> During 1942-43 airlift operations to supply encircled German units were decisive in bringing about a favorable solution near Demyansk in 1942 but they were unable to avert disaster at Stalingrad in 1942-43.* For this reason, fighter intervention during this period, when the Soviet fighters were the chief adversaries of the airlift pilots, was of particular importance. German Air Force commanders state[59] that near Demyansk Russian fighter attacks on Ju-52's flying at low level during daytime were at first insignificant. But before long, the Russians committed more I-16's (Ratas) in preplanned assaults, thus making such daylight transport flights impossible. From then on the Ju-52's were sent on such missions only under fighter escort, whereupon their losses from Soviet fighter attacks became relatively slight. Supplies could be airlifted to the encircled forces until they were able to break out of the pocket.

At Stalingrad the situation was different. There, also, supplies were airlifted to the encircled forces, even though losses increased steadily. Airlift operations were feasible so long as the Ju-52 and He-111 aircraft flying these missions were protected by German fighters and while the German fighters had at least temporary air superiority above the pocket. This situation changed radically as soon as the German fighters lost their bases to the Russian ground forces and could no longer secure the air above the encircled forces or land inside the pocket. As early as mid-November 1942, German transport units could no longer fly in close formation during daytime into the pocket; by the beginning of January 1943 daylight operations had to cease completely, even for individual aircraft, since overpowering Russian fighter interference interdicted access to the vicinity of Stalingrad. German transport aircraft losses from fighter interference had grown to intolerable proportions, accounting for one half and even more of the committed aircraft in some instances.╱ Once the German fighters had disappeared from the Stalingrad area,

---

* See Editor's Note, p. 167.
╱ For over-all Luftwaffe losses at Stalingrad, see Editor's Note, p. 168.

A German He-111 which was rammed over
Gorki by a Russian aircraft on 7 June 1943

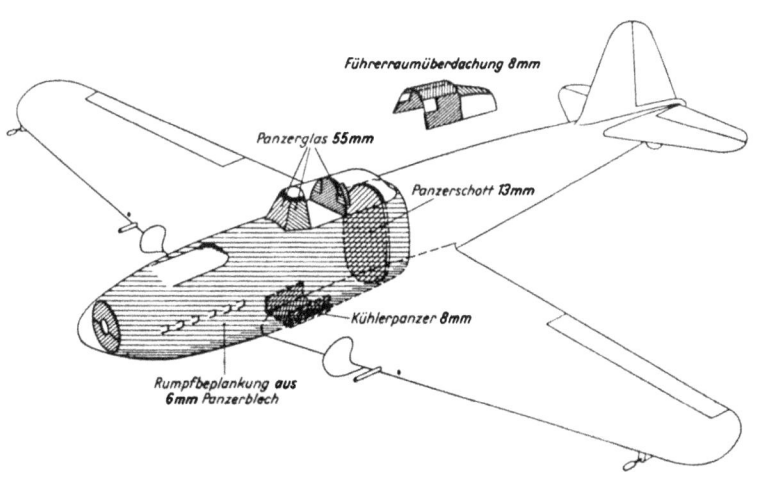

A diagram of the IL-2, ground-attack aircraft.
Shaded areas indicate armor (see page 227).

the Russian fighters reigned supreme. Even so, they did not take full advantage of their supremacy. Had they done a proper job, the entire German airlift supply effort would have collapsed by mid-December 1942.

The Russian fighters attacked the German transport aircraft usually in pairs or squadron formation within range of forward, operational airfields, in sectors where the flak defenses were poor, or above partisan-infested areas. Because of the weakness of ground and air defenses above the German pocket, the Russians preferred to attack there. They also made an effort to destroy the transport aircraft just before they landed or after they had taken off. While the transports broke formation or assembled, they suffered the heaviest losses. The Germans lost not only many personnel and much materiel, but the flow of supplies to the beleaguered Sixth Army was badly disrupted. Increasingly, the Russians combined fighter attacks on transport airplanes with sudden and clever fighter-bomber assaults. Soviet fighter attacks in daylight were generally unsuccessful if the Ju-52's flew individually in bad weather and hid behind clouds. In good weather the fighters, committed in units up to squadron strength, scored considerable successes, which were slightly reduced when the German transports flew in close-formation. The Soviet fighters attacked He-111's more carefully than they attacked Ju-52's, opening fire from greater distance. The concentrated defensive fire power of He-111 units often made Russian fighters reluctant to attack.

Russian night fighters rarely interfered with German airlift operations.

9. Russian Night-Fighter Operations. Nonexistent in 1941 and insignificant in 1942, Russian night-fighter operations were first improvised in the summer of 1943 after the Germans launched their first night-bombing attacks on Soviet war plants. After that, night-fighter aviation was actively organized.

Until mid-1943 the Russian command had obviously given a lower priority to night-fighter aviation as compared to daytime fighters.[60] The reason for this attitude might have been that the great majority of Soviet war plants were beyond the reach of the German bombers. Also, the German Air Force, much like its Russian counterpart, saw its principal mission in daytime support of the ground forces in the vicinity of the main line of resistance. It thus happened that German bombers flying night missions against, for instance, such minor objectives as airfields, roads, and railroad traffic, and billeting areas, very rarely encountered enemy fighters, even during clear nights. It was not until the summer of 1943 that the Germans concentrated strong forces for surprise night attacks on Soviet war plants at Gorki, Yaroslav, and Saratov which were then within striking range.* The Russians thereupon quickly organized night-fighter units, which suffered from all the deficiencies characteristic of such improvised measures. Since they had no trained night-fighter crews, they used pilots who had had a certain amount of night flying experience, but who usually lacked knowledge of fighter tactics. These pilots were committed from nearby airfields to protect the target area. They were, however, incapable of adjusting their speed to that of the German bombers so that they usually flew too fast. Moreover, they failed to take advantage of the light summer horizon in the north by approaching their target from the south, nor did they remain within the range of the Soviet flak. It was precisely over the target area that the night fighters had good opportunities of scoring hits because searchlights and burning fires lit up the vicinity. The silhouettes of the bombers were easy to distinguish. But no night-fighter attacks were launched within the range of antiaircraft fire. Whenever German bomber pilots encountered a Soviet night fighter, they nosed downward and turned abruptly toward the dark southern sector of the target area, whereupon their pursuers lost track of them. During the long approach and return flights the German bomber units rarely encountered Russian night fighters. The

---

*Editor's Note: In the latter half of June, 1943, Sixth Air Fleet launched several, improvised, night-bombing raids on the following targets: the tank factory "Molotov" in Gorki, the automotive plant "Molotov No. 1" in Gorki, a synthetic rubber plant in Yaroslavl, an asbestos plant in Yaroslavl and petroleum refineries in Saratov and Konstantinovski. Of these attacks, those on the two factories in Gorki were the most productive; the production of the tank factory was temporarily reduced by fifty per cent. As a result, the Luftwaffe High Command began to consider freeing its bomber forces in Russia from ground support missions and committing them exclusively in strategic operations. It was already too late in the campaign for such a fundamental change. For more details on these raids and a discussion of the planning for further strategic operations, see Generalleutnant a.D. Hermann Plocher, Der Feldzug im Osten, 1941-1945, Fuenftes Buch, Kapiteln 4 & 13 and Anlage 64, Karlsruhe Document Collection.

Russian command apparently relied on optical means of detection such as directional searchlights and on antiaircraft fire, not yet on radio location. The fact that the German bomber units almost always flew the same route facilitated the improvisation of night-fighter aviation by the Russians.

Major Brunner arrives at the conclusion that the Russian night-fighter aviation had excellent opportunities, for a short while, of inflicting heavy losses on the German bomber units flying night missions, but that the Soviet fliers failed almost entirely because of their tactical and probably also technical inability.

Other authors[61] are in general agreement with the above statements and mention that in spite of the progress made in the summer of 1943, Russian night-fighter operations remained primitive. They add, however, that a buildup on the Western pattern was underway.

10) <u>Fighter Operations in Combination with Other Air Arms.</u>
As escorts to Russian bomber or ground-attack units, the fighters performed their missions with increasing success.[62] Through the summer of 1942 Russian escort aviation was still very deficient. When attacked by German fighters they allowed themselves to be drawn off--leaving the unit they were to protect instead of guarding it--and formed a defensive circle before returning to their bases under the protection of their antiaircraft guns. Aside from lack of combat experience and tactical know-how, this conduct might also have been influenced by the escort pilots' confidence in the flight stability and armor of the IL-2's and the greater speed and defensive capability of the PE-2's--the tail gunner had a three-barreled machine gun--which made it seem less essential to carry out the escort mission.

During Operation Citadel* in the Kursk area in the summer of 1943 the German fighters were still absolutely superior to the Russian escort fighters; for this operation, however, the Germans had massed strong fighter units. At the same time, German fighters operating above the Kuban bridgehead/area were immediately involved in aerial combat by numerous Russian escort fighters, thus having

---

* See Editor's Note, p. 191.
/ See Editor's Note, p. 169.

no opportunity to carry out their mission of intercepting the Soviet bomber and ground-attack aircraft.

The above information indicates that the performances and success of the Russian escort fighters differed greatly, but were generally on the ascendancy after the summer of 1942. Some fighters stayed as close to the unit they were to protect as they possibly could, with other fighters providing protection from higher altitudes, flying up to 3,300 feet above the unit. After the summer of 1943 the Germans observed IL-2 and PE-2 units with up to 80 aircraft, being protected by direct and indirect fighter escort. The covering unit, stacked up high above and keeping down its speed, performed exactly like their German models, except that they rarely succeeded in carrying out their protective mission from above because their IL-2's were too slow. While on escort missions, the Russian fighters attempted repeatedly to neutralize German antiaircraft batteries by aircraft machine-gun fire and by dropping light bombs. Once the flak guns began to fire, however, they usually veered off immediately.

The Russian escort fighters for bomber and ground-attack units gradually improved so much that Colonel Kupfer,[63] commander of German close-combat aviation, in a lecture given in September 1943, considered them as exemplary. He stated that German ground-attack units could safely pass Russian bomber formations under fighter escort without any interference; the Soviet fighters remained obstinately with the unit they were ordered to protect.

Major Rall[64] agrees with other witnesses, but states that in spite of their progress, the Soviet fighters were rarely capable of warding off German fighter thrusts against the unit they were escorting so that Russian bomber losses still remained high.

11) Fighter Operations in Direct Support of the Ground Forces (Fighter-Bombers). Both Luftwaffe and Army officers agree[65] that Russian fighter operations in direct support of the ground forces and as fighter-bombers were insignificant during 1942-43, as they had been in 1941. In fact, low-level attacks by fighters decreased in proportion with the increasing commitment of IL-2 fighter-bombers for this type of mission.

The Soviet fighters generally caused little grief to the German ground forces. The damages caused by splinter bombs and a few short bursts of fire were slight. The Russian fighters flew singly, in pairs, or in fours, often taking advantage of dawn for low-level attacks. Fighter-bombers were directed by radio detachments on the ground so that a certain degree of concentration of forces could be achieved at the points of main effort.

Even in the southern part of the Russian theater, where most of the fighting took place in 1942-43, relatively few Russian fighter-bombers were employed, and the commitment of fighters in direct support of the ground forces was insignificant. Stalingrad was the only exception. There, the Russian fighters were active, switching from the northern to the southern pocket according to the momentary point of main effort. Continual interference and nuisance raids launched by Soviet fighters at the centers of the ground battle and above the city gave strong support to the ground forces' operations.

Except for Stalingrad, the generalization was valid that fighter operations in direct support of the ground forces, above all by fighters serving as fighter-bombers, were without consequence and had little effect on the German military effort.

12) <u>Fighter Operations under Special Weather Conditions.</u>
German commanders have almost no comments on this topic, a sign that no striking observations of any kind were made in this field. Opinions vary on the subject of Russian fighter operations conducted in bad weather. Some state that in bad weather no Russian fighters could be found in the air, while others say precisely the contrary: it was especially in very bad weather that the Russians would send out their fighters, launch fighter-bomber attacks from low clouds and during bad visibility from altitudes of 330 to 500 feet; such operations, however, suffered because the objectives could not be properly discerned and approached. [66]

For 1942-43, the assumption is probably correct that fighter operations under special weather conditions depended greatly on the training status and that there was no important difference between Russian and German procedures.

D. <u>Russian Fighter Aircraft, their Armament and Equipment.</u>

Soviet fighter aircraft in 1942-43 were in the midst of a progressive and even at times remarkable development of aircraft models, armament, and equipment. Modern airplanes encountered by the Germans gave very striking evidence of this evolution, which was accentuated by the increasing employment of Allied fighter aircraft.

Single-engine aircraft were still being used exclusively in fighter aviation; they were armed with machine guns and one cannon, sometimes even two cannons. German Air Force officers generally agree[67] that the older models--I-153 and I-16--had disappeared by the summer 1942. From that time on the various types of Mig, Lagg, and Yak models were encountered; by 1943 these were increasingly supplemented by Allied aircraft, such as Hurricane, Spitfire, Tomahawk, Kittyhawk, Airacobra, and even some Lightning models. Among the Soviet-constructed aircraft, the La-5, Yak-7B* and Yak-9 were the most advanced, being almost equal to the German Bf-109F and 109G models as well as to the subsequently committed FW-190's. The La-5's were capable of closer and faster turns than their German counterparts, which were unable to catch up with them in straight flight; the German fighters were faster only in oblique dives. The Lagg-3's and Yak-9's were equal to the Bf-109's in speed and armament (two machine guns and one or two cannons); these two types and the La-5 were the favorite Soviet aircraft, while the Mig-3's gradually disappeared.

The speed and rate of climb of the above-mentioned Allied aircraft, which played a decisive role in the Russian theater by 1943, were slightly below the Bf-109G's and FW-190's, even though there were certain differences between individual models.

According to available data Mig-3's, Lagg-3's, La-5's, Spitfires, PE-2's, and PE-3B's were used as night fighters. Statements by prisoners of war indicated that modern single and twin-engine night-fighter aircraft were being developed. The Soviet Air Force command considered the ideal prototype for night fighting to be a twin-engine, fast and maneuverable aircraft with a good rate of climb and good high-altitude performance as well as strong fire power. But no such aircraft were being mass-produced because final selection of a model had not been made.

---

* Editor's Note: Similar to the Yak-9, the Yak-7B was a single-place fighter plane which was equipped for night-time commitment.

The Soviet Yak-7B fighter

Another Soviet fighter, the Yak-9

Further progress had been made in the armament of fighter aircraft. The 7.6-mm machine guns were being replaced by 12.7-mm guns, and an increasing number of planes were equipped with 20-mm cannon, the Yak-9's even with 37-mm cannon. The highly explosive ammunition of the gas-pressure machine gun was very effective and was dreaded by the Germans.

No new information was gathered on the equipment of fighter aircraft, so that previously stated opinions retain their validity.

Thus, this period was marked by the modernization of Soviet fighters, which now were almost equal to the German models, the increased deliveries of Allied fighters and the improvement of armament on Soviet fighters. Their other equipment, however, showed no improvement and remained relatively simple.

E. Summary and Conclusions

Based on German observations and experience, the evaluation of Russian fighter aviation in 1942-43 can be summarized as follows:

1) The Russian fighter aviation recovered, first slowly then with increasing rapidity, from the disastrous setbacks of the first year of hostilities. Increasing combat experience, strong numerical superiority, and decreases in German operational strength resulted by the end of 1943 in the loss of clear air superiority by the Germans.

2) The personal conduct of Russian fighter pilots, insofar as it was determined by Russian characteristics, was still inferior to that of the Germans. But the successes they were achieving and the new models of aircraft with which they were equipped, strengthened the Soviet fighter pilots' confidence in their own performance as well as their self-assurance. They gradually lost their feeling of inferiority; as a consequence, the Russians developed an increasing number of good combat fliers and well-led fighter units.

3) The defensive attitude of Russian fighters was superseded by an offensive orientation. Committed within the framework of ground operations, the Russian fighter aircraft were concentrated above the points of main effort close to the main line of resistance. They operated primarily against German fighter, bomber, and ground-attack aircraft, acted as escorts for Soviet units, and occasionally as fighter-bombers. The operational principles, methods

of combat, tactics, and flying techniques were all geared toward attack.

4) The inferiority of materiel was overcome within a short time because of the technical progress in Russian aircraft construction and the Allied deliveries of planes. The up-to-date Russian aircraft were only slightly inferior to the German prototypes insofar as quality was concerned, while in quantity they were soon far ahead.

5) In combat with fighters the Russian pilots no longer avoided encounters, but on the contrary accepted and sought them out. The concentration of forces, numerical superiority, and flying experience of the Russian pilots led to success in aerial combat.

6) In combat with bombers the now aggressive Russian fighters hampered the execution of German bombing raids quite considerably.

7) In combat with dive bombers and ground-attack aircraft the Russian fighter pilots scored more and more victories because of their effective and stubborn attack methods. They no longer avoided encounters with German escort planes.

8) In combat with reconnaissance aircraft the Russian fighters increasingly hampered German strategic and close-reconnaissance flights, eliminating them almost completely at certain times at points of main effort.

9) In combat with transport aircraft the Russian fighter aviation scored so many victories that it eventually stopped all daytime airlift operations near Stalingrad.

10) Night-fighter operations--which did not get underway until the summer of 1943--did not show any significant results during this period.

11) Fighter operations in combination with other air arms made good progress, the Russian fighter pilots being generally capable of fulfilling their escort missions.

12) Fighter operations in direct support of ground forces and with fighter aircraft functioning as fighter-bombers were infrequent in 1942-43, showing little, if any, effect. Fighter operations in support of the Russian Navy were not observed.

In conclusion, Russian fighter aviation made progress during this period; its personnel, materiel, operations, command and staff procedures, flying techniques, and combat experience improved. The transition from defensive to offensive attitude and the growing numerical superiority brought about victories that eventually led to a limited superiority in the air, the effect of which was, however, circumscribed in space and time by the magnificent performances of German fighter pilots and units.

Section IV: The Ground-Attack Air Arm in 1942 and 1943

A. General

At the end of 1941, the Germans had observed that the Soviet ground-attack air arm was growing stronger. This tendency was accentuated during the following years, since the Russian command gave a particularly high priority to the development of ground-attack aviation. German Air Force commanders viewed this development along the following general lines:[68]

As early as the beginning of 1942 Russian ground-attack aviation had, for the most part, recovered from the defeat of 1941. During the course of the 1941-1942 winter operations, it proved to be even superior to the Luftwaffe on several occasions. From then on the Germans observed a gradual strengthening of Russian ground-attack aviation despite the personnel and materiel losses suffered. By the end of 1943 it had become the strongest Russian air arm. The Russian command still used its ground-attack forces against targets near the main line of resistance in support of the ground forces. Surprise, low-level strikes with bombs, rockets, and aircraft weapons, especially at points of main effort, were the usual form of these attacks. Often, however, the ground-attack aircraft did not fly their sorties in sufficient strength and with enough consistency. Their employment as "flying artillery" complied with Stalin's concept of the paramount importance of artillery, which in turn might have contributed to the high priority accorded the buildup of this type of aviation. Thus, Russian ground-attack aviation developed into a tough opponent, encountered wherever the struggle was hard and attacking dangerously wherever the German bombers had not previously destroyed the Russian airfields, whenever the German fighters did not enjoy air superiority, or whenever the German air warning service did not operate smoothly.

The dependable IL-2 remained the standard ground-attack aircraft during this period of development; they were committed in even greater numbers in more and more units. In 1943 some smaller, aggressive, and well trained units equipped with Lagg or Yak models were observed by the Germans who obviously had difficulty in deciding whether these were ground-attack or fighter-bomber units.

Stalingrad was the turning point for Russian ground-attack aviation. From then on this arm became an increasingly powerful element whose strength did not become fully effective, however, because of high personnel losses, the shortage of replacements, and the inexperience and lack of training of new crews. Victories were therefore primarily local and, even though this arm inflicted losses in personnel and equipment on the Germans, it did not impair their morale or cause panic. The general training status of Russian ground-attack aircraft crews, whose capability might have been limited by their innate deficiencies, had considerably improved, as had their ability to hit targets on the ground. Even so, they were no match for the Luftwaffe crews, whose performance remained unimpaired. For this reason the Russians could not employ their ground-attack potential at points where German air units interfered, such as near Kerch, Sevastopol,* and Leningrad. But in the summer of 1943, during Operation Citadel, the German air forces that had been concentrated for this offensive finally proved insufficient for preventing Russian attacks at certain times and places; this fact was acknowledged by the Germans.

In describing the development of Russian ground-attack aviation in 1942-43, Colonel von Beust[69] states that ground-attack aircraft played the most important role as early as 1942; this continued subsequently when they operated in conjunction with fighters. They became the decisive instrument of air warfare from the time the Russian command assumed the offensive. The development of ground-attack aviation is the best proof of the Soviet principle of warfare, according to which air operations were an integral part of the ground battle without separate strategic plans, missions or objectives. Ground-attack tactics were closely coordinated with ground operations; within these limitations they were well planned and developed from

---

* Editor's Note: Sevastopol, on the Crimea, was the chief Russian naval port on the Black Sea and was the scene of very heavy fighting in June and July of 1942.

experience that dated all the way back to the Spanish Civil War. The technical development that took place along parallel lines brought about the evolution of the IL-2 ground-attack aircraft whose design, capability, and usefulness were much more oriented to a single purpose than was the case with German ground-attack aircraft types. Low-level employment and attacks on ground targets were essential requirements so that strong armament and armor had priority over altitude performance, speed, and range. The potential targets were generally troop assemblies, fortified positions, artillery emplacements, antiaircraft positions, tanks, vehicles, and more rarely, for instance, railroad installations, trains, and airfields. In 1942, while the Russians were still on the defensive and their ground-attack aviation buildup was still underway, the number of their ground-attack units was still relatively low and the arm was not yet fully effective as an offensive instrument. By 1943, however, it was the essential instrument of air warfare of the Russian command, having no doubt a decisive influence on the course of operations.

These impressions and experiences of German Air Force officers are generally endorsed by Army commanders.[70] According to the latter, next to bombers, Russian ground-attack aviation affected the German ground forces more than any other air arm, while its operational principles of very close cooperation with the ground forces remained unchanged. The ground-attack units increased in strength over the two-year period, but large units were not observed until 1943. Whereas in 1942 the Russians sometimes did not commit any ground-attack units, --even during extensive offensive operations such as those that took place along the Volkhov river, to the east of Leningrad--they employed ground-attack aircraft everywhere after the end of 1942. This did not imply that the frequency and power of the attacks was distributed evenly along the entire frontline. On the contrary, the ground-attack units were concentrated at the points of main effort such as the Crimea, the Kuban bridgehead, Stalingrad, the Orel-Rzhev area on the central front, and Leningrad, but predominantly in the southern part of the theater. Meanwhile, the Russians had learned a lot; the ground-attack aircraft coordinated their assaults with those of the ground forces and executed them in a powerful and persistent manner. They did not, however, penetrate deeply into the German rear nor did they concentrate their force sufficiently. Without these deficiencies they would have interfered very much with the German withdrawal movements of 1943.*

B. Organizational Structure, Chain of Command, Strength Figures, and Methods of Assembly[71]

During 1943 ground-attack divisions were subordinated to ground-attack corps--three ground-attack divisions and one fighter division per corps--and by the end of that year five such corps had been identified in European Russia. In general, however, these divisions were the largest ground-attack organizational units. The divisions were usually composed exclusively of ground-attack aircraft and consisted of three regiments equipped with IL-2 aircraft; however, there were also composite ground-attack divisions with one fighter and two to three ground-attack regiments. The ground-attack regiment was composed of three squadrons (30 IL-2's) and one or two liaison aircraft (U-2's). Each squadron had three flights, the first of which had two, while the other two flights had four aircraft each.

On 1 July 1943 the average actual strength of aircraft per regiment was 28, and two months later it had dropped to 20 planes. The total number of IL-2 aircraft committed in autumn 1943 was estimated at 3,000, while the 1943 production was approximately 8,000.

The personnel strength of a ground-attack regiment

---

* Editor's Note: The year 1943 saw the Germans forced slowly but surely back towards the West. In the southern sector Stalingrad was lost (and with it about 90,000 German prisoners and 100,000 German dead), the Caucasus were evacuated except for the Kuban Bridgehead (see note, p. 169), which the Germans held until September, and the rich industrial area of the Donets Basin was lost. After the failure of Operation Citadel, the Russians pushed the Germans back to Kiev (which then changed hands twice) and finally, towards the end of the year, approached the old Polish border. Throughout 1943 German forces in the northern sector, by contrast, managed to hold the Leningrad front. In the southern sector they also managed to hold the Crimea, whose loss might have affected Turkish neutrality and would have put the Russian Air Force within easy range of the important Rumanian oil fields.

was about the same as that of a fighter regiment: the total of about 200 men was composed of approximately 33 pilots, 20 to 30 aerial gunners--depending on the number of two-seater IL-2's that gradually replaced the single-seaters--and 140 to 150 technical and administrative personnel.

By the end of 1943 the Germans, along their frontline in European Russia, identified 28 regular and 3 mixed ground-attack divisions. In general, two to three ground-attack divisions were assigned to each air army, but their number varied greatly. At the points of main effort of the ground battle, ground-attack regiments formed up to 40 percent of total air strength. On an average, air armies in the southern and central parts of the Russian theater had 11 to 13 subordinate ground-attack regiments, whereas those in the northern part had 3 to 5.

In a war of movement the airfields of ground-attack aircraft were situated about 20 to 25 miles behind the main line of resistance, during position warfare about 32 to 37 miles behind the forward lines. These airfields were so situated that intermediate landings could be avoided in the execution of missions. Whenever a Russian offensive operation was imminent, the Germans observed an unusual concentration of ground-attack aircraft, which indicated to them that an attack was being planned. For such offensives, the Russians improved and constructed numerous airfields near the contact zone in order to reduce approach flights to a minimum. These ground-attack airfields were often so close to the main line of resistance--10 to 12 miles-- that the German artillery was able to take them under fire successfully.

C. Ground-Attack Aircraft Operations

1. <u>Pilot Conduct</u>. The aggressiveness of the Soviet ground-attack pilots is favorably mentioned by most Luftwaffe and Army commanders reporting on the period 1942-43.[72] They were impressed by the pilots' increasing operational toughness, their stubborn execution of assigned missions despite heavy losses, and their "fighting heart and bold courage." At the same time, the conduct of Russian pilots was generally marked by respect for the combat-tested and better trained German crews. Only Major Meyer[73] criticizes the low morale and total lack of soldierly conduct of the Soviet pilots. According to him, the Russian was a man with plenty of natural instinct who lost all willpower under compulsion and developed into an animalistic and fanatical fighter under certain

circumstances. The attitude of complete resignation of crews that had been shot down seemed to indicate repeatedly their disinterestedness concerning the over-all situation. This opinion, however, is in direct contradiction to all the others and draws much too radical conclusions from the well-known Russian characteristics.

2) <u>General Operational Principles.</u> These remained unchanged during 1942-43, except that they were further developed on the basis of combat experience. The principal characteristics seemed to be: a) maximum cooperation with the ground forces whose requests and wishes pertaining to the commitment of ground-attack aircraft were mandatory; b) operations almost exclusively above the combat zone and the direct support zone against targets that had to be attacked within the framework of the ground battle; c) increasing emphasis on concentration of forces; d) transition to larger closed formations for attacks; e) attacks launched only in daytime, often in conjunction with bomber units.

German Army and Luftwaffe commanders[74] elaborate on the above points somewhat as follows:

The close cooperation between the ground-attack aircraft and the ground forces was emphasized by the air units purposely neglecting other targets and limiting their efforts almost exclusively to targets near the frontline. Concentrated on the same points of main effort as the ground forces, the attacks of the ground-attack aircraft were primarily aimed at the main line of resistance, troop movements and assemblies of any kind, artillery positions, antiaircraft batteries, heavy weapons emplacements, villages near the frontline, supply and service installations, road, rail and air traffic, and installations in rear areas. Surprisingly, these attacks rarely reached far in depth into rear areas. The German routes of withdrawal were not attacked so that the retrograde movements undertaken in 1943 never suffered, as they very well could have, from interference from the air. The operations of Russian ground-attack aircraft were often integrated into the artillery fire plan, so that this air arm could be considered as the extended, high-trajectory arm of the artillery.

Orders for operations were based either on instructions given directly by army group headquarters to air army or on requests made by Army agencies to the Air Force staffs responsible for coordination.

In the course of time the units conducting operations grew steadily in size, until they flew in closed formation in regimental strength and in tactical coordination with the concentration of ground forces. An individual ground-attack unit either had a separate mission, formed one attack wave among several, or it was integrated into a continuous attack. The forces assigned to such missions were often three or four times as many as the Germans would have committed against the same target.

Ground-attack units either approached their target under fighter escort or took advantage of the absence of German fighters by approaching at very low level. German light and medium flak, which was capable of defense and equipped with armor-piercing ammunition, forced the attackers to higher levels from which they were less effective. At points of main effort the Russians often launched continuous attacks over several hours with strong fighter escorts and, if a target was especially important, the combined high and low-level assault waves were composed of as many as 50 bomber, 60 ground-attack, and 100 fighter aircraft. Attacks in the combat zone were launched exclusively in daytime, either in closed formation with the aircraft veering off in low-level flight or individually by forming a chain, with the airplanes reassembling subsequently at maximum speed above the Russian lines. When German fighters were present, the ground-attack pilots showed a certain amount of reluctance to engage themselves fully, so that the success of the attack was jeopardized. If forced to give combat, the Russian ground-attack pilot first attempted to evade downward, and if that was not possible he would try to get rid of his pursuer by taking cover within the range of the extremely powerful Russian antiaircraft fire. In other instances, however, the pilot continued to carry out his mission, relying confidently on the armor plating of his IL-2 aircraft to protect him, so that the flight formation generally remained unchanged even under German fighter attack.

3) <u>Flying Conduct</u>. In 1942-43 the ground-attack operations were better planned and more effectively organized and directed than previously.[75] Before starting on a mission, the crews were thoroughly briefed. This briefing would be all the more detailed if little opportunity existed to change orders after the take-off, recall the unit, divert it to another target, or issue warnings of the approach of German fighters. Air-to-ground and air-to-air radio were not always available. The type of approach depended mostly on the distance from the target. Over long distances the V formation was usually preferred, with flights

flying at a certain distance behind or beside one another. The transition to the attack formation (row, double row, and latterly staggered row), which always took place before reaching the target area, did not involve any major complications or delay. The formation did not undergo any further change during the approach flight and above the target. Objectives beyond the main line of resistance were approached from an altitude of 3,300 feet and higher, with the sun in the rear, first flying in gentle turns, then straight ahead, using secondary targets if orientation was difficult. The various row formations were used from the start when approaching objectives in the combat zone, so that the execution of the attack did not require any changes. For this purpose, a formation designated "Peleng" was preferred, which consisted of a staggered row pointing left or right rearward; its order of approach indicated the direction in which it would veer off and thus also the direction the attack would take. If the formation was to veer off to the left, as it usually did, the approach formation pointed to the right rearward and vice versa. Formations flying the "Peleng" mostly placed new crews and single-seater IL-2's in the center. They flew in very detached formation over flak areas, constantly changing course. In so doing, they more and more frequently flew formations in which pairs gave each other mutual cover and support, eliminating most of the effect of surprise assaults by German fighters by continual weaving as soon as the Germans approached.

In carrying out their missions the Soviet ground-attack pilots demonstrated flexibility in their choice of tactics. Strikes took place at different times, from various levels, from different directions, and in ever changing formations. The principal attack formations were the circle and the row, often flown at low altitude, for which the IL-2 was particularly well suited. When low cloud formations predominated, the ground targets were attacked from an altitude of 330 to 500 feet, whereas with good visibility the altitude varied from 1,320 to 2,000 feet. By the end of 1943 the Germans observed that low-level attacks became less frequent and that there was a transitional tendency toward adopting the attack methods of close-support and dive-bomber aircraft with attack levels around 3,300 feet. In the event of mass, concurrent attacks from both high and low levels, the target was approached from different directions simultaneously. During the attack proper the IL-2's peeled off, fired from all fixed guns during their inclined oblique approach flight, dropped bombs or fired rockets--usually one after the other--and fired their mobile guns as they turned away. The attack was launched only once or repeated several times, depending on the intensity of the defensive fire, the location of the target in relation to the main line of resistance, and the type of mission. The attackers generally formed a circle, and if several attacks were launched, the aircraft would not leave until all bombs had been dropped, all rockets fired, and the ammunition expended.

The execution of the attack depended largely on the type and disposition of the target. Targets along the main line of resistance were usually approached at 2,310 to 2,640 feet altitude and attacked by pairs diving at a 30° to 45° angle. First, the rockets were fired, then the cannons, subsequently the machine guns; the bombs (usually two bombs weighing 220 lbs. and four 110 pounders) were dropped at an altitude of 825 to 1,000 feet, whereupon the aircraft pulled out of its dive. Tanks were approached at altitudes varying between 2,000 to 2,640 feet from a steep gliding flight or a dive. First there was gun fire, the rockets were released at about 2,310 feet then the bombs (preferably 220-pounders) were dropped, followed by cannon and machine-gun fire, and then the aircraft pulled out of their dive at about 800 feet. Vehicle columns were attacked from the closest distance with bombs and rockets and with all guns ablaze. March columns were often only strafed. Airfields were attacked with all weapons by diving from a 2,310 to 2,640 foot altitude. In order not to impair the maneuverability of the aircraft, the bombload consisted of small incendiary, high-explosive and fragmentation bombs totalling only about 660 lbs. in weight. The attack missions were broken down and assigned to individual pairs within the squadron. For instance, one pair was to attack the antiaircraft positions, another was to prevent the take-off of enemy aircraft, and a third pair was to attack parked aircraft.

At low altitudes the return flight was carried out in loose formation; at intermediate altitudes, however, the formation would turn immediately toward the main line of resistance in an effort to reach fighter or flak protected areas or control points by the shortest possible route and thus escape pursuing German fighters.

Soviet ground-attack pilots attempted to evade aerial combat with German fighters and, during low-level flights, they tried to avoid exposing their unprotected fuel tank that protruded from the belly of their aircraft. If attacked by fighters, they either flew a defensive circle formation or, if they recognized the German threat in time, a so-called snake formation that permitted them to move the scene of fighting more rapidly to their own territory than did the circle formation.

When encountering German reconnaissance aircraft of the FW-189 type, the IL-2's often proved aggressive. In such instances, they were confident of their armored protection, made oblique attacks from the rear from higher altitudes and fired cannons and machine guns. To make a kill they approached the German aircraft as closely as possible.

4) <u>Ground-Attack Operations on the Battlefield</u>. The great and steadily growing importance of Soviet ground-attack operations on the battlefield during 1942-43 is emphasized by German Army officers.[76] With the over-all shift in emphasis to the southern part of the theater during that period, the main effort of ground-attack operations was also to be found in that area.

In May 1942 south of Kharkov along the Donets, ground-attack aircraft operated in conjunction with attacking infantry and armor. These offensive operations were properly coordinated with regard to time and space, the targets were well selected, plans were effectively executed and correlated so that the operations produced a considerable effect on the Germans, especially on their morale. Along quiet sectors the Russian ground-attack aircraft were less active, launching mainly nuisance raids on rear area billets as well as supply and transportation installations. When major operations were imminent, the ground-attack aircraft concentrated their strikes on the combat zone; all identified targets on the battlefield were attacked. Gun emplacements were favorite targets, and neutralizing the artillery as soon as the infantry jumped off was the essential mission of the ground-attack aircraft which kept up a ceaseless bombardment for this purpose.

While the combat zone was thus subjected to intensive ground-attacks--marked by close cooperation with the ground forces--during Russian offensive operations, the German rear areas were relatively untouched, to the great surprise of the Germans. Moving up or withdrawing even major troop units was therefore no problem; the same was true of service units and supplies. The Russians' progressive achievements in supporting ground forces, however, were undeniable; the number and effectiveness of the ground-attack assaults increased steadily, particularly toward the end of 1943. Rigid control and concentration of forces, proper operational procedures, effective selection of targets, and planned execution of attacks at the right time and at the decisive point led to some considerable successes against German troops, even though they did not yet turn the tide of battle. Indeed, the German Army felt the change which had occurred since 1941. This was mainly the case in the Crimea and near Sevastopol, at the Kuban Bridgehead, near Stalingrad, and during the German withdrawal toward the Dnieper. In the Army Group Center and North areas, where there was less fighting, this change was not quite so obvious; but even in these areas improvements in ground-attack aircraft operations made themselves felt.

Luftwaffe officers[77] agree with Army commanders that ground-attack aircraft were committed by the Russians primarily in support of ground operations and that the close interrelationship between ground-attack aircraft and the ground forces they supported was noticeable everywhere, their operations being fully integrated.

Russian ground-attack operations in 1942 were marked by many improvisations. In the summer, for instance, they set fire to the dry steppe grass in the Don area, thus forcing the German troops to change positions and causing losses of ammunition. In the Kuban Bridgehead they fired phosphorous incendiary bullets at the forward lines, flak batteries, and across the terrain to prevent the reserves from moving up. They thus hampered the Germans in their freedom of maneuver and caused casualties from burns. Toward the end of 1943 the use of artificial smoke increased. A thick smoke screen, about 300 feet high, was put up above the main line of resistance by aircraft; the ground-attack aircraft emerged from that smoke screen by surprise, attacked the German positions along the screen, and disappeared in the smoke as soon as the German fighters counterattacked.

The opinion of Army and Luftwaffe officers that the support of ground forces was the essential mission of Russian ground-attack aircraft to which all other operations were subordinated is also confirmed by the very detailed Russian instructions on air-ground cooperation and by the Luftwaffe High Command's publication on Soviet ground-attack aviation.[78]

Air Force-Army cooperation followed the following pattern. Usually an air army instructed its subordinate units on the basis of orders from army group headquarters, but Air Force and Army staffs were joined together for limited offensive operations. They achieved effective cooperation by coordinating missions, conducting operations in close proximity, constantly exchanging information, and dispatching liaison officers to ground forces headquarters. In this connection, it was irrelevant whether the ground-attack units were subordinate to the ground forces headquarters for specific operations or whether they just coordinated their missions; the latter method of employment was the more customary, however. The intensified commitment of ground-attack aircraft for strikes on supply and service installations, troop units, billets and fortified positions began about two days before the offensive proper. During the artillery preparation the ground-attack aircraft directed their assaults particularly at targets on the battlefield that could not be reached by the artillery. Immediately before the infantry launched its attack, the ground-attack aircraft made a concentrated assault on the German forward line; and while infantry and tanks were engaged in a struggle for the forward positions, the ground-attack aircraft incessantly attacked German ground targets. During the battle for rearward positions of a defensive system, some of the ground-attack units always remained above the combat zone while others were held in readiness for new missions that might be requested by the ground forces.

5) <u>Ground-Attack Operations in Rear Areas</u>. There is general agreement[79] that ground-attack operations in rear areas during 1942-43 continued to play a relatively minor role. The majority of such attacks were directed against airfields, while others were aimed at supply installations, means of communication, and other rear area targets. Surprisingly enough, troop movements of even major units in rear areas were attacked only in isolated cases. For this reason, German Air Force elements that had to move cross country by road suffered few losses en route.

Russian ground-attack aircraft operating in rear areas usually appeared in squadron strength, rarely in larger units. They approached their targets either at a low or at an intermediate altitude, if possible under cover of clouds. When ground-attack aircraft launched attacks in regimental strength in the winter of 1942 in the Orel-Leningrad area against main highways, rail tracks, supply installations and dumps, the German Army suffered heavy losses. According to all available reports, however, operations directed against German airfields usually lacked proper planning and precision in execution so that only minor successes were achieved. Along the Stalingrad sector the initial Russian ground-attack aircraft missions to neutralize the departure airfields of the German transport aircraft were not very well planned, nor were they properly executed. Although they disrupted daytime operations and delayed the airlift, they remained ineffective. By the end of December 1942, however, the Soviet ground-attack aircraft, in squadron strength, attacked these same airfields almost daily, seriously hampering preparations, causing major losses, and disrupting the routine of the crews and ground personnel.

    6) <u>Russian Ground-Attack Operations by Night</u>. Records of German experts[80] give no information on night operations by Il-2's or other ground-attack aircraft units.

    Night sorties flown by U-2's are designated as ground-attack operations by night in several instances; but it would be more correct to consider the night nuisance raids flown by U-2's as bomber sorties, which is the procedure followed in this study.

    7) <u>Ground-Attack Operations during Special Weather Conditions</u>. The available data[81] justify the statement already made in the previous chapter, namely, that bad weather or winter conditions did not stop Soviet ground-attack aircraft operations. While there are statements that dusk attacks and bad weather sorties were outstanding features of Russian ground-attack operations, others indicate that they never witnessed such operations and that the flight training given to the crews would not have sufficed for the execution of such missions. But both Army and Luftwaffe officers emphasize that ground-attack aircraft appeared even in the worst weather to support the ground forces and that IL-2 units were operating even in 10:10 overcast with only 1,000 to 1,300 feet visibility. Freezing temperatures and snow seemed to affect the commitment of Russian ground-attack aircraft very little.

    8) <u>Ground-Attack Operations in Conjunction with Other Air Arms</u>. Earlier, this chapter has already dealt with combined operations of Soviet ground-attack and fighter aircraft. In addition to this information and with reference to joint ground-attack and bomber operations, German officers state[82] that as long as no German fighters interfered and the clouds were low, the Soviet ground-attack aircraft were apt to fly without escort. In most instances, however, they flew with strong fighter escort with whom they maintained radio contact. The ratio between fighter and ground-attack aircraft varied from 2:1 to 1:1. If time and location of rendezvous with this fighter escort were

not properly prearranged, the ground-attack aircraft often suffered heavy losses. The operating procedures frequently varied: sometimes the fighters flew above the ground-attack aircraft and sometimes below, and on occasions they flew some 4,000 to 6,600 feet to the side to escape the antiaircraft fire directed at the ground-attack aircraft. At times the fighter units formed three groups: one that flew in the rear and higher than the ground-attack unit, one close protection group that flew next to or immediately above, and finally a so-called top-level escort group that took off earlier in order to clear the sky above the target area at altitudes varying from 13,000 to 16,500 feet. At dusk the ground-attack aircraft fired flares to alert their fighter escorts flying at higher altitudes in case of a German fighter attack.

According to a captured special order issued by the Sixteenth Air Army on 17 July 1943, fighter escorts exercised some sort of control over ground-attack units since they were instructed to fire on the latter if they did not fulfill their mission.

Joint ground-attack and bomber operations increased steadily at the points of main effort, such as the Kuban Bridgehead, the Crimea, and near Stalingrad, where the airlift supply fields were the principal targets for such operations. During these offensive operations the Germans encountered some 80 to 100 ground-attack aircraft (one ground-attack aircraft division) and 60 to 100 bombers (1 or 2 bomber divisions) protected by strong fighter escorts. Whereas the bombers dropped their missiles from altitudes of 6,600 feet to 10,000 feet on the targets proper, the ground-attack aircraft assaulted primarily the ground defense weapons. Meanwhile, the fighters escorted the attack formations and were also committed in strikes against German fighter airfields in order to hamper the German planes from taking off or immediately involve them in aerial combat so that they would not disrupt the operations of the bomber and ground-attack aircraft. During such attacks, ground-attack and bomber aircraft dropped their bombs simultaneously or at short intervals. Often they flew several sorties in spite of heavy losses. The losses and damages inflicted on the Germans, however, were usually minor because the attacking units were in many cases too weak and in disproportion to the size of the target and the intensity of the defensive fire. Also, their attacks were inaccurate and did not last long enough to be effective.

D. **Types, Armament, and Equipment of Russian Ground-Attack Aircraft**

All German sources[83] agree that the IL-2 was the standard ground-attack aircraft in 1942-43; other models, such as fighters or U-2's, were used only in isolated instances. The IL-2 achieved remarkable success and was the principal antagonist of the German Army. The two-seater aircraft (IL-3) with rear gunner gradually took the place of the single-seater. The robust construction of the cantilevered, strongly armored, low-wing aircraft was kept intentionally simple in an effort to speed up production and employ partly untrained labor. While the original plane was all metal, the outer wing sections and tail were subsequently made out of wood. The extensive and good armor, consisting of welded steel plates and bullet-proof glass, protected all vital parts of the aircraft in one large armored "vessel" which contained, for instance, the cockpit, the rear gunner's area, the engine, the fuel and oil tanks, the water radiator, and oil cooler. The aircraft was thus secure from machine gun and light antiaircraft fire with small arm, high explosive, and tracer ammunition even when fired from close range. A German Air Force officer stated somewhat laconically and sadly[84] that the IL-2 "does not even tremble under sustained fire." Thus it was a dangerous adversary for the German FW-189 reconnaissance aircraft, which it often attacked. The two-barreled, rear machine gun of the FW-189 was ineffective against the IL-2's armor. The IL-2 could be hurt only by hitting its few vulnerable spots, such as the unprotected upper part of the cowl, the sliding window near the pilot's seat, the plywood tail assembly, and the roof of the cockpit where it slanted downward behind the pilot's seat.

The armament of the IL-2 consisted usually of two fixed 7.62-mm machine guns, model Shkas, with 750 rounds each, one mobile 12.7-mm machine gun, model BS or UBT, with three clips containing 70 rounds each, and two 20-mm cannons, model Shwak, or two 23-mm cannons, model VIA, with 200 rounds each. In some instances the armament consisted of two 37-mm cannons with 80 rounds each, instead of the 20-mm or 23-mm cannons.

The machine guns fired armor-piercing, incendiary, tracer, and high-explosive ammunition, while the cannon used fragmentation, fragmentation-incendiary, and armor-piercing incendiary ammunition. A reflector sight was used as aiming device, and a tubular sight had also been introduced. The cannons had a relatively low rate of fire, and their effectiveness in scoring hits was affected by training deficiencies. Under the wings there were launching rails for rockets; the rockets first used were of 82-mm caliber, later 132-mm caliber. Rocket projectiles of the fragmentation, armor-piercing, and high-explosive types were also available. The rocket release gear permitted individual release, bursts of fire, or salvos.

The bomb load averaged 880 lbs., with a maximum of 1,320 lbs. The bomb bays were capable of carrying bombs varying from 5.5 lbs. to 550 lbs. Considerably fewer duds were dropped than was the case earlier in the campaign. The light fragmentation bombs of the ground-attack aircraft were more effective and more feared by the German ground forces than the heavy fragmentation bombs used by bombers.

Other equipment consisted of a radio telephone set for air-to-air and air-to-ground traffic (models RSI-3 and RSI-4), customary flight and power plant control instruments, a reflector sight, oxygen equipment, and aerial cameras. Some ground-attack aircraft were also equipped with homing devices permitting instrument flight.

E. Summary and Conclusions

Based on German observations regarding Russian ground-attack aviation in 1942-43, the following evaluation seems justified:

1) Ground-attack aviation increasingly became the principal offensive arm of the Russian Air Force; it was also a valuable aid to the Soviet ground forces in decisive battles and inflicted heavy losses on the German ground forces. Although the Russian ground-attack aviation suffered considerable personnel and materiel losses, its buildup was hampered but not prevented by these losses.

2) The personal conduct of the Russian ground-attack pilots was generally characterized by aggressive vigor during attacks on targets on the ground, while a certain reserve was noticeable in aerial combat.

3) The principal mission of Russian ground-attack aircraft continued to be the support of the ground forces. By closely cooperating with the ground forces and concentrating their efforts at the centers of fighting, the Soviet ground-attack aircraft increased their influence on the outcome of combat operations, even though,

for a number of reasons, they were still incapable of deciding the issue.

4) The Russian ground-attack aircraft attacked primarily targets on the battlefield and achieved success by following proper procedures and executing their missions with stubbornness.

5) In contrast, attacks on rear area targets, which were mainly directed at German airfields, assumed a secondary role and usually produced little effect.

6) Flying technique and tactics had improved on the basis of experience, and were characterized by greater flexibility than previously. In most instances, units launching attacks were larger than before and were protected by correspondingly larger fighter escorts.

7) By developing the two-seater type IL-2 (or IL-3) and equipping and arming it better, the Russians seemed to have created a standard ground-attack aircraft that fulfilled all the requirements of that period.

8) The Germans did not observe night operations by Russian ground-attack aviation.

9) Russian ground-attack aviation made progress in operating jointly with other air arms. Both operations under fighter escort and in conjunction with bomber aircraft were usually conducted according to proper principles.

In conclusion, the improvements observed as early as 1941 with regard to making ground-attack aviation an effective offensive arm continued uninterruptedly during the period 1942-43. By introducing appropriate command and staff procedures as well as operational principles, and increasing and improving their personnel and materiel, the Russians made their ground-attack aviation capable of accomplishing its principal task--the support of the ground forces--with ever increasing success.

Section V: Bombardment Aviation

A. General

During the years 1942-43 Russian military leaders intentionally gave the buildup of the bomber arm a lower priority than that enjoyed by the fighter or ground-attack arms. Even though bombardment aviation also gradually grew stronger, especially after the spring of 1943, this progress was small compared to that of the two other air arms. According to the consensus of German Air Force commanders[85] this development took place in the following manner:

> Bombing operations of the Russian air forces could not compare with those of the Allies in the West insofar as commitment en masse and effectiveness were concerned. The targets of bomber raids were rarely deep in the German theater of operations. Usually, they were located in the combat zone. During this period, the principal mission of Russian bombers remained the direct and indirect support of ground operations in close cooperation with the Army. At the beginning of 1942 all long-range bomber and transport aircraft units, excepting those stationed in the Far East, were put under a unified command called the Long-Range Air Force. It was given specially qualified personnel who, however, were still not sufficiently trained. But even this newly organized command was employed for operations in conjunction with the ground forces, and not for strategic missions.
>
> Bombing attacks at points of main effort were usually well coordinated with the infantry, artillery, and armor so that, despite certain deficiencies, they were fairly successful. These successes, however, were not in proportion to the effort made.
>
> In the conduct of operations the crews' behavior was often passive, either a result of their lacking the essential mental ability, or an indication that the intricacies of navigational training could not be absorbed in so short a time.
>
> Modern bombing aircraft were in short supply, the available models being, on the average, too slow and generally inferior to German aircraft. The bombs and bomb sights were similarly deficient.
>
> Thus, the progress of the Russian bomber forces was hesitant and limited. Whether, and to what extent the expectation of Allied Lend-Lease shipments of bombers might have contributed to these deficiencies is difficult to say. The development and commitment of Russian long-range bomber aircraft give this idea some plausibility. Despite the slowness of their progress, Russian bomber forces were

capable of playing an important part during the Battle of Stalingrad, both by their bombing operations against the German airlift bases and by their relentless air supply sorties during which they moved up a constant flow of rations, ammunition, and equipment to the beleaguered city, before it was taken by the Germans. In 1943 they rendered similar services near Orel and Leningrad. There Russian bombers flew not only daytime missions, but also launched strong and well executed night raids with considerable success.

Even though the opinion[86] that Russian bombardment aviation was lagging behind the ground-attack and fighter arms during 1942-43 may be generally justified, the considerable progress made by this air arm after mid-1943 cannot be ignored.

According to Colonel von Beust,[87] Russian bomber units remained relatively weak and ineffective through 1942-43, despite certain improvements in training, equipment, and tactics. Their operations were almost exclusively directed against nearby targets in support of the ground forces and only rarely against long-range objectives, although German rear area logistical installations would have been excellent targets for systematic bombing operations. At Stalingrad, for instance, where the Russians completely stopped German airlift operations, they could also have inflicted a decisive defeat on German bombing and transport aviation. But the Russian bombers were not capable of carrying out such tasks. German Army officers generally agree with this description.[88]

B. Organizational Structure, Chain of Command, Strength Figures, and Methods of Assembly

According to the available, somewhat sketchy sources,[89] there was a distinction between close-support bombing units that were usually subordinate to air armies, and the long-range bombing and transport aviation units that had been unified under the Long-Range Air Force since the beginning of 1942. This command was subordinate to the Peoples' Commissariat for Defense and Central Headquarters. The units were controlled by the Long-Range Air Force headquarters, even though they occasionally flew ground-support missions, such as at Stalingrad.

Most of the bombardment divisions subordinate to the air army headquarters were composed of three regiments with two to three squadrons each; each squadron had ten aircraft; the ideal regiment was composed of three squadrons. The aircraft were PE-2's, PE-3's, DB-3's, DB-3F's (IL-4), and occasionally even SB's; for night missions, the Russians used U-2's, R-5's, R-Zet's,* TB-3's, and TB-7's. The relatively small number of aircraft made it difficult to equip bomber regiments uniformly, in contrast to fighter or ground-attack regiments. A few dive-bomber regiments were equipped exclusively with PE-2's--a very effective dive bomber-- but even these regiments lacked all other specialized equipment. The personnel strength of the bomber regiments depended on the aircraft models issued to them, with variations in numbers being shown only in the strength of flying personnel. In contrast to fighter and ground-attack units, bomber regiments had one additional aircraft mechanic per plane.

The Long-Range Air Force had divisions with two to three regiments each, a regiment being composed of three squadrons; guard regiments had four squadrons. Corps headquarters were being organized to assist the Command headquarters as tactical staffs. Apparently, future plans called for corps with two divisions composed of two regiments each, with each regiment consisting of two squadrons. By summer of 1943 there were seventeen long-range bombing divisions and one transport aircraft division under the Long-Range Command. The order of battle, however, varied constantly.

Each squadron had fifteen aircraft; regimental headquarters also had three command airplanes: one bomber, one transport aircraft (model PS-84), and one liaison aircraft (model U-2). The authorized strength of a regiment was therefore 46 bomber, one transport, and one liaison aircraft.

The personnel strength of a squadron consisted of 15 pilots, 15 observers, 15 radiomen, 15 gunners, and 90 men serving as technical ground personnel. Each regiment had 190 flying personnel, 291 technicians, and 27 other personnel, thus altogether 508 men. The flying personnel consisted of 8 field grade officers, 41 officers of other grades, and 141 NCO's. The corresponding

---

* Editor's Note: The R-Zet, R-Z, or R-5 as it was sometimes called, was a single-engine reconnaissance biplane which was also employed as a ground-attack, transport, liaison or night bomber aircraft, depending on the circumstances.

figures for technical personnel were 1 - 85 - 205, and for the other personnel 2 - 12 - 8. There were also four enlisted drivers and one female secretary.

The principal aircraft model used by the long-range bomber divisions was the DB-3F (IL-4). One division, composed of three regiments with two squadrons each, had American B-25's.

The Long-Range Air Force had its own ground organization, replacement regiments, and pilot schools, and was generally concentrated on airfields around Moscow. In case of necessity, the units could be shifted to airfields in the vicinity of the operational centers--the Stalingrad area in the winter of 1942-43, for instance-- or they could be moved up to advance air bases.

C. Bomber Operations

1) Personal Conduct. Opinions on this subject are at variance,[90] but it is generally emphasized that the close-support bomber pilots--similar to the ground-attack pilots--were aggressive and that they carried out their missions with remarkable courage and occasionally also with exemplary aggressiveness, so long as the fire from fighters or flak was not too intense. The rear gunner was still considered the best man in the crew, even though he opened fire from too great a distance. But he aimed well, fired relentlessly, and was usually the last to jump from a burning aircraft.

The general opinion on long-range bomber pilots was less favorable. They were more rigid, and their aggressiveness and conduct were below that of the average Russian pilot. Bomber crews employed for night sorties were especially noted for their lack of enthusiasm. When picked up by searchlights they would immediately jettison their bombs because of their fear of night fighters. Thus, the Germans often had the impression that the bomber crews were less interested in hitting their targets than in dropping their bombs as quickly as possible. Any generalization drawn from this statement would be unfair to the Russian bomber crews. But it cannot be denied that close-range bombers committed near the front in support of ground operations performed better and were more aggressive than the long-range bombers.

2) General Principles of Commitment. These were almost the same as during the first year of warfare in Russia. According

to German opinion, they showed the following characteristics: a) the bulk of the bomber units were committed as close-support aircraft, assisting the ground forces by hitting targets in the combat zone; b) units belonging to the Long-Range Air Force also flew most of their sorties against targets close to the front or in direct support zones, rarely striking rear area objectives, and only exceptionally attacking strategic targets; c) daytime bombing raids were carried out with fighter escorts, and, in the course of time, units grew in size and operated in conjunction with ground-attack aircraft; d) individual aircraft carried out night attacks as nuisance or bombing missions; after the summer of 1943, however, night attacks were conducted by major units.

The general principles, organization, and characteristics of Russian bombardment aviation underwent only minor changes during 1942-43.[91] The Russian conduct of operations resembled more and more that of the German. The principal mission was to attack nearby targets in support of the ground forces, so that Russian bombardment aviation acted really as reinforcement of the artillery and ground-attack aviation. The targets were either integrated into the artillery fire plan or they extended the artillery gun range beyond the capability of the ground weapons. Rarely did bombers attack rear area targets, such as railroad stations, supply installations, or airfields. Close-range bombers were used to overcome stubborn resistance or to accelerate an advance or a thrust in the direction of the main effort. Bombing raids in the contact zone were a sure indication of imminent ground offensives.

In accordance with Russian military doctrine and air army concepts, the bombardment regiments subordinate to an air army headquarters had only close-support functions and were therefore also designated as close-support bomber regiments. They operated generally in daytime, did not penetrate far beyond the main line of resistance, and flew in formations of from 12 to 20 aircraft. Smaller formations were exceptional, larger units were observed only at points of main effort or during operations launched in conjunction with ground-attack planes. Large units, such as those employed by the British or Americans, were not encountered in Russia.

Bombing raids were preferably staged in the early morning or at noon; they were often executed by attack waves and usually ended before dusk, the last raid of the day often being the most intense. Organic aircraft frequently carried out reconnaissance missions before the attack was launched. Along stationary frontlines attacks were often repeated against the same target, at the same time of day, along the same approach route, and in the same attack formation. Heavy Russian losses were the result of such repetitiousness. Bombs were dropped from horizontal flight, and were generally of medium size, while--on rare occasions--large numbers of small fragmentation bombs were used.

Long-range aircraft were employed, by preference, at points of main effort until the end of 1943 (for instance at Stalingrad, Orel, and Bryansk). These aircraft, operating in conjunction with mobile forces and spearhead armies, were supposed to prevent the moving up of German Army reserves and to disrupt the German supply services. Important rear area installations, such as communications centers and air force ground services, were preferred targets. Strategic bombing raids on the German zone of interior were limited in 1943 to isolated raids on East Prussian targets.

Night raids were mainly directed at targets in the combat zone; during these raids German airfields were bombed or nuisance attacks were launched by individual aircraft. After mid-1943 night-bombing operations were undertaken by larger-size units, and as the nights grew longer the Germans expected more extensive raids.

3) <u>Flying Technique</u>. In this field the Russian bomber pilots learned from wartime experience, by imitating their German adversaries, and by receiving instructions from Allied training teams.[92] Even though they were far from being as accomplished as their Western Allies--there were a few exceptions--the Russian bomber pilots progressed considerably in comparison to their 1941 methods.

Normally, the approach, attack, and return formation remained unchanged. The preferred unit formation became the V formation, with one V formation following the other at recognizable, at times even long, distances, sometimes echeloned in altitude. At first formations were made up of from 3 to 12 aircraft, but their strength soon averaged from 12 to 30 planes, sometimes even more. On occasion, entire units formed one V, but only if they did not exceed regimental strength. The handicaps of the V formation--inflexibility, difficulties of control, the need for superior flying ability--greatly inhibited the performance of the Russian bombing crews whose training was none too modern and whose ability was not very keen. Divisional formations--at that time very rare--

flew with regiments abreast, under heavy fighter escort.

Altitudes of flight and attack varied greatly according to the situation, the weather, and other circumstances. They varied from 1,000 to 26,500 feet, with both extremes being unusual. Targets near the main line of resistance were generally attacked from altitudes of 3,300 to 8,250 feet, objectives farther to the rear from 10,000 to 16,500 feet.

When attacking frontline targets the bombers flew straight toward the objective in fairly close formation; approaches from the side or rear were rare. The attacks were made by waves in regimental strength following one another at short intervals. At the end of the straight approach flight, apparently upon a signal given by the unit commander, the bombs--usually small and medium size-- were dropped; attacks being repeated until the bombers had emptied their entire load. Hits became more frequent. After the mission was accomplished, the aircraft immediately changed course, turned about, and flew straight back to their own lines. The same procedure was followed in attacking rear area targets; if these targets were difficult to find, the course was charted by reference points.

The Russian bomber pilots were about equal to their German counterparts in formation flying. On the other hand, their insufficient training in other spheres, such as their inability to take advantage of favorable weather conditions and their slow reaction to flak fire and above all to fighter attacks, proved a serious handicap. PE-2 units that were faced by German fighters often tried to keep their opponents away by firing rockets at them and dropping bombs into their approach route, tactics which were generally unsuccessful.

The conduct of night raids, which will be dealt with separately, was mainly left to individual aircraft flying at 5 to 15 minute intervals without bomb sights, radio direction or target finding devices. These aircraft flew at medium altitudes, following the same route on the approach and return flights during moonlit or at least starry nights, raids usually taking place from the beginning of dusk to shortly after midnight. Night attacks by major units flying in closed formation, in the fashion of Russia's Western Allies, began in mid-1943.

4) <u>Bombing Operations in Support of Army and Naval Operations.</u> The reports of Army officers[93] clearly indicate that strong Russian

bombing forces continued to support the ground forces in 1942-43. Whatever the difference between individual Russian bombing attacks and however varied the experiences of German Army officers may have been, it can be stated that, in general, the cooperation between bombers and ground forces was very close and that bombers were usually committed at points of main effort. This explains why certain German Army officers had no contact with Russian bombers from the spring of 1942 to the autumn of 1943, while others report that they were subjected to continuous bombing raids. Also, at certain times some sectors of the front were not attacked by any bombers whereas at other times Russian bombers predominated in the air. This indicates that the Russians concentrated their bombers for crucial operations more than ever before. During the Battle of Stalingrad Russian bomber activity increased from the end of August 1942; this intensification was steady, even though interrupted occasionally, until complete supremacy was achieved during the last weeks of the battle of encirclement. The Russian bombers usually attacked in squadron strength; they were so effective that the Germans occasionally rated their performance more highly than that of the ground-attack aviation. Other Russian bombing operations near Sevastopol, Kerch, at the Kuban Bridgehead, in the Caucasus and near Kharkov, Orel, and Leningrad (that is to say, everywhere that decisive battles were taking place) were executed with determination and in increasing strength in support of the ground forces.

Whereas sometimes the bombers attacked targets in the rear of the combat zone while the ground-attack aircraft concentrated on frontline objectives, at other times both the bomber and ground-attack aircraft would raid the same objectives. Quite frequently bomber units composed of some 30 aircraft would strike important objectives on or near the battlefield with flight altitudes varying according to the over-all situation and air and weather conditions. There was, however, a general tendency to attack from medium, and sometimes from high, altitudes.

The German losses suffered from such attacks continued to be low during this period, with the possible exception of the Battle of Stalingrad. Although personnel and materiel losses were higher than in 1941, they remained within acceptable limits; the effect produced on morale, however, was far more serious, although, in general, the German troops were not as greatly impressed by Russian bombing attacks as by the raids of ground-attack aircraft.

After the beginning of 1943, Russian bombing operations against German naval installations and operations multiplied.[94] High altitude raids, for instance, were directed by units of 20 to 30 bombers against harbor installations at Kerch and Feodosiya and at the ports of Anapa, Yalta, and Taman as well as against the German torpedo boat harbor at Ali Baba* west of Feodosiya. The effect of the bombings was generally minor because well placed flak fire often induced the Soviet bombers to drop their bombs prematurely. On the other hand, the Russian bombers succeeded in inflicting heavy losses on the German naval transports supplying the troops in the Caucasus. During the withdrawal of the German forces in the Caucasus the bombers again hampered the flow of supplies by repeated attacks on Kerch and Taman and partly destroyed the preparations for transferring the troops to the Crimea.

At the same time, Russian aircraft attacked German naval convoys between Constanta and Sevastopol, usually by dispatching torpedo bombers from Tuapse, which were generally loaded with normal aircraft torpedoes, occasionally also with parachute torpedoes. Although these operations were usually unsuccessful because the torpedoes were launched from too great a distance, the Russians did force the German Air Force commander to divert fighters to escorting the convoys, and these fighters were thus not available for other missions. A torpedo raid staged in the autumn of 1943 by a squadron of Douglas Bostons against the port of Constanta was totally ineffective. Whereas there was some bomber activity against the German Navy in the Black Sea area, according to available information the Russians did not undertake bomber operations in the Baltic or North Sea.

5) <u>Russian Bombing Operations in Rear Areas</u>. In 1942-43 Russian bombing operations in rear areas were mainly directed against tactical objectives. Supply, service, and transportation installations as well as billets and troop movements deep in the rear areas were among the chief targets, while missions aimed at Luftwaffe ground organization units focused mainly on airfields. Attacks on strategic objectives in the German zone of interior were

---

* Editor's Note: This must be a nickname for Ivan Baba, a small port located on a peninsula about a mile south of Feodosiya.

rare exceptions.

Opinions on the procedures used and effect produced by these bombing attacks vary. All Luftwaffe commanders agree, however, that gradually the planning improved, the attacks grew more intensive and became more successful. The Russian bomber attacks against the German airlift at Stalingrad[95] offer the best example of this. At first, the Russians did not launch any planned attacks by major units against those German loading airfields outside of the Stalingrad pocket. Instead, individual twin-engine aircraft made day and night attacks at irregular intervals, but their attempts to disrupt the flying activity failed. By mid-December 1942 bomber units in squadron strength appeared more frequently, and sometimes even larger units were employed. They attempted to disturb the airlift by dropping bombs from an altitude of 13,200 to 20,000 feet, flying in squadron V formation. Such attacks were almost continuous, and inflicted heavy losses of German aircraft, materiel, and irreplaceable personnel. Finally, the losses went as high as 50 percent of all the operational aircraft.

Simultaneous attacks against airfields situated in the pocket had a very detrimental effect on the landing and take-off of the transport aircraft, on the unloading of supplies, and on the evacuation of the wounded. Because of damage to the airstrips and uninterrupted attacks, take-offs and landings often had to be cancelled and airfields had to be temporarily closed down. The constant bombing attacks added to other causes finally led, in January 1943, to the complete stoppage of operations at the airfields in the Stalingrad pocket.

According to German Army and Air Force officers,[96] Russian bombing attacks in rear areas were still insignificant in 1942. When opposed by German fighters, the Soviet bomber units often suffered devastating losses. Although they carried out their missions without deviating, the bombers failed because they dropped their bombs indiscriminately, scoring few hits on the targets and producing little effect. A major attack[97] carried out by three waves of bombers against German billets along the Black Sea coast also produced little effect, except for some damages to buildings. By contrast, in the steppes along the Don River, German antiaircraft batteries that were repeatedly attacked, from an altitude of 5,000 to 10,000 feet, by Russian bombers during the summer of 1942 suffered considerable losses until the German troops were able to dig in, no cover or concealment being readily available.

During 1943 the situation changed profoundly.[98] Even then, Russian bombers scored little or no success if German Air Force units opposed them in strength. During Operation Citadel, for instance, the Russian bombers approaching German airfields were caught in time by German fighter aircraft and badly mauled. This did not stop the remaining bombers from stubbornly continuing their mission. Some elements reached the target and dropped their bombs despite continual fighter resistance; few hit the target, however, and the damage was slight.

During another attack of closed bomber formations flying under heavy fighter escort the targets were the airfields of the German 4th Bomber Wing in the Orel-Bryansk area. A major Russian success was prevented by well placed flak fire which impeded the aiming of Soviet bombardiers. During its return flight, this Russian unit was caught by German fighters which then shot down some 90 Soviet aircraft.

But the Russian Air Force was able to compensate for such losses by a continuous flow of materiel and personnel replacements. Russian bombing attacks spread to German rear area airfields and logistical facilities. Thus, the railheads at Orel and Bryansk were badly hit almost day after day with very noticeable effect. In Orel a train loaded with one million rations and part of an Army ration dump were bombed out, while at Bryansk the Germans lost 1,200 tons of ammunition. The Germans, as a result, were forced to disperse their supply and service facilities even wider, which again required more guard personnel, more supplies, and more POL, quite apart from the fact that the dispersed installations had no access to the railroad. This, in turn, affected the entire supply system.

The gradually improving performances of Russian bombers during attacks on rear area facilities of the Germans during 1943 are recognized by various German Air Force commanders.[99] According to them, the bombing operations were well prepared, based on good intelligence, reasonably planned from a tactical point of view, and carried out by surprise and at times when the German unit under attack was particularly vulnerable--immediately after landing, for example. Although German flak and fighters often succeeded in preventing the Russians from precision bombing, German personnel and materiel losses increased considerably because of the existing Russian numerical superiority, the growing strength of the units committed, and the Russians' steadily improving performance in dropping bombs and employing aircraft weapons. PE-2 units, up to 80 aircraft in strength, attacking in a steep dive, under direct and indirect protection of fighter escorts, were no longer exceptional.

A well executed Soviet bombing attack on the Stalino airfield in 1943, when no German fighters were present, was rather ineffective only because the German bomber group based on this field was away on a mission. When the Russians repeated the attack, their bombers were intercepted by German fighters that had been redeployed to this vicinity. The Russian bombers were dispersed before reaching their target and were almost completely annihilated.

A particularly instructive example of the improved Russian bomber operations was the raid on Kotly airfield, which was situated on the Bay of Finland and could be kept under observation by the Russian garrison in Leningrad. A few hours after the arrival of a German bomber group (1st Bomber Group, 1st Bomber Wing), the airfield was subjected to a classical bomber strike by 15 to 20 Russian aircraft approaching at low level from the sea. The antiaircraft fire by 4 four-barreled 20-mm machine guns was completely inadequate. German fighters were busy elsewhere at quite a distance, which was probably known to the Russians through intelligence channels. The small and medium bombs hit precisely between the parked aircraft and the billeting areas. After the bombardment the planes returned for low-level strafing attacks. Aside from considerable personnel losses, the Germans lost 10 Ju-88's that were either destroyed or heavily damaged. The same afternoon another attack was launched against the same airfield by 17 Russian bombers, and on the following day 24 bombers renewed the assault so that the operational readiness of the German bomber group was reduced to four aircraft. As a result, the entire unit had to be transferred to East Prussia for rehabilitation and replacement of losses. This was an irreplaceable loss because the unit had been an experienced bomber group. Even though no similar Russian successes have been registered, this event proves the capability of Soviet bomber units in 1943 under favorable circumstances.

In summary, during 1942 Russian bombing operations against German rear areas were primarily tactical. Aimed at supply installations and airfields, they were executed with far too few aircraft flown by poorly trained, inexperienced crews. As a result, losses were high and results were poor. By 1943, however, such attacks gained in power and were executed more skillfully because of the increased experience of the crews. Finally, although Russian losses to German fighter and antiaircraft defenses remained heavy, the Russians, in contrast to the Germans, were able to replace their losses within a short time. Thus, German defenses gradually weakened and Russian bombing operations improved.

6) <u>Night Bombing Operations</u>. Russian night bombing operations in 1942-43 were similar to those in 1941. They were either nuisance raids or attacks on tactical objectives near the main line of resistance, staged during the hours of darkness.

The methods of launching night nuisance raids changed little,[100] and the raids were still executed mainly by U-2 aircraft. The almost uninterrupted commitment of individual airplanes flying at low or intermediate levels during moonlit or starry nights was characterized by the aimless and nonselective dropping of small-caliber bombs on any identified target or ray of light. As a result, the bombers scored accidental hits, kept the frontline area under constant pressure, and disturbed the German troops' rest at night. As of 1943 they also dropped propaganda material and passes for potential deserters. For well-known reasons counteraction by German night fighters was hardly possible. The combination of 600-mm searchlights and light and medium flak had a deterrent effect and constituted a strong defense, but the existing shortage of equipment restricted its use to a few centers of ground fighting. Thus, the Russians could generally carry out their nuisance raids without being disturbed, scoring many successes, especially against service and supply installations. These night raids also affected the morale of the overextended German ground forces. Both Luftwaffe and Army officers agree that organizational improvements, proper training in dropping bombs, more adroit commitment, and the use of modern bombs and bombsights could have made these raids far more effective.

One author[101] very ably characterizes the nightly nuisance raids by stating that the nuisance bombing units were constantly being reinforced and reorganized. They appeared everywhere at night without any system, being used against any target of opportunity such as troop assemblies, occupied villages, rail or road traffic, airfields, and German night flying operations. Even though they did not score decisive successes--these were perhaps not sought--they produced a quite considerable and constant nuisance effect.

The Russian command issued detailed directives governing air-ground cooperation by night.[102] Very close contact between the appropriate Army and Air Force agencies, the attaching of Air Force liaison officers to Army staffs, the security of signal communications, the commitment of aircraft from advanced airfields, the installation of direction centers along the main line of resistance to orient and guide aircraft by flares, tracer ammunition, and searchlights, the marking of the main line of resistance by optical aids--all were spelled out in minute detail.

Whereas there were only a few changes in the execution of night nuisance raids in comparison to 1941, the bombing attacks on tactical objectives under cover of darkness increased considerably in intensity and importance both in the combat zone and in rear areas.[103] They were primarily directed against supply facilities and service installations as well as against German airfields and night air activity. The attacks were launched during clear, moonlit or starlit nights, primarily by individual aircraft--some obsolete four-engine planes, but mostly twin-engine PE-2's or DB's--that followed each other at short, regular intervals. They dropped their medium bombs and fired their guns from altitudes varying from 6,600 to 10,000 feet, often repeating their attacks on consecutive nights. During dark nights they lit up the target area with flares prior to dropping the bombs, but this was done so inaccurately and prematurely and without properly considering the wind that the bombs usually missed their target. The German ground defenses were occasionally deceived by Russian aircraft giving the proper German recognition signal before dropping their bombs.

The success achieved by these attacks varied greatly. For instance, during the period 16 to 26 June 1943 twin-engine aircraft flying individual missions attacked the East Zaporozhe* airfield during four nights for periods of two to two-and-a-half hours each time. A maximum number of 20 aircraft was employed; they attacked

---

* Editor's Note: Zaporozhe was important because of its location on the east bank of the Dnieper River bend, a natural barrier which figured importantly in the southern sector of the Russian campaign. Captured by the Germans in 1941, Zaporozhe remained in their possession until 14 October 1943. See Tippelskirch, pp. 342-43.

from about 6,600 feet altitude during clear nights, dropping a moderate number of bombs, many of which were duds. They did not cause any fires on the ground, but they damaged four aircraft and destroyed a small ammunition dump. In another instance,[104] IL-2's first attacked at dusk, followed by PE-2's, TB-3's, and DB-3's launching continuous raids, which completely immobilized the runway and the taxiway for half a day. Only because the wrong fuses had been used for the heavier-type bombs--producing deep bomb craters instead of fragmentation or splinter effects--did the damages resulting from the raids not turn out to be heavier.

Such night raids on German transport aircraft engaged in airlift operations near Stalingrad were, at first, rare and unsuccessful. But by December 1942 such raids grew in size and frequency, causing personnel and materiel losses that the Germans could ill afford.

Russian night raids on tactical objectives increased in intensity during 1943. In the northern sector of the Russian theater, for example, the main line of communications was severely disrupted by repeated attacks on the Dno railroad station. Such raids were particularly disruptive during Operation Citadel. Increasing night bombing attacks on the principal railroad stations and lines of communication led to long delays. Supplies had to be unloaded outside the stations or they had to be diverted to some other rail line, which then promptly became the main center of attraction for the Russian bombers. These continuous attacks finally forced the Germans to stop their supply trains as early as Roslavl and to transship the supplies via army group truck regiments or move them up by horse-drawn vehicles. Serious disadvantages of all kinds arose from this situation and were aggravated by the coordination and interaction of bombing attacks and partisan activities, the latter becoming more and more effective.

The Russians were hesitant to launch night attacks by major bombing units. By spring of 1943, however, such operations were observed by the Germans; during the summer of 1943, repeated night attacks by bombing formations took place in the Leningrad area. There, one or two squadrons would attack a single target from low altitudes with medium and heavy bombs. Before the start of the attack, the target area was illuminated by numerous flares. The attacks impressed the Germans by their vehemence, even though they did not achieve any results worth mentioning.

Since the Germans were short of antiaircraft guns, searchlights and (above all) night fighters, an effective defense against night attacks was difficult. Whenever the Germans were able to improvise night fighting operations by a combination of searchlights and night fighter aircraft, as for instance near Kerch, they shot down quite a number of Russian planes. The Russians contributed to these successes because their night attacks took place only during clear or moonlit nights, their aircraft used the same route for approach and return flights, and their twin- and four-engine bombers were easy to locate by their exhaust flame, which was clearly visible. Thus, the Russians stopped their night attacks near Kerch after repeating them for eight times and losing about twelve aircraft.

No Russian bomber raids at night on German naval targets were reported during the 1942-43 period, except for raids on German harbor installations in the Crimea, which were never too successful.

7) Operations under Special Weather Conditions. For the 1942-43 period there is very little information on Russian bombing operations under special weather conditions.[105] The conclusion that the training of most Russian bomber crews had not sufficiently advanced to permit carrying out missions under really bad weather conditions is based on the following facts: first, the Russians did not conduct strategic bombing operations and were therefore unable to obtain experience in flying under unfavorable weather conditions over long distances; second, night attacks were carried out only during spells of good weather; and finally, the bombing aircraft lacked adequate instruments and navigational aids to fly bad weather sorties.

Only for operations in the immediate combat zone could the weather be left out of consideration. There, the Russian bombing missions were adroitly and persistently executed under even the worst weather conditions and in the most severe cold. The same applied to the nuisance raids conducted by U-2's, which were practically unaffected by the weather. One report mentions, for instance, that a Russian nuisance raider attacked the Orsha airfield during weather that virtually excluded flying. The aircraft dropped small-caliber bombs, through a momentary opening in the clouds that covered the night sky, and hit a hangar, whereupon all aircraft inside the hangar burned to ashes.

Thus, during the period 1942-43 Russian bomber crews

were still generally incapable of carrying out flights over long distances in really bad weather; the night nuisance raids conducted by U-2's in all types of weather constituted the sole exception.

8) <u>Bomber Operations in Conjunction with Other Air Arms.</u> As stated earlier in this study, Russian combined operations of bombers and fighters were still inadequate until mid-1942. They led to high losses that could have been avoided and that were caused by the fighter escorts' inability to fulfill their mission and the bomber units' lack of cohesion. But after fighter and bomber crews had learned their lessons, cooperation improved considerably until, by the end of 1943, it reached a satisfactory level. Bombing operations without fighter escorts became a thing of the past.

D. <u>Types, Armament, and Equipment of Russian Bomber Aircraft</u>

There were few changes in the types of Russian bomber aircraft employed in 1942-43.[106] The antiquated SB and TB models were no longer used during daytime, and only occasionally used during the hours of darkness. The Russian daylight bomber units were therefore almost exclusively equipped with twin-engine DB-3's, DB-3F's (IL-4's), and PE-2's. In their performance these aircraft corresponded approximately to the Heinkel 111's with regard, for instance, to speed, maximum altitude, and bombload. They were therefore not up to modern standards. During these years the PE-2 remained the best Russian bomber: its armament consisted of two to three rigid and one to three mobile machine guns, it carried a bombload of 1,320 lbs., had a speed of 250 miles, a normal range of 250 miles, and carried a crew of three men. A great number of these aircraft were to be found in the immediate combat zone. Their powerful rear defenses of machine guns and rockets prevented German fighter attacks except from the side to the rear--in the blind spot caused by the tail assembly--or from above and to the side. Attacks directly from the rear were impossible. German fighters could score successes only by first eliminating the rear gunner and then setting one motor on fire, the rest of the aircraft being extremely fire resistant. It was known that the Russian Air Force command was trying to commit more modern bombers manufactured in the Soviet Union and in the United States. No such aircraft were encountered by the Germans during this period, however.

Russian medium and heavy caliber bombs, the Germans observed,[107] contained a disproportionately high percentage of duds. Thus, during an attack on the East Zaporozhe airfield in 1943, 8 out of 60 bombs were duds, during another raid as many as 30 out of 130. The light fragmentation bombs, however, detonated almost without exception and were quite effective. The Russians had a predilection for using captured German fragmentation bombs, with good effect.

No special information is available on the equipment of Russian bomber units in 1942-43. It seems improbable, however, that the backwardness in accessories and equipment--in comparison to Western standards--had been modified to any extent.

E. Summary and Conclusions

Russian bombardment aviation during 1942-43 can, on the basis of available source material, be evaluated as follows:

1) Despite some progress Russian bombardment aviation continued to be the weakest and intentionally neglected arm of the Russian Air Force.

2) The personal conduct of the Russian bomber crews, particularly in combat, was worthy of recognition.

3) In accordance with the general Russian doctrine on the conduct of operations, bombers continued to be employed exclusively for tactical and not for strategic missions. The creation, in 1942, of the Long-Range Air Force did not change this. Bomber operations, however, gave evidence of increasing adherence to the principle of concentration of forces.

4) Bombing attacks in the combat zone against tactical objectives in support of the ground forces constituted the main mission of Russian bombardment aviation. Cooperation with the Army was generally well organized and gradually produced results, particularly in the southern part of the theater.

5) Bombing operations in rear areas were also mainly tactical, being directed, for the most part, against service facilities, supply installations, and airfields. The effectiveness of these raids

grew considerably in the course of time, even though the successes often involved heavy losses.

6) Russian bombing operations against German naval targets took place only in the Black Sea area; there the results were negligible.

7) Night nuisance raids became more numerous; because of the continuous disturbance they created, they weakened the resilience of the German ground forces. Night attacks on tactical objectives were successful despite the Russian crews' deficiencies in training and experience.

8) The tactics and flying technique of Russian bomber crews had improved, even though there were still many weaknesses in the control of operations, as well as in technical ability and training. The size of the attacking units grew steadily, and operations were always conducted with fighter protection. Night operations were still predominantly conducted by individual aircraft.

9) Types, armament, and equipment of bombing aircraft showed little progress. The neglect of bombardment aviation in these fields manifested itself very clearly, affecting both operations and effectiveness.

10) The performances of Russian bombardment aviation in cooperation with ground-attack and fighter aircraft during combined operations improved in proportion to increasing experience.

Section VI: Other Flying Operations

A. General

There is little information on the use of Russian aircraft for other flying operations in 1942-43. The available data indicate, however, that considerable progress was made in air transport and courier flights and above all in airlift operations to and from partisan areas in the central and northern parts of the Russian theater. The successes achieved in transport and courier aviation were not as spectacular and perhaps less significant. But the rapidly growing partisan activity, which proved so harmful to the German troops, would have been altogether impossible without the continuous resupply and support by airlift.

B. Transport Aviation

Russian military transport aviation[108] was at first expanded by the employment of large civil aviation elements. They were used for carrying light express goods in rear areas, wounded personnel, and supplies to partisan-infested areas. For these missions the Russians often still employed the antiquated TB-model aircraft. In supplying the Russian ground forces at Stalingrad, Russian transport aviation also played an important and successful part. By contrast, the Soviet transport aircraft did not succeed in flying adequate supplies to the Russian bridgehead south of Kerch in November 1943. The supply containers they dropped often landed within the German lines, some of the aircraft were shot down, and finally the Russians were forced to abandon the bridgehead.

By summer of 1943 the Germans had identified one long-distance transport division with three regiments operating within the framework of the so-called Long-Range Air Force. This division was also occasionally committed for bombing missions. It was equipped with PS-84* model aircraft, and its crews had been transferred from civil aviation. Aside from carrying out supply functions, especially for the long-range bomber units, these transport aircraft were used for dropping leaflets and propaganda material, as for instance in January 1943 near Orel and Bryansk.

C. Courier, Liaison, and Command Missions

Russian courier and liaison missions increased in importance because of the vast expanses of the theater and the long distances to be covered in the combat zone as well as in the zone of interior. This type of aviation was therefore correspondingly enlarged.[109] Its principal objectives were the rapid transmission of information, the delivery of courier mail, the transporting of light loads and passengers, and to a minor degree the maintenance of liaison with the partisans or the setting down of agents behind the Germans lines. These courier,

---

* Editor's Note: A twin-engined transport, the PS-84 was the Russian version of the American C-47.

liaison, and command missions were unified within the framework of the Russian Air Force and subordinated to the Intelligence and Liaison Branches within the Soviet High Command staff of the Air Force. Beginning in 1943, each air army was given a courier aircraft regiment as well as a varying number of separate courier squadrons and flights. The latter were attached to army staffs in accordance with the over-all situation. Supply and personnel matters for those units were handled by the air armies in the combat zone, whereas, in the zone of interior, air force staffs in the military districts had this responsibility. The models used were mainly U-2's, with a few R-5's, UT-1's, and UT-2's. Captured German Fieseler Storch aircraft were observed occasionally. During the last few weeks of the period under review a new type of aircraft was identified by the Germans, the JA-6.* It was built of lumber, had twin-engines, a crew of two or three, and could carry a payload of 1,100-1,320 lbs.

Russian courier and liaison aircraft were often encountered by German reconnaissance planes during 1943, usually along railroad tracks. The dirty gray-green camouflage paint of these aircraft made them difficult to observe in bad weather when the sky was overcast. In sunshine they could be identified by their sharp silhouette. The Russians flew skillfully, taking advantage of favorable terrain features. On these aircraft, the rear seat was often equipped with a machine gun mounted on a rotating gun ring for defensive protection against attacks from the rear and above. If they recognized an attacker in time, the Soviet courier pilots would change course abruptly as soon as the opponent opened fire and disappear behind groups of trees, villages or in forest fire-breaks. The Germans shot them down only if they could catch them by surprise in a low-level attack from the rear by suddenly reducing altitude and speed.

D. Airlifting Supplies to Partisan Units

In 1942-43 the cooperation between the Russian Air Force and partisan units expanded gradually, especially in the extensive areas of the central and northern parts of the Russian theater, which were infested by partisans. This cooperation resulted in extremely heavy

---

* Editor's Note: English designation may be YA-6. No additional data available.

losses and damages to the Germans.[110] Continuous airlift supported the partisans with rations, weapons, medical supplies, and many other supply items, and at the same time provided them with key personnel and important orders and information. The methods of executing these operations had remained essentially unchanged, i.e. aircraft and cargo gliders landed by night on emergency airfields--during the winter on the ice of frozen lakes--which were also used for airdrops. This support enabled the partisans to carry out successful attacks on railroads, roads, airfields, bridges, convoys, march columns, rear area command agencies, and even troop units. As a result, the Germans suffered heavy losses of personnel and materiel. In addition, they had to devote considerable forces to countermeasures. These extensive, time-consuming operations resulted in an attrition of forces. For instance, security troops had to be committed more extensively and vehicles had to move in guarded convoys. The Germans flew reconnaissance missions to discover airdrop and landing fields in partisan-held areas, attacked airlift operations wherever they had been identified, used deception by setting up dummy airfields and giving fake signals, and finally activated a special anti-partisan wing of 100 Arado-66's. The results achieved--especially in the central part of the theater--remained unsatisfactory. In the final analysis, this use of airlift by the Russian Air Force must be considered a success, for the relentless night airlift operations enabled the partisans to carry out their tasks.

Section VII: <u>Air Force Ground Organization, Technological Development, and Supply Services</u>

A. <u>General</u>

There is relatively little information on the ground organization, technological development, and supply services of the Soviet Air Force during 1942-43. The available data indicate that with considerable simplicity in these spheres the Russians demonstrated remarkable adaptability and an admirable capacity for improvisation. To an increasing degree, their methods were tailored to fit the requirements of the Russian theater of war in general and the Soviet Air Force in particular.

B. Air Force Ground Organization

1) **General.** The Soviet Air Force ground organization recovered fairly quickly from the reverses of 1941. It was realistically organized, adjusted to constantly changing circumstances, and it perfected itself on the basis of practical experience.[111] In establishing airfields, the Russians often disregarded the lack of railroad sidings and in many instances even the absence of improved roads leading to the facility. Instead, they preferred more and more to build airfields close to the frontline. The increasing number of flying units, the necessary decentralization in assembling air force units, and the absence of a great number of large peacetime airfields that had fallen into German hands, gradually led the Russians to use almost exclusively advance airfields for Air Force operations. Thus, in the summer of 1943, there were only two fixed installations among the sixteen Russian airfields in the area south of Orel.

2) **Operational Principles, Organization, and Chain of Command.** German officers had no insight into these matters during 1942-43. They did know, hoever, that the chief of rear area services at an air army headquarters directed his entire ground organization, including supply, in accordance with regulations prepared by the Central Administration of Rear Area Services in the Central Administration of Red Army Air Force Units. Each chief of rear area services had a subordinate branch for ground organization.[112]

3) **The Airfields and Their Facilities.** In describing the conditions which prevailed in 1941, we noted that the unpretentiousness of the Russian ground organization had many advantages and that the Russians had demonstrated particular ability and talent for improvisation in this sphere. These observations are equally valid for the period 1942-43.[113] Advance airfields were literally roughed out with complete disregard of the prevailing season. On a flat surface having the required dimensions--about 1,100-1,320 yards in length and 176-220 yards in width--heavy rollers were used to establish a runway in an east-west direction which was the predominant direction of winds in Russia. These airstrips could be used even in bad weather; they also proved effective when covered by snow. The dispersal areas were well camouflaged; in winter they were under a cover of snow. The troops usually lived in dugouts, not in fixed or barrack-type billets. Some advance airfields were completely integrated into the surrounding countryside. Wherever splinterproof shelters were available for aircraft, the opening

passages were shifted from time to time to confuse reconnaissance pilots. In the course of time, however, the Russians almost completely stopped building revetments for aircraft. Ammunition, bomb, and POL dumps were dug into the ground away from the airstrips. The airfields were usually protected by one or two antiaircraft batteries.

Air Force ground personnel operated efficiently. The flight operations, particularly take-offs, took place rapidly and without incidents. Bomb damages were repaired within a short time. Thus, for instance, the last airfield near Sevastopol was repaired again and again despite repeated German air attacks. While the airfield was thus kept operational, the planes were distributed among the covered shelters and were moved at frequent intervals.

The Russians were also very skilled in installing dummy airfields. As an example, the Germans made several saturation bombing attacks on an airfield near Kerch until they discovered, during a low-level attack, that this was a dummy installation on which Russian ground crews were continuously moving well imitated dummy aircraft from one end to the other. On another advance airfield the Russians intermingled real and dummy aircraft so skillfully that they could not be distinguished from one another.

C. Air Force Technological Development.

We have already discussed the individual types of aircraft and the related technological development for 1942-43 in another section of this chapter. From an organizational point of view,[114] technical matters were controlled by the Central Administration of the Aviation Engineer Service within the Central Administration of Red Army Air Force Units. It was from this agency, then, that a chief engineer at an air army headquarters would receive his directives. The fixed aircraft repair shop within his jurisdictional area dispatched a maintenance and a repair battalion to satisfy all immediate requirements up front. The testing and introduction of technical innovations and improvements and the execution of repairs were particularly stressed. Subordinate specialized inspectors were responsible for constant technical supervision.

D. The Supply Services.

Despite many difficulties, Russian supply services generally fulfilled their functions, even though they had to improvise constantly.[115] The replacement of aircraft was well organized since, despite heavy losses, no decrease in operational strength of fighter aircraft was felt in the field. Aircraft replacements were flown in great numbers directly from the factory to airfields in the combat zone to fill existing gaps. Thus, in the summer of 1943, entire groups of aircraft arrived at airfields in the Orel area, even though they had not yet received their coat of camouflage paint.

Materiel was, by preference, transported by truck. The availability of railroad connections, therefore, was relatively unimportant. Personnel replacements were made through air force replacement regiments. During the very tenuous situation in the spring of 1942, for example, the reconnaissance replacement regiment had sufficient personnel for five to six reconnaissance regiments. Up until the autumn of 1942, however, these regiments could only be activated very slowly, one at a time, because the necessary aircraft were lacking. By 1943 this bottleneck had been overcome.

The Central Administration for Rear Area Services--a part of the Central Administration of Red Army Air Force Units--controlled the entire supply system as well as the ground organization. A chief of rear area services at each air army headquarters directed all supply services at the lower echelons.

Section VIII: <u>Air Force Signal Communications</u>[116]

Russian Air Force signal communications, during this period, shared in the general progress achieved by the Russian Air Force; this was particularly noticeable in radio communications and organization, and in the operational principles followed. The signal traffic was smoother since detailed directives on signal communications within the Air Force had been issued. Allied materiel assistance might also have been of importance. In comparison to German Air Force signal communications, the Russians were still considerably retarded; no step had been taken to form separate air force signal units as an arm of the service.

In the organizational field the remarkable feature was that signal communications included not only radio, radar, telephone, teletype, and other means of communicating, but also all media of transmission such as liaison, courier, and command aircraft. There was therefore no differentiation between the transmittal of a message, an item or a person, all these services being accomplished by signal communications. The Signal Communications Service Branch in the Central Administration of Red Army Air Force Units, was the control agency for these operations. A chief of signal communications and liaison service acting as the chief of the signal communications and liaison branch at each air army headquarters, directed, according to the regulations and orders issued by the central control agency, all radio, telephone, teletype, courier, and liaison services within the air army. The cryptographic service, an exception, formed a separate branch.

The most obvious progress had been made in the transmission of radio messages.[117] In radio traffic among aircraft in flight and, above all, in air-ground communications, there had been considerable improvement since 1941. In May 1943, for instance, at the Kuban Bridgehead all Russian fighters were equipped with radio sets. Russian fighter and ground-attack aircraft were systematically and consistently directed by radio control stations established along advance positions at the points of main effort. These radio control stations assisted the Russian fighters in locating German formations in flight, informed Soviet ground-attack and close-range bombers of worth-while targets along the German main line of resistance, provided information on the air and ground battle, and warned Russian ground-attack and bomber aircraft of the approach of German fighters. The radio control stations supervised the operations of Russian aircraft in flight and were even authorized to reprimand or punish crews while they were still in the air, if they had made a mistake or their failure to carry out a mission had been established. In addition, the radio control stations attempted to enter German radio traffic circuits, threatening or misleading the German crews. But despite all these measures, the radio discipline of the Russian Air Force units was still far from perfect. This enabled the German radio intercept service not only to establish the assembly preparations of Russian Air Force units in many instances, but also to direct the German fighters toward the approaching Soviet units or to warn German headquarters and troops of the impending danger.

The existence of a Russian Air Force radio intercept service was known to the Germans who, however, had no knowledge of details because of the strictly imposed secrecy. But the Germans had reason to assume that the Russian radio monitoring service was inferior to their own and that it did not produce any significant results or information on the situation in the air.[118]

Even though the Russian Air Force organized its own organic telecommunications units on a major scale in 1943--a development that affected the German reconnaissance and bombing aircraft, often very disagreeably--this sphere of activity was still retarded. The same can be said about the radar service. Radar instruments were available and mass production of new sets was apparently underway for sets that could detect the appearance and number of enemy aircraft apparently within 70 to 90 miles' distance. To judge by the operations of the Russian Air Force and especially by the performance of the night fighter aviation, Soviet radar development must still have been at a very elementary stage.[119]

Section IX: <u>Training</u>[120]

As already stated, German officers had little insight into Russian training methods. The deficiences which obtained in this field during 1942-43 were certainly caused by lack of sufficient time to thoroughly train personnel before sending them into combat. This was not surprising after the losses and reverses of the first year of the Russian campaign, quite apart from the fact that the Soviet Air Force had to base its training on gradually obtained experience in combat.

The much abbreviated training course consisted as a rule of the following: after premilitary training in flying clubs and associations, suitable personnel were sent to pilots' schools, and from there to the specialized schools of the different air arms. The personnel that had completed these training courses were assigned to air replacement or training regiments from which they were transferred to combat units. There were no specialized training courses for observers.

The flying and ground personnel were concentrated in air replacement regiments, where they were either subjected to further training or retrained by special instructors. Then they were used to activate new units, to rehabilitate units that had suffered heavy losses or to serve as individual replacements of crews with combat units.

There were two air academies: the Command, Staff, and Navigational Academy of the Red Army Air Force at Chkalov trained staff officers, regimental and divisional commanders, air attaches, navigation officers and field-grade officers (in the supply services and ground organization) in command, staff, and operational principles, whereas the Air War Academy Zhukovski at Sverdlovsk--previously located in Moscow--trained primarily members of the higher technical staffs.

There was no detailed information on training by Allied instructors. But the Germans had established the fact that at Kostroma Russian pilots were retrained by British instructors to fly British aircraft.

From these relatively scarce data it can be gathered, however, that the Russian Air Force's efforts to bridge the existing gap in the training of its personnel were gradually proving successful.

Section X: <u>Paratroops and Airborne Forces</u>

In 1942-43 there were no basic changes in the organization and employment of Russian paratroops and airborne forces. They remained directly subordinate to Red Army headquarters, i.e. to the Peoples' Commissar for Defense.

By the end of February 1942 the activation of 10 airborne corps--ordered in the autumn 1941--had been completed. Almost all of these units were assembled in the area east of Moscow; during the following months, particularly in January and May 1942, they were committed on a small scale at various sectors of the front. These operations had a very detrimental effect on the flow of German supplies, since they were directed against the German lines of communication, traffic centers, and other man-made facilities, thus disrupting the few railroads and highways that were available. In August 1942, under the effect of the German advance on Stalingrad, the airborne corps were reorganized into seven guards rifle divisions, one guards artillery division, and one guards armored corps, all under the command of the First Guards Rifle Army, which was immediately sent into combat near Stalingrad. At the same time the Russians resumed the activation of airborne corps which in turn were employed in ground combat near Demyansk and at Staraya Russa in February 1943. Further activations taking place after April 1943 had generally been concluded by the end of 1943.[121]

The units activated after April 1943 were no longer organized as airborne corps; the new units were airborne brigades with about 3,500 men each. By autumn of 1943, 7 out of 20 airborne brigades, which the Germans assumed were then in existence, were ready for commitment. An airborne brigade was composed of four airborne battalions of 700 men each, one engineer company, one signal, one machine-gun antiaircraft, and one bicycle-reconnaissance company as well as one antitank battalion. Each airborne battalion had three rifle companies as well as one machine-gun, one mortar, and one bazooka company and one reconnaissance, one engineer, and one signal platoon. At that time all airborne forces were paratroops.

The Flying Units of the Red Army Airborne Forces had probably also been considerably reduced by the spring of 1943, being essentially limited to two training glider regiments and the glider school at Saratov. The mission of the glider regiments was: to carry airborne forces, cargo, ammunition, medical supplies, and rations; to evacuate the wounded from partisan-held areas; and to airlift supplies of all types to the partisans during the hours of darkness. They also attempted to undertake surprise night-bombing attacks, after having been towed to high altitudes.

The airborne forces had no organic transport aircraft capable of carrying troops for major operations. For this reason, transport units of the Long-Range Air Force, occasionally augmented by Red Army Air Force transports or civilian aircraft, had to be employed for large-scale operations. Obviously, this led to major complications and resulted in failures, like the operation in the Kanev area during the night of 24-25 September 1943. During that operation the Russian paratroopers jumped too far east of the Dnieper from too high an altitude (5,000 feet). When they landed, they were so dispersed that the Russian commander was unable to concentrate his forces within a short enough time and commit them at the decisive point on the battlefield.

Whereas personnel selection, training status, and above all the high priority enjoyed by the airborne forces ought to have produced a powerful instrument of war, these forces were greatly hampered in their usefulness because of inadequate leadership, defective cooperation between the air and ground forces, and improperly coordinated commitment both with regard to time and space. The result was piecemeal employment.[122]

Section XI: <u>Aircraft Production, Armament Industry, and Communications Network</u>

Information in these areas remained scant during 1942-43. German officers, however, provide the following general indications:[123]

Russian aircraft production reached its lowest point in the autumn of 1942. The Soviet production figures that became known to the Germans at that time indicated that for many months the number of aircraft shot down exceeded the number being produced. The Germans arrived at the somewhat hasty conclusion that the number of aircraft in the Soviet Air Force was gradually shrinking. But the contrary was actually the case. The total production of fighters in 1942, for instance, numbered--quite apart from 2,200 imported Allied aircraft--9,300 planes as against about 4,600 German fighters produced during the same period. As to the number of frontline aircraft, the Russians had some 10,000 to 12,000 planes by the summer of 1943, so that they were practically independent of aircraft imported from the United States or Great Britain.

The Russian armament industry was generally capable of fulfilling the wartime requirements. Several armament plants in the Volga area, in the Urals, and in Siberia, which had hitherto remained unknown to the Germans, proved that the armament production capacity was far greater than they had assumed. Another surprise was that, despite having lost 60 percent of its iron and steel capacity by the end of 1941, the Russian armament industry was able to continue production without reduction because of the extensive quantities of iron and steel it had stockpiled. German leaders, however, hoped that the continuation of hostilities and the loss of the Caucasus area would lead to a breakdown of the Russian armament industry because of insuperable difficulties in the production of iron, steel, fuel, and food.

As part of the transportation network, the Russian railroads continued to fulfill their functions despite technical and mechanical difficulties. Whereas damage to tracks could usually be repaired within a few hours, air attacks on railroad stations and yards, especially when signal facilities had been hit, proved often of very lasting effect. The Vyazma railroad station, for instance, was out of order for 14 days after one such attack.

Civilian air traffic was fully geared to military requirements.[124] The Civil Air Fleet, which, at the beginning of hostilities, had already been subordinated to the Central Administration of Red Army Air Force Units, was more completely integrated into that organization. The mission of the Civil Air Fleet was essentially military, consisting mainly of courier and transport services. More and more of its groups were transformed into air regiments, redesignated, and integrated into air armies. Even though personnel replacements and supply were still the responsibility of the central administration of the Civil Air Fleet, all other matters, including ground organization, were taken care of by the military agencies. The completion of the Civil Air Fleet's integration into the Red Army Air Force, it was thought, would be achieved in a short time.

One author[125] succinctly summarizes the situation as follows:

> The German hopes of severing the enemy from his principal resources or of destroying his production facilities were buried at Stalingrad and along the edge of the Caucasus. Russia's aircraft production plants and armament industry operated almost without disturbance, well supported by Allied deliveries of raw materials and of other types of products.

Section XII: <u>Allied Assistance</u>

Even though German officers did not know the details of Allied assistance to the Russian Air Force, the effect of this assistance made itself felt at the front. They agree that Allied assistance became increasingly noticeable after the spring of 1942.[126] Most of the British and American aircraft were in action near Leningrad and at the Kuban Bridgehead. This could probably be explained by the fact that Leningrad was favorably situated near the termini of the northern entry routes which passed through Murmansk and Archangel, while the Kuban Bridgehead was easily accessible from the southern entry route that began at the Persian Gulf and passed through Baku. Along the Kuban Bridgehead, British and American aircraft models-- Airacobra-type fighters and Boston and Mitchell type bombers--were at times more numerous than Russian planes.

The northern routes, via Alaska to Eastern Russia or via Great Britain to Murmansk, carried the greater share of aircraft imports into the Soviet Union. Losses on the Murmansk route from submarines and air attacks on convoys were at times quite considerable.* The southern ferrying route led via Miami, Natal, Ascension, Cairo to Abadan on the Persian Gulf, where the Americans had built large installations. From there, shipments passed via Baku into southern Russia. Along this southern route, 1,702 aircraft were transported by ship, while 602 were transferred by air up to 1 September 1943. Of the total number of American aircraft delivered up to that date 20 percent were P-40's (Curtiss Tomahawk), 25 percent were P-39's (Bell Airacobra), 49 percent A-20's (Boston III), 5 percent B-25's (Mitchell), and 1 percent AT-6's.[127]

Because of the great number of British and American aircraft appearing in the Russian theater, Luftwaffe officers felt sure that the delivery of aircraft and flying equipment was probably the most important Allied assistance to the Soviet Union. It contributed very considerably to the growth of the Russian Air Force during 1942-43, even if the quota of aircraft required according to the Lend-Lease agreements was not fulfilled.

Section XIII: Conclusions

German officers' evaluation of the Russian Air Force in 1942-43 can be summarized as follows:

1) The recovery of the Russian Air Force--a process that had begun already in the autumn of 1941 after the devastating blows of the German offensive--continued, at first slowly then gaining momentum during the following years. Whereas in 1942 this development did not seriously affect the existing German air superiority, by the end of 1943 the situation had changed significantly. By then the Russians, benefiting from a considerable numerical superiority, were able to dominate the air space at certain times and in certain places under

---

* Editor's Note: The most successful German attack on an allied convoy in this region occurred in July 1942 against convoy P.Q. 17, which lost 23 of its 37 ships. See Denis Richards and Hilary St. G. Saunders, Royal Air Force, 1939-1945, Vol. II, The Fight Avails, Her Majesty's Stationery Office (London, 1954), p. 81.

certain conditions. The growth of Russian air power extended over all spheres, showing particular progress in command and staff procedures, technology, and the conduct of air operations; this was quite apart from the steadily increasing number of aircraft. Less progress was made in such fields as education and training or personnel, and in the evaluation of combat experience. As a result, the Luftwaffe--though numerically inferior--was still capable of holding its own in aerial combat at points of main effort and even of achieving temporary air superiority at specific intervals during 1943.

2) In 1942-43 Russian air operations continued to emphasize direct support of the ground forces. The growing intensity of Russian air attacks and their concentration at the decisive points of the ground battle, impressed the Germans and, in addition, gave the Russian ground forces moral and material support. The general trend characterizing Russian air operations was the gradual change from defensive operations--forced upon the Soviet Air Force in 1941--to offensive operations in all spheres.

3) The combat behavior of Russian flying crews continued to be determined by inherent Russian character traits. The increasing number of successes and the growing confidence in their new aircraft models strengthened their self-assurance and promoted their aggressiveness. The Soviet airman thus developed into an opponent who could no longer be disdained.

4) Reconnaissance aviation was employed essentially in support of the ground forces, becoming more and more effective in close and battlefield reconnaissance operations, whereas strategic reconnaissance was relatively retarded by comparison. Despite much progress since 1941, however, the over-all performance of reconnaissance aviation was still not satisfactory, mainly because of personnel deficiencies. Training of crews remained inadequate.

5) Fighter aviation dropped its fundamentally defensive attitude and switched everywhere to the offensive. In their operations against German fighters, reconnaissance aircraft, dive-bombers, bombers, and transport planes, the Russian fighter crews benefited from such factors as more modern types of aircraft, proper command and staff procedures, and growing experience in combat. These factors, in turn, improved the crews' performances and gave them more and more self-assurance, with the result that

they scored more successes. These developments, together with the great numerical superiority of Russian fighters, were the primary causes for the German loss of undisputed air superiority in 1943.

6) Ground-attack aviation, being the top-priority arm of the Soviet Air Force, was further developed and formed the principal attack weapon from the air during the execution of ground operations. Ground-attack aircraft were concentrated at the points of main effort and employed tactically in support of the ground forces, both for offensive and defensive purposes. Their ability to influence the course of the ground battle was gaining. But, while they scored successes, they did not achieve decisive results.

7) In 1942-43 bombers continued to play a role secondary to that of fighter and ground-attack aviation; this was exactly what Russian military leaders intended. Bombardment aviation was used almost exclusively for tactical purposes in support of the ground forces and frequently in conjunction with ground-attack aviation. While the conduct of day and night bombing attacks improved steadily, the effectiveness of these attacks was limited by the restrictions imposed on Soviet bombardment aviation.

8) Combined operations of fighter, ground-attack, and bomber aircraft and their joint operations with ground forces developed gradually, until they reached satisfactory and in some instances even remarkably high standards.

9) The use of aircraft for other flying operations, such as transport, courier, and liaison missions, was expanded on a large scale according to plan. The major successes scored by the partisan units in the extensive areas they dominated would not have been possible without large-scale assistance from the Soviet Air Force, particularly in airlifting supplies.

10) Air Force ground organization, technological development, and supply services, although steadily improving, remained relatively primitive by West European standards. They did satisfy the requirements of the Soviet Air Force, however.

11) Air Force signal communications, particularly in the field of radio communications, participated in the general progress of the Soviet Air Force. Nevertheless, the difference between Russian and German or Allied Air Force signal communications remained

considerable.

12) Although German military experts had no way of evaluating the Russian training system in its step-by-step procedures, they did not doubt that the over-all status of training had improved.

13) Paratroops and airborne forces continued as elite units, but they were primarily employed during critical situations in the ground fighting so that they were dissipated and decimated. No major parachute operations took place during the period under review.

14) Aircraft production, the armament industry, and the transportation network overcame the difficulties of the first year of German-Russian hostilities rather quickly and fulfilled their requirements, insofar as German military experts could judge.

15) Allied assistance, consisting of aircraft and flying equipment, increased steadily after the spring of 1942, and made itself felt on German forces in combat.

In summary, the Russian Air Force in 1942-43 can be characterized as follows: During this period it was almost exclusively employed as a tactical instrument of ground warfare and as such scored an increasing number of successes. It recovered progressively from the disastrous events of 1941, switched to the offensive in all spheres, and achieved equality in the air during 1943, primarily because of its great numerical superiority. It was only because of the wider combat experience and the better performances of the German crews that the Luftwaffe, despite its numerical inferiority, was still capable of holding the initiative at the operational points of main effort.

Chapter 4

THE RUSSIAN AIR FORCE ACHIEVES AIR SUPERIORITY

Section I: <u>The Course of the Air War in 1944-45</u>[1]

As in the previous years of the war, Russian air operations remained contingent upon the operations of the ground forces. Throughout the war the Soviet Command adhered to its basic point of view: that air power be employed primarily and almost exclusively to support the Army. Even during the last phase of the war the Soviets made only very occasional use of their air forces for quasi-strategic* missions. It might be added here that the same applied to German air power in the Eastern Theater, the only difference being that the scope of Soviet air operations was intentionally restricted, whereas that of the Luftwaffe was restricted, in the last two years of the campaign, by the exigencies of the situation. ⱡ

To understand Russia's use of her air force it is thus important to review the decisive battles on the ground during this last year and a half of the war. In chronological order, they were:

<u>1944</u>

January - March	Severe German defensive battles all along the line, particularly in zones of Army Groups South and North
April - May	German evacuation of the Crimea and Sevastopol
20 June	Opening of major Soviet offensive in Center; annihilation of German Army Group Center

---

* See note below, p. 348.

ⱡ Editor's Note: For an opposing opinion and a brief account of the Luftwaffe's attempts at strategic bombing in Russia see, Richard Suchenwirth, <u>Historical Turning Points in the German Air Force War Effort</u>, USAF Historical Studies: No. 189, USAF Historical Division (Maxwell AFB, 1959), pp. 76-90.

17 July	Opening of major Soviet offensive in the South; evacuation of Rumania, Bulgaria, and parts of Hungary by German troops
August	German defensive battles and delaying actions all along the line
September	Establishment of German main line of resistance in Poland at the San and Vistula Rivers
October	Soviet forces isolate the Baltic and open their drive into East Prussia
1945	
12 January	Soviet forces break through Vistula line and advance against Oder River
February	German defense of Oder River line
March	Soviet drive into Pomerania and Hungary; German loss of East Prussia
April - May	Soviets break through Oder line; capture of Berlin

Whereas the main emphasis in ground operations in 1942-43 was in the southern part of the Eastern Theater, calling for a corresponding shift of emphasis in air warfare to that part of the front, the picture changed in early 1944 and more pronouncedly so from the middle of the year on. In accordance with the day to day development of the tactical situation, main emphasis in ground operations from then on shifted back and forth from area to area, until, as Soviet superiority mounted, decisively important battles were in progress in various areas at the same time.

The Soviet air forces were required to adapt their activities to the requirements of these circumstances, and their mounting strength enabled them to do so. Thus, apart from a few exceptions, air warfare was almost exclusively restricted to those areas in which decisive ground operations were in progress, while elsewhere air activities came to an almost complete standstill.

The growth of Soviet air power in 1942-43, which had already led to a gradual balance of power in the air--as described in the previous chapter--, increased in the months which followed. The Soviets were favored here by the growing need for German air power in other theaters of operations. At the same time the operable strength of the Luftwaffe in front line units was decreasing because of diminishing aircraft production, the growing German shortage of fuel, and the concomitant rapidly mounting strength of the Soviet air forces.

According to Luftwaffe commanders,[2] by the end of 1943 the Soviets already had achieved a large numerical superiority in air power, and this superiority increased considerably up to the end of the war. Their almost unlimited resources in manpower, materiel, and fuel enabled the Soviets to isolate the areas of main effort from the air by large concentrations of bombers and ground-attack aircraft, with fighter escorts. While the Soviet air forces were becoming increasingly aggressive, the Luftwaffe, conversely, was forced onto the defensive: the picture had changed radically since 1941. Nevertheless, right up to the end of the war the Soviets failed to achieve absolute air superiority because the individual Soviet fighter pilot remained inferior to his German counterpart in air combat and was unable to prevent completely German bomber and dive-bomber units from executing their assigned missions. Still, the continuing decrease of German ground-to-air and air-to-air defensive power resulted in a considerable Soviet air superiority in the last phase of the war.

Luftwaffe commanders agree that up to the end of the war the primary mission of the Soviet air forces was that of supporting the ground forces. Concurrently with a step up in attacks against targets in the German near-front areas, went an increase--although only on an appreciable scale from the summer of 1944 on--in missions against traffic targets, supply installations, Luftwaffe ground installations, and similar objectives in the German rear. At no time did the Soviets engage in strategic air warfare of the type waged by the Western Allies.

The ceaseless commitment of heavily massed air power in the areas of main effort, to achieve which the Soviet Command practically stripped secondary tactical areas of air support, constituted extremely effective support for all operations on the ground and contributed heavily to the success achieved by the Soviets in their offensives. In this connection the Soviets made a steadily increasing use of fighters in fighter-bomber missions, a use which proved highly effective.

In actions in which the Soviet Command sought to force a major decision, it deliberately withheld its air power during the initial stages of the operation in order then to throw its strength into the battle in a sudden heavy concentration, always in closed formations. When the attack on the ground began to make good progress, air power was again withheld, to be committed later only when German resistance stiffened.

According to Luftwaffe commanders, from 1944 on the Soviets, in addition to the effort they spent on their fighter and ground-attack arms, began to pay more attention to the development of their bomber and reconnaissance arms. Through the commitment of an overwhelming numerical superiority of highly developed types of aircraft, the Soviets in 1944 achieved equality in the air with their German opponent. In the last phase of the war they even sometimes achieved a slight technical superiority, but were unable to take advantage of this because of personnel inadequacies.

Finally, commanders state that in the last phases of the war the training and fighting qualities of flying personnel remained the weak points in Soviet air power. Although training standards, morale, and aggressiveness of aircraft crews improved with the change-over to offensive warfare, they failed to keep pace with the increasing numerical strength and modernization of the Soviet air force's equipment. Thus, Soviet airmen up to the end of the war frequently displayed a reluctance, which occasionally assumed critical proportions, when they encountered German defenses of any considerable strength.

The above consolidated opinions of Luftwaffe officers are supplemented and confirmed by excerpts from descriptive accounts by two Luftwaffe commanders. Captain von Reschke describes the behavior of Soviet air forces in the northern area from early 1944 to the end of the war approximately as follows:[3]

The quality of Soviet air forces' materiel in the spring and summer of 1944 almost equalled that of their German opponents.

In numbers, the Russians had such a pronounced superiority that they could afford to develop clearly defined power concentrations. Nonetheless, German air units were still able to execute their missions successfully.

In the summer and autumn of 1944 the heavily massed Soviet fighter-interceptors in Courland* and East Prussia seriously hampered German air activities and inflicted heavy losses on the German air forces besides enabling the Soviets to secure periodical air superiority over the general battle areas.

After the close of the Soviet autumn offensive the air situation returned to normal and remained unchanged up to the opening of the Soviet drive into East Prussia which, in January 1945, ushered in a period of major battle that lasted right up to the end of the war. Soviet air activities increased steadily, with massed units committed to isolate the individual zones of attack. At the same time ceaseless attacks were flown against the German troops on the line and in the near front areas, while the German ground organization was kept under such close and constant observation by day and night that German air operations were hampered seriously and, by the spring of 1945, the Soviets succeeded in achieving air superiority in East Prussia.

Reschke's opinion is that the Soviets' success was due to their steady increase in strength, plus the exemplary cooperation existing between the various arms of their air forces, their able development of areas of main effort, their illimitable replacements in materiel and personnel, their technological progress, Allied deliveries, and the steadily declining German defense capabilities. Superior German training and other advantages of German flying personnel, according to Reschke, were no longer important factors. He comes to the conclusion that, although committed exclusively in support of the ground forces and not in strategic missions, the Soviets, through their steadily mounting air superiority, achieved cumulative results

---

* Editor's Note: This is the historic name for the southwestern portion of Latvia. Courland was bordered on the west by the Baltic Sea and to the north and east by the Western Dvina River. German Army Group Courland held a bridgehead with an area of about 900 square miles in the western part of Courland until the end of the War.

equalling those of their western allies.

Major H. J. Jaehne, whose return to the Eastern Theater in January 1945--after a lengthy assignment in the Western Theater--afforded him a particularly good opportunity to draw comparisons between the Soviet and the western air forces, reaches similar conclusions.[4] He states that in this period the Soviets were achieving air superiority in East Prussia but that there was a vast difference between air superiority in the East and air superiority as it existed in the West. For example, in the Western Theater supply routes were practically impassable for supply columns during daylight, whereas in East Prussia supply traffic proceeded almost undisturbed in the rear areas. In the West, German fighters as a rule found themselves engaged in combat almost as soon as they left the ground and consequently were unable to execute their assigned missions; in the East they generally still found it possible to execute their missions, although within limited areas and subject to limitations in time. Air units of the Western Allies were in evidence at all times of the day, in all combat areas and over Germany; the Soviets endeavored only to achieve and maintain air superiority at and near the front and to destroy the German front line Army units.

In spite of growing combat strengths, improved training standards and combat morale of personnel, increased output and better technical performances of aircraft, and refined tactics, Soviet airmen were still a bit cautious in combat. This was due primarily to the effective action of German fighters and German antiaircraft artillery. Even during the battles around Berlin and in Mecklenburg in April 1945, the Soviet air forces restricted their operations to the front areas, but it must be admitted that in doing so they achieved the desired result--that of effectively supporting all operations of the Army.

In spite of their enormous numerical superiority, concludes Jaehne, the Soviets did not succeed in achieving absolute air supremacy until the last German aircraft had disappeared from the skies.

Jaehne's picture of the operations and effectiveness of the Soviet air forces is rounded out by field commanders of the German Army with similar experience.[5] According to their reports, strength ratios in air power were more in favor of the Soviets in 1944, and particularly so in 1945, than they had been in 1943. With each successive major offensive, Soviet air attacks increased in frequency and size and the concentration of air power in areas of main effort became more pronounced. Air power was massed in the areas where the command on the ground sought to force a decision. In Cherkassy,* for example, Soviet fighters were superior in strength and destroyed numerous German transport planes, while Soviet bombers seriously depleted the two enveloped German corps. Also, during the bitter battles fought for Sevastopol in the spring of 1944 Soviet air support was impressive. Another example was the large offensive against Army Group Center. Four Soviet armies attacked the German lines in succession, one each day from 20 to 23 June 1944. These attacks on the ground were supported by masses of air units, which operated with particularly effective results against the German artillery. Against this crushing superiority the German Sixth Air Fleet had only 40 operable fighters. Yet even prior to their 1945 offensive the Soviets had had a large enough numerical superiority to maintain air supremacy.

In quiet sectors of the front the Soviet air forces remained remarkably inactive, as was the case during the last German offensive in Hungary in February 1945, where Soviet resistance in the air was practically non-existent. This was in sharp contrast with focal points of combat, where, during the spring of 1945, the Soviets launched almost ceaseless day and night air attacks. By this time, the Soviets, in the areas of main effort, had begun committing larger numbers of fighter-bombers with which they frequently brought all traffic to a complete standstill to a depth of up to 12 miles in the German rear.

In spite of this change in the air situation in favor of the Soviets, field commanders of the German Army agree unanimously that air warfare in the West produced far more telling effects on the German troops. As one source puts it: ". . . Soviet air attacks were mere pinpricks compared with those by the Anglo-Americans . . . ."[6]

---

* Editor's Note: Towards the end of January 1944 the 11th and 42d Corps of the German 8th Army were surrounded in the Cherkassy, Korsun'-Shevchenkovskiy area, north of the Dnieper River bend. Air supply of the beseiged corps was attempted, but had to be given up when they lost control of the last airfield in the pocket. Most of the two corps (about 30,000 men), minus their artillery and tanks, were able to break out during the night of 16-17 February. Cherkassy, according to von Tippelskirch and von Manstein, was another example of Hitler's ill-conceived and stubborn ground-holding tactics in the Russian campaign.

On the whole, the losses inflicted by Soviet air attacks remained within tolerable limits and the German troops were able to carry out their movements even during daylight without appreciable interference and at only a small cost in losses. Although the defending German fighters were weak in numbers, wherever they did put in an appearance they proved superior and swept the skies clear of Soviet air forces. The Luftwaffe not only held its own against the numerically far superior Soviet air forces, but was even able at this late stage to deal powerful blows. The opportunities for such action, however, became steadily rarer, both in respect to limits of time and space.

The above findings of the German ground forces apply primarily to 1944, but also can be applied conditionally to 1945.

Air operations in support of the Soviet Navy also increased in scope and importance in the last two years of the war, but on a scale not even approaching the operations in support of the Soviet Army. In spite of their great superiority in numbers and materiel, the results achieved by Soviet air forces in naval support operations were very modest.

German naval commanders[7] consulted agree that Soviet air activities at sea intensified gradually, and that a certain degree of systematic planning for operations, together with the proper tactical cooperation between the Soviet air forces and the Soviet Navy, became evident. These latter features, however, were not achieved until the final phase of the war, at a time when German seaborne transportation in the Baltic, in the Black Sea, and at the German ports of embarkation and debarkation, were exposed--practically without defenses--to repeated heavy Soviet air attacks. Until then Soviet air activities at sea remained restricted primarily to reconnaissance, escort missions for Soviet seaborne transports, and occasional attacks against German seaborne transports, without any signs of organized integration between the Soviet air and naval units involved.

The 1944 operations against the Crimea were an exception. Here, the tactically well integrated action of the Soviet air forces contributed largely to the success achieved by the Soviet Army and Navy in their amphibious operations. The Soviet naval air arm, which considered itself an elite force, generally proved to be quite aggressive during these operations. This applied particularly to the naval bomber and torpedo-bomber units, which gave a good account of themselves, even in critical situations.

The Soviets, in 1944-45, continued to develop their antiaircraft artillery arm, with most of their heavy equipment patterned on foreign models. Although they at no time achieved the standards of performance of the German fire control equipment, the Soviet antiaircraft artillery forces as a whole were not to be underestimated as an opponent. The characteristic features of Soviet antiaircraft artillery operations were: 1) massed concentration close to the target defended; 2) action in defense of the concentration of ground and air forces prior to offensive operations; 3) action in defense of the foremost infantry and tank units spearheading an attack both during the initial attack and during the breakthrough operations; and 4) speedy and frequent displacement of units, particularly in areas near the front.

In their operations, as characterized above, Soviet antiaircraft artillery forces often placed Luftwaffe units in difficult situations and in some areas inflicted losses which were by no means inconsiderable. Towards the end of the war, however, the effectiveness of antiaircraft artillery defenses was less important when compared with the effectiveness of the Soviet defensive fighter forces.[8]

Section II: Command and Operations

In the last two years of the war the command and operations of the Soviet air forces continued to improve. German field commanders assess them broadly as follows:[9]

1) The Soviet Command continued to adhere to the doctrine of planned cooperation of the air forces with the Army. Air operations, including those of bomber forces, were governed by the principle that air power should be used exclusively to support the Army.

2) In line with the basic principle stated above, the Soviets committed their air power in accordance with the requirements of operations by the ground forces, and thus principally in tactically defined missions in the front areas, with a decided emphasis on the principle of power concentration. Measures to increase long-range

reconnaissance and fighter patrol activities, action against traffic and supply targets in the German rear, and offensive operations against German shipping and airfields, all served the same purpose: direct support of the Army.

3) The orders of higher command echelons improved in clarity and decisivensss, but they lacked flexibility. Commands at lower levels gave evidence, up to the end, of lacking the requisite versatility and the ability to take quick and independent action consonant with the requirements of current situations. These defects may have been largely due to the generally accepted military formalism, and to the intellectual level of the troops and their officers, which, at best, can only be described as average.

4) The offensive action taken by the Soviets in the battle for air supremacy differed widely from that taken in the West. It was in consonance with the basic Soviet doctrine of employing air power in the near front areas that the Soviet Command rejected the idea of operating against the German air armament industry or against the German ground service organization. Instead, the Soviet Command committed its fighters against the German front-line air forces and its ground-attack and bomber units against the German Army. For these reasons the battle for air supremacy in the Eastern Theater was restricted primarily to the front areas.

Section III: <u>Organization and Chains of Command</u>

No important changes have become known regarding the organization and chain of command of Soviet air forces during the last two years of the war.[10] The Soviet Command continued to adhere to the system it had found suitable in the past. This meant that the air forces remained under the Army and the Navy, and that the Air Arm of the Red Army remained organized in air armies, corps, divisions, regiments, and squadrons. The same organization was retained for the air forces assigned to the Navy.

In 1945 it was estimated that the Soviets had 10 to 13 air armies, approximately 30 air corps, 130 to 150 air divisions, and roughly 650 air regiments.

Based primarily on smooth and close cooperation between the Army--or the Navy--and its assigned air forces, the flexible command system, instead of rigid command controls, remained in force in 1944-45 and apparently was found suitable up to the end of the war.

The only major change planned was a reorganization of the air regiments. Still under question was whether the air regiments, with an authorized strength of forty aircraft each, should continue to be organized into three squadrons, each containing twelve aircraft, plus a headquarters flight of four aircraft, or be organized into four squadrons. It appears, however, that no final decision was reached on this point by the end of the war.

Available information on the organization and chains of command of the Soviet air forces, as they existed in 1944-45, is relatively sparse. In general, the description given in Chapter 3 can be considered equally valid for the last year of the war. No reports which would contradict this assumption have been received.

Section IV: <u>Strength and Distribution</u>

Little information is available on the strength of the Soviet air forces in 1944 and 1945. That which we have indicates that the numerical strength continued to gain.[11] Different estimates indicate that the Soviets had approximately 13,000 aircraft committed in the field at the beginning of 1944 and an average of about 20,000 at any given time from autumn 1944 to the end of the war. In April of 1945 the Luftwaffe High Command gives a total figure of 17,000 Soviet aircraft in the field, broken down as follows: 8,000 fighters, 3,900 ground-attack aircraft, 5,000 bombers, and 800 transport and other types. The overall number of combat aircraft in the Soviet Union was estimated at 39,700; thus, a very large combat reserve was apparently available.

The same source indicates Soviet aircraft losses of 2,700 per month during the last few months of the war, of which 1,500 were lost at the front and 1,200 in the Zone of Interior. New deliveries were estimated at 3,700 aircraft per month, meaning a monthly increase in aircraft strength of 1,000.

Strength ratios at the front developed steadily in favor of the Soviets. For example, in the northern area in February 1944 the ratio of Soviet aircraft to German aircraft was still only approximately 5 or 6 to 1; by summer it increased, in areas of main effort, to 10 to 1 and even more. By February of 1945 the ratio was estimated at 50 to 1 in favor of the Soviets!

Few reports are available concerning the distribution of Soviet air power, which was just as difficult for German field commanders to estimate as were Soviet strengths. Those reports we do have agree that the disposition of air power reflected the areas of main effort in ground operations.[12] Prior to each major Soviet offensive all Soviet airfields near the front became crowded with aircraft. By this time, however, the Luftwaffe was too weak to launch heavy attacks against the crowded fields.

Soviet air units always displaced in accordance with the main direction of the attack on the ground. Nevertheless, the air units usually had difficulty keeping up with the army's advance, as was the case during the Soviet summer offensive of 1944 against German Army Group Center.

At the end of September 1944 the movement of strong air forces to the Bulgarian area, the westward transfer of units committed against Hungary, and the arrival of new units to reinforce the already heavy concentration of air power north of the Beskid Mountains served to indicate an imminent Soviet offensive directed at the southeastern area. In a similar manner the concentration of Soviet air forces in any area could always be taken as an unmistakable indication of what was to come. The last Soviet concentration of air power, at the end of April 1945 (involving the Fourth Air Army, with 1,600 aircraft in Pomerania, the Sixteenth Air Army, with 2,600 aircraft in the Mark /Brandenburg/ area and in Western Prussia, the Second Air Army, with 2,100 aircraft in Silesia, and another air army presumably transferred from Eastern Prussia to Upper Silesia) was an immediate prelude to the all-out offensive across the Oder River directed at Berlin.

Section V: <u>Aircraft Types, Weapons, Other Equipment</u>

German field commanders and other authorities[13] are of the opinion that the Soviets, in 1944-45, continued the further development of tested aircraft models, their weapons, ammunition, and other items of technical equipment. The types used included the Lagg and Yak fighters, the IL-2 ground-attack plane, and the DB-3, DB-3F, PE-2, and B-25 bomber and reconnaissance planes.

In line with Soviet air power doctrines, main emphasis was on the development of fighter aircraft, and in this field the latest La-9* and Yak-9 fighters in evidence at the front were not only high-performance aircraft but in some respects superior to the German Focke-Wulf and Messerschmitt fighters.

Over-all technological developments, particularly in the construction of aircraft, provided evidence of the importance the Soviet Command attached to tactical air power and also revealed that in 1945 Soviet planning still put main emphasis on the development and production of tactical types. There was no evidence of any intention to increase appreciably the strategic air arm.

The Soviet Command held its latest aircraft models in reserve, making only small use of them at the front, until the old types committed were depleted or until they could commit the new types simultaneously in large numbers. Because of this method, eventually only new types were in action at the front.

By the end of 1942 the output of the Soviet aircraft industry exceeded losses at the front and in the Zone of Interior. The steadily increasing number of aircraft available and their continued improvement, as compared with the models used by the Germans, were indisputable ingredients of the mounting Soviet air superiority.

The development of the Soviet air forces from early 1944 to the end of the war can be summarized broadly as follows:

1) Retaining their existing organization, chains of command, and command and tactical principles, the Soviet air forces were committed almost exclusively in support of the Army in pronounced concentration in the areas of main effort on the ground and thereby contributed largely to the Soviet successes and the German defeat. Heavy and effective air attacks against the immediate rear of the German front lines increased from mid-1944 on. The scope of air operations in support of the Soviet Navy increased considerably towards the end of the war, but remained relatively insignificant in the overall

---

* Editor's Note: The La-9 was a further development of the La-5 and La-7 series. A single-engine, low-wing monoplane, it was introduced very late in the war.

picture.

2) The air situation changed slowly but continuously in favor of the Soviets. The steady improvement in the numerical strength and performance of the Soviet air forces, together with the steady decline of German air power, resulted in a crushing Soviet air superiority. Although this was already noticeable in 1944, by 1945 it became the dominant feature of the air war in Russia.

3) The now-decisive factors which enabled the Soviets to achieve air superiority had been present in previous years. They were:

a) The modernization and accelerated expansion of the Soviet air forces.

b) The increased and undisturbed production of aircraft, and the consequent rapid increase in the numbers of aircraft in the field.

c) The aggressive, ruthless, and unremitting commitment of air units in massed operations--in which they possessed a crushing numerical superiority--to support the Army in consonance with logically developed principles of command.

d) The improved combat experience, mounting confidence, and growing aggressiveness of flight personnel. Weaknesses still remained noticeable, however, in respect to training, tactics, and the capabilities of the personnel.

e) The decrease in properly planned German counter-air action due to the rapid decline in German operable strengths and general German shortages in manpower and fuel.

4) Contrary to Anglo-American air superiority in the West, Soviet air superiority in the East was due solely to numbers and therefore was restricted in time and area. In the execution of their missions German fighters, reconnaissance units, bombers and dive-bombers were, right up to the end of the war, able to maintain their own. This was due primarily to the abilities and better performances of German crews. Owing to the small operable strength of German air units, however, the opportunities to contest local Soviet air

superiority became increasingly rare.

A German field commander[14] ably describes the situation as it existed towards the end of the war, with the remark that German airmen had the knowledge that they were inferior but had no feeling of inferiority.

5) Even in 1944-45 the Soviets made practically no strategic use of their air power.

6) The Soviet antiaircraft artillery remained a source of grave concern to German air forces. Towards the end of the war, however, the results achieved by Soviet antiaircraft artillery forces were relatively small in comparison with the results obtained by their air forces.

Section VI: <u>The Reconnaissance Arm</u>[15]

The importance attached by the Soviet Command to air reconnaissance in 1943 continued to increase in 1944-45. This became particularly evident when combat shifted to non-Russian territory and a substitute had to be found for the declining intelligence activities of partisans and agents.

On the basis of sources presently available, Soviet air reconnaissance can be assessed in broad outline as follows:[16]

Once the Soviet Command had realized the importance of systematically conducted air reconnaissance, they not only directed such operations in accordance with proper planning, but also took appropriate measures to build up their air reconnaissance arm. It was quite evident that, with some modifications, they had adopted the German patterns of reconnaissance. This was true, for example, in operational principles and in the organization of the reconnaissance forces into strategic and tactical air reconnaissance regiments. Thus, the strategic regiments were in some respects similar to the German strategic reconnaissance groups and the tactical regiments to the German tactical reconnaissance groups. A point in which the Soviet system differed from the German, however, was that the Soviets made liberal use of fighter and ground-attack air regiments for tactical and battle reconnaissance. This may have been the outcome of the Soviet principle that every plane over the battlefield had a reconnaissance function in addition to its combat function.

Just as was the case in the overall conduct of air operations, the Soviets employed their air reconnaissance forces in concentration in support of the Army, and thus in the areas of main effort in ground operations. Whereas reconnaissance units in general remained relatively inactive, reconnaissance activities increased suddenly just prior to each major offensive. These took the form of thorough tactical and battle reconnaissance missions, with a gradual increase in the effort spent on large area reconnaissance against road, rail and airfield targets. Reconnaissance activities continued during the actual offensive and lessened only when the situation became relatively quiet in the sector involved. During the last months of the war, when large area reconnaissance continued, inferences usually could be drawn as to the direction of future Soviet attacks. The fact that Soviet air reconnaissance produced no exceptionally noticeable results for the German Army or Luftwaffe cannot be considered as proof that it was inadequate or unsuitably conducted. It can be assumed, nevertheless, that a very systematic program of air photo and target reconnaissance and of air artillery fire directing would have produced more noticeable effects.

It was difficult to obtain a clear picture of Soviet reconnaissance activities because of the lack of German superiority in fighters in the front areas and the impossibility of intercepting Soviet reconnaissance planes in the German rear owing to fuel shortages. One can, perhaps, assume that Soviet reconnaissance planes towards the end of the war found conditions in the German rear approximating those conditions which German reconnaissance units had found in the Soviet rear at the beginning of the campaign, so that the Soviet Command had a general knowledge of the measures taken by the Germans on land and at sea.

In the meanwhile, Soviet reconnaissance airmen had improved considerably in training, although they at no time achieved the high performances of German units in actual reconnaissance operations and frequently failed in air combat because of their poor gunnery.[17] The ratio of newly trained to seasoned reconnaissance aircraft crews was approximately 1 to 1. Late in the war the replacements arriving at the front were adequately trained and were employed systematically in progressively difficult missions. The practice of giving air reconnaissance personnel preferential treatment in the form of better pay, better rations, more leave and more decorations was maintained.

A. Organization, Chains of Command, Strengths

According to sources available at writing,[18] the organization, chains of command, and strengths of the Soviet air reconnaissance forces in former years remained in force with only relatively unimportant changes.

The highest command authority within the reconnaissance forces was the Commander of Reconnaissance of the Soviet Army within the Central Administration of the Air Forces of the Soviet Army. He was also Chief, Reconnaissance Division, Main Administration of the Air Forces of the Soviet Army. This meant also that he was Chief Intelligence Officer, in which position he was able to exert an important influence on the employment of the air reconnaissance forces, something which his counterpart in the Luftwaffe was unable to do.

The organization into separate long-range and tactical regiments was retained, with composite air regiments becoming less frequent. Only long-range air reconnaissance regiments of the Central Administration of the Air Forces of the Soviet Army were employed in missions extending farther into the operational field. The original intention had been to employ one such long-range air reconnaissance regiment in the zone of each air army, but up to the end of the war one of these regiments had to cover the zone of each two air armies. This probably was due, at least in part, to two factors: 1) adequate intelligence coverage was secured from the widely ramified network of agents in Soviet territories and from partisan activities; 2) the Soviet methods of air warfare did not require strategic target data.

The organization of long-range air reconnaissance regiments was not based on a uniform wartime table of organization. As a rule these regiments contained three squadrons each, a squadron consisting of two flights of three planes and one flight of four planes. In addition, the regiment usually had two U-2 liaison planes. Some regiments, however, had an entirely different organization. Thus, it was known that the 47th Guards Long-Range Air Reconnaissance

Regiment, acknowledged as the best reconnaissance unit of the Air Forces of the Soviet Army, was organized as follows:

	Aircraft Types	Missions
1st Squadron	PE-2	Intermediate-range reconnaissance up to 210 miles.
2d Squadron	IL-4*	Night reconnaissance up to a range of 450 miles.
3d Squadron	PE-3 & TU-2	Long-range reconnaissance.
4th Squadron	PE-2	Reserve and training squadron.
5th Squadron	Li-2⁄	Transportation and partisan supply missions.
6th Squadron	unknown	unknown

Some long-range air reconnaissance regiments were also identified organized into five squadrons (for example: two PE-2, two Boston III, and one Yak-9 squadrons) and others into four squadrons.

A long-range air reconnaissance regiment of three squadrons had a personnel strength of approximately 300 men, of whom 100 were flight personnel. Each squadron had ten 3-man crews. With the exception of radio-operator gunners all flight personnel were commissioned officers. The regiment had 110 technical, 35 weapons, 25 photographic, and 30 general purpose personnel. Actual strengths in 1944 as a rule were approximately 20 percent below authorized strengths, but in this respect a gradual improvement was noticeable.

---

* Editor's Note: This was an improved version of the DB-3F. See note above, p. 189.

⁄ Editor's Note: This was an armed version of the PS-84 (DC-3).

The Russian Mig-3,
one-place fighter

A Soviet Li-2 transport

When not committed in missions directly assigned by the High Command of the Air Forces of the Soviet Army, long-range air reconnaissance regiments were assigned tactically and administratively to the air armies and were employed in tactical reconnaissance missions within the scope of the appropriate air army in precisely the same manner as the tactical air reconnaissance regiments. Each air army had one long-range or one tactical air reconnaissance regiment; when committed in an area of main effort it sometimes had two or more reconnaissance regiments.

Like the long-range air reconnaissance regiments, the tactical air reconnaissance regiments normally assigned to air armies had, as a rule, three squadrons. Of these, however, two were usually PE-2 squadrons and one had either fighter or ground-attack aircraft. In aircraft strength the tactical air reconnaissance regiment approximated the long-range air reconnaissance regiment of three squadrons, as described above.

In May 1944 German intelligence had identified 21 Soviet air reconnaissance regiments, 9 of which were long-range, and 12 of which were tactical. In September the total number identified was 31--10 long-range, 18 tactical, and 3 naval air reconnaissance regiments. On the whole, this strength remained unchanged up to the end of the war.

B. Soviet Air Reconnaissance Operations

Luftwaffe field commanders and other sources[19] are in agreement that even in the last years of the war the Soviets restricted their efforts primarily to tactical air reconnaissance or, strictly speaking, to tactical and battle field reconnaissance, and that in this area they operated very much in accordance with German principles. The aircraft most often used for long-range and at times also for close-range tactical reconnaissance remained the PE-2 model, whereas battle reconnaissance in the stricter sense was still performed by the IL-2 ground-attack units, as had been the case in the first part of the campaign, and in a growing measure by fighter aircraft, primarily of the Yak-9 model. Owing to the relatively weak German defenses, these aircraft were quite capable of executing their missions.

No important new features were observed in the tactical

execution of reconnaissance missions by the Soviets, except that the number of such missions, during both the day and night, was steadily increasing. Efforts were directed primarily at obtaining information on the following points, all relating to targets within the main battle areas: the location of the forward German lines; German strongpoints, pockets of resistance, mortar and artillery firing positions, and antitank defense lines; supply movements; rail and road movements close behind the German main line of resistance to ascertain the nature, direction, and volume of such movements; motor vehicle and armored concentrations; settlements occupied by German troops; airfields, supply depots, defense installations, river crossing points, and the location of higher level headquarters staffs. Main emphasis was on overall reconnaissance of the assigned combat area, with less stress on the detection of individual targets. Air photos were always taken of airfields and rail depots and settlements; panorama photos of rail routes or roads were made only rarely. With very few exceptions the maximum depth to which long-range reconnaissance penetrated behind the German lines was approximately 180 miles; the average depth, which was maintained with remarkable regularity, was 120 miles. In tactical and battlefield reconnaissance the maximum depth was around 36 miles, the average around 24 miles.

In carrying out their reconnaissance missions, Soviet airmen adhered to the same principle as their German opponents: they avoided air combat if at all possible. Right up to the end of the war Soviet air reconnaissance units showed a marked respect for German fighters; on encountering German aircraft they almost invariably endeavored to escape by nosing down, if at all possible eastwards. The Soviet reconnaissance forces developed no specific tactics for defense against German fighters. Seasoned crews had their own methods of combat, developed from their personal experience. The normal procedure for Soviet reconnaissance airmen under attack was to open fire with their machine guns at a range of approximately 550-660 yards, with their rockets--directed to the rear--at ranges between 660 and 1,300 yards; occasionally they would drop parachute fragmentation bombs against an attacker coming from below and rear.

In the last phases of the war it was a great advantage for Soviet reconnaissance units that German fighters no longer could be committed against single planes operating at high altitudes, because of the shortage of ammunition and fuel on the German side.

In reconnaissance over targets strongly defended by antiaircraft artillery, Soviet reconnaissance aircraft usually made their approach run at the highest possible altitude from the direction of the sun, gliding in with engines throttled down. The moment German antiaircraft guns opened fire the Russians would nose down and, after flying over the reconnaissance target, would then regain altitude at top speed. While over the target area the planes never changed their course. If they encountered unexpected but poorly aimed defense fire, they usually carried out no evasive maneuvers, although sometimes they immediately changed their direction, altitude, and speed.

At the highest command level, missions were assigned in the form of reconnaissance programs established by the Operational Staff of the Air Forces of the Soviet Army. These programs were issued at irregular intervals as a broad general directive to the air armies, which were allowed a lot of latitude in carrying them out.

Based on these directives and on the requests from the appropriate army group headquarters, the intelligence officer of the air army concerned assigned the daily reconnaissance missions to the subordinate air reconnaissance regiments. It should be noted here that as a rule the army group addressed its desires and requests to the air army, and only in very rare cases directly to an air reconnaissance regiment.

The mission assignment allowed the regimental commander wide scope for personal initiative in its execution. In areas where the front was stable, missions were assigned in very broad outline. During an attack, in contrast, or in other cases when the front was fluid, reconnaissance missions were assigned in great detail, mentioning each individual target to be covered.

After receiving his mission assignment the regimental intelligence officer, or the regimental commander, prepared the detailed orders accordingly and assigned missions to his individual squadrons, and only in special circumstances directly to the individual aircraft crews. The officer preparing the detailed orders was required to consult the regimental weather reporting unit, most of which are said, by prisoners of war, to have performed unsatisfactory work. For this reason more reliance was placed on the weather reports turned in by returning aircraft crews.

As a rule the squadron leader oriented his individual crews on the basis of maps with a scale of 1 : 200,000, in which all details known concerning the enemy were marked, including the positions of antiaircraft batteries or single guns. General discussions between participating crews were the exception rather than the rule, and by German standards preparations for the mission were frequently somewhat superficial. The individual crews usually were allowed to select their own operating altitudes and their routes.

To facilitate the transmittal of information and contact in general, the air reconnaissance regiment always had its headquarters in the vicinity of the headquarters of the air army, while the squadrons were based on various airfields distributed along the line.

In the reporting system radio played a significant role, with a constant flow of messages taking place between reconnaissance planes and the regimental radio station. As a rule, reconnaissance planes were not allowed to operate unless radio contact existed. Air-to-air radio communication was also maintained with escorting fighter aircraft. Long-range reconnaissance was controlled by wireless telegraphy, tactical reconnaissance by voice radio. Air army, army group, and frequently army and tank force headquarters were tuned in to receive messages on the main channel used by the reconnaissance units.

In the last phase of the war radio messages were transmitted in the clear with increasing frequency, but weather reports and special messages on technical matters were always sent in special codes.

During their approach flight reconnaissance planes always reported when they were crossing over the front lines; while over enemy territory they transmitted only particularly important messages; and as soon as they were over friendly territory on their return trip they turned in a summarized report of their findings. Each reconnaissance pilot reported orally and in writing to the appropriate command post after his return from a mission.

The regimental photographic section was responsible for

the development and initial interpretation of aerial photos; the detailed interpretation and all major work was handled in the photographic staff section at air army headquarters.

The Soviets continued to attach great importance to air photo reconnaissance, but obtained by this means intelligence which was far less precise than that obtained by the German air photo reconnaissance units.

The regimental intelligence officer reported in writing to air army headquarters on the day's reconnaissance operations and the results obtained, thus rounding out the day's reconnaissance findings.

1) <u>Long-Range Reconnaissance</u>. The few reports available on Soviet long-range reconnaissance activities reveal that operations of this type increased during the last years of the campaign, but that the methods employed remained unchanged.[20] As previously mentioned, long-range reconnaissance was an exclusive responsibility of the strategic reconnaissance regiments--controlled directly by the High Command of the Air Forces of the Soviet Army--which were distributed along the entire line and committed within the zones of the individual air armies.

The Soviet Air Command, in their references to long-range reconnaissance, differentiated between what they called strategic reconnaissance and what they called operational reconnaissance. Strategic reconnaissance was carried out exclusively by the long-range air reconnaissance regiments of the High Command of the Air Forces of the Soviet Army. Their aircraft penetrated beyond 240 miles into enemy territory. In daylight types PE-3 and Tu-2 planes were used, at night types B-25 and IL-4. By way of contrast, the reconnaissance regiments attached to air armies were to furnish the main forces for operational reconnaissance, up to 240 miles, which was to be carried out by PE-2 planes. In practice, however, air armies paid hardly any attention to long-range reconnaissance, restricting their efforts primarily to tactical and battlefield reconnaissance.

In the last years of the war the main target categories assigned to long-range reconnaissance units remained the same as they had been before. As a rule these missions were flown without fighter escorts. The intensity and regularity of Soviet long-range reconnaissance increased steadily as the fronts moved westward and farther away from Soviet-Russian territory. This tendency became increasingly evident from August 1944 on and at the end of 1944 and early 1945 took the form of a close-meshed, wide-area air patrol activity which was repeated frequently and concentrated chiefly against rail and road routes, and airfields in the Government General* and the Courland areas, East Prussia and West Prussia,† the area adjoining the Warta River, Upper and Lower Silesia, and finally westward across the Oder River.

In some cases these reconnaissance operations were carried out with a regularity and obstinacy by no means suited to the purpose. For example, in April 1944 a Soviet PE-2 reconnaissance plane--jokingly called the reconnaissance duty officer because of its regularity--put in an appearance every morning without fail between 0700 and 0800 hours over Duenaburg, †† at the time about 150 miles behind the German main line of resistance; invariably it approached from the German rear at an altitude between 13,000 and 16,000 feet and departed in the direction of the front lines; its reconnaissance targets unmistakably were the Dvina River crossing points, rail traffic, and German airfields. No successes by German antiaircraft artillery are recorded against long-range reconnaissance aircraft of this type.

---

* Editor's Note: The central section of Poland which remained after German and Russian annexations of Polish territory in World War II. The Government General was occupied and administered by Germany.

† Editor's Note: Prior to World War I West Prussia was a Province of Prussia located roughly between Pomerania and East Prussia. The Treaty of Versailles ceded most of this territory to Poland and it then became the Polish Corridor. In 1939 it was annexed to Germany and now it is again a part of Poland. West Prussia, together with East Prussia, which after the War was divided between Poland and Russia, constitute what Germans today refer to as East Germany. What is popularly called East Germany in America is, by contrast, termed Middle Germany by Germans.

†† Editor's Note: Duenaburg is located in Southeast Latvia on the Western Dvina River. In Latvian it is called Daugavpils, in Russian, Dvinsk.

To what extent Soviet long-range reconnaissance units showed any real improvement in the execution of their missions is a subject German field commanders were unable to judge. From the measures taken by the Soviet Command in the last two years of the campaign it is safe to assume, however, that the command on the whole received a relatively accurate report on conditions in the German rear from its long-range reconnaissance forces.

2) <u>Short-Range Reconnaissance.</u> All sources available at writing[21] agree that in the last years of the campaign Soviet short-range air reconnaissance activities were more intense than before, that stronger and better qualified forces were employed for the purpose, and that on the whole the results obtained substantially aided the Soviet Army.

The categories of target reconnaissance remained practically unchanged. A difference was noticeable, however, in the priority of the various categories, which changed according to the current tactical situation.

Also noticed was the increasing use made of normal reconnaissance planes for general tactical reconnaissance and of fighter and ground-attack planes for specific battlefield reconnaissance. Nevertheless, this was only the general rule, as these two types of missions frequently overlapped. Thus, fighter and ground-attack planes sometimes engaged in general tactical reconnaissance, particularly in unfavorable weather and when the cloud ceiling was low. As a rule, however, the division of missions was noticeable.

Normal reconnaissance planes were employed primarily on air photo reconnaissance missions while fighter and ground-attack planes had to rely largely on visual observation.

The plane most frequently used in daylight tactical reconnaissance was the PE-2, with Boston III planes used in individual plane reconnaissance missions. The first plane took off in the early morning and had the added mission of carrying out weather reconnaissance. Other planes followed at intervals throughout the day, with main emphasis on the forenoon. In order to avert too pronounced a regularity in their operations, the planes took off at varying times and frequently changed the point at which they crossed the front lines, making efforts to select weakly defended German sectors. Operating altitudes were usually between 16,000 and 26,000 feet, descending to just beneath the clouds when the cloud cover was heavy, but rarely below 4,000 feet, for which reason tactical reconnaissance was primarily an air photo operation. During the approach the planes changed their course frequently, and after executing their mission returned by a different route.

On an average, PE-2 planes flew missions lasting two and never more than two-and-three-quarter hours. Douglas Boston planes, which could operate only when the cloud ceiling was at least 6,600 feet up, carried out missions lasting approximately three-and-one-half hours. Air photo mosaics were taken only in the proximity of the main line of resistance, and the interval between the operations of the individual planes participating increased in proportion to the strength of the German defenses encountered. Whether one and the same crew was committed repeatedly in succession or a number of crews were employed for the purpose depended on current circumstances.

When on photo reconnaissance missions in the near front areas, Soviet reconnaissance planes were usually escorted by fighters. This also applied to all missions flown at altitudes below 16,500 feet.

Other short-range reconnaissance was performed by IL-2 ground-attack planes on normal tactical reconnaissance missions, usually during morning and evening dusk or in unfavorable weather conditions. These were, for the most part, visual observation missions, with occasional oblique photographic operations. Operating altitudes varied between 160 and 6,600 feet.

What has been said above concerning the tactical reconnaissance missions of ground-attack planes applies equally to fighters. One occasion on which fighters were employed in a mission of this type was in April 1944, when Soviet fighters singly or in pairs flew daily reconnaissance missions[22] at an altitude of roughly 3,300 feet over the Idritsa airfield, 18 miles in the German rear. Similar observations were made time and again in other areas, and it was noted that the information these reconnaissance units can be assumed to have gathered in many cases was translated speadily into fire action. A striking example of this occurred at the few airfields still in German hands in East Prussia: each time work was just about completed on repairing the runways, the Soviets attacked them with aircraft and long-range artillery. On one occasion a pair of Soviet reconnaissance planes observed a German fighter group arriving on the Orsha airfield early on 25 June 1944, and at midday the fighter group came under attack by Soviet bombers. A similar incident occurred on 16 October 1944 in Trankein.[23]

Battlefield reconnaissance was carried out principally by fighter and ground-attack units. Experience having shown that the assignment of dual missions--combat plus reconnaissance--to fighter and ground-attack units did not produce satisfactory results, the Soviet Air Command from the spring of 1944 selected, in an increasing measure, the best pilots from these two arms for exclusive use and specialized training in reconnaissance operations. This practice was applied more frequently in the case of fighters than in that of ground-attack units. Thus, according to available reports,[24] approximately 60 percent of all Soviet fighters and about 35-40 percent of all Soviet ground-attack units received reconnaissance missions in addition to their normal activities.

When employed on reconnaissance missions, fighters operated primarily for the various headquarters staffs of the air commands, while ground-attack units also performed frequent reconnaissance missions for the Army. Both types also flew weather reconnaissance.

No difference was noticed between the reconnaissance targets assigned to fighter or ground-attack units.

Fighter units committed in reconnaissance missions avoided air battle and also did not attack ground targets. At most they would attack German transport or courier planes if the attack did not divert them from their mission. They operated most frequently in pairs, less frequently in swarms of about five. Approximately 50 percent of their missions involved air photography. They penetrated to a depth of about 36 miles, approached at altitudes between 16,500 and 18,000 feet, dived steeply to between 6,600 and 10,000 feet over the target area, and returned to their bases at altitudes between 5,000 and 6,000 feet or even at ground level.

Ground-attack units, in contrast, almost invariably carried out armed reconnaissance and attacked worth-while ground targets. They operated most frequently in swarms of 4 to 6 planes, the unit leader being responsible for reconnaissance of the assigned ground targets while the rest of the planes observed the air and were responsible for the protection of the lead plane. In most cases the activities of such units included air photo reconnaissance. They penetrated to an average depth of 24 miles and usually carried out their reconnaissance missions at low altitudes. They preferred to operate without escort fighters, fearing that these would betray their approach. When operating at altitudes above 3,300 feet, however, each IL-2 swarm was given an escort of two to four swarms of fighters.

Both the mission assignment and reporting systems for fighter and ground-attack units employed in reconnaissance were approximately the same as those of normal reconnaissance forces. The only real difference was that the regimental commander or regimental intelligence officer gave the participating crews a more detailed briefing and did not allow them as much initiative in the execution of their missions. Very often such items as the approach and return routes, the direction of target approach, and the altitude were prescribed.

As a rule the air regiment dispatched units on reconnaissance twice daily, once in the forenoon and once in the afternoon, the take-off time varying from one to two hours. Then, during their return flight, the planes usually sent in a brief radio message, making their full report orally to the regimental intelligence officer after landing.

Radio communications by fighter and ground-attack reconnaissance units remained a weak point up to the end of the war. Usually the units maintained communications while airborne through their air directing team on the ground or through an advanced division or corps command post, but contact was frequently lost when the planes penetrated to a depth of more than 18 to 30 miles. Radio communications were usually in the clear and the messages sent mentioned reference points and target numbers.

The regimental photographic section handled the development of air photos, but it remained uncertain whether photo interpretation was handled at the regimental, division, or air army level. It seems safe to assume, however, that the regimental photographic section interpreted only the more important features, leaving the detailed interpretation to the air division or air army.

Night reconnaissance and artillery target spotting were fields of endeavor which had their appropriate share within the scope of tactical and battlefield reconnaissance, indicating the general improvement in Soviet air reconnaissance activities. In March 1945, for example, an IL-2 plane, from an altitude of about 6,600 feet, directed night artillery fire against the German airfield at Pillau.* In another case artillery spotting planes even directed the fire of long-range artillery at night.

Night reconnaissance activities by Soviet nuisance-raider planes continued to increase, but played only a minor role in the overall pattern of Soviet air reconnaissance up to the end of the war.

In contrast, the Soviets made remarkable progress in tactical air reconnaissance during bad weather. Thus, Soviet planes, usually fighters, were observed on reconnaissance over the battle area during weather conditions so bad that all other air operations were called off. However, reconnaissance of this type failed to produce really worth-while results.

3) <u>Appraisal by German Army and Navy Field Commanders</u>. Reports by German Army field commanders, which time and again stress a considerable increase in Soviet air activities, strangely enough make very little mention of Soviet air reconnaissance.[25] Reports on operations in the Crimea, Courland, East Prussia, and Hungary, for example, contain practically nothing on Soviet air reconnaissance. This applies also to military writers who have published accounts of the Russian campaign.

This can be explained partly by the fact that, owing to the nature of air reconnaissance activities, such operations were far less spectacular than those of, for example, the fighter forces. Nevertheless, it must be pointed out that in 1944-45 Soviet air reconnaissance had not attained the degree of importance which would have been appropriate within the overall pattern of the Soviet

---

* Editor's Note: Baltisk, formerly a part of East Prussia and called Pillau by the Germans, was the port through which supplies for Army Group North passed. In March and April of 1945 the area between and adjacent to Baltisk and Kaliningrad (Koenigsberg) was the scene of heavy fighting.

military endeavor.

While the Soviets undoubtedly had made progress in the field of cooperation between air reconnaissance and operations on the ground, deficiences were, nevertheless, frequently apparent. Thus, owing to inadequate reconnaissance results, the Soviet air force frequently failed to attack at the most appropriate time; for instance when the withdrawing German forces had only a few roads and bridges available for their movements. This is the reason German Army field commanders, even during the last phase of the war, did not consider Soviet air reconnaissance as a serious hazard for the German ground forces. It should be noted in this connection, however, that it was exceedingly difficult for Army field commanders to form an appropriate opinion concerning the effectiveness of Soviet air reconnaissance.

Available German sources[26] reveal an unmistakable improvement in 1944-45 in Soviet air reconnaissance for the Soviet Navy and against the German Navy and its installations, as well as against German shipping. Main emphasis in Soviet naval air reconnaissance was on the detection of German convoys and shipping movements in ports, on air photo reconnaissance before and after attacks against seaborne targets and German ports, and on weather reporting. In the summer of 1944, for example, a certain degree of regularity was observed in Soviet naval air reconnaissance. On the Polar front this regularity took the form of daily long-range reconnaissance over the areas off the German-held coastline between Petsamo /Pechenga/* and North Cape to the west (and occasionally extending farther west), and north as far as Barents Island. The reconnaissance flights were followed up by Soviet air attacks against submarines, E-boats, and shipping in general, particularly when shipping was lively or when Allied incoming or outgoing convoys were on the approach.

In the Baltic, Soviet long-range air reconnaissance concentrated on the Gulf of Finland, and increased its activity in the Bay of Danzig and in the middle reaches of the Baltic only shortly before Germany's collapse. In the western parts of the Baltic, the Soviets carried out no organized naval reconnaissance.

In the Black Sea the Soviets maintained lively long-range

---

* See note above, p. 128.

air reconnaissance. During the German withdrawal from the Crimea these activities were directed continuously at the Rumanian coastline, with main emphasis on the area between Constanta and the mouth of the Danube River, and served the purpose of providing data for the preparation of air attacks against German retrograde transportation shipping between Sevastopol and Constanta. Once they detected German convoys or other floating targets, the Soviets left contact planes in the area to transmit to the bomber or torpedo bomber units the required data for the setting of their bombing sights. Communication with the ground was by means of wireless telegraphy. Soviet reconnaissance planes, in addition to directing bombing and torpedo bombing attacks against German convoys, directed attacks against ships traveling alone.

Soviet naval air reconnaissance cannot be described as perfect. The arm had made, however, indisputable progress against its former performances in spite of still evident weaknesses. This cannot disguise the fact that the Soviet Command, in its general disregard for naval warfare--something which, incidentally, it shared with the German Command--hampered the development of the Soviet marine air reconnaissance arm and other air reconnaissance over the sea and coastal waters.

C. Aircraft Types, Weapons, Other Equipment.

As was the case throughout the Soviet air forces, the principle in air reconnaissance was to develop and perfect the existing types of aircraft instead of adopting entirely new models.[27]

Right up to the end of the war the previously mentioned and generally satisfactory types of aircraft were retained in operations. These types were as follows: PE-2, PE-3, Tu-2, B-25, Boston III, and IL-4 for long-range reconnaissance (IL-4 exclusively for night reconnaissance); PE-2, Boston III, IL-2, Lagg-3, La-5, Yak-7, Yak-9, and U-2 for general tactical and battle reconnaissance (U-2 exclusively for night operations); Boston III, IL-4, PE-2, PE-3, Yak-9, Spitfire, and Kittyhawk aircraft, MBR-2, and GST (Consolidated) seaplanes for naval reconnaissance.

They can be considered generally to have met the requirements for which they were intended. This applies particularly to the Tu-2 planes employed in long-range reconnaissance, and the

PE-2, Yak-7, and Yak-9 planes employed in general tactical and battle reconnaissance.

In the last years of the war no major changes occurred in the weapons mounted by Soviet reconnaissance aircraft, light and heavy machine guns still being the standard armament. Reconnaissance planes also frequently carried four rockets suspended under the wings. These rockets had a rearward line of fire and an effective range between 1,900 and 4,000 feet. Use was also made of parachute-suspended fragmentation bombs (AC-2). The bombs were released from a container holding ten. They had a weight of 3.3 pounds, were released two at a time and detonated three seconds after release, approximately 1,000 feet behind the releasing plane. No case is on record of reconnaissance planes armed with cannon, and even the fighter aircraft employed as reconnaissance planes usually carried cameras instead of cannon.

Strenuous efforts were made to improve photographic equipment. Thus, fighter regiments employed in reconnaissance missions received three sets of photographic equipment of the model IL-2, intended for oblique and vertical photography.*

In March 1944 the Soviets were found to be using a new type of pendulum camera, which they called Nachalka, Russian for "swinging." Through a pendulum movement while in operation, this camera covered an area six times as wide as that covered by a rigidly installed camera, with an overlap varying between 30 and 60 percent. Owing to the inadequate lenses available to the Soviets, however, the results obtained were not quite satisfactory. In order to obtain

---

* The types of photographic equipment most frequently in use were the following:

Type	Focal Length	Lens	Purpose
AFA-1	F=30	1:4.5	Panorama photos
AFA-13	F=30	1:4.5	" "
	F=50	1:5	
AFA-27	F=21	1:4.5	Hand camera

Improvised rollers fashioned from tree trunks, used by the Russians in airfield construction

A Russian parachute bomb container which releases small caliber fragmentation bomb

clear photos, planes using the camera had to operate at altitudes between 13,000 and 16,000 feet, an altitude at which they were particularly exposed to fire from the ground. This naturally had adverse effects on the results obtained.

In a steadily growing measure fighter regiments, and less frequently ground-attack regiments, were assigned photographic sections to enable them at least to develop their air photos and carry out the initial interpretation.

An item of standard communications equipment was the RSB radio instrument, with a telephonic communication range of 360-420 miles. On the whole this instrument was found satisfactory, which also can be said of the RPK radio target finding instrument.

The maps most frequently used were color prints with a scale of 1:500,000 or 1:200,000 and grid squares. With the exception of photographic instruments, fighter and ground-attack regiments employed in reconnaissance missions had the same equipment.

D. Evaluation of Soviet Air Reconnaissance Activities

In an overall critique of Soviet air reconnaissance activities in the last two years of the war, the information available from German field commanders and other sources make it clear that strenuous efforts by the Soviet Command to promote and develop its air reconnaissance forces in training, tactics, and technology were very successful. To the end of the war Army support remained the primary mission of the reconnaissance arm but large area and long-range reconnaissance increased. One feature was the great use of fighter and fighter-bomber units to conduct battlefield reconnaissance. As before, night air reconnaissance was of minor importance.

In conclusion, the improvement of Soviet air reconnaissance, which commenced in 1942-43, continued on an increasing scale. As a result, Soviet air reconnaissance units were able, usually, to execute their missions, although they did not achieve the high standards of performance of their German opponents or of their Western Allies.

Section VII: <u>The Fighter Arm</u>[28]

Apart from a few inconsequential differences of opinion, German air commanders in the field unanimously express more or less the following opinions on the Soviet fighter forces during the last years of the war:[29]

The Soviet Command continued to concentrate on building up its fighter arm and developing it to a high standard. Therefore, the arm had a privileged position, both in respect to its numerical increase and the attention it received, and could be considered as the favorite of the Soviet air forces. Numerous fighter corps, divisions, and regiments were awarded the honor title of "Guards Fighters" and most of the air force personnel awarded the title of "Hero of the Soviet Union" were from the fighter arm.

The best aviation trainees were drafted into this arm for training. Too, a steadily improving training program, the adaptation of operational principles to western patterns, and a marked progress in the development of fighter aircraft models did much to develop the fighter arm into an especially strong member of the Soviet air forces.

Fighter forces were committed in consonance with the main effort in operations on the ground and were designed primarily to provide protection for the Soviet attack armies during their assembly and breakthrough operations, and to protect other types of air forces supporting the operations on the ground. The scope of fighter operations was, therefore, primarily tactical, so that their action had an indirect rather than a direct impact on the German ground forces, with the exception of the fighter-bomber attacks which were developed later.

Owing to the continuous expansion of the fighter arm the Soviet Command, from the summer of 1944 on, was able to make adequately strong fighter forces available in all sectors of the front and thus gradually to achieve and maintain general superiority in the air.

It should be stressed, however, that the improved and in some cases very good results achieved by the Soviet fighter arm would not alone have sufficed to achieve air superiority for the Russians. A simultaneous reduction in the number of Luftwaffe forces committed in the Eastern Theater, because of excessive requirements in other theaters, contributed substantially to this situation.

In 1944 the German fighter forces available still were able to cope with their Soviet counterparts, but in 1945 the success achieved by individual German fighter units no longer constituted a serious hazard to Soviet fighter forces.

From the summer of 1944 on the numerical superiority of the Soviet fighter forces became more and more noticeable. For example, Soviet fighters commenced to appear much more frequently and in heavier concentrations along the approach route and over the target areas of German bombers, and created a situation in which German Ju-88 and He-111 bomber units could no longer be committed in daylight missions. German air reconnaissance units also were able to execute their missions only within a restricted scope, operating, from the autumn of 1944 on, [30] "like hunted hares," as a German squadron leader puts it.

German ground-attack and dive-bomber units on every mission they undertook during this period encountered strong Soviet fighter forces, which displayed continuously improving flying ability, tactics, and combat morale.

In their efforts to create a more closely meshed air defense in all fields, the Soviets also made strenuous endeavors to develop and make more use of their night fighter arm. However, they achieved only modest results.

Work proceeded uninterrupted on improving the training of fighter airmen, and by mid-1944 the Soviets created conditions which put an end to their period of experimentation. Approximately 36,000--over 50 percent of the total number--of the trainees in aviation schools at the time were in fighter training establishments. The motivating idea here was to create a corps of versatile, aggressive, and well-disciplined fighter personnel who would be proud of their arm and eager for action; a goal which the Soviets were only partially able to achieve. Because of existing weaknesses, the capabilities and performances of the individual Soviet fighters continued to vary widely up to the end of the war. For example, in spite of the large number of fighter units in existence, very few Soviet air aces became known. This circumstance, however, cannot obscure the fact that on the whole the behavior and the performances of Soviet fighters improved considerably.

The above development of the Soviet fighter arm from the summer of 1944 on is described by Captain von Reschke, who, in his report[31] on operations in the northern area of the Eastern Theater, states that in August 1944 the Soviet Fighter Command committed strong fighter forces to screen off the areas east of the Vistula River. In contrast hardly any defense by Soviet fighters was encountered over the Baranow bridgehead* or over German territory.

Strong fighter forces supporting the Soviet drive on East Prussia in October 1944 secured air superiority and almost completely precluded German air reconnaissance. Soviet fighters also appeared over the German rear, while German air units were able to operate almost without interference in the Soviet rear outside the areas of main effort.

From February 1945 on German fighters were even unable to prevent the Soviets from maintaining constant fighter patrol, combined with fighter-bomber attacks, over the German airfields in East Prussia. Reaching their aircraft on the ground or taking off or landing were all bigger problems for German personnel than their combat mission once they were airborne. The era of Soviet air superiority thus had arrived.

H. E. Schlage gives a very similar account of conditions in

---

* Editor's Note: The Russian bridgehead across the Vistula at Baranow (Baranow Sandomierski, about 110 miles south of Warsaw) was one of several important bridgeheads they secured in the summer of 1944 and from which they would launch their massive offensives after the turn of the year. Through hard fighting the German 4th Panzer Army managed to contain the Baranow bridgehead during the late summer. But on 12 January 1945 Marshal Konev's First Ukranian Front (consisting of 60 guard divisions, 8 armored corps, 1 cavalry corps and 8 independent armored units) burst out of the Baranow bridgehead, overrunning not only the 4th Panzer Army but also some strong German mobile reserves behind the front, and headed towards Breslau and the Upper Silesian industrial area. By this time Upper Silesia was the last, intact, German industrial area (the Ruhr had been badly crippled by Allied air attacks) and therefore constituted a strategic target for the Russian forces.

the central areas of the Eastern Theater.[32] According to him, the numerical superiority of the Soviet fighters began to make itself felt in this area at the beginning of the winter battles of January 1944 and increased by the end of the war to a crushing superiority. Schlage considers the summer of 1944 as the turning point in the history of the Soviet air forces, and adds that in the winter and summer offensives of 1944 clearly defined areas of main effort were discernible in Soviet fighter operations. In order to develop these concentrations of power, adjacent areas were stripped of fighter support. As time passed the picture changed completely until the Soviets were able to maintain fighter activities in practically all areas simultaneously, culminating in the last few weeks of warfare during which Soviet fighter superiority was at a ratio of 50 to 1.

From the summer of 1944 on the Soviets apparently had no supply and replacement problems. Schlage's impression was that they had adequate numbers of suitable fighter aircraft and well-trained pilots, as well as sufficient weapons and ammunition.

In Schlage's judgment, fighter pilots seemed to have improved in training, but it remained an open question whether this was due to Soviet accomplishments alone or to Allied assistance. Be that as it may the fact remains that Soviet fighter pilots now were highly qualified personnel. This was a development which the German command had expected and feared, and in view of the other changing circumstances in the Soviet fighter arm it caused no surprise.

In connection with the above, a report[33] addressed to Goering by the Commanding General, Sixth Air Fleet, on 8 January 1945 concerning fighter operations in the Eastern Theater reveals that not only German fighter pilots but even the highest levels of command in the Eastern Theater still were convinced in the spring of 1945 that, in spite of the crushing numerical superiority of Soviet fighters, they could beat their Soviet opponent if only a reasonably adequate number of German fighter units and the necessary fuel could be made available.

Only very few and incomplete accounts are available from German army field commanders on the effectiveness of Soviet fighter action during this period.[34] These accounts state that Soviet fighter operations had no decisive impact on military events, and that no signs were evident of Soviet fighter power concentrations or of Soviet fighter action in the German rear. This assessment can be considered too general and therefore does not do justice to the Soviet fighter arm in the final phase of the war. It is probably due to the fact that--with the exception of fighter-bomber activities--Soviet fighter action as a rule had no direct impact on the German ground forces.

A. Organization, Chains of Command, Strengths, and Distribution

According to German field commanders and other sources,[35] no significant changes occurred in the organization and chains of command of the Soviet fighter forces during 1944-45. As was the case with the other arms of the Soviet air forces, the fighter arm had a Chief of Fighter Forces within the Inspectorate General of the Air Forces of the Red Army at the Central Administration of the Air Forces of the Red Army. Besides exercising supervision over the training of the rising crop of fighter airmen, this officer was required to inspect the training status, operability, and combat morale of the fighter units and their appropriate commitment, and to assure the existence of good relations between the tactical command staffs and their fighter units. He exercised a considerable influence on appointments to command positions in the fighter arm, submitted recommendations for the activation of new units, the rehabilitation of depleted units, the equipment or reequipment of existing units, and similar matters. However, he had no direct influence on the actual employment of fighter forces and was able to make his influence felt only indirectly by means of his reports and recommendations to the Inspector General.

The several Fighter Corps, as the highest level of command within the fighter arm, received their operational directives from the air armies. An attempt was usually made to keep the two to four divisions and regiments assigned to a fighter corps headquarters together with the headquarters when it was necessary to transfer them from one area of the front to another. Corps headquarters were organized specifically as tactical command staffs and were kept as small as possible. They were relieved of all responsibilities in the fields of supply and replacement and ground service organization, the latter being a responsibility of the air armies.

At the next lowest echelon were the fighter divisions, which were approximately equivalent in strength to German fighter wings and consisted exclusively of fighter units. They were assigned directly to fighter corps or to air armies. Under directives from either fighter corps or air army the division committed its regiments in action closely integrated with that of the ground forces or of bomber, ground-attack, or air reconnaissance units. Fighter division headquarters also had no organic administrative or supply and replacement sections. Their supply and technical requirements were an exclusive responsibility of the air armies.

The distribution of responsibilities within the headquarters staff of a Soviet fighter regiment* approximated that customarily within the headquarters of a German fighter wing headquarters, the only real difference being that the Soviet staff had a considerably larger number of officer personnel.

Of these, the deputy regimental commander, a post which did not exist in German fighter wing headquarters, played an especially important role. Besides having full authority to act on behalf of the commander, this officer had the responsibility, as his main mission, of combat orientation for pilots newly assigned to his regiment and of giving their training the final touches. Newly arriving crews could not be committed in combat action without his prior approval and they carried out their first few missions under his supervision.

The technical personnel, of whom only an irreducible minimum were assigned to fighter regiments, were experienced and capable. They performed only first echelon maintenance and very minor repairs, all major repairs being a responsibility of the mobile repair platoons of the appropriate airfield operating battalion. Because of the system of fixed ground service organizations and because Soviet fighter regiments had so little technical and aviation equipment, they were extremely mobile.

As the output of the Soviet aircraft industry grew and Soviet combat losses decreased, unit strengths in the Soviet fighter arm increased steadily. It is estimated that the fighters on line in February-March 1944 totalled 4,543 or 37 percent of the overall strength of the entire Soviet air forces. Of these fighter aircraft, 485 were

---

* See Figure 6, Organization of a Soviet Fighter Regiment Headquarters Staff, Status 1 July 1944.

older models, 3,228 were new types from Soviet production, and 830 were from the Western Allies. The estimated strength in September 1944 and in the spring of 1945 was approximately 8,000 fighter aircraft. This considerable increase in the number of fighter aircraft available resulted on the one hand in increased actual strengths available in regiments--the average in August 1944 being 37 aircraft per regiment--, and on the other hand in the arrival of newly activated or rehabilitated fighter regiments at the front. According to available reports there were 197 Soviet fighter regiments in July 1944, 223 in August, and 290 in September. These figures include the fighter units allocated to the Home Air Defense Command (PVO) /Protivo-Vozdushnaia Oborona/, which contained approximately 1,500 fighter aircraft, some of which were stationed deep in the rear of the combat areas and some even close to the fighting front.

In September 1944 German intelligence identified 16 Soviet fighter corps and 60 fighter division headquarters. The mounting strength of the Soviet fighter arm also was reflected in Soviet aircraft losses. Even as late as in 1943 these totalled 8,500 fighters, against only 6,200 fighter aircraft lost in 1944.

Whereas the actual aircraft strength in a fighter regiment totalled 35 and sometimes more in the autumn of 1944, the authorized strength remained 30 fighter aircraft plus 1 liaison and 1 training plane per regiment. Measures to increase the authorized strength were under consideration but were not introduced formally. The average actual strength of the Soviet fighter squadron varied between 6 and 8 fighter aircraft.

Nothing was changed in the assignment of night-fighter forces[36] to the Commander of Home Air Defense Forces. It seems, however, that there was a division between those night-fighter units in the operational zones and night-fighter units in the Zone of Interior. The PVO or Home Defense Air Armies, as higher level headquarters, controlled night-fighter corps, antiaircraft artillery corps, or divisions including both of these arms, and in addition sometimes also had temporary control over antiaircraft searchlight, barrage balloon, and aircraft reporting units if the situation required such control. The fighter corps and divisions of the Home Defense Command contained daylight and night-fighter units. What percentage of the overall fighter strength was represented by night fighters is not known. At the time only night-fighter regiments or squadrons had been identified as

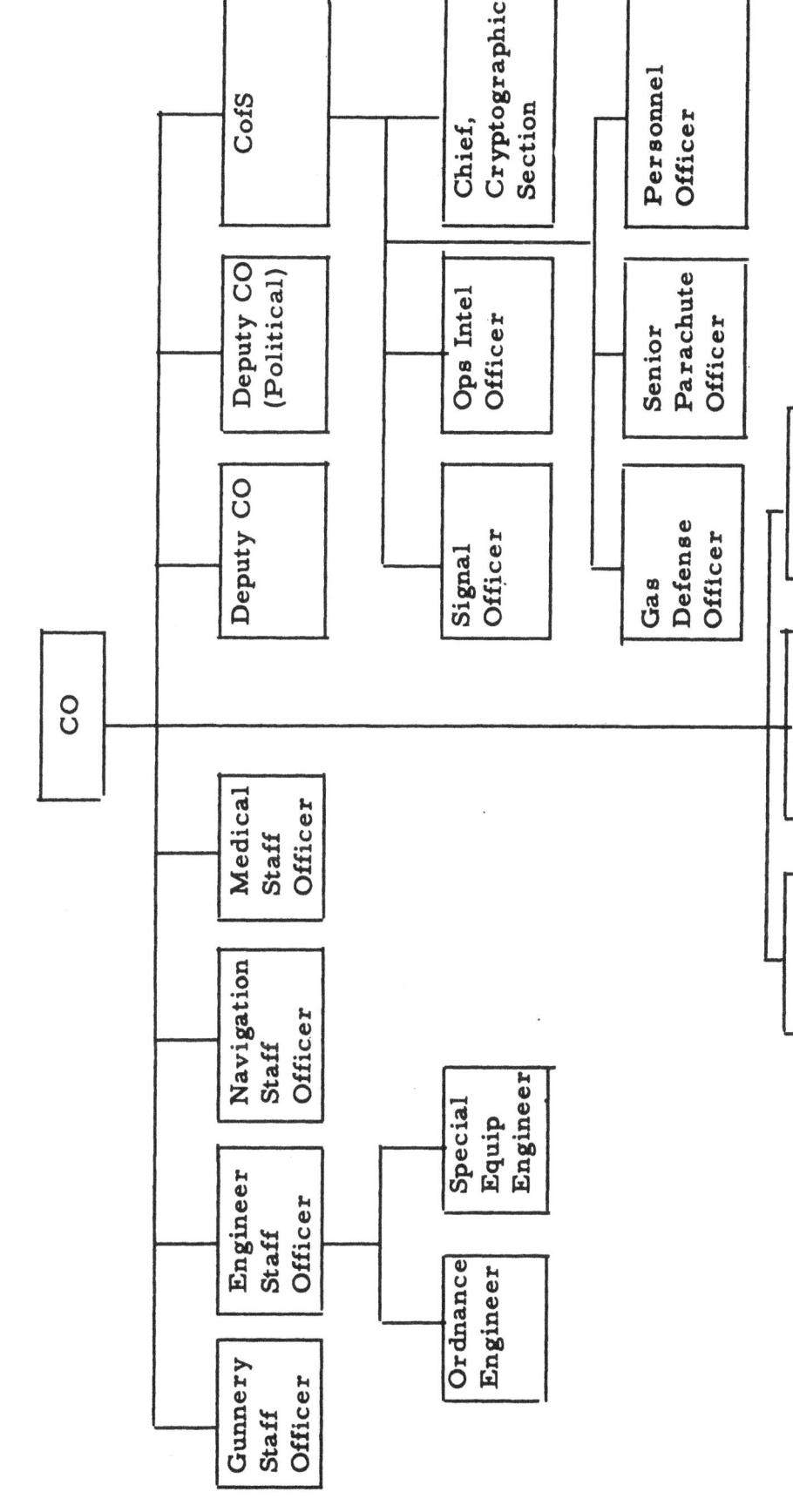

Figure 6

specific night-fighter units, some of them being permanently assigned to specific localities. The system of holding night-fighter units under constant alert at replacement and training regiments was retained.

The distribution or concentration of fighter forces was always in accordance with the areas of main effort in the tactical situation on the ground and in the air.

B. Fighter Forces in Operations

1) <u>Personal Behavior</u>. German field commanders differ on the subject of the personal behavior of Soviet fighter pilots in 1944-45. However, the majority report a considerable improvement in combat morale.

Those reporting adversely on Soviet fighter pilots[37] state that they were not very aggressive nor persistent enough in attack, that they lacked spirit in their attacks and only attacked when in superior strength. They also contend that Soviet ground control stations, by radio, accused their fighters of cowardice. Fighter pairs or flights, according to these same sources, only followed in an attack if their squadron leader led the way with determination, and the failure of a unit almost always was due to the personal failure of the unit leader. It was thought that the reason for the relatively small success achieved by Soviet fighter forces resided in a characteristic feature of the Russian personality, the habit of not carrying an undertaking through to its logical conclusion.

Those sources which report[38] favorably on Soviet fighter pilots emphasize that from 1944 on Russian fighter airmen displayed a completely different attitude, that they were determined in combat and disregarded danger to the point of self-destruction. They even broke through well placed defensive fire, and, with all guns blazing, flew in to close range of their opponents. In spite of heavy losses their personal aggressiveness and combat morale improved steadily because of their constantly growing numerical superiority and their achievement of technical parity, because of their improved training, and, last but not least, because of propagandistic influences resulting from reports on the inferiority of the German Air Force and the imminent final victory of Soviet Russia in her "patriotic battle" for liberation of the homeland from the German conqueror. These, it is considered, were the factors which contributed to impart to Soviet fighter pilots--who were the cream of Soviet air personnel, and who

were being trained in an ever increasing measure to act independently--
the feeling that they were masters of the heavens, a feeling which
received no small measure of encouragement from the fact that German
opposition was almost non-existent.

There can thus be small doubt that, in spite of certain individual weaknesses and failures, and in spite of the varying quality of individual units, the Soviet fighter arm had--at least from the summer of 1944 on--made marked progress insofar as the performance and attitude of its members were concerned and had developed into a serious opponent.

2) <u>General Operational Principles</u>. The improvement in the command and operations of fighter forces which had been noted in 1942-43 continued steadily during the last two years of the war. In general, Soviet fighter operations were characterized by the following features.

    a) Aggressive conduct, with main effort over the front lines and in the near front areas.

    b) The commitment of large masses of fighters in roving and patrol missions to completely seal off the battle area during major offensives on the ground.

    c) Increasingly frequent penetrations into the German rear by growing Soviet fighter forces. These culminated in air superiority for the Soviets in the spring of 1945.

    d) Concurrently with the above missions fighters flew strong fighter escorts for bomber and ground-attack units and later also for fighter-bomber units.

    e) Increasingly frequent commitment in fighter-bomber missions from mid-1944 on.

    f) Appropriate operations which were tailored to appropriate tactics. The units were directed in accordance with plans by ground control stations.

These findings are confirmed by Luftwaffe field commanders.[39] Soviet airmen, however, could not be considered genuine fighter pilots in the German or Anglo-American sense; the actions of all

Soviet fighter units were at all times subject to current expediencies, which occasionally included the tactical evasion of combat with German fighters.

The sudden appearance of a fighter corps in a focal area of attack was for the purpose of consolidating, under uniform direction, the efforts of all fighter forces present and was almost always the sign of an imminent Soviet offensive.

During offensive operations the fighter forces--in pronounced concentration over the immediate front and the close rear--assumed responsibility for the protection of the Soviet assembly of ground and air forces, the units spearheading the attack--usually armored forces--, and for sealing off the battle area during major engagements. This latter part of the mission was accomplished by fighter patrols and by fighters assigned roving missions at all altitudes up to 20,000 feet. The fighters participating were relieved on station, thus maintaining a constant and almost complete canopy over the entire area of attack in ground operations. This type of fighter support operation was carried out by individual squadrons or by regiments and extended either parallel with the main line of resistance or at right angles to the front for a distance of approximately 12 miles. When a number of regiments participated each regiment had its assigned zone. Towards the end of the war, operations of this type enabled the Soviets to achieve mastery of the air not only over the immediate front areas but even far into the German rear, with Soviet fighters engaging in pursuit actions which frequently carried them as far as German airfields heavily defended by antiaircraft artillery. In the meantime, Soviet rear-area air defenses became a secondary consideration and resembled the quiet sectors of the front where Soviet fighters behaved in a markedly passive manner.

In addition to sealing off the front and near front areas, Soviet fighters were assigned the important concurrent mission of providing escorts for ground-attack, bomber, and fighter-bomber units. With growing frequency the Soviets committed massed bomber and ground-attack units under fighter escort. In East Prussia in the spring of 1945, for example, such attacks were repeated several times daily. The tactics employed were practical and with the steadily increasing technical performances of their aircraft, Soviet fighters adhered more and more closely to these tactics.

The direction of fighter operations by radio became the

general rule, particularly in areas of main effort. In numerous cases fighters and fighter-bombers were guided by radio to a meeting point and then employed in a joint operation.

    3) <u>Execution of Fighter Operations.</u> Although field commanders of the German Air Force differ, according to their personal experience, on some points concerning the execution of Soviet fighter operations, their general opinion is that by 1944-45 Soviet fighters had adapted themselves to the requirements of modern warfare and had learned much.[40]

Usually, fighter units conducted their operations cleverly, although frequently they still became scattered after only brief combat action and were rarely observed reassembling over German held territory. They had adopted the western flight formations of pairs, flights, and squadrons, but occasionally were still observed operating in large, loosely organized, and unsteady formations.

Fighters usually operated in units of eight to ten aircraft, which were combined to form an attack group approximately 30-50 strong.

The approach was usually at medium altitudes but occasionally also at altitudes up to 23,000 feet.

The defensive circle was still the favorite formation. From it, the fighters would emerge singly at brief intervals in order then to attack the hostile aircraft from all sides.

In air combat Soviet fighters still made the mistake of opening fire at excessive ranges, but gunnery training, including the subject of fire discipline, had improved markedly.

Generalmajor Uebe[41] gives a highly graphic account of the flight behavior of Soviet fighter pilots in the last two years of the war.

According to his description, Soviet fighter units operating in strengths of more than 30 aircraft under a single command and uniformly directed were a rare occurrence. In areas of main effort as many as 100 fighters were committed at times, which equalled the strength of three air regiments. In such cases, however, the attack and defense groupings were only loosely linked, and the individual planes roved singly within the assigned area without direct mutual contact. The combat formation in 1944-45 was based on the pair system, as was the case in the German fighter arm. The flight of two pairs flew in relatively loose formation with a frontal spacing of 500 to 600 feet between planes; lateral and altitude spacing between the elements of the normal operational units--consisting of seven to eight flights and thus of approximately thirty aircraft--depended on weather conditions. Very frequently a lone plane followed in the rear of the Soviet fighter unit, obviously with the mission of maintaining rearward and upward observation. This plane was jokingly referred to by German airmen as the "wooden eye" of the unit.

Late in the war the Luftwaffe adopted a basic flight formation of three aircraft for units with a cruising speed of more than 300 miles per hour in order to secure flexibility. This system was not adopted by the Soviets.

A certain measure of nervous jerkiness remained a characteristic feature of Soviet fighters up to the end and made it possible to identify an approaching fighter unit as such even at extremely long ranges. Soviet fighters also favored the forming of a defensive circle before attacking. Fighter operations by independent pairs or flights of aircraft taking advantage of hazy weather, sunrise or sunset were a rare occurrence. When on escort missions Soviet fighters remained in the immediate vicinity of the escorted unit as long as possible.

4) <u>Soviet Fighters in Combat against German Fighters</u>. All field commanders of the German Air Force unanimously emphasize that German fighters had to the end a feeling of superiority in air combat,[42] in spite of the growingly unfavorable numerical ratio and in spite of certain technical advantages of the Soviet fighter aircraft over German models in the last year of the war. There can be no doubt that the German fighter units had a better command, wider combat experience, and greater tactical ability, factors which proved decisive in air combat. This fact was admitted by the Soviets. A captured Soviet lieutenant from a guards fighter unit for example stated as follows: "The fighters from the (German) 54th Fighter Wing are usually in the minority in combat. But when they are present things get hot. All of them are aces."[43]

The individual superiority of the German fighter, however, was not enough to prevent the gradual achievement of air superiority by the Soviets through their crushing numerical superiority. This development also was favored by the fact that German fighter operations became less and less frequent, while German losses, particularly in new fighter personnel, mounted steadily.

Their strong numerical superiority and their modern aircraft gave Soviet fighter pilots an advantage over the German fighter arm. This knowledge in some cases made them over-confident, intrepid, and obstinate, at times even stupid. While in combat they would give an exhibition of acrobatic flying in order to display the maneuverability of their planes.

The maneuverability of the German FW-190 was superior to that of the Soviet Yak-9, and the Soviet La-5 was better than the German Me-109. The German FW-190, however, was superior to the Soviet Yak-3.

In combat against German fighters, Soviet fighters were occasionally not ruthless enough in the attack. On the other hand, they would fire continuously even though they had no targets in their sights.

The above observations, however, cannot obscure the fact that the Soviet fighter arm had improved considerably its performances against German fighters, and that the command made proper use of its great numerical superiority.

A typical example of Soviet fighters in operations against German fighters near the end of the war is given in an account of an air battle at Zinten,* East Prussia, in February 1945.[44] The description is an example of numerous such encounters:

The lead plane of a German BF-109 flight attacking a formation of Soviet ground-attack aircraft came itself under attack from the rear and below by two Soviet Yak-3 fighters and had to break off engagement because of hits in its engine and steering gear. Flying alone the German fighter again came under attack by two Yak-3 planes, this time from above. One of the Soviet planes passed the crippled German fighter and, coming into its sights immediately ahead, was shot down almost simultaneously with the downing of the second

---

* Editor's Note: Now Kornevo.

Soviet plane by the rest of the German BF-109 flight, also on their return trip by this time. Whereas the crippled lead plane of the German flight was forced to make an emergency landing, the leader of the pair which had shot down the second Soviet plane was pursued and shot down by another six Yak-3 planes.

At the time of the above air engagement approximately 40 Soviet fighters and 20 Soviet ground-attack aircraft were in the air in the Zinten area against only one swarm and one pair of German fighters. Of the German airmen involved the only one to survive was the swarm leader, who reached his squadron base safely after his emergency landing; all others were killed in action.

The above example offers a striking illustration of the terrific Soviet superiority in fighters towards the end of the war. It also reveals how this superiority resulted unavoidably in intolerably heavy German losses in fighter pilots, losses which could not be replaced.

5) <u>Fighter Operations against German Bombers</u>. From available reports[45] it is evident that Soviet fighter attacks against German bombers, which had commenced in 1943, continued on an increasing scale in the following years.

The impact of these fighter attacks in the summer of 1944 precluded any possibility of committing the older German He-111 and Ju-88 bomber models in daylight operations. Even Ju-188 bomber units came under persistent attack at altitudes of 30,000 feet and above. Only He-177 bomber units above flight strength and in close formation were safe, because of their very effective defensive fire power, from Soviet fighters. Still, it is remarkable that Soviet fighters did not even attempt to attack such units. It seems almost as though they had instructions to attack He-177 units only in exceptional circumstances or not at all. In spite of their heavy defensive firepower, however, He-177 planes flying alone invariably were shot down by Soviet fighters.

In this connection Lieutenant Colonel von Riesen[46] even reports what was unmistakably a simulated attack by Soviet fighters against an He-177 bomber group, 18-20 aircraft strong, in the Minsk area in the summer of 1944. A formation of some thirty Soviet fighters curved in a wide sweep from starboard to the rear of the He-177 group, which was flying in close formation.

Instead of attacking, however, the Soviets passed over the German group some 6,000 feet higher up after firing with all guns into empty space. At such an altitude an observer on the ground must have gained the impression that the shells from the Soviet planes were exploding among the German planes. After carrying out this maneuver, the Soviet fighter formation descended in a steep dive far ahead of the German planes.

The above description of a simulated attack is the only one on record. In general, reports emphasize time and again the tenaciousness of Soviet fighters in their attacks against German bombers. This was particularly true of those fighter units led by a determined commander. It was by no means rare for two or even three squadrons to attack simultaneously. In spite of all this, however, the losses due to Soviet fighter attacks remained small when the bomber unit was flying in a close, properly echeloned formation, and if the bomber unit protected itself with well-aimed, sudden defensive fire. In such cases the Soviet fighters usually failed to repeat their attack.

Soviet fighters were committed against German bomber formations either as a result of air situation reports or as a natural outcome of regular fighter patrols, as was the case above the Kerch Peninsula, where fighter patrols were employed to prevent the bombing of Soviet amphibious operations.

In evaluating Soviet fighter operations against German bombers it should be borne in mind that such action was hardly possible after September 1944, because from then on, the Luftwaffe, faced with absolute Soviet numerical superiority, was rarely able to employ its bomber units.

6) <u>Soviet Fighter Operations against German Dive-Bombers.</u>
Soviet fighter action against German dive-bombers continued to increase considerably in the last two years of warfare and seriously complicated the execution of dive-bombing missions. [47] Dive-bomber units were a highly favored target for Soviet fighters and the losses they suffered were by no means inconsiderable, particularly late in the war when they frequently had to operate without fighter escorts because of fuel shortages.

Soviet fighters not only flew patrols over the battle areas but also endeavored to intercept German dive-bomber and ground-attack units while still on the approach over the German rear and drive them off before they could even reach their assigned target areas. In these operations Soviet fighters preferred to operate in a formation based on pairs, strongly echeloned in altitude--between 6,600 and 20,000 feet--while cleverly exploiting weather conditions and the sun. Frequently, they were able to attack German dive-bombers by surprise, approaching simultaneously from various directions and various altitudes.

When in a favorable position Soviet fighters during this period always sought combat and in most cases no longer gave evidence of fearing the German FW-190 aircraft, especially when they identified them as bombers.

As long as the German units remained in a well closed formation, Soviet successes remained within modest limits. The strong Soviet fighter defenses compelled German dive-bomber and ground-attack units to approach at very high altitudes and descend at high speeds when close to their targets in order to break through the Soviet fighter defenses, a tactic which was usually successful. It is only natural, however, that the precision and effectiveness of the German attack suffered as a result.

The general experience outlined above is confirmed in all points by Colonel Rudel[48] on the basis of his highly diversified experience during the last two years of the war. Rudel writes that in endeavoring to execute their missions, German dive-bomber units found themselves almost hopelessly outnumbered by opposing Soviet fighters. Air battles between flight or at most squadron-sized German dive-bomber units and Soviet units or 15 to 30 Airacobras, La-5, or Yak-9 fighters were by no means rare; on the contrary, they were a daily occurrence. In these engagements Soviet fighter pilots as a rule were extremely aggressive and showed far better performances than in former years. They had mastered both the aviation and combat aspects of their job.

In these air engagements, which frequently developed into fantastic battles of maneuver down to tree-top levels, the Soviet pilots pressed their opponents mercilessly, attacked from all sides, and were relentless in pursuit. Rudel states that he hardly ever returned from a mission without at least one hit in some part of his plane, and reports on one air battle in the spring of 1944 in which his plane was literally riddled with 20-mm and 37-mm missiles. The German Ju-87 was a relatively slow and somewhat cumbersome plane and, particularly after the appearance of the Yak-3 model, could no longer be considered a match for the modern Soviet fighters; when loaded, it was inferior in every respect. The only chance of success was in a maneuver of close curves, in which the Soviet's speed carried them too far outward and robbed the pilot of his fire power.

Dive-bombers which became separated from their formation were invariably shot down by Soviet fighters. Losses remained relatively small, however, as long as dive-bombers kept their formation.

The reequipment of the dive-bomber units with FW-190 aircraft improved the situation somewhat, and units of these aircraft even succeeded in shooting down a considerable number of Soviet fighters. However, operational conditions for the dive-bombers deteriorated steadily in the spring of 1945. Whenever a unit left the ground on a combat mission it found American fighter units waiting on the West and Soviet fighter units on the East and the unit had to "run the gauntlet" in the truest sense of the word as long as it was in the air. The air was swarming with hostile fighters, and continuous air combat during the approach flight, during the attack within the target area, and during the return flight, was the order of the day. Units returning from combat missions had to fight their way home through fighter patrols and on reaching their bases could not land until antiaircraft guns cleared the air of Soviet fighters.

7) <u>Soviet Fighter Operations against German Air Reconnaissance Forces</u>. Soviet fighters in 1943 already proved a serious impediment to German air reconnaissance activities. According to the unanimous opinion of all German air commanders consulted, the effects of Soviet fighter operations on German air reconnaissance increased steadily and in the spring of 1945 brought German air reconnaissance to an almost complete standstill. [49]

In the first few months of 1944 German air reconnaissance units as a rule still succeeded in executing their assigned missions, although with growing difficulty. Above all, encounters with Soviet fighters were not too frequent in the Soviet rear or in quiet areas of the front. Heavily outnumbered, German reconnaissance units had no chances of success in air combat against Soviet fighters, but experienced crews usually managed to repel Soviet fighter attacks and return safely to their bases. It was only on rare occasions that

German reconnaissance units succeeded in shooting down Soviet fighters, and this took place only in the far rear areas. The Soviet fighter patrols, under constant alert in these areas, apparently were manned by inexperienced and not very well trained crews. In areas of main effort at the front and at well established penetration points, German reconnaissance units were always seriously hampered in their operations by Soviet fighters on permanent patrol or roving missions.

Up to mid-1944 the Me-109 planes employed in reconnaissance were able to escape the Soviet fighters then committed at the front. The fighters were faster than the Me-109 in a short steep climb, and just as fast in a dive, but in a gradual long climb at a top speed of 180 miles, the Soviets as a rule gave up the chase at an altitude of around 20,000 feet. Captain von Reschke[50] reports how his pair of Me-109 reconnaissance planes on one occasion came under a surprise attack by eight Soviet fighters striking through a thin veil of clouds. The reconnaissance planes were cruising at an altitude of about 13,000 feet and immediately turned in on the Soviet fighters with their guns blazing. The fighters scattered at once and made no effort to follow the two German planes in their gradual climb.

In the summer of 1944, with the appearance of the new Soviet fighter models, particularly the Yak-3, the use of tactics of the above type was at an end. From then on it was impossible, because of the heavy losses incurred, to employ the FW-189--the standard German reconnaissance plane--in daylight missions. It had to be replaced in part by the single-seater Me-109 and in part by the twin-seater Me-110. Gradually it even became impossible to employ the FW-189 with fighter escorts.

Another modification which the introduction of the fast and modern Soviet fighters made essential was the removal of bombing equipment from German reconnaissance planes and its replacement by longer range instruments for panorama photography. This was necessary because reconnaissance planes now were forced to operate at higher altitudes: above 20,000 feet on strategic reconnaissance missions, and between 13,000 and 16,000 feet on tactical reconnaissance missions.

Soviet interception of German reconnaissance planes increased steadily from the summer of 1944 on. Almost all German reconnaissance units found themselves involved in air battle whenever they reached their target areas. This shows that the Soviet aircraft reporting service identified the German planes while these were crossing the front areas. Soviet antiaircraft directional fire, used to indicate approaching German aircraft, usually brought speedy intervention from Soviet fighters on patrol in the area.

During major offensive operations the Soviets employed such strong fighter forces to screen the front areas that German battle reconnaissance near the front was practically impossible, even over German-held terrain. The only possible tactic here was what was called "pin-point reconnaissance," in which the plane would approach its reconnaissance target at a great altitude from the Soviet rear. Flying at top speed it then would dive down through the Soviet fighter screen and return to the German lines at practically ground level. Naturally, the results obtained by such means were not very satisfactory.

A certain relaxation in the Soviet fighter effort was noticeable only during periods of quiet in ground operations or for brief intervals when fronts had become fluid and properly integrated fighter patrol operations had not yet been reorganized.

In their encounters with German reconnaissance planes, Soviet fighters fought with the utmost determination at any altitude, and occasionally even tried to ram German planes under attack.

If German reconnaissance planes were operating with fighter escorts, the Soviet fighters would engage the German fighters in combat in order then to shoot down the reconnaissance planes.

From the accounts given by German reconnaissance airmen concerning their air battles against Soviet fighters it is obvious--and this is substantiated by all available sources--that Soviet fighters usually operated in squadrons or flights. For the actual attack run the flight would scatter and then approach the target from all sides, including the front. Adopting the German tactics of attack, they would fly to within the closest range of the German reconnaissance plane with all guns firing, and would pursue it persistently as far as and even beyond the front lines. Attacks by units of 10 to 15 Lagg or Yak fighters were by no means rare. The number of reconnaissance planes damaged by enemy fire, and also the number of planes lost, together with their crews, increased alarmingly in the second half of 1944.

Soviet fighters also displayed a remarkable ability to adapt themselves to current circumstances in the battle against the German air reconnaissance arm. Thus, He-111 planes in September 1944 had succeeded in the execution of photo reconnaissance missions at altitudes between 20,000 and 23,000 feet. As soon as this became known to the Soviet Command it dispatched fighters on missions calculated to prevent any repetition of such German reconnaissance operations. No Soviet fighters remained at these altitudes once these German reconnaissance missions ceased.

From early 1945 on the numbers of Soviet fighters committed in patrols over the focal points of battle were so overwhelmingly superior that German air reconnaissance activities were suppressed to the point of insignificance, and finally the situation was so bad that reconnaissance planes were being intercepted just after taking off for their missions.

Conditions in East Prussia during this last phase of the war are described in their full, tragic implications by Captain von Reschke[51] according to whom Soviet fighters and fighter-bombers were the first aircraft in the skies over the German airfield each morning. They remained posted over the airfield virtually throughout the day, keeping it under such close observation that it was absolutely impossible for reconnaissance planes to take off except during the very early morning dusk. The returning planes came under attack by Soviet fighters and fighter-bombers immediately after landing, and in some cases were shot into flames even before they had taxied to a standstill.

At times airmen based near the Baltic found it less hazardous in the air than on the ground at their own base. If a pilot succeeded in taking off, he first flew out to sea a distance of approximately twelve miles at ground level. At sea he climbed to cruising level and then flew at top speed to his assigned reconnaissance area, where he was relatively immune from interference, but only while operating at extreme altitudes. Reconnaissance units rarely succeeded in executing their mission without becoming engaged in air combat, and the results they obtained were relatively insignificant.

8) <u>Soviet Fighter Operations against German Airlift</u>. No new features of any great significance are reported concerning Soviet fighter operations against German air transport in 1944-45.

Major Brunner[52] reports that already in the summer of 1944 the Soviet fighter defenses had become so effective that He-111's no longer could be employed in daylight air transport missions. For this reason all airlifts had to be restricted to the hours of dusk, primarily in the evenings, and air drops were made from altitudes of between 500 and 700 feet in single plane missions. These circumstances presented exceptionally favorable opportunities for intercept action by Soviet fighters, who, for inexplicable reasons, failed to exploit these opportunities. The constant recurrence of the air drops at known points and at regular times plus the vulnerability of the He-111 plane when operating alone should have facilitated Soviet fighter attacks greatly. Possibly the Soviet fighter pilots were reluctant to accept the risks of landing at night after the attacks.

9) <u>Night-Fighter Operations</u>. The efforts of the Soviet Command, noticeable at the end of 1943, to expedite the development of its night-fighter arm continued on an increasing scope in 1944. Some measure of success was achieved in the field of illuminated night fighting, but dark night fighting did not progress beyond the incipient stages up to the end of the war. From the autumn of 1944 on, however, the subject of night fighting again became one of minor importance for the Soviet Command as German night air attacks against targets in the Soviet rear became less and less frequent and finally ceased altogether.

Major Brunner,[53] who commanded a bomber group of the IV Air Corps in night bombing attacks in the Eastern Theater during the summer of 1944, reports that up to the summer of 1944 Soviet night-fighter activities increased week by week. In the beginning, the effects of these activities were noticeable only in the target areas and occasionally along the approach and return routes. From May 1944 on, however, Soviet night fighters were encountered throughout the entire combat areas west of the Dnieper River, particularly during moonlit nights.

The aircraft employed in night-fighter operations were chiefly single-engine day-fighter models, such as the La-5, but twin-engine PE-2 fighters were also encountered occasionally. Combined twin- and single-engine night-fighter operations also were observed several times. A refinement of tactics and efforts to operate by flights or pairs soon became noticeable.

As a rule Soviet night fighters attacked from various

directions while climbing. The approach was from the rear and above, and at the proper moment the night fighter would move into position below the German bomber in order to climb with guns firing.

Flares were dropped in efforts to light up the surroundings and thereby make the attacking German bombers visible.

Soviet night-fighter activities were directed primarily at German pathfinder and target marking planes rather than at the actual bomber formations. German planes flying singly were pursued persistently and on some occasions Soviet fighters were observed repeating their attack run as often as five times.

In some cases Soviet night fighters awaited the German bombers as far forward as the light beacons, thus forcing the Germans to fly without position lights even while over German held territory. In a similar manner fighters endeavored to intercept German bombers at turning points in their course marked by light flares.

It can be assumed that the Soviet system of directing night-fighter operations still relied primarily on visual and optical aids plus voice radio, and was not supported by the use of radar. This seems obvious from the fact that the night fighters often passed German bombers in the dark and made futile efforts to find them, sometimes even employing airborne searchlights. The assumption is also substantiated by the fact that bombers were able to escape weapons fire through evasive maneuvers.

Considerable progress was made in organizing the direction of night-fighter operations from the ground, use being made of directional searchlights, together with lamps of various colors and in various color combinations, as well as specific light signals of all types. The various optical signals and aids presumably served the dual purpose of providing reference points for ground orientation-- particularly during very dark nights--, and of signalling the approach and direction of German bombers.

All of the above were signs of the Soviet effort to improve their night defenses. No appreciable results were achieved, and Soviet night fighters did not make any great impression on German air crews. Nevertheless, it must be admitted that the Soviet's development of their night-fighter arm was correct, logical and methodical.

In August 1944 the 55th Bomber Wing flew its last night missions against the Soviets. In the four months from May to August the wing had lost a total of fourteen aircraft over hostile territory during night attacks. How many of these planes were lost to Soviet night fighters, AA fire, or because of engine or other technical failures is unknown.

The above observations by an experienced bomber group commander, whose units in the summer of 1944 executed numerous night bombing missions in Russia, are confirmed in all essentials by other available sources. [54]

From these additional sources, the organization of the Soviet night-fighter service can be roughly determined.

The air defense zones were sub-divided into quadrilateral areas, which were allocated night-fighter regiments as the situation required. These zones committed their forces by squadrons or flights in their sub-areas in accordance with a standardized plan. Each such defense unit included a ground-control station, a light beacon, and a searchlight.

The control center of Home Air Defense Headquarters issued orders for the aircraft to take off, and the operations of the air units thus committed were directed individually by the ground-control station of the sub-area concerned by means of voice radio. The ground-control station, as well as the aircraft reporting service, received their orders from the control center of Home Air Defense Headquarters. The aircraft reporting service was organized in aircraft reporting companies controlling individual reporting posts, and had improved its performances considerably through the use of radar.

The Soviets also differentiated between illuminated and dark night-fighter operations. In dark night-fighter operations they did not progress beyond the beginning stages during the war and therefore achieved no particular success. The use of radar to guide fighters to their targets and of radio direction finding apparatus to track targets remained in the experimental stages.

For the above reasons Soviet night fighters were employed

almost exclusively in illuminated night-fighter operations. The fighters were guided to their targets either by forward ground control stations using voice radio or by an optical system employing light beacons--coupled with searchlights--, and vari-colored lights and signals to indicate the direction of the German bombers. At the control center of the Home Air Defense Headquarters all reports received from the aircraft reporting service concerning penetrations by hostile aircraft were posted on a master air situation map. The speeds of German aircraft were given on the situation map, thus enabling the control center and the various ground-control stations to keep track of the movements of the German bombers within margins of error tolerable for operational purposes. At regimental headquarters the navigational staff officer kept the air situation map currently posted on the basis of the computed courses and altitudes of hostile and friendly aircraft and thus provided the necessary data to guide the night-fighter units to their target by means of voice radio messages.

Night fighters usually were committed in action over the target area, advantage being taken of moonlight, searchlight illumination, and the light from German flare bombs, since any of these sources of light served to reveal the attacking German bombers clearly.

Soviet night fighters, usually single-engine Yak-1 and La-5, but also twin-engine PE-2 planes, operated in some cases with position lights burning. Even when this was not the case they were visible at a great distance because of their exhaust flames.

No clearly defined attack tactics were developed for night-fighter operations. Owing to the lighted condition of the ground the fighters frequently made their attack run from the rear and above; when the target was illuminated by searchlights or on very dark nights they also sometimes attacked from the rear and below, adapting their speed to that of the plane they were attacking.

As a rule the attack was flown by a single plane, less frequently by a pair of fighters. At times, but only rarely, they were observed attacking in flight formation echeloned to the right.

If a Soviet night fighter ran into the line of fire of friendly antiaircraft artillery fire, he immediately banked down, giving the identification signal. On one occasion it was observed that Soviet night fighters used signal lights and searchlights mounted under their wings, together with other identification signals, to request specific limitations of antiaircraft artillery fire.

Besides these night-fighter operations within target areas, cases are also on record, although on very rare occasions, of night fighters attacking German bombers during their approach or departure, and in some cases for short distances over the German lines. The Russians showed a preference in these attacks for German bombers flying with position lights. In such cases the night fighters would, from the outset, take up stations at altitudes known to be used by the German bombers.

No case is on record of Soviet intruder planes infiltrating German formations during night operations. In contrast, it was noted occasionally that PE-2 night fighters were committed as contact planes even at great distances from the defended target area with the mission of transmitting radio messages guiding the single-engine night fighters to their target. On reaching the night-fighter zone these contact planes dropped flare bombs enabling the other night fighters, who had meanwhile arrived on the scene, to engage in illuminated night-fighter operations.

In the last few months of warfare Soviet long-range night-fighter operations gained some measure of importance. In the summer of 1944 the Soviet Command had organized a number of what were called long-range night-fighter patrol regiments as part of the existing long-range bomber arm. The majority of these regiments were equipped with Boston-A-20-G planes, some of them temporarily with B-25's and IL-4's. These units were not intended for escort purposes but for specific offensive actions supporting the Soviet night-bomber units in the execution of their missions.

The missions of the newly created night-fighter patrol regiments were more or less as follows: a) to neutralize German night-fighter bases while Soviet bombers were carrying out their attacks. For this purpose the regiments involved maintained patrols over the German night-fighter bases around the target area starting ten minutes prior to the scheduled time of the bombing attack and lasting as long as circumstances required. The patrolling planes were to attack all German planes taking off and were to bomb the airfields; b) to carry out low-level attacks, using weapons fire and bombs, against German AAA and searchlight positions within the target area. For this purpose units had to maintain observation over the entire target area and immediately eliminate all firing batteries and searchlights which went into operation; and c) to carry out low-level attacks against moving targets. For this purpose units were assigned roving missions with instructions to attack with weapons and bombs all German movements detected on rail and road routes.

In executing these missions the night-fighter patrol units operated at altitudes between 330 and 1,300 feet. The results achieved were extremely modest.

The experience gained concerning the training status of Soviet night-fighter personnel was very moderate. The bulk of the personnel assigned to the new arm came from the instructor staffs of the various replacement and training regiments with a sprinkling of newly trained personnel considered particularly capable. In the last years of the war pilots considered to be aces were also withdrawn from the fighting front for employment in night-fighter operations.

There can be no doubt that the capabilities and performances of Soviet night fighters had improved, although they by no means equalled those of their German counterparts or of their counterparts in the night-fighter forces of the Western Allies.

On the basis of these very detailed and exhaustive reports the Soviet night-fighter arm in the last years of the war can be evaluated approximately as follows: a) The Soviets succeeded, by the summer of 1944, in achieving a relatively high standard of performance in illuminated night fighting, but in the field of dark night-fighter operations they did not progress beyond the first stages of development. b) The direction of night-fighter operations remained restricted primarily to the use of voice radio and optical aids. For this reason, and because of the still very imperfect performances of the Soviet aircraft reporting services, the results obtained in night-fighter operations necessarily remained within modest limits and had no noticeably retarding effect on German night-bombing attacks. c) In the final phase of the war the Soviets also committed long-range fighters in support of their night-bombing attacks. There are no records, however, of any particular success achieved by the Soviets in this field.

10) <u>Soviet Fighter Cooperation with Other Elements of the</u>

<u>Soviet Air Forces</u>. German field commanders.[55] express the opinion that, as the war progressed, cooperation between the Soviet fighter arm and the rest of the Soviet air forces improved. It is necessary to distinguish between two fundamentally different types of operation a) the escort mission, and b) the combined combat mission.

Escort missions were executed either in the form of unit escort duties or in the form of air patrols maintained over the area in which the protected units were to operate.

If reconnaissance units required escort protection, the escort fighters either joined the escorted unit over the fighter base, which the reconnaissance unit was required to cross on the way to its target area, or the reconnaissance unit made a stopover at the fighter base to pick up its escort. It was only on rare occasions that the juncture was made en route at some predetermined spot.

As a rule Soviet ground-attack and bomber forces during the last two years of warfare always operated under fighter escort. It was only in exceptional cases and in very quiet areas that Soviet ground-attack or bomber forces were observed operating against the German communications zone without escorts.

When escorting ground-attack or bomber units, fighters usually remained as long as possible in the immediate vicinity of the protected unit but at higher altitudes, varying between several hundred feet and 7,000 feet. Thus, in the autumn of 1944 ground-attack formations of 60 to 80 aircraft were escorted by fighters in equal strength. The latter restricted their action to the execution of their escort missions and made no effort to dive down and join the attack. In other cases it was observed occasionally that the escort fighters remained over the target area after the attacking Soviet bomber formation had departed.

Soviet fighters had learned the art of properly escorting bomber and ground-attack units during offensive operations and of protecting them against attack by German fighters, functions in which the Soviet fighters were favored greatly by their crushing numerical superiority.

Combined combat action, in which bombers, ground-attack units, and fighters--usually the fighter-bomber type--were assigned separate attack missions within separate target areas, became increasingly frequent in the last years of warfare, and particularly so in the spring of 1945. As a rule these attacks were well integrated in timing and area and in some cases produced decidedly adverse effects on the German ground forces.

Coordinated action between fighter and bomber units was also observed repeatedly in attacks against German reconnaissance planes. It was by no means rare, for example, for a pair of La-5 and a pair of IL-2 planes to combine in action against German reconnaissance planes.

11) <u>Fighter-Bomber Operations in Coordination with the Army and the Navy.</u> In the last years of the war Soviet fighters were committed more often in direct support of the Army and in fighter-bomber missions than previously. This development became more and more pronounced as the gradual cessation of German air activities released Soviet fighters from their normal missions, a fact which is emphasized unanimously by field commanders of the German Army and Air Force.[56] Here again it is necessary to differentiate between defensive or protective and offensive missions.

The protective mission of Soviet fighters in cooperation with the Army called primarily for large-scale fighter attacks to seal off the approach, regrouping, assembly, attack, and break-through areas in major offensives so effectively that operations on the ground would be largely secure against German air attack.

Special importance was attached to air support for those units--particularly tank units--which spearheaded an offensive; in consequence, German dive-bomber and ground-attack aircraft found it exceptionally difficult and at times completely impossible to subject such units to effective attack. It was by no means rare during such operations for Soviet fighter units to be assigned tactically to the tank units and controlled by forward air direction teams. In operations of this type the supporting fighters usually were assigned roving missions or patrol missions with main concentration over the main line of resistance, extending approximately 12 miles in depth on both sides of the front. From the spring of 1944 on Soviet fighters were employed in missions of this type with increasing frequency and on a steadily increasing scale. The attacks were directed chiefly at such targets as German forces spearheading an attack, centers of defense, individual and pinpoint targets of all types, vehicles and concentrations of all sorts, near front supply installations and supply routes, road traffic installations--with emphasis on narrow road sections, culverts, rail traffic, rail installations, locomotives, and other rolling stock left standing in shunting yards.

Although Soviet fighters at no time achieved the high degree of perfection attained by their western allies in operations of the type discussed above, their attacks in the main areas of military action towards the end of the war produced results which completely stopped German road traffic and almost all other traffic during daylight as far back as 12 miles in the German rear. During the battles for Pillau, for example, all avenues of traffic to Pillau /Baltisk/ led through Fischhausen /Primorsk/.* On the first day of the Soviet attack, massed Soviet fighters and fighter-bombers subjected Fischhausen to such heavy and continuous attacks that the whole town very soon was reduced to rubble and was completely impassable to traffic of any type. The result was that all German troops committed forward of Fischhausen had to leave all vehicles and heavy weapons behind in their withdrawal and only with extreme difficulty and at the expense of heavy losses did they manage to escape with their lives.

Through action of the above type Soviet fighter-bombers seriously affected the morale of the German troops and inflicted considerable losses in men and materiel.

German airfields now also came under frequent attack by Soviet fighter-bombers. Cleverly exploiting terrain cover and the cover afforded by built-up areas at the airfields, the fighter-bomber units even succeeded in breaking through strong ground defenses by light and heavy AA guns and in numerous cases inflicted heavy losses.

In attacking airfields Soviet fighters and fighter-bombers often began by circling around the airfield at an altitude of approximately 5,000 feet--outside the range of light antiaircraft guns--in order then suddenly to dive down, individually or by pairs or flights, to attack the airfield with weapons fire and bombs and then immediately climb back to a higher altitude.

In operating against traffic targets, the planes made their attack run lengthwise along, at right angles to, or obliquely across

---

* See note above, p. 293.

the route according to the local situation, weather conditions, and the position of the sun.

In 1944-45 the Soviets also made increasing use of fighter forces in support of naval operations, primarily in the form of protective missions. [57] The primary missions were those of providing air defense for naval units, convoys, port installations and other important naval targets, as well as for bomber, ground-attack, and torpedo bomber units employed at sea.

Some of the fighter regiments committed in operations such as those described above were equipped with modern Soviet aircraft models, such as the Yak-7 and Yak-9, others had American Airacobra aircraft.

When on escort missions at sea one formation usually flew close escort in the immediate vicinity of the escorted unit while another formation maintained station 2,000 to 2,600 feet higher up and to the rear, echeloned either towards the sun or towards the shore, ready to engage German fighters which might attempt an attack. On approaching the target, the escort fighters if at all possible remained beyond the range of hostile ships' or port antiaircraft guns in order again to take up escort stations with the attacking bomber or other unit after it had released its bombs.

In addition to their protective missions, Soviet fighters were employed in attack missions integrated with Soviet naval operations. These missions were either fighter-bomber attacks against ships or port targets, or attacks against German airfields. In attacks against ships or port targets, the fighter-bomber usually made its attack run in a glide from an altitude of between 1,300 and 2,600 feet, and released its bomb--usually of the 550-pound type--at an altitude of 1,000 feet. The approach and departure were at low levels as a rule and, if circumstances required, the bombing plane was escorted by other fighters. The attacks against German airfields occurred during large-scale attacks against convoys and served the purpose of preventing the take off of German fighters or of intercepting any which had succeeded in taking off.

Night-fighter support of naval operations was observed in only a few isolated cases. Presumably the aircraft involved were day fighters temporarily employed in night operations. No records are available on the existence of night-fighter squadrons or regiments with the Soviet Navy.

12) *Soviet Fighter Operations under Exceptional Weather Conditions.* The few reports available from German field commanders[58] concerning the behavior of Soviet fighters during unfavorable weather produce a somewhat contradictory picture, similar to that of previous years.

Whereas some sources maintain that neither cold nor any other conditions of weather--with the exception of fog--could prevent the operations of Soviet fighters, other sources emphasize that bad weather operations were unpopular with Soviet fighter pilots, that a certain measure of reluctance to operate was noticeable during spells of bad weather, and even that there was definitely no risk of encountering Soviet fighters during periods of really unfavorable weather. In like manner, these sources maintain that Soviet fighters if at all possible avoided missions during morning and evening dusk.

In contrast, Soviet fighters could always be expected in the air when there was a cloud ceiling of up to 5/10 at an altitude between 2,600 and 3,300 feet with solid clouds higher up.

The evaluation of former years, namely that the behavior of Soviet fighters under exceptional weather conditions was an individual matter of training and approximated the behavior of German fighter pilots under similar circumstances, can therefore be considered to apply equally to the later phases of the war, with the possible reservation that, in line with their general improvement, Soviet fighters now operated on a larger scale during bad weather than had been the case formerly.

C. *Fighter Aircraft Types, Weapons, Other Items of Equipment*

The efforts expended by the Soviet Command during the last years of the war to develop existing types of fighter aircraft and their armament and other equipment, together with the measures taken at the turn of 1944-45 to reequip the fighter arm with the most up-to-date types of aircraft show the extreme importance which the command attached to this arm and its expansion. As a result, Soviet aircraft models became gradually more noticeable than the aircraft supplied by the Allies. This is confirmed by practically all German sources available at writing, and is supplemented in some detail:[59]

The fighter models produced by the Soviets in the last two years of the war were good on the whole, and in some ways better than those received from the Western Allies under the Lend-Lease Agreement. Soviet fighter types had excellent maneuverability and great climbing power at lower altitudes. Performance dropped off at altitudes above 20,000 feet, however, and they were a little too slow in horizontal flight.

As such, the Soviet fighter aircraft in the field by the end of 1944 were equal in quality to the German models then in use. In fact, the Soviet Yak-3 must be considered as superior to the German Bf-109-GVI and the FW-190, although this did not become so clearly evident because of the small numbers of Yak-3's that were committed at the front.

The models most preferred by Soviet fighters during this period were the La-5, the Yak-7 or Yak-9, and the Airacobra. Units equipped with these types proved serious opponents in combat: the planes were highly maneuverable and fast and had generally good flight characteristics. They were very rugged, relatively insensitive to weapons fire, and did not catch on fire easily. Whereas the German Bf-109-G and FW-190 models were equal to any of the above Soviet models in all respects, this can not be said of the Soviet Yak-3 (initially designated Yak-11) which made its first appearances at the front in the late summer of 1944. This plane was faster, more maneuverable, and had better climbing capabilities than the German Bf-109-G and FW-190, to which it was inferior only in point of armament. The same applies to the Soviet La-7.*

The aircraft models encountered as night fighters in the summer of 1944 included Mig-3, Lagg-3, La-5, Spitfire V (single-engine model), PE-2, and in some cases a twin-engine version of the Boston III in the front areas, and Yak-2, ⫟ Yak-7b, Mig-3,

---

* Editor's Note: The La-7, which was developed from the La-5 in 1944, had a more powerful engine (2,000 h.p.) than its predecessor and an additional 37 mm. cannon.

⫟ Editor's Note: No data currently available on this model.

Lagg-3, Hurricane and, only rarely, Airacobra and La-5 planes in home defense areas. It seems that the Soviets had made progress in the development of modern planes for use as night fighters, and it is alleged that the Mig-5* and TU-2 showed good performances as such. However, by the end of the war nothing indicated that these aircraft types were in serial production.

The weapons and ammunition of the Soviet fighter arm were not up to date. As an example, it was a long time before they developed a really serviceable aircraft cannon. When a cannon finally was introduced its rate of fire was too slow. The effects of the armor-piercing shells used were by no means impressive, but the explosive shells caused very serious wounds. All in all, however, the armament of Soviet fighters with machine guns and cannon participated in the general progress made, and the weapons in use were commensurate with the requirements of air warfare in the Eastern Theater.

In all other points fighter equipment had improved considerably. Especially the personal equipment of fighter personnel must be considered excellent; this applies in particular to the fur and leather clothing issued.

D. General Appraisal of the Soviet Fighter Arm in 1944-45

On the basis of data available at writing the Soviet fighter arm as it existed in the last two years of warfare can be evaluated as follows:

1) Continued technological development, additional combat experience, and above all a quickly mounting numerical superiority all contributed to bring about a steady increase in the preponderance of Soviet fighters in 1944, culminating in 1945 in the achievement of an air supremacy which from then on was rarely jeopardized.

2) The development of Soviet air power and the increasing successes of Soviet arms had a favorable impact on Soviet fighter personnel. Towards the end of the war, the average Soviet fighter

---

* Editor's Note: The Mig-5 was the first twin-engine, single-place fighter built in Russia.

pilot was a worthy opponent.

3) The aggressive trend, already noticeable in fighter operations in 1943, became increasingly evident. In addition to the concentrated commitment of fighter forces over the main battle areas and the near front areas (to prevent German air attacks and German air reconnaissance), and the assignment of strong fighter escorts to attacking Soviet air formations, fighter-bomber attacks and fighter penetrations into the German rear gradually mounted in significance. On the whole, the tactical principles, the behavior of the units while airborne, and the fighter operational control were sound.

4) The original Soviet technological inferiority had been reversed. The latest Soviet fighter models were in some respects superior to the German models in the field at the time. From the summer of 1944 on the numerical superiority of the Soviet fighters became overwhelming.

5) No important changes took place in respect to the organization, chains of command, unit strengths, or distribution of forces in the fighter arm apart from a steady increase in the number of units in existence.

6) Soviet fighters conducted their operations against the German fighter arm aggressively and with determination. Although still tactically inferior in individual air combat to their German opponents, their great numerical superiority enabled them to decrease their own losses and simultaneously increase the number of German planes they downed.

7) Soviet fighters finally made it impossible for the older types of German bomber aircraft to engage in daylight missions. German bombers flying in unit formations, however, incurred only small losses.

8) Fighter action against German dive-bomber and ground-attack forces was conducted with the utmost rigor and produced better results. Towards the end of the war the Soviet's crushing numerical superiority in fighters almost completely prevented missions by German ground-attack and dive-bomber forces.

9) Fighter action against German air reconnaissance

hampered such activities more and more, finally creating a situation in which all possibilities of German air reconnaissance in areas of main effort at the front were practically eliminated.

10) Fighter action against German air transport made it practically impossible for transport aircraft to operate during daylight, so that German air drops had to be made during morning or evening dusk or during the night.

11) Everything possible was done to develop night-fighter capabilities. Modest success was achieved in illuminated night-fighter operations, but dark night-fighter operations did not progress beyond the initial stages. Toward the end of the war the Soviets initiated long-range night-fighter operations, which did not, however, attain any significance by the end of the war.

12) In cooperation with other elements of the Soviet air forces, the fighter forces successfully executed both protective and, with growing frequency, aggressive combat missions.

13) Fighter operations to protect army operations against interference and fighter-bomber operations in support of army action increased steadily, both in scope and frequency, and often produced telling results, especially towards the end of the war. The same applies, in far smaller measure, to fighter cooperation with the Soviet Navy.

In conclusion, the strength of the Soviet fighter arm grew at a steadily increasing rate. In the interplay of all military arms, the fighter's contribution toward the overall successes achieved was by no means small. From the summer of 1944 on the Soviet fighter arm achieved a numerical superiority which was fatal to the German side and which finally resulted in Russian air supremacy. Only by means of increasingly rare concentrated fighter attacks was the German Command able to obtain air superiority of a temporary nature in locally restricted areas.

Section VIII: <u>The Soviet Ground-Attack Air Arm in 1944-45</u>[60]

Apart from minor deviations due to local circumstances, field commanders of the German Air Force almost all agree in their evaluation of the Soviet ground-attack air arm in the last years of the war. Their opinions can be summarized as follows:[61]

In 1944-45 the Soviet Command continued its vigorous development of ground-attack aviation, which made further sound progress. The number of ground-attack units in existence steadily increased. With a few technical modifications the IL-2 /Stormovik/ was retained as the standard ground-attack aircraft model.

The main purpose for which ground-attack units were to be committed--support of army operations on the ground--remained unchanged. This meant that ground-attack units were directed primarily against all manner of targets within the main line of resistance and the immediate vicinity. An example of this was the Soviet Crimean offensive of April 1944. There the Soviet Command sought to force a decision and strong ground-attack forces were committed against the German front line troops, but not against the retreating German columns.

Later in the war, however, ground-attack units extended their operations to include targets in the German rear, particularly such targets as rail and road traffic, supply and traffic installations of all types, and the ground service installations of the Luftwaffe. These attacks in the German rear, which were aimed primarily at targets directly effecting land operations, began, in the autumn of 1944, to increase in both scope and frequency.

By 1945 all troop movements and all military installations in the near German rear--including shipping in the Bay of Danzig and across the Baltic--were raided daily by Soviet ground-attack units from morning to night. An evident lack of proper planning, however, lessened the effectiveness of these raids.

As long as German fighters could mount fighter missions in adequate strength against the Soviet ground-attack forces, the latter suffered considerable losses. These losses were increased by German medium and heavy antiaircraft guns. As a consequence, the results achieved by the Soviets remained small. The ratio of German defensive fighters to attacking Soviet ground-attack aircraft, however, became less and less favorable to the Germans. Thus, approximately from the end of 1944 on, the Russian ground-attack units were able to secure more effective results.

Soviet ground-attack aircraft frequently employed deceptive

tactics designed to out-maneuver their German opponents. They executed their main attack, for instance, when the German fighters were already departing or were engaged in other sectors of the front. One factor militating in favor of the Soviets here was the German shortage of fuel, which was beginning to become acute.

In spite of all German defensive measures, the Soviet ground-attack air arm steadily improved in the last two years of warfare, although it lagged far behind its Anglo-American counterparts in the scope and effectiveness of its attacks. One reason for this was probably the inadequate training given to newly assigned personnel.

An Army spokesman, Generalleutnant Huffmann[62] confirms the above findings, adding that the IL-2 was always available in adequate numbers in spite of the large numbers lost.

The large majority (and the most impressive) of all air attacks executed in support of operations on the ground were flown by the Soviet ground-attack air arm. Its numerical strength was increasing continuously so that at the end of the war it was frequently able to commit as many as fifty planes, or even more, against a single target.

A massed commitment of ground-attack air units in action coordinated with the army was always observed at those points where the Soviet Command was seeking to force a decision, while only small forces were committed in areas of secondary importance. Nevertheless, in most cases the effects achieved were of a psychological rather than a material nature.

In all justice to the Soviet ground-attack air arm, and in spite of the indisputable results it achieved, it at no time during the war played a decisive role.

> A. <u>Organization, Chains of Command, Strengths, and Distribution</u>

From available data[63] it appears that no basic changes occurred in the organization and chains of command of the Soviet ground-attack air arm in 1945.

Ground-attack air corps were assigned to air armies, ground-attack divisions to air armies or to ground-attack air corps headquarters, with ground-attack air regiments and squadrons retained in the original form and with the original strengths.

The repeatedly reported intention to give ground-attack regiments an authorized strength of two ground-attack squadrons plus one fighter squadron was not put into effect.

On numerous occasions ground-attack air units were assigned directly to army headquarters during decisive phases of a battle, and particularly to tank commands responsible for the execution of clearly defined combat missions. In such cases the operations of the ground-attack air units thus assigned were usually directed by liaison officers at advanced command posts.

At the beginning of April 1944 the Soviet ground-attack air arm had an estimated strength of 2,683 aircraft, the large majority of them modern ground-attack models. In mid-September 1944 it was known that 7 ground-attack air corps, 35 ground-attack divisions, and approximately 130 ground-attack air regiments were in existence; by the end of the year these figures mounted to 11 corps, 41 divisions, and approximately 160 regiments. Losses in action totalled approximately 7,300 as against approximately 6,900 in the previous year. Weighted against the increased numbers of aircraft available and the increased commitments in 1944 the increase in losses appears relatively slight and provides further evidence of the mounting Soviet air superiority.

In distributing its ground-attack air units, the Soviet Command adhered to its established principle of basing the bulk of the units on airfields close to the front as soon as these airfields were developed, so that the units would be as close as possible to their targets.

B. <u>Ground-Attack Air Forces in Operations</u>

1) <u>Personnel</u>. As was the case with Soviet fighter personnel, German field commanders are not quite uniform in their appraisal of the conduct of Soviet ground-attack airmen in the last years of the war.[64] Here again, however, the positive opinions are in the majority.

As captured Soviet airmen put it, Soviet ground-attack personnel considered themselves as the "cannon fodder" of the Soviet air forces, and had no desire to be shot down just "before the victorious end of the war." This apparently general attitude--and the fact that flight personnel punished for cowardice were afterwards transferred as gunners to ground-attack air units to rehabilitate themselves at the front--had in some cases unfavorable influence on morale and thereby on the personal behavior of ground-attack personnel.

On the whole, however, the unexpected success achieved in the large offensives and breakthrough battles had done much to improve morale so that ground-attack personnel were carried along by the general current of elation in the summer of 1944. They executed their missions purposefully and with determination, displaying courage and aggressiveness, qualities which are especially emphasized by German army field commanders.

It can thus be said that the Soviet ground-attack air arm proved a robust and worthy opponent, which admittedly produced no surprises up to the end of the war. Performing its missions without much shouting or ado, the arm remained what might be called the "infantry of the skies."

2) <u>Commitment</u>. The basic principles governing the commitment of Soviet ground-attack air forces in former years remained practically unchanged in 1944-45. For the most part these principles coincided with German views, and they were applied practically, logically, and with due consideration for current circumstances.

The main feature was the employment of ground-attack forces in extremely close coordination with army operations, primarily against targets in the main battle area, but, with increasing frequency as time went on, against targets in the German rear. Adherence to the doctrine of power concentration, to the rule that ground-attack units should operate with fighter escorts, and to the pattern of attacks integrated with the action of bomber and fighter units, remained unchanging ingredients of the Soviet concepts for the conduct of ground-attack air operations in 1944-45. All of this is confirmed by German field commanders. [65]

In the employment of ground-attack air forces, the basic trend of Soviet conduct of air warfare became most clearly evident. In the execution of the arm's primary mission--that of supporting the army through air strikes against near front targets--the main emphasis was on extending the effective range of the ground-based weapons and eliminating hostile resistance in areas of terrain closed to observation from the ground.

No matter what the circumstances were, first priority was always given to operations in the main battle area against such targets as tanks and assault guns, heavy infantry weapons, infantry positions and field-type fortifications, troop movements and assemblies, unit headquarters and command posts, and shelters. It was only as a secondary consideration that attacks were directed against targets in the rear areas, such as rail traffic and installations, vehicle and troop columns on the march, detraining, detrucking, and assembly movements, supply and service installations, and airfields.

The failure to conduct systematically planned attacks against German withdrawal movements remained an almost incredible flaw in the Russian exercise of command in 1944-45.

At sea the targets most frequently selected for attack by ground-attack air units were outpost patrol boats, small merchant vessels up to 1,000 tons displacement, and light naval units.

Initially the trend was to support the ground forces by means of a few concentrated air strikes. Early in 1944, however, the Russians began to commit small units in continuous--if possible, overlapping--consecutive waves designed to wear down the German resistance and silence or drive under cover the hostile infantry.

Soviet ground-attack air formations smaller than group size were rarely observed, although the squadrons or flights within the group attacked separately.

The timing of attacks varied--according to the current situation and the assigned mission--from early morning to late evening. Efforts were made to avoid areas protected by antiaircraft guns. During major offensives, however, the first strike was launched against previously detected and reconnoitered AA positions. In other attacks, a special pair of planes was detailed with instructions to keep the target area under observation and take immediate action against antiaircraft guns which opened fire.

Ground-attack air forces were committed in line with the principle of power concentration. The transfer of a ground-attack air corps or of ground-attack air divisions therefore usually indicated a Soviet decision to develop a new area of main effort in ground operations.

While airborne, ground-attack air units received their instructions by voice radio from air liaison officers attached to the appropriate command posts of the ground forces or from special air directing aircraft.

3) <u>Flight Conduct of Ground-Attack Air Units</u>.[66] The methods applied by the Soviet ground-attack air forces in 1944-45, although modified and improved in some respects, differed very little in their essentials from those of 1943. Unit formation, tactics of attack, and mode of approach and departure remained essentially the same. Thus, the procedure in the commitment of Soviet ground-attack air forces, whose excellent maintenance of unit formation while airborne is stressed repeatedly by German commanders, was approximately as described below.

Units were assigned their targets before the take off, or air directing teams established far forward transmitted them their target data by voice radio while they were on the approach. On the approach route the units usually travelled at altitudes between 3,300 and 5,000 feet and echeloned to right or left, less frequently echeloned by flights, according to weather conditions, the cloud ceiling, terrain features, and the resistance expected. The unit did not always adhere rigidly to the formation assumed immediately after take off.

On arrival in the target area, the actual attack run was carried out in an oblique dive from the approach altitude of between 3,900 and 5,000 feet or, if the approach was at low levels, from altitudes between 1,000 and 1,300 feet, to which altitude the planes first climbed. For the attack run spacing between the individual planes was increased to between 160 and 660 yards, so that each plane could aim its bombs individually.

The strength of attacking formations varied between 25 and 60 planes and the attack run was carried out in waves of 4 to 8 planes or, in unfavorable weather, by pairs. On a few occasions an entire unit was observed diving in a concentrated attack on the target.

Using bombs, rocket projectiles, and weapons fire, the unit repeated its attack run persistently until the target was eliminated, and it was noted in many cases that even highly effective defensive fire from the ground and heavy losses failed to deter the unit in the execution of its mission. After the attack, the planes usually departed at low levels and in a straight line back to the front.

Navigation, habitually visual and by dead reckoning, was an exclusive responsibility of the individual pilot. For this purpose various orientation marks, such as visual signals, smoke, and light beacons were used. In unfavorable weather the pilot depended on his radio direction-finding instrument and sometimes oriented himself by extraneous information picked up in his voice radio.

As time passed Soviet ground-attack airmen made noticeable progress, both in the clever exploitation of cover during the approach to the target and in the finding of the target. They were highly flexible in the execution of their missions and very observant in their search for suitable targets.

Even during the last years of the war Soviet ground-attack units, when pursued by German fighters, endeavored to escape at ground levels, firing rocket projectiles rearward, rigidly maintaining their unit formation, and relying largely on the protection afforded by their heavy armor plating.

Although inferior to German fighters in air combat, their clever flight performances, exploitation of cover, and strong protective armor enabled them to resist attack for a long time, so that the only really effective tactic for a German fighter was to attempt a surprise attack.

For passive defense against lively fire by antiaircraft guns, Soviet ground-attack units repeatedly changed their course and employed other evasive maneuvers. These took the form of short, sharp curves, side-slipping at top speed--carried out either by individual planes or by the entire attack wave if not in too close formation--and similar maneuvers. Massed fire by medium and light antiaircraft guns, or by heavy infantry weapons at lower altitudes, frequently forced Soviet ground-attack forces to climb to higher altitudes and thereby lessened the effectiveness of their attack.

In summary, then, the flying conduct of Soviet ground-attack units in 1944-45 were marked by the following features:

a) The existing principles and methods of approach, attack, and departure for ground-attack air forces were retained and improved.

b) Multi-wave attacks by large units became increasingly frequent in place of the former squadron-size attacks.

c) Attacking units exploited weather and terrain conditions appropriately, and found their targets more easily.

d) Soviet ground-attack aircraft avoided combat with German fighters and, as far as possible, avoided massed fire by antiaircraft guns.

4) <u>Ground-Attack Units in the Battle Area in Cooperation with the Army and the Navy</u>. The principles governing the commitment of ground-attack air forces in action integrated with army operations during 1944-45 remained unchanged. The ground-attack air arm's increasing strength, however, did affect the form and frequency of its operations. The following is offered from accounts by field commanders of the German Army[67] to supplement what has been said in previous chapters.

A good example of the employment of ground-attack air forces in support of the army in an attack with limited objectives is found in the battles around Sevastopol in the spring of 1944.*

---

* Editor's Note: On 8 April 1944 elements of the Fourth Ukranian Front managed to cross the Sivash or Putrid Sea and gain entry into the Crimea. This maneuver made German defensive positions on the Perekop Isthmus and the Kerch Peninsula (see notes above, pp. 86 and 120) untenable and forced the German and Rumanian forces to retreat to the Fortress of Sevastopol. The operations described here by the author were costly to the Germans as well as to the Russians. Of approximately 200,000 men at the beginning of April, the Germans and Rumanians lost over 60,000 before the evacuation of the Crimea was ended. In addition, 10,000 men who defended Sevastopol during its evacuation had to surrender to the Russians. Russian ground-attack air operations figured significantly in this German defeat. See Kurt von Tippelskirch (1959 ed.), pp. 378-79 and Wolfgang Pickert, <u>Vom Kuban-Brueckenkopf bis Sewastopol</u>, Kurt Vowinckel (Heidelberg, 1955).

During the first phase of the battle--a Soviet surprise advance in an attempt to enter the fortress while the German troops withdrew--no ground-attack air forces were committed. During the second phase--a Soviet attempt to take the fortress in a brief battle--attacks by strong ground-attack air forces were restricted to the foremost German line of defense, the targets being fortified positions, and battery and antiaircraft gun firing positions. No attempt was made by the aircraft to attack the German rear. No cooperation with Soviet fighters was evident and as a result the Soviet ground-attack air forces suffered considerable losses. It was only at the beginning of the third phase--the opening of a thoroughly prepared attack after a proper build-up on the ground--that ground-attack air forces had adequate fighter protection. In the first few days of this phase, ground-attack strikes remained restricted almost exclusively to the front areas, and it was only when the decisive all-out attack opened early on 8 May that the ground-attack aircraft extended the range of their operations to include all jetties in the port. In spite of the large number of Soviet planes downed--German fighters downed 90 and German antiaircraft fire another 30 on this one day alone--it was no longer possible to cope with the vast numerical superiority of the Soviet forces. In the final phase--German evacuation of the fortress and withdrawal of the German troops across the Black Sea--the departure of the last German fighter group left the entire area defenseless against Soviet air attack except for fire from some antiaircraft guns. Then the Soviet ground-attack air forces directed their effort against the departing German convoys, achieving numerous hits but failing to sink any of the ships. Smaller ships, particularly the naval barges with their strong antiaircraft defenses, were rarely hit. Nevertheless, the continuous massed attacks by Soviet ground-attack aircraft inflicted exceptionally heavy personnel losses.

As the war continued, cooperation between the Soviet ground-attack air arm and the Soviet army improved steadily and, during major offensives, produced correspondingly good results.

Above all, the use of ground-attack air units to support tank forces and to repel German counterattacks increased significantly. Frequently, in order to secure the closest possible cooperation, ground-attack units were assigned tactically to the appropriate army headquarters.

Finally, the numerical superiority of the Soviet ground-attack forces reached such proportions that Soviet attacks and breakthrough operations on the ground received almost ceaseless support of this type. The ground-attack units concentrated on targets within the main battle area, but as time passed they also, with increasing frequency, penetrated as far as 36 to 42 miles into the German rear. In these attacks the Soviet ground-attack forces gradually attained high standards of performance and inflicted significant losses on their German opponents.

In spite of this, many large-scale daylight German troop movements, which could not be concealed, occurred right up to the end of the war without interference from Soviet ground-attack forces. A case in point was the retreat across the Western Dvina River at Riga, in which German troops crossed the river by only two bridges in dense masses moving ceaselessly for five days and nights.*

Luftwaffe field commanders[68] express opinions similar to those of German army officers above concerning the employment of Soviet ground-attack forces in the battle area.

Anti-tank air operations, a field of activities hitherto badly neglected by the Soviets, began to receive attention early in 1945, and from then on the Soviet ground-attack air forces engaged in this form of action on a steadily increasing scale and at times achieved good results.

In former years there had been no evidence of ground-attack air forces cooperating with the Soviet Navy, but this changed in 1944-45. In addition to the previously mentioned operations against German ships during the battle for Sevastopol, Soviet ground-attack aircraft operated against convoys and other naval targets at sea and in ports, both in the Black Sea and later also in the Baltic, although such operations were never on a very large scale.[69] The units assigned to support the Navy also had IL-2 aircraft and employed very much the same tactics as those used by units supporting the Army: approach in unit formation echeloned far forward, with planes closely interspaced, at low altitudes or behind cloud cover; ascent to

---

*Editor's Note: This occurred in September 1944. Russian operations in this area gradually drove a wedge between German forces in Western Courland and East Prussia. See note above, p. 269.

altitudes of between 1,300 and 2,000 feet just before the target was reached; attack run if possible from direction of the sun in successive waves at intervals of between 2,000 and 2,300 feet-- this repeated several times--each plane diving individually to attack with 55 to 220 pound bombs, rocket projectiles, weapons fire, and occasionally phosphorous spray equipment. In operations of this type the attacking air units always had fighter escorts.

To summarize, the employment of Soviet ground-attack air units in the battle area on the ground and in cooperation with the Army and Navy in the last years of warfare was marked by the following specific features:

a) Action in close and direct support of the Army remained the primary mission and towards the end of the war resulted in a crushing Soviet superiority on the field of battle. As a part of this mission, cooperation with tank forces was given first priority.

b) Although main emphasis was placed on targets within the central battle area, attacks also were launched with increasing frequency at targets in the German rear.

c) The tactical principles and the methods of operation remained practically unchanged and were adapted to the requirements of current situations.

d) During this period ground-attack forces were observed for the first time in operations integrated with those of the Soviet Navy, but these activities were of minor scope compared to those in support of the Army.

5) <u>Operations of Soviet Ground-Attack Air Forces in the German Rear</u>. The opinion of practically all German field commanders[70] is that in the last two years of warfare the operations of Soviet ground-attack air forces against targets in the German rear, and particularly against service installations of the Luftwaffe, increased in scope, but at no time achieved anything like the significance of their operations in the battle area. Still, these attacks against supply and traffic installations, shelters and command posts, and other important rearward installations and establishments frequently produced very noticeable results. In some cases these operations proved exceedingly costly to the German Army, as for example at the time of the collapse of German Army Group Center (June 1944),

when Soviet ground-attack forces attacked traffic bottlenecks in the German rear, such as the bridges over the Berezina River.

Attacks against moving German trains and vehicles were, as a rule, only effective in the absence of defensive antiaircraft guns, the presence of which had, at all times, a markedly deterrent effect on Soviet ground-attack aircraft.

Operations against German airfields were still a relatively rare occurrence in early 1944 but increased as time went on, culminating in the spring of 1945 in Soviet ground-attack forces raiding the few airfields still available to the German side almost daily. Units of 40 to 60 aircraft, escorted by fighters in equal strength, used light and medium weight fragmentation bombs, rocket projectiles, and weapons fire to attack buildings, taxiways, runways, and aircraft on the ground. These attacks disrupted servicing activities and inflicted considerable losses on flight and ground service personnel and materiel. As a result, the operability of German air units steadily declined.

In the final phase of the war, when ammunition shortages compelled the German side to restrict antiaircraft fire by light and medium weapons to aircraft targets within a range of 550 yards, Soviet ground-attack aircraft frequently began to attack from higher altitudes, where they could operate without interference. Such an attack by Soviet ground-attack aircraft against Littausdorf airfield (in the Warta River bend) April, 1945, resulted in the destruction of 72 out of 78 aircraft on the ground.

6) <u>Night Operations by Soviet Ground-Attack Air Forces.</u> In 1944-45 Soviet ground-attack units equipped with IL-2 aircraft were not employed systematically in night operations. According to German field commanders,[71] such employment was unnecessary, since the special U-2 harass-bomber units created for the purpose took care of night-nuisance raids, and other night attacks were carried out on an adequate scope by normal bomber forces. Some reports indicate that in a very few cases IL-2 aircraft were observed in night operations and that some IL-2 units received special training for such operations.

7) <u>Operations under Exceptional Weather Conditions.</u>[72] The operations of Soviet ground-attack aircraft under exceptionally unfavorable weather conditions in the last two years of warfare

were similar to those in previous years. According to German field commanders, unfavorable weather conditions did not prevent the employment of ground-attack air forces, although conditions of rain, low-hanging clouds, heavy snow storms, fog, and haze did reduce their activities considerably. This applied in particular to strikes in the German rear and against German airfields. Closer to the front, in contrast, unfavorable flying weather brought no relief for the German troops, since Soviet ground-attack air units continued to operate.

In the mountainous Carpathian and Beskid regions, the Soviets profited from meteorological conditions, since the weather was usually favorable for aviation east and very unfavorable west of the mountain ranges.

8) <u>Employment in Cooperation with Other Elements of the Soviet Air Forces.</u> Cooperation with the other air arms continued to improve in 1944-45. The scope of such operations grew considerably, particularly when the war was drawing to a close, although, according to German field commanders,[73] no essential changes occurred in the methods employed.

Coordinated action with fighter forces was primarily in the form of operations under fighter escort, as previously described. It had become a standing rule to assign fighter units to protect ground-attack forces against interference from German fighters. The ratio of ground-attack to fighter escort aircraft varied between 2 to 1 and 1 to 2. As in former years fighters occasionally were assigned what could be called an extended, protective mission besides their normal escort mission; in such cases a fighter assault group was dispatched ahead of the ground-attack force to neutralize the German defenses in the target area.

When fighter-bombers and IL-2 units engaged in a joint mission, the fighter-bombers assumed the role of escort fighters in addition to their corollary mission of bombing. Over the target the fighter-bombers usually first carried out a dive-bombing attack, the ground-attack aircraft following up with low-level attacks.

Combined bomber, ground-attack, and fighter-bomber attacks increased considerably in scope, frequency, and effectiveness towards the end of the war. If the strike was against a single target area, the IL-2 units attacked the antiaircraft gun positions to enable the bomber units to make their attack run without interference. Frequently, however, the targets assigned in such joint operations were distributed within a larger area, particularly during German retrograde movements. In Samland, for example, during operations on the attenuated Fischhausen-Pillau Peninsula* (April 1945) Soviet bombers were assigned a 1,600-yard zone immediately behind the German main line of resistance, the next zone of 1,600 yards was assigned to ground-attack units, and a third zone, also 1,600 yards deep was attacked by fighter-bombers. Within their separate zones the three air arms used bombs and all other weapons available in practically nonstop attacks against the German troops, concentrating their efforts primarily against troop concentrations and pockets of resistance. After one to two hours, the fighter-bombers shifted farther forward to attack a new 1,600-yard zone, their old zone being taken over by the ground-attack units, whose old zone, in turn, was taken over by the bomber units. The combined attack was maintained in this form from early morning to late evening, inflicting considerable losses. One factor which contributed to increase the German losses here was that the congestion in the German withdrawal movements was further complicated by the constant stream of refugees.

C. Aircraft Types, Weapons, Other Equipment [74]

The two-seater model IL-2 remained the standard ground-attack aircraft of the Soviet air forces in the last phase of the war.

The technical and combat features of the IL-2, already discussed in Chapters 2 and 3, underwent only slight improvements and modifications and proved adequate for the conditions of air warfare in the Eastern Theater. It remained a relatively clumsy plane and was correspondingly vulnerable to fighter attack. It could, however, be considered adequately maneuverable and its excellent protective armor largely compensated for its other weak points.

Only slight changes were made in the calibers and mountings

---

* Editor's Note: The Pillau (now Baltisk) Peninsula is on the eastern edge of the Gulf of Danzig--now the Kaliningradsk region of the U.S.S.R. (formerly East Prussia). The Pillau Peninsula extends southward along the Vistula Lagoon from Samland, a peninsular area between the Courland and Vistula Lagoons. See note above, p. 293.

of the machine guns and cannon and the ammunition used. The reequipment of some units with 37-mm recoil-operated guns--in place of the former 20-mm and 23-mm blowback-operated guns--which commenced in the spring of 1944, introduced a new feature. The guns were on rigid mounts under the wings, and 55 to 80 rounds of ammunition were carried for each gun. The rate of fire was approximately 6 rounds per second. Planes with this type of gun, however, were not popular with Soviet airmen because the plane was too awkward to handle, and the recoil gave the plane a swaying motion. Furthermore, the bombload was reduced to 110 pounds and such planes were unable to carry rocket projectiles. For this reason plans existed--but were not carried out--to replace the two 37-mm guns by four 23-mm guns. No noticeable changes occurred in the types of bombs, rocket projectiles or ammunition carried, nor in the methods of loading and use. The authorized payload was exceeded quite generally by up to 100 percent.

The most frequently used aiming device was the WW-1 ring sight. The rigidly installed weapons were adjusted to a range of 440 yards, the rocket projectiles to a range of 880 yards.

Radio equipment had progressed so far that each plane had an RSI-4 receiver, and each swarm leader a RSI-3 transceiver. Only lead planes were equipped with radio locator instruments (Type RPK-10), and the last plane of each tactical wave carried an AFA-12 camera to photograph target results. The planes also had, for example, adequate panel instruments, oxygen equipment, and auxiliary equipment for night landing.

When necessary, IL-2 units carried equipment for smoke screening--two planes could lay down a smoke screen in an area 3,000 by 200 yards that would last for fifteen minutes in a slow wind--which could also be used for emitting phosphoric gas sprays.

D. <u>Summary Appraisal of the Soviet Ground-Attack Air Forces</u>

Sound development and logical employment by the Soviet Command, combined with the steadily increasing numerical superiority, enabled the ground-attack air arm to operate with ever improving effectiveness in 1944-45 and thereby make an important contribution to the overall Soviet victory.

Section IX: Soviet Bomber Forces[75]

Although on a much smaller scale than fighter and ground-attack aviation, the Soviet bomber arm participated in the general progress of the Soviet air forces in the last two years of warfare. It appears that various factors contributed to retard the growth of the bomber arm in comparison with the other two air arms. First, the Soviets apparently were unable to promote all arms of the air forces simultaneously and with equal vigor; secondly, the expansion of the bomber arm presented especially difficult problems. In the third place, the ruling views of the Soviet Command exercised a decisive influence in the matter; in view of the paramount importance of land warfare in Soviet military doctrine the development of a bomber arm was consciously given less priority than the fighter and ground-attack air arms and no provisions at all were made for strategic air warfare, a concept which was proved to be sound by the progress of military events in the Eastern Theater. Finally, the Soviet Air Command was able to dispense with the development of a strong bomber arm because it could depend on support from the Western Allies in this field.

Thus, the Soviet bomber arm was far behind the fighter and ground-attack air arms in 1944-45. While stating these limiting factors, German field commanders[76] nonetheless agree unanimously that the Soviet bomber forces made remarkable progress in the last two years of warfare and in doing so were able to take advantage of the gradual decline in German fighter defense activities.

In 1944-45 Soviet bombers still had as their primary mission the support of army operations on the ground. Continuous, concentrated attacks in the near German rear at points of main effort in the various offensives and breakthrough battles played a major role. As time passed, however, operations were stepped up considerably against German Air Force installations and other targets in the far German rear.

Even during the final phase of the war the use of Soviet bombers in quasi-strategic* missions was a rare occurrence. On the whole no

---

*Editor's Note: "Quasi-strategic" is used in this section to translate the German operativ, which sometimes indicates an intermediate degree of importance between strategy and tactics. For a discussion of the terms Strategie, Operationen and Taktik see Albert Kesselring (Generalfeldmarschall a. D.), Gedanken zum zweiten Weltkrieg, Athenaeum=Verlag (Bonn, 1955), p. 44.

significant changes were noted in the Soviet commitment of bomber forces right up to the end of the war.

Within the limited scope of their pattern of air warfare, the Soviets made sound use of their bomber forces, and thus increased the scope of their victories on the ground. The technical equipment of Soviet bomber aircraft was adequate for such limited employment.

German losses due to Soviet bomber attacks increased as the effectiveness of German fighter and AAA defenses was impaired by strong Soviet fighter escorts and the higher altitudes at which Soviet bombers operated.

The Soviet long-range bomber arm (ADD) also had to adapt its operations to the basic concepts of the Soviet Command on the use of bomber forces. Originally established as a strong force independent of the army and designed for the purpose of conducting quasi-strategic air warfare at night, plans for this use of the arm had to be abandoned at an early stage because of technical and training difficulties and probably also because of the fundamental views of the Soviet Command.

The Soviet long-range bomber arm was committed almost exclusively in missions of direct and indirect support for the army. These missions included targets at the point of main effort, targets in the central battle area, and such targets as German traffic installations, supply establishments, and the ground service organization in the German rear. Accordingly, the long-range bomber corps, which for a long time remained stationed in the general area of Moscow, was later distributed all along the line and employed in concentration in those areas in which the Soviet Command launched its major attacks. This use of the bomber arm became evident at the opening of the Soviet offensive on 22 June 1944. The offensive received support from very strong bomber forces, which had hitherto generally been held in reserve.

A few night attacks carried out against Koenigsberg /Kaliningrad/, Berlin, Bucharest, and other large cities with explosive and incendiary bombs showed features of strategic operations and could be considered as exceptional performances. Frequently, however, only one-third of the aircraft dispatched on missions of this type reached the target area, and the results achieved were insignificant. This applies also to the terror attacks launched against Finnish towns, particularly Helsinki, Turku, and Kotka, in the spring of 1944, which were designed to serve political purposes.

Because of the lack of long-range escort fighters, the Soviet long-range bomber arm carried out no long-range daylight attacks, but the bombers were used largely in supply missions.

During the last two years of warfare, Soviet bomber operations against German seaborne supplies and port installations in the eastern parts of the Baltic as well as in northern waters grew to such proportions that in some cases German shipping was seriously affected.

On the whole, Soviet bomber aviation thus can be considered to have made some progress in 1944-45. However, intentional neglect of the arm, inadequate training, inadequate measures to equip the units with modern bomber aircraft and other materiel, and, last but not least, the limited use made of bomber forces, all contributed to prevent the Soviet bomber arm from achieving the standards and importance of the Soviet fighter and ground-attack air arms.

A. Organization, Chain of Command, Unit Strengths, Distribution

According to available sources,[77] the chain of command of the Soviet bombers forces in 1944-45 remained approximately what it had been the year before. This applies both to the support bomber forces assigned to air armies and the long-range bomber arm (ADD) controlled directly by the Soviet Supreme Command.

The consolidation of divisions under corps headquarters became the general rule and was applied with particular firmness to the forces intended for long-range operations. Each long-range bomber corps had as a rule two divisions, each consisting of two (later three) regiments. In the case of the bomber forces assigned to air armies, the number of divisions per corps varied according to the current situation. Each of these divisions usually had three regiments. Towards the end of the war plans existed, but were not put into effect, to establish a new unit, the Eighteenth Air Army, consisting exclusively of long-range bomber corps.

The numerical strength of the Soviet bomber arm in March 1944 was estimated at 4,561 aircraft, broken down as follows: 530 aircraft from Allied deliveries (45 DC-3, 100 B-25, 385 Boston III);

2,213 aircraft from Soviet production (68 TB-7, 309 PS-84, 543 DB-3F, 1,293 PE-2); 1,818 night harassing planes from Soviet production (70 SB-2, 1,624 U-2, 124 other models).

The long-range bomber arm was estimated at 860 aircraft in February 1944, 1,100 in June, 1,300 in August, and 1,400 in September of the same year, and at 1,600 in January 1945, so that it had almost doubled its strength within one year.

In mid-September 1944, 6 bomber corps, 30 bomber divisions, and 110 bomber regiments were known to exist. Towards the end of the year these figures had increased to 7 corps, 35 divisions, and 135 regiments. The comparative figures for the long-range bomber arm in mid-September 1944 were 9 corps, 18 divisions, and 48 regiments; no changes occurred here in the number of corps and divisions, but the number of regiments increased to 58 by the end of the year.

As a rule the actual aircraft strength per squadron at the end of 1944 exceeded the authorized strength of 33 by 3 to 5 aircraft; in addition, most squadrons had a number of crews in reserve.

Approximately 70 per cent of the crews were old personnel and the aircraft in the units were the same models as in previous years, but with some technical improvements.

Bomber aircraft losses totalled 5,100 in 1943 and 5,200 in 1944. This slight increase in the number of planes lost was completely out of proportion to the large increase in numerical strength and provided proof of the improvement in Soviet bomber aviation.

The distribution of Soviet bomber forces depended largely on the current areas of main effort in ground operations. This applied not only to the units assigned to air armies, but also to the long-range bomber arm. Whereas most of the long-range bomber units at the beginning of 1944 were still concentrated in the northern areas for their attacks against Finland, from April 1944 on more and more of them were transferred to the southern areas. There they were placed under six long-range bomber corps headquarters and from June on they operated from airfields in the general area of Kiev in support of army operations. During the summer, these forces were employed in concentrated attacks in the southern and central areas, and in the autumn almost all of them moved north for action against German Army Group North.

All of the above changes in the distribution of long-range bomber forces were due to the requirements of the army on the ground and not to any planning for strategic air warfare.

B. <u>Soviet Bomber Forces in Action</u>

1) <u>Combat Behavior of Bomber Personnel.</u> The somewhat reserved opinions expressed by German field commanders in former years concerning the Soviet bomber forces remained unchanged in 1944-45.[78]

On the one hand it was admitted that in many cases Soviet bomber crews executed their missions with persistence and determination, even at the cost of heavy losses; on the other hand, it is maintained that they were over-cautious in the execution of attacks, that they released their bomb loads prematurely when they encountered antiaircraft fire, and that they lacked aggressiveness and confidence in their own capabilities.

The growth of the Soviet bomber forces was still overshadowed by the build up of the fighter and ground-attack forces, and bomber units were not receiving the best personnel. There can be no doubt that these factors and the frequently noticed inadequate intellectual capabilities of bomber personnel had an adverse effect on the combat morale and aggressiveness of the force as a whole.

It is generally agreed, nonetheless, that bomber personnel improved in combat morale and self-confidence as a result of the weakening German defenses and the increasing scope of Soviet victories. As time passed this impression was confirmed by the behavior of the captured crews of downed Soviet bombers; they displayed considerably more self-assurance than formerly and were firmly convinced of a final Soviet victory.

2) <u>General Principles of Commitment.</u> According to available sources,[79] the general principles governing the employment of Soviet bomber forces remained essentially unchanged up to the end of the war. This means that the bulk of all bomber forces, including the units of the long-range bomber arm, still were used to support the operations of the army on the ground by bombing targets in the near German rear and deeper in the German communications zone,

while bombing missions of a quasi-strategic nature remained the exception.

In contrast with the above, bomber units attacked targets in the German rear with growing frequency, insofar as such targets were related to operations on the ground.

Close cooperation with the army on the ground resulted in a steadily increasing commitment of bomber units and in more firmly controlled missions. Air strikes by bomber forces, during the last two years of the war, were rarely under regimental strength, with the regiments following one another into the attack at brief intervals.

Bombers in operation were always protected by fighter escorts or, if they were executing missions in the near front areas, by fighter patrols.

Because the Soviet Command considered that a quasi-strategic use of its long-range bomber forces would have no important impact on military developments, no basic changes occurred in the tactical or technical methods of operation. Nevertheless, the methods of attack were gradually refined and improved. Bombers now carried out night attacks in sizeable units, with the individual strikes following successively at shorter intervals than formerly, and in accordance with more modern concepts.

The types of missions executed by the long-range bomber forces included night harassing attacks over the German main line of resistance area, which were usually carried out by single planes, strikes by complete units against targets in the German rear, and supply missions. As a rule, night operations, particularly long-range night missions, were executed only during good weather.

In other points, the principles governing the employment of Soviet bomber forces, as already described in Chapter 3, applied equally in 1944-45.

3) <u>Flight Conduct in the Execution of Missions by Soviet Bombers.</u> [80] No notable changes occurred in this field in the last years of warfare. What has been said in Chapter 3 on the subject of formation during the approach, attack, and departure; cruising and attack altitudes; execution of attack missions; and behavior in unit formation and in air combat therefore can be considered as generally applicable here.

Attacks were usually carried out in waves of regiment strength--the squadrons following each other at brief intervals within the regiment--at medium altitudes of between 6,600 and 13,000 feet. The unit generally flew in close formation and all planes released their bombs in horizontal flight on receiving the appropriate order from the lead plane. On the whole, the accuracy and effectiveness of bombing showed signs of improvement. Very often the attacking unit approached the bombing run in such a way as to be able to fly off towards the front lines immediately after the bomb release.

As the German defenses weakened towards the end of the war, Soviet bombers attacked at lower levels with increasing frequency. The awkward and clumsy behavior of Soviet bombers in air combat had not been quite surmounted, but this behavior no longer had decisive results because of the growing numerical strengths of the individual units and the decrease in German defensive fighter activities.

In the spring of 1945 Soviet bombers carried out morning and evening dusk attacks against targets in East Prussia. These attacks were executed by twin-engine, long-range bombers, each plane approaching individually at altitudes of between 2,600 and 3,300 feet and at intervals of five minutes for a stick bomb release of three or four 550-pound bombs. These attacks were not very successful, however, because of the effectiveness of the German fighter and AAA defenses in this area.

The only real difference noticed was in the execution of night missions. With the exception of night harassing raids (still carried out by single aircraft), bombers now commenced operating in larger units in accordance with more modern principles. In cases where attacks were still carried out by single planes, the tactics previously described were employed.

Thus, Soviet bombing operations in 1944-45 were marked by the following characteristic features: a) the existing tactics were retained and improved in respect to formation, cruising and attack altitudes, approach, bombing run, departure, formation flight, and air combat, but nothing essentially new was introduced; b) bombing attacks during daylight were carried out by increasingly large, closed units with fighter escorts; c) night bombing missions, with the exception of harassing operations, were no longer carried out by single planes but in a growing measure by complete units in accordance with western patterns.

4) <u>Bomber Operations within the Battle Area on the Ground and in Cooperation with the Army and the Navy</u>. Soviet bomber activities over the battle areas on the ground and in coordination with the army in 1944-45 were similar to those of 1943, the only difference being that they gradually became more frequent, more powerful, and more successful.[81] Both in timing and location of attacks, the Soviets adhered to the principles of power concentration. Therefore only little remains to be said in addition to that which has been stated in Chapter 3.

During the battles in the Crimea and for Sevastopol in the spring of 1944--previously mentioned in the discussion of Soviet ground-attack air forces*--Soviet bombers operated in a manner similar to that of the ground-attack units. In the first phase of the operations on the ground--the German withdrawal to Sevastopol and the Soviet attempt to enter the fortress in a sudden surprise drive--bombers did not participate at all. In the second phase--the Soviet attempt to take the fortress in an immediate assault--Soviet long-range bomber units operated from airfields in the general area of Kiev in day and night attacks against targets deep inside the fortified area. Bomb aiming was poor in these attacks and the German losses were correspondingly small. In the third phase the bombers carried out similar, preplanned attacks against the fortress, extending their operations to the German airfields. In the fourth phase--German evacuation of the fortress and withdrawal of the German troops across the Black Sea--the Soviet bombers directed their attacks primarily against embarkation operations and troop transports in the port of Sevastopol. Here they achieved considerable successes, sinking the <u>Totila</u> and the <u>Teja</u>, each of 3,000 tons displacement, and a number of ships in the 1,000 ton class, and inflicting heavy casualties.

In the period which followed, the commitment of bombers increased steadily--frequently in cooperation with ground-attack and fighter-bomber forces--in support of army operations in areas of main effort during offensive actions. The attacks here were directed against targets within the main battle area and in the

---

* See above, p. 340 ff and note, p. 340.

German rear. Like ground-attack forces, the Soviet bombers rarely, and never in systematically planned operations, attacked the withdrawing German columns.

It can be said both of the establishment of the German defenses in Courland* and of the German withdrawal from Estonia to Riga, that continuous attacks by Soviet bombers in appropriate strength could have seriously jeopardized the German operations involved. During the withdrawal to Riga, for example, a complete German division in the autumn of 1944 crossed the Dvina River between the Baltic and Riga by ferries and boats on a clear sunny day without any interference by Soviet air forces. Later, Soviet bombers attacked Libau /Liepaja/ innumerable times without achieving any really effective results.

Even as late as in the spring of 1945, Soviet bombers attacking Bromberg /Bydgoszcz/, a fortified city, unloaded their bombs indiscriminately on residential quarters, while no attacks were flown against the German command post in the local barracks or against the electric power station, the gas works, or the bridges across the Brahe /Brda/ River. Even later, when the German garrison fought its way out of Bromberg, the troops completed their march northward without interference from Soviet air forces.

Single bombers and harassing planes continued to be the only planes committed in night operations in the near front areas.

Thus, the employment of Soviet bombers in cooperation with the army on the ground increased and achieved some measure of success during the last years of warfare. Bomber operations per se, however, did not achieve decisive importance, even though they no doubt could have in view of the Soviet numerical superiority and the declining effectiveness of German resistance in the air. Apart from the lack of system, inadequate training, and insufficient experience, this may have been due to the way in which the Soviet Command had continually neglected its bomber arm in the past.

German commanders agree that Soviet bomber activities in cooperation with the Navy increased quite considerably in the last two years of warfare.[82] In 1943 the Black Sea was the only area

---

* See note above, p. 269.

where Soviet bombers attacked German shipping and port installations, but in 1944-45 these activities were extended to the Baltic and the Arctic Ocean. The attacks were directed primarily against seaborne transportation, such as convoys, supply ships, and troop transports, and less frequently against naval units, or naval and supply installations in ports.

Specific targets attacked included seaborne supplies en route from Odessa and Constanta to the Crimea; convoys off the Norwegian coast; seaborne withdrawal movements during the German evacuation of the Latvian coast; German and Rumanian naval units off Constanta; German mine sweepers operating in the eastern parts of the Baltic--the operations of which were seriously hampered by these attacks; port installations at Odessa, Constanta, Riga, Windau /Ventspils/, Libau /Liepaja/, Koenigsberg /Kaliningrad/, Danzig, and other ports.

In the beginning, attacks of the above types were characterized by a dispersal of effort and poor planning, so that they were not very effective. Towards the end of the war they were carried out on a larger scale and with more system and reached the apex of effectiveness in the very last phase of the war, when German shipping was practically undefended.

Naval bombers operated in regiment, squadron, or flight-size units according to the nature of the target. The usual approach and bombing run was at altitudes of between 10,000 and 13,000 feet, and the most usual form of attack was that of horizontal area bombing. In rare cases, PE-2 units carried out low-level or dive-bombing attacks at a dive angle of approximately 60 to 70 degrees. The individual planes of each flight followed their flight leader and released their bombs--usually of the 330 to 550-pound category--from an altitude of 3,300 feet. Units engaged in these operations always had strong fighter escorts and carried parachute fragmentation bombs for their own defense.

Towards the end of the war, torpedo bombers, as a rule IL-4 or Boston A20G planes, also began operating at night and were employed in mine-laying missions. Such missions, formerly rare, increased in frequency and scope and were directed at off-shore shipping routes, port entries, anchorages, and in some cases at river estuaries and navigable rivers. The mines were laid at night or during bad weather by single planes or small units. The drop altitude depended on the type of mines used, some of which were British ground mines of the magnetic type, while the others were from Soviet production. In a very few cases, towards the end of the war, Soviet bombers were observed using depth charges in anti-submarine operations.

Operations against German convoys were tightly integrated in timing and were carried out simultaneously by bomber, torpedo-bomber, ground-attack, and fighter aircraft together with submarines. Immediately prior to the bombing run the attacking units separated to attack their targets simultaneously in small groups from various altitudes and directions, using bombs, weapons fire, air torpedos, and in some cases phosphorus bombs. A reconnaissance plane posted over the target area kept the command post directing the air attack currently informed by means of a running report on such items as bomb aiming, the effects achieved, mistakes made, losses incurred, German fighter and antiaircraft artillery action, and personnel in distress at sea. This enabled the air command to take immediate and appropriate action as required. During operations of this type, the Soviets usually directed simultaneous holding attacks against German airfields.

Although the Soviets committed very strong air forces, they achieved relatively small results in their attacks against German convoys. Losses due to German fighter action proved seriously discouraging and occasionally resulted in a premature cessation of the attack. For example, on 17 June 1944 a force of approximately 100 Soviet aircraft (Boston, IL-2, P-40, Yak-9, and Airacobra (P-39)) attacked a German convoy of 10 transport ships and 20 escort units off the Norwegian coast. The attack was carried out in four waves and lasted altogether 25 minutes. Losing 40 aircraft themselves, the Soviets downed two German fighters, sank one transport ship with a displacement of 1,600 tons, and damaged one merchant vessel.

In the light of what has been said, Soviet bomber operations over the battle area and in cooperation with the army and the Navy in 1944-45 can be said to have been marked by the following features:

    a) Soviet bomber forces, including long-range bomber units, were employed in concentration to support the army on the ground, achieving growing successes, but never on a scale which could have decided the outcome of the battle.

b) They attacked targets within the main battle area as well as targets in the German rear. Right up to the end of the war, however, their inadequate air action against German retrograde movements remained an inexplicable error of omission of the Soviet Command.

c) Combined bomber, ground-attack, and fighter strikes in support of the army on the ground gradually became the most important feature in bomber operations.

d) Bomber operations in support of the Soviet Navy gained considerably in significance and were extended to include northern waters and the Baltic Sea. Besides bombing and air torpedo attacks, bombers engaged in mine-laying operations on a steadily growing scale. The operations of Soviet bombers, however, did not interfere seriously with German naval operations.

5) <u>Soviet Bomber Operations in the German Rear</u>. With very few exceptions bombing operations in the German rear were directed against the German Air Force ground service organization or against targets in direct or indirect support of Army operations. The unanimous opinion of German field commanders[83] is that no important changes occurred in this field in 1944-45 except that the attacks were more frequent, were carried out with stronger forces, and were more effective than in former years. In planning and execution, however, they differed little from the operations described in detail in Chapter 3.

Soviet bomber operations in the German rear began to increase in 1943 and continued until they reached a peak in the spring of 1945. Ceaseless bombing during daylight, and sometimes also at dusk and during the night, directed at the last German airfields still in operation in East Prussia finally had a serious effect on German air operations and periodically prevented German air activities altogether. The same can be said of Soviet bombing attacks against port installations and other targets in the Baltic ports.

It is probably due alone to their wariness in this new field of endeavor--i.e. operations in the German rear--that the Soviet bombers did not achieve even more effective results. Occasionally, in attacks of this type a Soviet plane would appear at a very high altitude for last minute reconnaissance followed by a small bomber unit dispatched for the purpose of drawing the German fighters into air combat prior to the arrival of the main body of bombers. The latter approached on a different course, waiting to exploit the situation and attack at the most favorable moment. Tactics of this type, however, were relatively rare.

6) <u>Night-Bombing Operations</u>. In 1944-45 harassing bombing and attacks against tactical targets in the zone of army operations still played the major role, but two new features were noticeable: strikes against quasi-strategic targets, and attacks by complete units in accordance with western patterns.

No changes occurred in the planning and execution of night harassing attacks,[84] already described in Chapter 3. They remained the most frequent type of Soviet night air operations in stabilized front areas. Most of these harassing attacks were carried out by U-2 planes. Apart from a certain impact on supply and replacement movements, the main effect of these attacks was through their continuous disturbance of the troops, who were subject to severe psychological strains anyway because of the uninterrupted combat in which they were engaged. In the last years of warfare it was still impossible to find an effective remedy against these nuisance raiders.

Night bombing attacks against tactical targets gained in significance.[85] They were designed to support army operations on the ground and were directed against such targets as traffic, supply and servicing installations, billets and shelters, bridges and other river crossing points, airfields, and unit headquarters. In this way, for example, the Soviets directed attacks against the headquarters of Provisional Army Group Heinrici in Northern Hungary in mid-December 1944, and, early in 1945, against the headquarters of I Air Corps and those of Air Administrative Area Command Hungary in Veszprem, Papa, Oedenburg /Sopron/, and Steinamanger /Szombathely/. The bombs were not badly placed in these attacks, as the present author can testify from personal experience of the attacks at Steinamanger, but the results were relatively insignificant.

In support of current operations on the ground, the Soviet bombers directed numerous attacks of this type against a large number of towns, including Sevastopol, Lvov, Riga, Dvina, Libau /Liepaja/, and later in the war against Koenigsberg /Kaliningrad/ and Danzig. At the same time the frequency and scale of attacks against German airfields in the near front areas and also farther in the German rear grew. In September 1944, for example, 17 bombing attacks involving approximately 3,200 bombers, plus 12 penetrations by approximately

200 planes engaged in partisan supply operations are reported, excluding operations within the area of the main line of resistance. The effects of these attacks varied, but on the whole they became increasingly effective.

Some of these missions were flown by individual planes, others by complete units, which tried to increase their effectiveness by concentration of their force. Individual planes usually attacked targets near the front, while complete units hit targets in the German rear, but exceptions to this rule were noted occasionally. Towards the end of the war unit attacks increasingly took the place of attacks by individual aircraft.

An increase in the frequency and scope of night attacks against quasi-strategic (or political) objectives[86] is reported for the first time in 1944-45. In the spring of 1944 such attacks were directed against towns in Finland and were designed to break the morale of the Finnish population. Later they were directed against Koenigsberg /Kaliningrad/, Budapest, and other densely populated cities and centers of government and administration.

These attacks, which were an exclusive mission of units of the long-range bomber arm, were carried out as a rule by complete units and not by individual planes. Compared with the night attacks by air forces of the Western Allies, the results achieved were not impressive. They did show, however, a considerable improvement over operations in former years. Nevertheless, right up to the end of the war the Soviets did not succeed in removing the existing deficiencies in organization, training, and combat experience.

Insofar as night harassing and single-plane operations are concerned the reader is referred to the description given above in Chapter 3.

Night-bombing missions by complete units corresponded largely to the western pattern for such operations and in general were executed in the manner now described:[87]

The sub-units participating in the operation took off from various bases widely distributed along the front, navigating by their own radio bearings supplemented by dead reckoning and orientation by ground features, and following as direct a course as possible to their assigned target. The entire unit did not assemble prior to the attack nor were diversive or deceptive maneuvers employed. The individual attack waves were directed at the target concentrically and in closed formation. The direction and altitude of attack were prescribed by orders for each participating sub-unit. As a rule the attack altitude was between 13,000 and 17,000 feet, the departure frequently as low as 6,600 feet. The prescribed duration of a division-size attack was approximately twenty minutes, but the attack often lasted longer. The regimental marker planes had orders to light up the target one minute prior to the bombing run, and to drop new marker flares at intervals of three to four minutes. The use of pathfinder planes with special Rotterdam type equipment /airborne navigational and blind flying set/ was not observed.

The type of bomb used depended on the kind of target under attack, but preference was shown for 110- and 220-pounders, and only a small quantity of 550- and 1,100-pound bombs were carried. The usual method of bombing was by stick release, which meant that a plane carrying ten 220-pound bombs released at intervals of one to two seconds could cover a strip 330 to 1,150 yards long.

Well placed defensive fire by antiaircraft guns frequently resulted in a premature bomb release. To evade such fire Soviet bombers pushed down their noses, losing as much as 3,300 feet in altitude, or held their altitude and flew in curves. Long-range bombers had no night-fighter escorts in 1944, but were supported by fighters on patrol missions over their home bases, both during their take off and their subsequent landing.

According to the nature of the target and the distance involved, the attacks were sometimes repeated. However, the repeat attacks were not flown by the entire unit but by individual planes at irregular intervals, which took off as soon as they had refueled and taken on a new load of bombs. In such cases the duration of the mission for individual crews sometimes lasted eight to twelve hours. Operations of this type were carried out on light and dark nights but not when weather conditions were really bad.

Apart from a few isolated torpedo bombing attacks and mining missions, Soviet bombers were not observed in night operations at sea.

On the basis of available data Soviet bomber operations at night in 1944-45 can therefore be evaluated as follows:

a) They consisted of harassing operations, attacks against tactical targets and--in contrast with former years--attacks against quasi-strategic targets.

b) The methods employed in night-harassing operations and night attacks against tactical targets remained the same as in former years, but were executed with stronger forces and increasing success. These attacks constituted the bulk of night operations carried out by bombers.

c) From the spring of 1944 on Soviet bombers engaged in night attacks against quasi-strategic targets, but not on any appreciable scale. Although properly planned, the attacks were not strong enough.

d) Besides single-plane missions, attacks by complete units in accordance with western patterns--particularly when committed for quasi-strategic purposes--played a role of steadily growing importance.

e) Inadequacies in training and combat experience, coupled with the former hesitancy to commit bomber forces in night operations, produced results which were not commensurate with the amount of effort expended.

7) Bomber Operations under Exceptional Weather Conditions.*
The few reports available on the subject[88] show that even in 1944-45 Soviet bomber forces avoided missions during really bad weather, showing a marked preference for fair to medium-fair weather, that they were no longer hampered in their operations by very dark nights, and, above all, that they carried out their missions in the same manner in winter as in summer. Nigh harassing raids and missions in the immediate vicinity of the front were executed in practically all weather conditions.

---

* What has been said on this subject concerning 1942-43 in Chapter 3 applies equally to the 1944-45 period.

8) <u>Bomber Operations in Cooperation with Other Elements of the Air Forces.</u>* In the last years of warfare cooperation between bomber forces and other elements of the air forces improved markedly, and was characterized by the following features:

a) In cooperation with daylight fighters, Soviet bombers always received adequate protection in the form of direct or indirect escorts. The attacking formations maintained unit cohesion even when attacked by German fighters.

b) Soviet bombers engaged in night operations received night-fighter protection while taking off from the bases and while landing. Towards the end of the war night fighters also patrolled over and attacked German night-fighter bases in the vicinity of the bombers' targets, and also attacked German antiaircraft artillery and searchlight positions within the target area.

c) In cooperation with ground-attack and fighter-bomber forces, combined bomber attacks increased in frequency, concentration, and effectiveness.

C. <u>Aircraft Types, Weapons, and Other Equipment</u>

Reports on the types of bomber aircraft and their weapons and equipment in use in 1944-45 are not very numerous,[89] but all agree that no innovations worthy of note occurred in these fields.

As in the past, the plane used most frequently in night harassing raids was the U-2. It was admirably suited for such use because of its easy handling in flight, the small amount of servicing and maintenance it required. In addition, its ability to take off and land at very small emergency air strips, made it possible to dispatch it several times in the course of one night.

The planes used in normal bombing missions were the Li-2, IL-4, PE-2, TB-3, TB-7, Mitchell B-25, Douglas A-20

---

* Bomber cooperation with fighters--including night-fighter, ground-attack, and fighter-bomber forces--has been already treated in the present chapter so that no further discussion is needed here.

(Boston III) and, as the only new Soviet-produced model, the TU-2. Of these types, the TB-3 and TB-7, being outdated models, were dispatched only on night-bombing missions, while the Douglas-Boston was committed primarily in night-fighter missions. The planes available in the largest numbers were the IL-4, Li-2, PE-2, and Douglas-Boston.

The above types of aircraft were adequate for use as medium bombers in the execution of tactical bombing missions. They were too light for strategic purposes.

The modern TU-2 was faster and had a greater maximum operational altitude than the IL-4. It appears to have been adequate for requirements in the Eastern Theater, but was not in evidence in large enough numbers to permit a definite appraisal. Soviet experts also were not uniformly in favor of this model.

Soviet bombers in the last two years of warfare did not achieve the results expected of them. This was probably owing in part to the types of bomber aircraft in use, which were not in all respects suitable under conditions of modern warfare.

No important changes are reported in the types of bombs in use in 1944-45 or in the methods of their use. In some cases the Soviets were observed using captured German 2,200-pound bombs in night attacks, having equipped Li-2 planes with special bomb clips for the purpose. The authorized bombloads were frequently exceeded. Detonators seem to have improved, since the number of duds declined. Soviet long-range bombers frequently used a rotating bomb container. This was a container filled with small caliber bombs which were ejected from the container (known as the PRAB) some time after the release. One innovation was a projectile similar to a rocket projectile, released in night raids by U-2 planes at altitudes of between 1,600 and 2,000 feet. It left no fire trail behind and was released with a faintly audible report.

D. Summary Assessment of the Soviet Bomber Forces in 1944-45

A final evaluation of the Soviet bomber forces in 1944-45 can be stated as follows:

1) The Soviet bomber arm showed considerable improvements in the execution of missions and general performances but was unable to catch up to the fighter and ground-attack air arms.

2) Soviet bomber personnel still showed a few defects, but on the whole their combat morale, aggressiveness, and self-assurance were improved.

3) The organization and chains of command in the arm underwent only small changes, unit strengths increased steadily, and the distribution of forces--including the units of the long-range bomber arm--was predicated on the current areas of main effort in operations on the ground, and on the principle of concentration of forces.

4) The primary mission of the Soviet bomber forces remained that of supporting army operations on the ground by bombing targets in the near front areas and in the German rear. In the execution of this mission those tactical principles which had proved to be sound in the past remained in force. This use of bomber forces in proper cooperation with the ground forces and on a steadily mounting scale resulted in growing successes.

5) The employment of bombers against German naval units and other seaborne targets also increased in the Baltic and in northern waters, and towards the end of the war proved fateful to weakly defended German transports in the Baltic.

6) Bomber attacks against the German ground service organization hampered German air operations considerably, and helped to bring about the paralyzation of the German Air Force in the spring of 1945.

7) Soviet bombers rarely flew quasi-strategic daylight missions. At night, however, they carried out such missions with increasing frequency and power, but without achieving any appreciable measure of success. Such attacks were directed primarily against large towns considered important because of the size of their population or because of their functions as administrative centers.

8) Night harassing raids and night attacks against tactical targets increased in scope and effectiveness.

9) Cooperation with other elements of the Soviet air forces advanced considerably. The fighter escort system functioned smoothly, and combined attacks in which bomber, ground-attack, and fighter-bomber forces participated were carried out with greater concentration and more effective results.

10) In the field of aircraft types, weapons, and equipment no appreciable progress was achieved. This was one of the reasons why the success of the Soviet bomber forces remained limited.

In conclusion, during 1944-45 Soviet bomber aviation showed considerable progress, both in daylight and night operations. That the Soviets did not achieve results equalling those of their Western Allies in this field is, among other reasons, primarily owing to the way in which the Supreme Soviet Command had for many years neglected the development of bomber aviation.

Section X: Special Air Missions[90]

Little information is available concerning special air missions. What is available indicates that operations in this field continued to improve. Signs of this were the successes and constant growth of the partisan movements, made possible by special air-support missions.

A. Air Transportation

No spectacular changes were observed in this field.[91] The use of units of the Long-Range Air Force for transport operations continued to increase. Reports confirmed both the existence of a 3-regiment air transport division within the Long-Range Air Force and the use of twin-engine aircraft in transport missions. Units of the Long-Range Air Force supplied surrounded army units by airdrop in night operations. The drop sites were marked by light signals, and the supplies were dropped by aircraft flying singly at altitudes of between 1,000 and 1,600 feet. Transport aircraft rarely landed inside a pocket.

In addition to supplying surrounded units, the Soviets succeeded in keeping their troops supplied by air when rail and road routes were damaged and when mud conditions made transportation on the ground impracticable.

B. <u>Courier, Liaison, and Command Planes</u>.

Soviet courier and liaison operations[92] in 1944-45 were not marked by any special features. Courier traffic was, nevertheless, quite lively. In Courland* in the spring and summer of 1944, for example, heavy courier traffic was necessary to secure cooperation with the many partisan units in the areas around Dvina. While on courier missions of this type, Soviet pilots occasionally lost their way and fell into German hands.

The same principles of organization which governed courier planes in 1943 applied in 1944-45. The commitment of these planes, largely U-2's, and their organization into separate units attached to air armies followed the already established patterns.

Airfields were detected which were reserved exclusively for use by liaison units. In December 1944 Soviet liaison planes landed at special ice air bases on frozen lakes in East Prussia.

C. <u>Partisan Supply Operations</u>

Closely linked to large-scale Soviet offensive operations on the ground, the air movement of supplies to partisan groups[93] increased considerably in 1944. With increasing frequency, transport planes penetrated the German rear areas carrying weapons, ammunition, explosives, medical supplies, and command personnel to the partisans. In the zone of German Army Group Center, for example, several hundred Soviet planes were reported in the German rear flying such missions nightly prior to the Soviet offensive of 1944. This is the only explanation which can be found for the ability of the partisans to blow up railroad tracks at approximately 4,000 points during the two nights preceding the opening of the June 1944 offensive against Army Group Center. Operations on such a scale would not have been possible without support from the Soviet air forces.

In order to supply the partisans, the Soviets used makeshift airstrips secluded in vast, forest covered areas. Supplies were usually brought in at night by either powered aircraft or cargo gliders. Improvised lighting made landings, or in some cases air

---

* See note above, p. 269.

drops, possible. The magnitude of these efforts can be judged by the results of a large-scale German counter-partisan operation near Lepel. On one of the partisan airfields in the area German troops found more than one hundred cargo gliders. The air drop points, of which only very few were detected by the German forces, were marked by special signals, usually open fires, the number and pattern of which changed daily in accordance with a pre-established plan.

Units of the Long-Range Air Force also participated in these nightly supply operations. On long-distance missions they usually flew in formation, crossing the German lines at an altitude of about 13,000 feet. When they reached the target area they were guided either by radio signals or light beacons.

Besides flying supplies to the partisans, Soviet air units flew in large numbers of paratroopers, who gave direct support to the partisans, thereby increasing their combat strength.

Partisan operations were combatted (as in 1943) by committing strong German fighting forces in countermeasures. These, however, produced only partially effective results. It was not until the war moved into German territory that these partisan activities and the concurrent Soviet air-support operations ceased. Up to then, however, the Soviet air forces contributed very largely to the success achieved by the partisans.

Section XI: <u>The Ground Service Organization of the Soviet Air Forces; Soviet Air Force Technology; the Supply Services</u> [94]

As in 1942-43, the Soviets were undemanding, extremely adaptable, and able to master problems as they arose with the simple means available. No spectacular innovations were noted, but the application and continued development of tried and tested principles made it possible to meet the requirements of the troops.

A. <u>Ground Service Organization</u>

In the opinion of German field commanders,[95] the Soviet ground service organization was more flexible, more adaptable, and thus performed better than its German counterpart under existing conditions in the Eastern Theater. Repeatedly, the Soviets established airfields in a surprisingly short time in terrain considered by the Germans to be completely unsuitable for even make-shift type airfields. The Soviets did have the advantage, however, that their aircraft were, in general, lighter than those in use by the Germans.

The Soviet system, observed already in 1943, of dispensing with permanent type air bases in favor of an extensive network of temporary airfields--to which they constantly added new fields while moving the network closer to the front--was continued and intensified in 1944-45. In the zone opposite German Army Group Center in the summer of 1944, for example, only two of the sixty-four airfields detected were of the permanent type and these were at Smolensk North and Smolensk South.

In the development of the Soviet network of airfields, the organization, scope, speed of operations, and sequence of the various construction phases, provided reliable indications on the location, and frequently on the timing, of impending, large-scale offensives. This was found to be the case time and again in Courland, Hungary, Poland, East Prussia, and Silesia, in fact, in all areas of the Eastern Theater. Air units moved on to the airfields only shortly before the opening of the actual attack.

Difficulties in the development of the ground service system during rapid forward movements, or in the quick transfer of air units to airfields closer to the front, were hardly noticeable. What has been said here, also applies very largely to the progress made in ground organization facilities for night operations.

As time passed, the Soviets overcame their reluctance to use former German airfields. When they entered German territory, they found numerous airfields available, which they immediately put into operation. Frequently, however, Russian carelessness made it possible for German air units to achieve good results right up to the end of the war by attacking these overcrowded fields.

1) <u>Operational Principles, Organization, Chains of Command.</u>
By rapidly extending their system of advance airfields, the Soviet air forces were able to provide the necessary air support for the units spearheading the attack on the ground. Furthermore, the resulting dispersion of the Soviet air units made them less vulnerable to attack. During Army advances, Soviet air forces operated almost exclusively from these temporary airfields. Their construction and expansion

was indicative of the increased capabilities of the ground service forces. Opposite German Army Group Center, for example, it was observed in September 1943 that 290 airfield construction battalions established 183 airfields; in July 1944, in contrast, it took only 211 airfield construction battalions to construct 310 airfields within an area of the same size. This means that each airfield construction battalion on an average completed one-and-one-half airfields in one month. The large overall performance was due to the existence of numerous airfield operation, airfield construction, technical, and transport units. The total number of new airfields constructed in August 1944 was 506, quite a commendable performance.

Prior to the opening of the summer offensive against German Army Group Center in June 1944, the Soviets had more than 64 airfields in the area, 62 of them of the temporary type. Of these, only seven were not in operation at the time. These seven fields, less than nine miles from the front lines, were put into operation immediately after the offensive began. Of the remaining 57 fields, 42 were between 9 and 27 miles from the front and each had between 25 and 30 aircraft (i.e., one air regiment).

The organization and chains of command within the ground service system remained unchanged. Each air army was assigned an average of four regional air bases, the number varying according to the mission and the current situation. Each regional air base, in turn controlled a number of airfield operating and airfield construction battalions, besides airfield technical companies, motor transport battalions, captured materiel salvage companies, and signal companies.

In addition to the above, each air army had a number of station-type and mobile aircraft repair shops, station-type and motorized motor vehicle maintenance shops, independent technical companies, and terminal supply depots. The functions of these various establishments were as follows:

Regional Air Bases were responsible for the proper employment of its assigned units, for the allocation of supplies, and the execution of unit transfers.

Airfield Operating Battalions were responsible for the maintenance and operation of their assigned airfields. This included the refuelling and loading of units, housekeeping and medical services for the air units stationed on the field; transportation, guard, weather, and radio and wire communication services.

Airfield Construction Battalions were responsible for the construction and repair of airfields.

Airfield Technical Companies were responsible for the maintenance of the technical installations at existing airfields and for the technical equipment of newly constructed fields.

Captured Materiel Recovery Battalions handled the identification, sorting, and evacuation of captured enemy air materiel.

Signal Companies established and operated the wire and radio installations required for ground communications.

Motorized Aircraft Maintenance Shops handled the overhauling and general maintenance work which exceeded the capabilities of the technical personnel assigned to the air units.

Station-Type Aircraft Maintenance and Repair Shops repaired aircraft damaged beyond the repair capacity of the motorized aircraft maintenance shops.

Motorized and Station-Type Vehicle Maintenance Shops performed the same services for motor vehicles as the aircraft maintenance shops did for aircraft.

Independent Technical Companies were responsible for the installation and improvement of navigational aids.

Terminal Supply Depots handled the supplies intended exclusively for the air forces.

Air units assigned to the Navy were serviced by naval air bases, the responsibilities and functions of which approximated those of the regional air bases of the air armies. There was, however, one important difference: the naval air bases were organic to the units they serviced. In general, they came under an air regiment for tactical control, while administratively and in matters of supply they were directly subordinate to an air division.

In the Home Defense Area the air force ground organization was of a locally permanent type, in contrast with the organization at the front which changed with the military situation. Thus, the various units were permanently attached to replacement air units and aviation schools.

2) <u>Airfields and Their Equipment</u>.[96] In 1944-45 the Russians gave renewed proof of their ability to construct and place in operation airfields of the simplest type within an incredibly short time. By making use of labor and machinery from the civilian population, particularly from nearby collective farms, and by employing tractors and special levelling vehicles, they were able to construct a runway with the essential subsidiary installations within ten to fourteen days. As soon as a runway 330 yards wide was ready, it was placed in operation. It is only natural that the airfields constructed in this manner were extremely makeshift and primitive, but they served the purposes for which they were intended.

The Russians were equally quick to repair demolished former German airfields and to improvise what were called ice airfields, which could be used by the heaviest types of aircraft.

Through the clever adaptation of their airfields to the surrounding terrain, and through the use of dummies and the creation of dummy airfields, the Russians again proved that they were masters in camouflage of all types.

In general, Soviet airfields and airfield equipment in 1944-45 differed little from the description given for 1943 in Chapter 3. The same applies to the defense of airfields by antiaircraft artillery.

No new experience was gained on the subject of the personnel employed in the ground services of the Soviet air forces.

B. <u>Soviet Air Force Technology</u>[97]

Only very little insight could be gained in 1944-45, as was the case in former years, into the field of Soviet air force technology.

The Soviets proved to be extremely good in the art of technical improvisation. They were quick to master the technicalities of captured German materiel, using German bombs, for example, with excellent results. The use of rollers and piles made from tree trunks, wooden rafters, planking, twigs, sawdust, and tree trimmings in the construction of runways, and the use of truck motors to start aircraft engines in winter--by transmitting the truck engine power to the propellor hub via the drive shaft and some pulleys--are examples of the primitive but highly useful improvisations and inventions employed by the Russians. In any case, technology as applied in the Soviet air forces in 1944-45 was equal to all requirements.

C. Supply Services[98]

In 1944-45, the supply situation of the Soviet air forces was improving steadily, supplies of all types seemed to be plentiful, and no shortages were evident. Apparently, the need for support from the Western Allies, in the form of air force supplies no longer existed.

The Russians used rail transportation to move various aircraft parts separately to air bases in the field for assembly on the spot. Among the parts thus moved forward were fuselages, wings and engines.

Being content to adhere to the proven methods of the past, the Russians introduced no changes in the organization and operations of their air force supply and replacement services during the last two years of warfare.

Section XII: Air Signal Communications[99]

Sources available reveal that the Soviets made further progress in this field. By cleverly applying foreign experience to Russian conditions, they succeeded in bringing about a general improvement in capabilities, particularly in the field of radio communications. The over-all structure of the air signal services assumed forms approximating those of an independently functioning Air Signal Corps. This development, however, was not quite completed by the time the war ended.[100]

In the organizational field,[101] the most important and most incisive measure was taken in mid-1944: the air signal units were removed from Army Signal Corps control and placed under the Administration of Signal Communications Services of the Air Forces of the Red Army. This established an independent air signal force, a development which resulted in a general expansion of radio communications and a reduction of wire communication facilities.

Up to the end of the war there were no clear signs that the aircraft reporting, air traffic control, and radio intercept services would be incorporated in the new signal communications services.

The air signal services were headed by a Chief of Air Signal Troops of the Air Forces of the Red Army, who at the same time was Signal Staff Officer to the High Command of Air Forces of the Red Army.

The air signal troops were organized into air signal regiments controlled by the air armies, and air signal regiments controlled by the High Command of the Air Forces of the Red Army.

An air signal regiment comprised one headquarters company, one telephone operating company, one radio operating company, one telephone construction company, and one telephone-cable laying company.

Each air corps, each air division, each regional air base, and each airfield operating battalion was assigned an independently operating air signal company consisting of: one headquarters platoon, one radio platoon, one telephone platoon, and one telephone construction platoon.

In September 1944 the overall strength of the air signal forces--excluding those signal units in the Long-Range Air Force, those serving with naval air forces, the signal troops of the Home Defense Command and those of the High Command of the Red Army Air Forces--was approximately 90,000 personnel.

The signal officer of each air unit was subordinate to the chief of staff of the unit. He received his orders from the chief of staff as well as from his next superior air signal officer. He was responsible for the proper employment of the assigned air signal personnel and the use of signal equipment, as well as all unit signal operations.

Each headquarters was responsible for the establishment

and operation of communications with the next lower echelon. This responsibility included the establishment and operation of communication centers (at headquarters), radio communications, wire communications, and other signal devices (optical and movable).

In contrast with the German use of wire communications--which played a primary role in their exercise of command--the Soviets attached major importance to radio.[102] The scarcity of permanent telephone lines in Russia and the enormous distances compelled the Soviet Command to such wide use of radio communications, which thus became the main medium for air-to-air communication, for the direction of operations, and for transmission of reports on the air situation.

In contrast to the German side, the Soviet radio warning service and the radio directing service included the radio installations of the Army. The establishment of radio networks and radio channels, however, corresponded to German usages. Ground-attack, bomber, and escort fighter units participating in an operation, and the radio stations on the ground, all used the same frequency. Only the unit lead planes maintained contact with the ground. Once a unit was outside the normal range of radio communication--if operating at an altitude of 3,300 feet, approximately 30 miles--no further efforts were made to exchange messages with the ground station. Radio traffic was usually in the clear, the risk of interception being considered the lesser of two evils compared with the possibilities of error and loss of time resulting from communications in code. Reconnaissance aircraft conducted their radio communications in the same manner as described above.

By the spring of 1944 the Soviets used radar[103] to detect German aircraft and to guide their fighters to within close range of their targets. No information is available, however, on the nature of Soviet radar units and their control. In the field of high frequency radio technology the Soviets still were in the initial stages of development. Therefore, all radar instruments known to exist throughout Russia, even as late as in the autumn of 1944, were ground-based instruments of British manufacture or instruments copied in the Soviet Union from British models. Although the existence of airborne radar instruments was not established at the time, there was unmistakable evidence that radar was being used in the control of fighter operations.

No new information of any significance was obtained concerning the Soviet radio intercept service.

As for wire communications,[104] lines of the existing basic network were generally used in the establishment of command communication channels. Only an exceedingly wide-meshed wire network was available for long-distance communications. The Russian Air Force, Army, and Navy all had to depend on this one network because no separate networks existed for the individual services. In establishing wire communication lines, the air signal service, when possible, took advantage of existing networks of the civilian postal services and of the various Army headquarters, thus reducing construction work. Women were employed with particular frequency in the wire and radio communications services.

No new information of any importance was obtained in the last years of warfare concerning other mediums of communication or concerning the signal equipment in use. The signal equipment used by the Soviet air forces was not equal in quality to that produced in western countries. This can be assumed with particular certainty since the standards achieved by the Soviet radio industry were far lower than those reached in other fields of technology in the Soviet Union. Nevertheless, the equipment available was, no doubt, adequate to the none too excessive demands of the Soviet air forces.

In an overall evaluation of the Soviet air signal services in 1944-45 approximately the same features prevail as in 1942-43: progress in the field of organization towards the establishment of an independent Air Signal Corps; notable improvements in the field of radio communications; and adequate capabilities in the fields of radar, wire communications and equipment. This means, essentially, that the Soviet air signal services could meet the requirements of the Soviet air forces, although they by no means could have met western standards or coped with conditions in the West.

Section XIII: <u>Training Activities</u>[105]

In the last phase of the war, as in the earlier phases, German field commanders gained no direct insight into the training of Soviet air forces. Instead, in forming their opinions they had to rely on deductions based upon the behavior and performances of Soviet airmen. These performances, however, clearly indicated that the training standards of the Soviet air forces had improved considerably.

In the training of aviators the Soviets adhered to their existing system, under which trainees progressed in succession through an Aeroclub, elementary aviation school, service school, replacement training regiment (air), air training regiment, and finally to a front-line unit. This program was extremely flexible and was adapted to current circumstances.

The training program was well thought out and systematic, but the results achieved remained far below German or Anglo-American standards. Since they had no manpower problems--the increase in pilots exceeded the output in aircraft considerably-- the Russians were able to extend the training period again, and thus give longer training to pilots who proved less capable than the average. This was an important advantage over the Germans, who could not afford to spend so much time in training, and who had no such reserves in personnel.

After the reverses they suffered in the first years of the war, the Soviets shifted the main responsibility for flying training from the flying schools to the replacement air units. This measure was reversed in the summer of 1943. In like manner it was noticed that the flying schools, transferred into the Russian interior after 1941, began to move back to the west in 1943.

The length of the preliminary flying training course in the aeroclubs was curtailed seriously during the war, and the course did not have nearly the importance it had had prior to the war. For this reason flying training now began in earnest in the primary flying schools, of which there were 130, and lasted on an average of from nine to twelve months. The trainees then entered the service schools, of which there were 60 for the fighter forces, 30 for the bombers, 30 for the ground-attack force, and 8 for the long-range bombers. Training in a service school lasted between twelve and fourteen months. In addition there were service schools for naval aviation, night flying and instrument navigation, as well as special schools for navigation and bombing.

The number of trainees at the individual schools varied widely, from as few as 200 to as many as 2,000. In fighter schools the average number of trainees was 750.

Apart from service schools for flight personnel, schools

existed for airborne radio operators, air gunners, ordnance, photographic, and other highly specialized personnel. The organization within the school system was very flexible and frequently brought about the fusion of schools from the various services.

After leaving the service schools, trainees spent two to six months in a replacement air regiment. These regiments consisted of from two to six squadrons and gave advanced training, refresher courses, and complete crew training. Another responsibility of the replacement air regiments, at least fifty of which were identified, was to refit existing front-line units, activate new units, and rehabilitate worn out units.

Training in a replacement air regiment was frequently followed by assignment, lasting between one and four months, to an air training regiment. One of these was assigned to each air army. The main mission of the air training regiment was to retrain and familiarize personnel with the types of aircraft being used by the air army to which it belonged. The regiment usually contained five squadrons, two of them equipped with fighter, one with PE-2, and one with IL-2 aircraft. The fifth squadron was reserved for the training of flight leaders. Towards the end of the war some of the air training regiments were disbanded, their functions being assumed by the replacement air regiments.

Flying personnel received their final training in front-line units, before being sent into action. This phase, lasting from one to three months, was rigorous and intensive, every effort being made to simulate actual combat conditions.

The training of the Soviet air forces was well organized and certainly provided adequate time to give flight personnel a thorough preparation for their coming duties. This was reflected in a general improvement of training standards.

Section XIV: Airborne Forces[106]

The overall organization of the Soviet parachute and other airborne forces remained practically unchanged in 1944-45, these troops still being organized in what were called airborne brigades. They were intended exclusively for use as paratroopers, and the brigades still had no organically assigned air transport.

Within the brigade itself, in contrast, a number of changes occurred which will now be enumerated.

Each airborne brigade was assigned a light tank battalion (with Model T-26 tanks); an artillery battalion of two 76.2-mm gun batteries and one 120-mm howitzer battery; and one light AA battalion of one 37-mm gun battery and two antiaircraft machine gun companies. In addition, the existing antitank battalion was increased in strength from two to four batteries. The strength of the brigade thus increased from 3,500 to approximately 4,200 combat personnel.

It was estimated in mid-1944 that the Soviets had a total of 23 airborne brigades, most of them concentrated in the Moscow area. This represented a combat strength of approximately 100,000 combat troops.

No reliable information was obtained concerning transportation methods. Plans existed to use gliders and PE-8* and Li-2 powered transportation aircraft for the purpose. Soviet paratroopers were armed with the most up-to-date small arms (submachine guns and carbines). Their jump training was very thorough, but allegedly was restricted to daytime practice jumping.

The well-equipped and well-trained airborne brigades represented a considerable power factor for use in airborne and conventional ground combat. However, in 1944-45, as in former years, they were not committed in airborne operations on any appreciable scale.

The failure to employ these troops in airborne operations may have been due to the Soviet Command considering difficult and costly operations of this type inappropriate, to a reluctance to undertake such operations because of a lack of adequate experience, or to other reasons.

The only fairly large scale use made of paratroopers was to reinforce partisan forces. Thus, as many as 300 paratroopers were landed in some of the daily drops within a large area in the central sector in the summer of 1944.

---

* Editor's Note: Previously designated as the TB-7, the PE-8 was a four-engine bomber which was later employed as an air transport plane.

Section XV: <u>Air Armament Industry, Military Economy, and Transportation</u>[107]

What is known concerning developments in these three fields has been gathered from diverse sources, and the account which now follows is not based on information from German field commanders, who had no insight into such matters.

<u>The Air Armament Industry.</u>[108] The Soviets continued their program for the rapid expansion of their air armament industry in 1944-45. Their output in aircraft per month increased from approximately 700 at the time when they evacuated the western territories in 1941-42 to 1,900 by early 1943, 2,400 by early 1944 and 3,400 by the autumn of 1944. In September 1944, as an example, they produced 1,450 fighter, 1,025 ground-attack, 460 bomber, 150 transport, and 390 training aircraft. These overall figures remained practically unchanged up to 1945.

To increase production, the number of types was severely restricted. Special stress was placed on the production of single-engine and thus on fighter and ground-attack aircraft, which made up approximately 75 percent of the entire output in aircraft. Most fuselages constructed for single-engine planes were of mixed construction /metal and wood/, those for multi-engine planes were all metal. The aircraft engines produced were almost exclusively of the carburetor type. By mid-1944 the existence of nine aircraft engine factories was established. It was also known that 21 fuselage factories existed, of which 8 produced fuselages for fighters, 2 for ground-attack aircraft, 5 for bombers, and 6 for training or transportation aircraft. Other factories were still under construction.

The lack of skilled labor was a serious problem for the Soviet aircraft industry. All in all it was estimated that the industry employed roughly 500,000 personnel, the majority of them women and children. All factories were producing at top capacity.

The main factors contributing towards the favorable development of the Soviet aircraft industry were: 1) the progressive expansion of existing factories; 2) the importation of the most up-to-date installations for serial production; 3) the establishment of new factories plus the reestablishment of evacuated factories in their former locations, after the retreat of German forces from the western territories (thus the Moscow area again became a center of the aircraft industry); and 4) the fact that the industry was able to function without any interference.

The large-scale expansion of the air armament industry not only enabled the Soviets to replace, within a relatively short time, their at times exceedingly heavy losses, but it enabled them to increase steadily their current strength in aircraft and completely modernize their entire air force. For quite some time the Soviet industry had been producing more than enough aircraft to replace its losses, so that the Russians no longer had to depend on Allied deliveries.

The Military Economy. In 1944-45 the entire Soviet military economy was also making steady progress towards the stage at which it would be able to meet all requirements for the conduct of the war. The main emphasis was on Army ordnance, with air force requirements taking second place.

The output in steel increased from 10 million tons in 1943 to 11.8 million tons in 1944 and 12.3 million tons in 1945. This was sufficient for the manufacture of 30,000 armored vehicles, 40,000 aircraft, 120,000 artillery pieces, 450,000 machine guns, 2,000,000 submachine guns, and 100,000 mortars, plus the necessary amounts of ammunition.

In developing their armament industry, the Soviets displayed a genius for improvisation on a scale which German authorities would have considered inconceivable. Thus, complete factories were dismantled within a few days, loaded for transportation--together with the necessary workers--, shipped to a new location, reestablished there and placed in operation within an incredibly short time. Once reestablished the factories very shortly not only achieved their former production capacity but in addition were able to make up for lost time and increase their output considerably.

In recaptured towns where the power plants had been destroyed prior to the German evacuation, the Soviets moved in complete power stations mounted on railway trains. Moving right up to the spot where electricity was required, these mobile power stations made it possible for the industries to resume operations almost immediately.

In any case it must be said that the Soviet armament industry was capable of meeting requirements during the last years of the

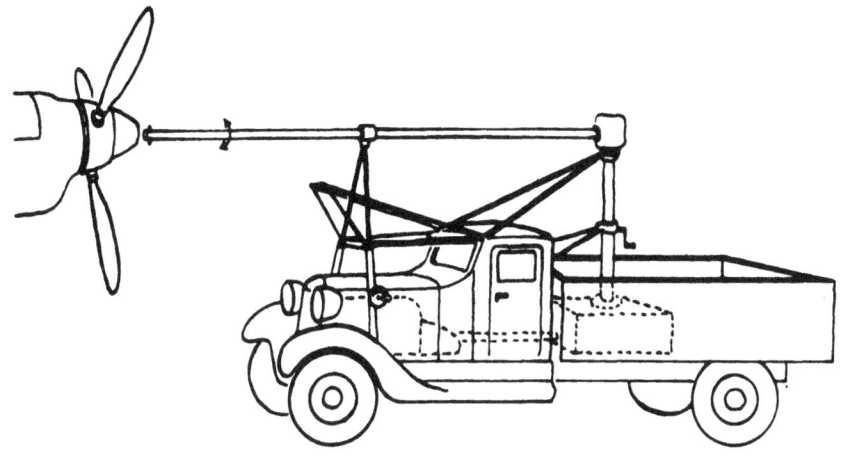

Diagram showing how the Russians used truck motors to start aircraft engines in winter

Drawing showing a mobile power station. These were used by the Russians to supply electricity to damaged factories.

war, and the hopes which the German military command had harbored that the Soviet industry would slow down or even come to a complete standstill were not realized.

Transportation. No major changes in the Soviet transportation system were observed in 1944-45, and all difficulties which might have been encountered in this field were mastered by normal means. Even the rapid Soviet advances in 1944-45 were not hampered materially by transportation difficulties.

In line with the general developments of the past civil aviation had been made a part of the military force and no new features of any special importance were noted in this field.

It was thus evident that the air armament industry, the military economy as such, and transportation and communications met all requirements of the Soviet command and forces and thereby made a large contribution to the overall Soviet victory.

Section XVI: Allied Support [109]

Allied assistance to the Soviet air forces continued to play a considerable role in the last third of the war and took the form of direct and indirect support. Direct support was primarily in the personnel field, indirect support in the field of materiel supplies.

One measure of direct support was that of the employment of French fighter forces.[110] Up to the summer of 1944 the French Normandie Fighter Regiment and the "Lorraine" and "Bretagne" squadrons were known to be in action. The Normandie Regiment, originally equipped with Yak-1 and later with Yak-9 aircraft, proved quite a problem to German fighter pilots, and was considered almost their equal. Fighter-bomber attacks by this unit against German airfields in East Prussia in the spring of 1945 were carried out very cleverly, efficiently, and with determination. French ground service personnel had proved less satisfactory and allegedly had been replaced by Soviet personnel and returned to Britain.

Another form of direct support was by American bomber and fighter formations flying from airfields in Italy and Britain to Soviet Russia.[111] After the establishment of an appropriate ground service organization in the Poltava area,* the first American bomber and fighter units landed there from Italy on 2 June 1944 to return to their Italian bases on 11 June. Very soon units flew the first triangular route, in which 200 bombers from Britain flew to Soviet Russia, where those not destroyed by German counteraction on the way landed on 21 June 1944 to take off for Italian bases five days later.

The small use made of the Anglo-American air bases established in the Soviet Union for operations against Eastern Germany and the Balkan area gave rise to the assumption that the whole arrangement was tailored to political propaganda rather than military purposes. It must be admitted, however, that some of the attacks carried out under the arrangement did have seriously disturbing effects, as was the case with the missions flown by U.S. fighter forces from bases in the Poltava area against German airfields in Poland.

Another item of personnel support which merits mention is that of the training given Soviet personnel in the air forces of the Western Powers. The changes in the Soviet air forces, which became increasingly marked from 1944 on, seemed largely due to this training assistance. It would be difficult, however, to determine to what extent this assumption is correct.

---

* Editor's Note: Bases were also established at Mirgorod and Piryatin. One of the factors which discouraged more extensive use of these bases by American aircraft was the Russian failure either to provide adequate defenses for the bases or to allow the Americans themselves to defend the bases. The indirect result was a brilliant night-raid (22 June 1944) by the Luftwaffe on the Poltava base which resulted in the destruction of 43 B-17's, 15 Mustangs and some miscellaneous Russian aircraft and the damaging of 26 additional B-17's. Also destroyed by the raid were quantities of American ammunition and 450,000 gallons of gasoline. After the war, General Spaatz told prisoner Hermann Goering that this was the best attack the Luftwaffe made against the Army Air Forces. For an interesting account of this attack, American shuttle bombing between Italy, Russia, and England and the problems connected with the American bases in Russia, see, Craven and Cate (eds.), The Army Air Forces in World War II, Vol. III, Europe, Argument to V-E Day, University of Chicago Press (Chicago, 1951), pp. 308-319.

Indirect support assumed a far greater scope than direct support.[112] This indirect support was in the form of materiel supplies. Intended originally only as an emergency measure to relieve a temporary shortage in military equipment, the assistance program was expanded to compensate for shortcomings in the Soviet program of production and the deliveries made under the program did much to enable the Soviet Union to continue resistance and later assume the offensive. Gradually, emphasis in the materiel support program shifted from the delivery of specific military materiel to the delivery of supplies needed indirectly for the conduct of the war.

Aircraft constituted the most numerous item in the supplies delivered under the assistance program.* Monthly deliveries in aircraft averaged 150 in 1941, 300 in 1942, 500 to 600 in 1943 and the first half of 1944, and then fell again to an average of 300 per month. By 1 January 1944 Soviet Russia had received from the Western Allies a total of approximately 10,000 aircraft, consisting of 6,000 fighters, 2,600 bombers, 400 transports, and 1,000 training aircraft. Of these deliveries, 60 percent came from the United States and 40 percent from Great Britain, or, to be more precise, 6,003 aircraft from the United States and 4,101 aircraft from Great Britain. By 1 October 1944 the Soviets had received from the Western Allies a total of approximately 14,700 aircraft-- 8,734 from the United States and 6,015 from Great Britain. The total of 14,700 aircraft consisted of 8,200 fighters, 3,600 bombers, 100 reconnaissance planes, 1,200 transports, and 1,600 training aircraft. Losses during transportation amounted to an average of 20 percent. Britain halted deliveries in the summer of 1944.

During the time in which these deliveries were made, the Soviet industry produced 97,000 aircraft, so that Allied deliveries amounted to roughly 15 percent of the overall Soviet output.

Aircraft delivered, in the order of their numbers, were: Airacobra, followed by Spitfire, Hurricane, Kittyhawk, and Mustang fighters; Douglas Boston III, Mitchell, Marauder, and Hampden

---

* Editor's Note: The approximate total of American planes given to Russia during the war was 14,612, according to Craven and Cate (eds.), The Army Air Forces in World War II, Vol. VI, Men and Planes, University of Chicago Press (Chicago, 1955), pp. 352, 405.

bombers; Catalina seaplanes; and Douglas C-47 transports. Only a small number of four-engine planes were delivered.

Next in importance to aircraft were Allied deliveries of specialized machinery and high-octane aviation gasoline. The latter item in particular could not be produced in adequate quantities within the Soviet Union. After the Western Allies, in 1943, had supplied the necessary technical installations for a number of refineries, it was to be assumed that Soviet industry soon would be able to cope with these bottlenecks.

The routes used by the Western Allies for the movement of deliveries to the Soviet Union are generally known and also have been mentioned previously in this study. The northern route through Murmansk and Archangel lost steadily in importance to the Persian Gulf route. The sea routes to Far East ports, and the Alaskan route for the delivery of aircraft by air gained steadily in importance.

From what has been said no doubt can exist that in 1944-45 Allied support in terms of materiel and, to a lesser degree, personnel, again proved to be invaluable to the Soviet air forces and made a decisively important contribution to their successes.

Section XVII: Summary

The opinion of German field commanders concerning the Soviet air forces in 1944-45 resulted, among other things, from constant encounters with those forces in the air. In its essence, that opinion can be formulated as follows:

1) The shift in power ratios in favor of the Soviets commenced as early as 1943 and accelerated steadily during the last third of the war. Soviet successes on the ground and in air warfare, Soviet numerical superiority, progress in the field of technology, and the increasing combat experience of Soviet airmen all contributed to bring about a gradual overall strengthening of the Soviet air forces.

These developments naturally culminated in Soviet air superiority. This air superiority, however, did not amount to absolute air supremacy of the kind established by the German Air Force at the opening of the Russian campaign. Whenever German and Soviet airmen encountered each other in air combat right up to the very end of the war, and their equipment was technically equal, the superior intellectual and combat capabilities of the German airmen always decided the action in their favor, in spite of crushing Soviet superiority in numbers. Owing to the rapid disappearance of German air power, however, the possibilities for such successful encounters in the air became less and less frequent.

2) As had been the case in the past, Soviet air power served almost exclusively to provide direct or indirect support for the army on the ground and made a decisively important contribution to the final Soviet victory.

The salient features of the Soviet air forces in this phase of the war were their aggressive conduct of operations, their adherence to the principle of power concentration, and their retention of organizational and operational methods which had proved sound in the past.

In contrast with former times, the Soviet air forces engaged in strategic missions, although only on a moderate scale. However, the results achieved in attacks of this type, most of which took place in the night, were not impressive.

3) The personal behavior of Soviet pilots in this period is reflected in their increasing successes, their growing self-assurance, their mounting aggressiveness, and their improved combat morale. Nevertheless, right up to the end they were unable to surmount completely their feeling of inferiority to their German opponents. This was one of the fundamental causes for the failure of the Soviet air forces to achieve absolute air supremacy.

4) In addition to performing their former tasks, Soviet reconnaissance units were committed increasingly in wide area reconnaissance missions. Through systematic action and the intensity of their operations they produced results which were adequate for the Soviet conduct of operations.

5) The Soviet fighter forces increased their efforts and improved their performances and methods in all fields. These factors, coupled with their crushing numerical superiority, enabled them to achieve and maintain air superiority and thereby contribute greatly to the final Soviet victory.

6) The Soviet ground-attack air forces continued to adhere

to the tactical principles which had proved sound in the past. Through their persistent and successful attacks in support of major operations on the ground, they contributed a decisive share in breaking German resistance. The Soviet Command's continual emphasis of ground-attack aviation thus achieved the desired result.

7) Soviet bombers were more in evidence in this period than in the early years of the war, and they achieved a commendable measure of success in operations supporting the army on the ground. The effectiveness of night-bombing operations, by contrast, did not assume major proportions. In spite of its improvement, the bomber arm, right up to the end of the war, remained inferior to fighter and ground-attack aviation.

8) Fighter, ground-attack, and bomber cooperation with each other and with the army continued to increase and improve, and produced good results. Cooperation with the Navy, neglected in the past, also gained a certain measure of importance.

9) The employment of aircraft in special-type missions increased. Partisan supply operations, in particular, made a decisively important contribution to the success achieved in partisan activities.

10) The ground service organization, air force technology, and the supply services continued to adhere to their simple basic principles and participated in the general development of the Soviet air forces. They were able to meet all demands in their fields.

11) The air signal services gained a larger measure of independence and showed signs of becoming a separate air signal corps. Concentrating primarily on the development of radio communications, the service was able to meet all requirements of the Soviet air forces, although it did not achieve western standards.

12) In training activities the Soviets could proceed without interference and in accordance with a long-range program. As a result, they were able to assign well prepared personnel to their front-line units.

13) Paratroopers and other airborne troops were well trained and equipped, but were not committed in any sizeable airborne or ground combat missions; it was only in the field of partisan operations

that the employment of paratroopers played a significant role.

14) The Soviet aircraft industry, military economy, and transportation system were able to develop and expand without enemy interference and thus could meet all requirements for the conduct of the war.

15) Support from the Western Allies continued right up to the end of the war, particularly in the form of materiel supplies, which were primarily aircraft. This support was a large factor contributing to the final Soviet victory.

As in the past, the Soviets in the last third of the war continued to employ their air power primarily to serve the purposes of operations on the ground. The rapid decline of the German air power potential, the progressive development of the Soviet air forces in all fields, their growing combat experience, and their vast numerical superiority enabled them to make a vitally important contribution towards final victory.

At the end of the war Soviet air superiority was securely established. Although German airmen still had the advantage of superior operational and combat experience, their small numbers towards the end of the war prevented them from exploiting these advantages.

CONCLUSION

The Soviet air forces, inferior to the German Air Force in every respect except that of numerical strength at the beginning of the Russian campaign, were almost completely paralyzed in 1941 by the Luftwaffe's powerful blows and by the loss of their ground service system to the German Army. This resulted in temporary German air supremacy.

The decreasing frequency and power of German air attacks, however, and the undisturbed Russian Air Force training activities and aircraft production coupled with support from their Western Allies enabled the Soviet air forces to make rapid progress towards complete recovery in 1942-43. Their transition from a strictly defensive attitude to a fundamentally offensive one, and their mounting numerical superiority, finally enabled them to achieve parity in air power.

In 1944-45, the progressive development of the Soviet air forces was accelerated. In spite of this, Soviet air power continued to be employed almost exclusively to support operations on the ground. The further decline of German air power and the concomitant increase in Soviet air power finally resulted in uncontested Soviet air superiority, which, in turn, became an essential ingredient of the Soviet victory.

World War II is the firm foundation upon which today's Soviet air strength rests. In response to German aggression and with decisive Allied support, the Russian Air Force, by the end of the war had grown into an arm of impressive proportions.

FOOTNOTES

Chapter 1

1. This section is based on: Contributions by Generalingenieur a.D. Otto R. Thomsen and Lieutenant Colonel a.D. Douglas Pitcairn (General Staff); Ingenieur R. Lusar, "Die Sowjetunion auf dem Wege zur Luftmacht" (The Soviet Union on the Road to Air Power), Militaerpolitisches Forum, Vol. 12 (Munich, 1953); Helm Speidel (General der Flieger a.D. Wilhelm Speidel), "Reichswehr und Rote Armee" /Reichswehr and the Red Army/, (hereinafter cited as RRA), Vierteljahreshefte fuer Zeitgeschichte, Vol. 1 (Stuttgart, 1953); Asher Lee, The Soviet Air Force, Duckworth (London, 1952) (hereinafter cited as Lee). Unless otherwise noted, documents cited in this study are to be found in G/VI/1 through G/VI/9 (consisting of 29 German loose-leaf notebooks), Karlsruhe Document Collection, Archives Branch, USAF Historical Division, Maxwell Air Force Base, Alabama.

2. RRA.

3. Thomsen. General Thomsen spent three years at the Junkers plant in Fili, from 1924-27. His account is a valuable source of information on the early collaboration between German and Russian aircraft engineers.

4. Pitcairn.

5. This section is based on: Contributions by Generalleutnant a.D. Heinrich Aschenbrenner (pre-war German military attache in Russia), Generalingenieur a.D. Kurt Breith, Colonel a.D. Kurt Gottschling, Colonel a.D. R. von Heimann, Pitcairn, and Colonel a.D. Lothar Schuettel; Orientierungsheft Union der Sozialistischen Sowjetrepubliken (UdSSR), Der Oberbefehlshaber der Luftwaffe, Fuehrungsstab Ic/IV No. 3500/41 geh. (German intelligence digest on Soviet Russia, 1941, hereinafter cited as OUSS); OKL, Gedanken zur Beurteilung der Luftlage von 1939 (Luftwaffe High Command, Thoughts on an Appraisal of the Air Situation, 1939, hereinafter cited as GBL); Russische Luftwaffe 1941, a study of 8. Abteilung, Generalstab der Luftwaffe (Russian Air Force 1941, hereinafter cited as RL 41);

5. (cont'd)
"Ausbildungswesen" SU-Fliegertruppe, Luftwaffenfuehrungsstab, Ic/Fremde Luftwaffen Ost, No. 3000/44 geh. (A Luftwaffe intelligence bulletin on training in the Russian Air Force); Beurteilung der Nachrichtenquellen aus Sowjetrussland and Das russische Kriegspotential, F. Greffrath (appraisal of intelligence sources in Russia and the Russian war potential, both compiled by Lieutenant Colonel a. D. Greffrath from Luftwaffe High Command documents, hereinafter cited respectively as BNS and DRK); Beurteilung der sowjetrussichen Luftwaffe in 1941, Plocher (appraisal of the Russian Air Force in 1941 by Generalleutnant a. D. Hermann Plocher, hereinafter cited as BSL); "Die Luftgeltung der Sowjetunion" and "Die Luftwaffe der Sowjetunion," Handbuch der neuzeitlichen Wehrwissenschaften 1938, n. p., n. pub. (Russian air power and the Russian air force, hereinafter cited as HNWLS and HNWLW respectively); Annex F, Command and Employment of Air Forces, World War II and Korea, Air War College, Air University (Maxwell AFB, 1952); Georg W. Feuchter, Geschichte des Luftkrieges /"History of Air Warfare"/, Athenaeum Verlag (Bonn, 1954), (hereinafter cited as Feuchter); Adolf Galland, Die Ersten und die Letzten /Available in an abridged English edition, The First and the Last, Henry Holt & Co. (New York, 1954). Most of the English editions referred to in these notes are shorter than the cited, original German editions./, Schneekluth (Darmstadt, 1953), (hereinafter cited as Galland); R. L. Garthoff, Soviet Military Doctrine, The Rand Corporation (Santa Monica, 1953), (hereinafter cited as Garthoff); Lee; Trial of the Major War Criminals before the International Military Tribunal, (Nuremberg, Germany, 1947) hereinafter cited as IMT.

6. BNS; BSL, p. 4.

7. OUSS, pp. 71, 73-74, 81-82.

8. Ibid., p. 73.

9. RL 41.

10. 1938, n. p., n. pub.

11. Gottschling, p. 11.

12. Feuchter, p. 195.

13. OUSS, p. 64.

14. BSL, p. 21.

15. Lee, pp. 56-68.

16. OUSS, pp. 75-81.

17. GBL.

18. Breith and Heimann.

19. This section is based on OUSS.

20. OUSS.

21. This section is based on: Heimann and Schuettel; RL 41; OUSS; "Luftlandetruppen," SU Fliegertruppe, Luftwaffenfuehrungsstab, Ic/Fremde Luftwaffen Ost, No. 39896/43 geh. (a Luftwaffe intelligence publication on Russian airborne troops, hereinafter cited as SUFL); Garthoff; Alkmar von Hove, Achtung Fallschirmjaeger /"Attention! Paratroopers"/, Druffel Verlag (Leoni am Starnberger See, 1954); Lee.

22. SUFL, p. 9.

23. Ibid., p. 11.

24. OUSS, pp. 53-55.

25. This section is based on: Heimann, Schuettel and Thomsen; OUSS; BSL; Lee; HNWLS and HNWLW.

26. OUSS, pp. 106-9.

27. HNWLS, pp. 1-5.

28. Schuettel, pp. 14-15.

29. Ibid., p. 15.

30. Aschenbrenner.

31. Ibid.

32. Ibid.

33. IMT, Vol. IX, pp. 81-82.

34. Schuettel, p. 15; Aschenbrenner in a letter to the author (n.d.).

35. This section is based on: OUSS; GBL; BNS and DRK.

36. OUSS, pp. 104-06, 109-18.

37. BNS, pp. 7-8.

38. This section is based on: OUSS; BSL; HNWLS.

39. OUSS, pp. 118-27.

40. Ibid., pp. 84-87.

41. HNWLS, pp. 3-4.

42. This section is based on: Contributions by Colonel a.D. Freiherr (Baron) Hans-Henning von Beust (General Staff), and Pitcairn; Galland.

43. v. Beust, pp. 9-10.

44. OUSS, p. 82.

Chapter 2

1. This section is based on: Contributions by Colonel a.D. Freiherr Hans-Henning von Beust, Major a.D. Arnulf Blasig, Major a.D. Manfred von Cossart, Colonel a.D. Heinz-Joachim Jaehne, Captain a.D. Otto Kath, Lieutenant Colonel a.D. Helmut Mahlke (General Staff), Generalmajor a.D. Fritz Morzik, Captain a.D. Herbert Pabst (deceased), Generalmajor a.D. Horst Parrisius, Major a.D. Guenther Rall, Captain a.D. Volker Reschke, Lieutenant Colonel a.D. Horst von Riesen (General Staff), Major a.D. Hans-Egon Schlage, Major a.D. Egon Stoll-Berberich, General der Flieger a.D. Paul Deichmann; Generalleutnant a.D. Hermann

1. (cont'd)
Plocher, Erfolge deutscher Jagd-und Zerstoererverbaende gegen die russische Luftwaffe im Nordabschnitt der Ostfront bei Kriegsbeginn (German single and twin-engine fighter successes in the northern sector of the Russian front at the beginning of the war, hereinafter cited as JZGNOK); Generaloberst a. D. Hans Juergen Stumpff, Gedanken zum Kampf der deutschen Luftwaffe im Gebiet noerdlich des Polarkreises (Thoughts on Luftwaffe operations north of the Arctic Circle, hereinafter cited as GKLGP); Generalmajor a. D. Klaus Uebe, Der taktische Einsatz der russischen Luftwaffe zur Unterstuetzung des Heeres (The employment of the Russian Air Force in ground-support missions, hereinafter cited as ELUH); Kapitaen zur See a. D. Wilhelm Moessel, Einsatz der russischen Luftwaffe ueber See. Lehren und Folgerungen (Over-water employment of the Russian Air Force. Lessons and Conclusions, hereinafter cited as ERLUS); Vizeadmiral L. Buerkner, Sowjetische Seefliegeroperationen im 2. Weltkrieg einschliesslich Heeresfliegeroperationen zur Unterstuetzung von Marineunternehmungen (Russian Navy and Army air force operations in World War II in support of Russian naval operations, hereinafter cited as SSHUM); Auszug aus den Aussagen des Reichsmarschalls Hermann Goering vor den Alliierten am 1. Juni 1945 (Extract from Goering's interrogation by the Allies, 1 June 1945); Dr. K. Bartz, Als der Himmel brannte /Available in translation under the title, Swastika in the Air, W. Kimber (London, 1956)/, Sponholtz (Hannover, 1955), (hereinafter cited as Bartz); G. W. Feuchter, Geschichte des Luftkrieges /"History of Air Warfare"/, Athenaeum Verlag (Bonn, 1945), (hereinafter cited as Feuchter); Adolf Galland, Die Ersten und die Letzten /English edition bears the title, The First and the Last, Henry Holt & Co. (New York, 1954)/, Schneekluth (Darmstadt, 1953), (hereinafter cited as Galland); H. Knoke, Die grosse Jagd /Available in translation under the title, I Flew for the Fuerhrer, Henry Holt & Co. (New York, 1954)/, Boesendahl (Rinteln, 1952), (hereinafter cited as Knoke); Hans-Ulrich Rudel, Trotzdem /Published in English under the title, Stuka Pilot, Euphorion Books (Dublin, 1952)/, Duerer Verlag (Buenos Aires, 1949), (hereinafter cited as Rudel); Heinz Guderian, Erinnerungen eines Soldaten /In English published as Panzer Leader, Dutton (New York, 1952)/, (Heidelberg,

1. (cont'd)
   1951); Erich von Manstein, Verlorene Siege /An abbreviated translation bears the title, Lost Victories, Henry Regnery (Chicago, 1958)/, Athenaeum Verlag (Bonn, 1955), (hereinafter cited as v. Manstein); Albert Kesselring, Soldat bis zum letzten Tag /In translation this appears as, A Soldier's Record, Morrow (New York, 1954)/, Athenaeum Verlag (Bonn, 1953); H. S. Koch, Flak, die Geschichte der deutschen Flakartillerie 1935-1945 /"Flak, the History of German Antiaircraft Artillery"/, Verlag Hans-Henning Podzun (Bad Nauheim, 1954).

2. Orientierungsheft Union der Sozialistischen Sowjetrepubliken (UdSSR), der Oberbefehlshaber der Luftwaffe, Fuehrungsstab Ic/IV No. 3500/41 geh. (German intelligence digest on Soviet Russia, 1941).

3. Rall, p. 10.

4. v. Cossart, pp. 1-2.

5. Kath.

6. v. Cossart, pp. 8-9.

7. v. Riesen, II, pp. 1-5.

8. Pabst diary, p. 6.

9. Generalleutnant a. D. Hermann Plocher, Der Kampf um die Luftueberlegenheit bei Beginn des Russlandfeldzuges im Bereich der Luftflotte 1 (Battle for air superiority in the First Air Fleet area at the beginning of the Russian campaign), pp. 2-3.

10. Mahlke, p. 1.

11. ELUH, I.

12. v. Beust, pp. 11, 13-14.

13. v. Heimann, pp. 3-5.

14. Vernehmung des sowjetischen Fliegerobersten Wanjuschkin (Interrogation of the Russian Air Force Colonel Vanyuschkin, hereinafter referred to as VSFW), pp. 9-10.

15. Jaehne, p. 2.

16. Bartz.

17. Rudel, pp. 37, 46-47.

18. v. Cossart, pp. 3, 7-8.

19. Rudel, p. 35.

20. Pabst diary, pp. 11, 20, 23, 27, 32-33.

21. v. Riesen, II, pp. 1-5.

22. Huffmann (compilation of Army officers' contributions), I, pp. 4-7, (hereinafter cited as Huffmann (compilation)).

23. Ibid., p. 20.

24. v. Manstein, pp. 225-26.

25. Huffmann (compilation), I, pp. 21-36.

26. Ibid., pp. 30-31.

27. Ibid., pp. 6, 34.

28. ERLUS.

29. SSHUM.

30. Rall, pp. 1-2.

31. Stoll-Berberich, pp. 1-3.

32. v. Cossart, pp. 4-5.

33. v. Beust, pp. 12-13.

34. Morzik, p. 1.

35. v. Heimann, pp. 3, 7; Jaehne, p. 2; Galland, p. 163.

36. v. Heimann, p. 3.

37. Reschke, p. 6.

38. ELUH, I., pp. 9-15.

39. Huffmann (compilation), I, pp. 4-6, 11-14, 20-36.

40. Jaehne, pp. 2-3.

41. The smallness of this number illustrates the effectiveness of the first German attacks on the Soviet air force.

42. v. Heimann, pp. 3, 8.

43. <u>Galland</u>, p. 130.

44. VSFW, pp. 2, 8.

45. <u>Feuchter</u>, p. 195.

46. v. Beust, p. 13.

47. Blasig, p. 1; Morzik, p. 1; Reschke, p. 3; Stoll-Berberich, p. 1; Jaehne, p. 4; <u>Galland</u>, p. 130.

48. Kath, pp. 4, 6.

49. ELUH, I, p. 2.

50. VSFW, p. 3.

51. This section is based on: Contributions by v. Beust, Generalleutnant a. D. Bruno Frankewitz, v. Heimann, Huffmann, Jaehne, Kath, Reschke, Lieutenant Colonel a. D. Fritz Wolff; ELUH; Generalmajor a. D. Klaus Uebe, Reaktionen und Haltung (Benehmen) der russichen Flugzeugbesatzungen im Gefecht (a questionnaire on the combat reactions and behavior of Russian air crews, dated 1 Feb 1950, hereinafter cited as RHRFG); ERLUS.

52. v. Beust, p. 16.

53. v. Heimann, p. 10.

54. Jaehne, pp. 7, 9.

55. RHRFG, p. 5.

56. v. Beust, p. 15.

57. Jaehne, p. 7.

58. Jaehne, p. 7; ELUH, II, p. 1; v. Heimann, p. 10.

59. Reschke, p. 1.

60. ELUH, II, pp. 1-2.

61. Huffmann (compilation), I, pp. 7-8.

62. Ibid., p. 24; Huffmann (contribution), pp. 1-2.

63. Frankewitz, pp. 2-3, 6.

64. ERLUS, pp. 5-6, 9, 14.

65. Jaehne, pp. 7-8.

66. This section is based on: Contributions by v. Beust, Blasig, v. Cossart, Frankewitz, v. Heimann, Huffmann, Jaehne, Kath, Morzik, Pabst, Parrisius, Rall, Reschke, v. Riesen, Schlage, Thomsen, Wolff; Major a. D. Joachim Joedicke, in a letter to the author; ELUH; RHRFG; Bemerkungen fuer den Einsatz der Luftwaffe Nr. 20, Luftwaffenfuehrungsstab, General von Waldau, 20.1.1942 (Bulletin no. 20 on air force commitment, hereinafter cited as BEL); Einsatzerfahrungen im Osten (Russland) Winter 1941/42, Kriegstagebuch des Jagdgeschwaders 54 (Combat experience in Russia, winter of 1941-42, an extract from the war diary of 54th Fighter Wing, hereinafter cited as EOW); GKLGP; Auszug aus Ausarbeitung des Generalmajors a. D. Walter Grabmann, 15.6.1953 (extract from a draft by General Grabmann, 15 June 1953, hereinafter cited as AAG); Major a. D. Arnulf Blasig, Die Luftschlacht ueber Kirkenes am 1.8.1941 (the air battle over Kirkenes, 1 Aug 1941, hereinafter cited as LUK); Taktische Erfahrungen im Kampf gegen russische Jaeger (tactical experiences from combat with Russian fighters,

66. (cont'd)
hereinafter cited as TEKRJ); UdSSR-Ausbringungs- und Einfuhrprogramm 1941 und 1942 fuer Jagdflugzeuge, in Anlage zu OKL Ic/Fr. Lw. Ost 1403/45 g. Kdos. und Der Chef des Generalstabes der Luftwaffe vom 8.7.1945 (Russian production and import program for fighters, 1941 and 1942, hereinafter cited as RAE); Knoke; Rudel.

67. For example, v. Beust, p. 17; RHRFG, pp. 1-3.

68. Jaehne, p. 10.

69. Morzig, p. 3.

70. RAE.

71. v. Beust, p. 17.

72. Blasig, p. 1.

73. Morzig, p. 1; v. Riesen, p. 1; ELUH, p. 8; EOW, p. 3.

74. v. Cossart, p. 4; GKLGP, p. 3.

75. RHRFG, pp. 1-2.

76. v. Cossart, pp. 4-5.

77. Reschke, p. 3.

78. Rall, pp. 1-2.

79. EOW, pp. 2-5.

80. TEKRJ, I, pp. 1-10.

81. Rall, pp. 2-6.

82. ELUH, I, p. 8.

83. v. Beust, p. 18; Kath, p. 5; Blasig, p. 2; Reschke, pp. 2-3; ELUH, I, p. 8; ELUH, III, pp. 2-4.

84. v. Cossart, pp. 3-9.

85. v. Beust, pp. 18-20.
86. v. Riesen, pp. 1-3.
87. Joedicke letter, pp. 1-3.
88. Rall, pp. 2-3, 6.
89. TEKRJ, I, pp. 4, 16-17; Morzik, p. 1.
90. BEL, pp. 16-17.
91. Pabst diary, pp. 8-11, 13, 33.
92. LUK, pp. 2-4; Blasig, pp. 1-2.
93. TEKRJ, I, p. 18.
94. Rall, p. 4.
95. Schlage, pp. 1-2.
96. Jaehne, p. 11.
97. Reschke, p. 2.
98. v. Beust, p. 19.
99. Jaehne, p. 11.
100. v. Cossart, p. 10.
101. ELUH, I, p. 8; III, p. 5.
102. EOW, p. 4.
103. Reschke, p. 2.
104. Rall, pp. 7-8.
105. Wolff, p. 2.
106. Frankewitz, pp. 3-4.

107. Huffmann (contribution), pp. 8-9, 22, 24, 29 ff.

108. Jaehne, p. 11.

109. Rall, p. 7; Blasig, p. 2.

110. TEKRJ, I, pp. 8-9.

111. v. Beust, p. 19.

112. Rall, p. 7.

113. TEKRJ, I, pp. 4-5.

114. Kath, p. 8.

115. Rall, p. 8.

116. Reschke, p. 2; Jaehne, p. 11.

117. Thomsen, p. 6.

118. TEKRJ, I, pp. 3-4.

119. Kath, p. 5.

120. Rall, p. 4; Reschke, p. 2; Jaehne, p. 11.

121. TEKRJ, pp. 5-6.

122. Rall, p. 8.

123. Jaehne, p. 11.

124. v. Heimann, p. 12.

125. Blasig, pp. 1, 4; EOW, p. 4.

126. TEKRJ, II, pp. 6-7.

127. ELUH, III, pp. 4-5; v. Heimann, p. 12; Reschke, p. 2; Rall, p. 9; Jaehne, p. 11; GKLGP, p. 3.

128. EOW, p. 5.

129. BEL, pp. 20, 22-24.

130. v. Beust, p. 20.

131. This section is based on: Contributions by v. Beust, Frankewitz, v. Heimann, Huffmann, Jaehne, Pabst, Reschke, v. Riesen, Stoll-Berberich, Thomsen, Wolff; ELUH; RHRFG; General der Flakartillerie Wolfgang Pickert and General der Flakartillerie a.D. von Axthelm (in supplements to ELUH), (hereinafter cited as: ELUH (Pickert supplement) and ELUH (v. Axthelm supplement)); EOW; General der Infanterie a.D. Hans von Greiffenberg, Taktik russischer Tiefflieger bei Bekaempfung von Erdzielen (tactics of Russian ground-attack aircraft, hereinafter cited as TRTBE); Rudel; v. Manstein.

132. v. Beust, p. 21.

133. v. Heimann, p. 13.

134. Jaehne, p. 13.

135. ELUH, II, p. 2.

136. Reschke, p. 4; Pabst diary, p. 18; Jaehne, p. 13; Stoll-Berberich, p. 4.

137. RHRFG, pp. 3-4; ELUH, I, p. 8.

138. Stoll-Berberich, pp. 2-3, 5.

139. Frankewitz, p. 7.

140. Huffmann (contribution), pp. 9-10, 13.

141. ELUH (Pickert supplement), p. 1.

142. Jaehne, p. 13.

143. Huffmann (contribution), p. 10.

144. ELUH, I, p. 9; ELUH, II, pp. 3, 6; RHRFG, pp. 3-4.

145. TRTBE, p. 3.

146. EOW, p. 4.

147. Reschke, p. 4.

148. Stoll-Berberich, pp. 3-4.

149. Pabst diary, pp. 17-18.

150. Frankewitz, p. 3.

151. Wolff, p. 3.

152. Huffmann (contribution), pp. 4, 9-13, 24, 30, 33-34.

153. TRTBE, pp. 1-3.

154. ELUH (v. Axthelm supplement), p. 6.

155. ELUH, II, p. 4.

156. Stoll-Berberich, p. 2.

157. Reschke, p. 4.

158. Stoll-Berberich, pp. 3-4.

159. Pabst diary, pp. 27-28.

160. Thomsen, p. 7.

161. Rudel, p. 20.

162. Jaehne, p. 13.

163. Huffmann (contribution), pp. 9-10.

164. Jaehne, p. 13.

165. Huffmann (contribution), pp. 9-10.

166. Reschke, pp. 4-5.

167. Huffmann (contribution), p. 11.

168. ELUH, II, p. 6.

169. See above, pp. 101-02.

170. Jaehne, p. 14.

171. ELUH (Pickert supplement), p. 1.

172. TRTBE, p. 2.

173. EOW, p. 7.

174. Stoll-Berberich, p. 1.

175. Jaehne, p. 14.

176. This section is based on: Contributions by v. Beust, Bläsig, v. Cossart, Frankewitz, v. Heimann, Huffmann, Jaehne, Kath, Mahlke, Morzig, Pabst, Reschke, v. Riesen, Thomsen, Wolf; ELUH; RHRFG; ELUH (Pickert supplement); ELUH (v. Axthelm supplement); EOW, I and II; JZGNOK; ERLUS; Rudel; VSFW.

177. Huffmann (contribution), pp. 14-19.

178. v. Heimann, p. 14; Jaehne, p. 15; EOW, p. 16; Rudel, p. 20.

179. v. Beust, p. 23.

180. v. Beust, p. 24; Reschke, p. 8.

181. v. Heimann, p. 16.

182. v. Beust, p. 23.

183. Reschke, p. 8; Kath, pp. 1-3; Huffmann, p. 4; TEKRJ, I, pp. 11-12.

184. RHRFG, pp. 4-5.

185. Reschke, pp. 6, 8.

186. Pabst, p. 24, v. Beust, p. 25; v. Cossart, p. 12.

187. Mahlke, pp. 3-4.

188. Jaehne, p. 15.

189. v. Riesen, p. 3; v. Beust, II, p. 2.

190. Reschke, pp. 7-8.

191. Huffmann (contribution), pp. 17, 19.

192. Kath, p. 2.

193. Pabst, pp. 2-3, 17.

194. v. Heimann, pp. 13-14.

195. Kath, pp. 1-4; Thomsen, p. 8; v. Riesen, p. 3; Blasig, p. 3; v. Cossart, pp. 11-12.

196. EOW, p. 6; TEKRJ, I, pp. 11-12, 15.

197. ELUH, II, pp. 11-12.

198. ERLUS, p. 19.

199. v. Beust, pp. 23-25.

200. Frankewitz, pp. 6-7.

201. Wolff, pp. 4-5, 9

202. Huffmann (contribution), pp. 14-19, 24-25, 30, 36.

203. v. Manstein, pp. 225-26.

204. v. Heimann, p. 13; Reschke, p. 6; Pabst diary, pp. 2-3.

205. ELUH, II, p. 11.

206. ERLUS, pp. 7-8, 11, 16.

207. v. Beust, p. 25; v. Heimann, p. 13.

208. Kath, pp. 1-2; JZGNOK, p. 1.

209. Pabst diary, pp. 17-18, 21-27.

210. v. Riesen, p. 3.

211. v. Cossart, pp. 11-12.

212. Thomsen, pp. 8-9.

213. ELUH (v. Axthelm supplement), pp. 2-3, 5.

214. v. Heimann, p. 14; Morzig, p. 1; Mahlke, pp. 5-8; ELUH, III, pp. 8-9; ELUH (Pickert supplement), p. 1; Rudel, pp. 20-21.

215. Huffmann (contribution), pp. 4, 14, 19.

216. ERLUS, p. 20.

217. Reschke, p. 7.

218. Pabst diary, p. 34.

219. Thomsen, p. 9.

220. v. Beust, pp. 22, 25-26.

221. Huffmann (contribution), p. 18.

222. TEKRJ, I, p. 11.

223. ELUH, II, pp. 12-13; EOW, p. 6.

224. v. Heimann, p. 14; Reschke, p. 8; v. Beust, p. 23.

225. v. Heimann, p. 14; Reschke, p. 7; Kath, p. 5; Jaehne, p. 15; v. Beust, p. 23; TEKRJ, II, pp. 11-12; EOW, p. 6.

226. RHRFG, p. 5.

227. This section is based on: Contributions by Blasig, v. Heimann, Huffmann, Mahlke, Reschke and Thomsen.

228. Thomsen, p. 11.

229. v. Heimann, p. 16; Reschke, p. 9.

230. Blasig, p. 3.

231. Mahlke, pp. 9-16.

232. This section is based on: Generalingenieur a. D. Kurt Breith, Major a. D. Bruno Meyer, Parrisius, v. Heimann, Huffmann, Jaehne, Kath, Pabst, Reschke, Thomsen; GKLGP; ELUH.

233. Breith and Parrisius in letters to the author; v. Heimann, p. 5; Kath, p. 3; Pabst diary, p. 6; Huffmann, p. 3.

234. Kath, p. 3.

235. v. Heimann, p. 15; Jaehne, p. 16.

236. v. Heimann, pp. 14-15; Thomsen, p. 12; Reschke, p. 9; Breith, p. 1; Pabst diary, pp. 13, 16; Parrisius, p. 1; Meyer, p. 3; GKLGP, p. 2.

237. Breith, p. 2; ELUH, II, p. 12; Jaehne, p. 6; Thomsen, p. 14; Parrisius, p. 1; GKLGP, p. 3.

238. Breith, p. 2; Jaehne, pp. 5, 9; Thomsen, p. 15; Parrisius, p. 1; v. Heimann, p. 4.

239. This section is based on: Contributions by Colonel a. D. Kurt Gottschling, Huffmann, Jaehne, v. Riesen, Stoll-Berberich.

240. Huffmann (contribution), p. 20; Gottschling, pp. 8-9, 15; Jaehne, p. 4; v. Riesen, pp. 1-3, 5; Stoll-Berberich, p. 4.

241. Gottschling, p. 9.

242. This section is based on: Colonel a. D. Lothar Schuettel, Russische Fallschirm- und Luftlandetruppen (Russian parachute and airborne troops); contributions by v. Heimann, Huffmann and Mahlke.

243. "Luftlandetruppen," SU Fliegertruppe, Luftwaffenfuehrungsstab, Ic/Fremde Luftwaffen Ost, No. 39896/43 geh. (a Luftwaffe intelligence publication on Russian airborne troops), p. 16.

244. This section is based on: Bericht des Wehrwirtschaft- und Ruestungsamtes beim Oberkommando der Wehrmacht ueber die wehrwirtschaftliche Lage der UdSSR Anfang 1942 (an Armed Forces High Command report on the Russian military economy in early 1942); contributions by v. Heimann and v. Riesen.

245. This section is based on: v. Heimann, Huffmann and Blasig.

Chapter 3

1. Contributions by: Colonel a. D. Freiherr Hans-Henning von Beust (General Staff), pp. 27-33; Major a. D. Richard Brunner, pp. 4-6; Major a. D. Manfred von Cossart, pp. 13-18; Major a. D. Heinz-Joachim Jaehne, pp. 18-22; Captain a. D. Otto Kath, pp. 7-11; Major a. D. Bruno Meyer, pp. 3-9; Lieutenant Colonel a. D. Horst von Riesen (General Staff), Part I, pp. 4-6, Part II, pp. 7-12; Major a. D. Hans-Egon Schlage, pp. 8-13; Major a. D. Egon Stoll-Berberich, pp. 6-7; Captain a. D. Dr. Karl-Heinz Wilke, pp. 2-7; General der Flieger a. D. Paul Deichmann.

   Also: Captain Herbert Pabst (deceased), Pabst Diary, pp. 45, 59, 67, 75, 80; Generalmajor a. D. Klaus Uebe, Der taktische Einsatz der russichen Luftwaffe zur Unterstuetzung des Heeres (The employment of the Russian Air Force in ground-support missions, hereinafter cited as ELUH); Generaloberst a. D. Hans Juergen Stumpf, Gedanken zum Kampf der deutschen Luftwaffe im Gebiet noerdlich des Polarkreises (Thoughts on Luftwaffe operations north of the Arctic Circle, hereinafter cited as GKLGP); Russische Luftwaffe Ende 1943 (Russian Air Force, end of 1943), in Wochenbericht Nr. 6 der Presseabteilung der Kriegswissenschaftlichen Abteilung der Luftwaffe vom 31. 10. 1943, ObdL, Luftwaffenfuehrungsstab Ic, p. 1; Generalleutnant a. D. Herbert J. Rieckhoff, "Geheimnisse um die Luftwaffe der Sowjetunion" /"Secrets surrounding the Soviet air force"/, in Flugwehr und- Technik (Arme et Technique de l'Air), Huber & Co., Frauenfeld, Switzerland, No. 8, Aug. 1948, (hereinafter cited as Rieckhoff), pp. 182-85; K. W. Streit, "Der Flug aus der Hoelle" /"Flight from Hell"/ in Der Frontsoldat erzaehlt, 17 Jahrgang, Nos. 4, 5, 6 (1953), n. place, n. pub., (hereinafter cited as Streit), pp. 140-42.

2. Jaehne, pp. 18-22.

3. Schlage, pp. 8-11.

4. v. Cossart, pp. 13-16; Stoll-Berberich, pp. 6-7.

5. Wilke, pp. 2-7.

6. Rieckhoff, pp. 183-84.

7. v. Riesen, p. 12; Kath, p. 11, Schlage, pp. 12-13; Meyer, p. 6; ELUH, Part I, p. 5; Rieckhoff, p. 183.

8. v. Beust, pp. 27-29, 31-33.

9. Contribution by Generalleutnant a.D. Helmuth Huffmann, Part II, pp. 2-5, 27-29, 42-44, 49.

10. Contribution by Generalleutnant a.D. Bruno Frankewitz, pp. 13-14.

11. GKLGP, p. 17.

12. Konteradmiral a.D. Otto Schulz and Colonel a.D. Helmut Schalke (General Staff), in their letter to the author; contributions by: Colonel a.D. Kurt Gottschling, p. 17; and General der Flakartillerie a.D. Wolfgang Pickert, p. 4.

13. v. Cossart, p. 14; Huffmann, pp. 4-5; Pabst Diary, pp. 41, 67; v. Riesen, Part I, pp. 5-6; Schlage, pp. 9-10; Wilke, pp. 2-7.

14. v. Beust, pp. 29-32; Brunner, pp. 1-4; v. Cossart, pp. 13-14; Kath, pp. 9-11; Pickert, p. 2; v. Riesen, pp. 7-10; Schlage, p. 12; Stoll-Berberich, p. 6; Wilke, pp. 16-18; Rieckhoff, p. 183.

15. "Zusammenwirken der Fliegertruppe mit den Erdtruppen" /"Russian air-ground cooperation"/, SU Fliegertruppe, ObdL, Luftwaffenfuehrungsstab Ic, No. 53210/44 geh., (hereinafter cited as ZFME).

16. Schlage, p. 12.

17. Stoll-Berberich, p. 6.

18. Wilke, pp. 16-17.

19. Generalmajor Herhudt von Rohden, Die Luftwaffe ringt um Stalingrad /"The Luftwaffe fights for Stalingrad"/, Limes-Verlag (Wiesbaden, 1952), (hereinafter cited as v. Rohden), p. 34; Streit, pp. 140-42; Huffmann, Part II, pp. 36-37, 42.

20. ELUH, Part I, pp. 11-15.

21. v. Beust, pp. 29-31.

22. Jaehne, p. 20.

23. "Kriegsgliederung, Stand Juni 1943" in SU Fliegertruppe (Russian Air Force order of battle, June 1943), ObdL, Luftwaffenfuehrungsstand Ic, No. 20547/43 geh., (hereinafter cited as KSUF), pp. 9-15, 31, 37-42, 45-46, 61-63, 71-72, 75, 99, 104-11.

24. Ibid., pp. 46-54, 60, 66.

25. Ibid., p. 64.

26. v. Beust, p. 31; Jaehne, p. 20; Schlage, p. 10; Deichmann, p. 2; ELUH, Part I, pp. 3-4; KSUF, p. 63.

27. Wilke, p. 24.

28. KSUF, pp. 50-51, 59-60.

29. Ibid., pp. 53-54, 60.

30. Jaehne, pp. 22-23; Wilke, pp. 16, 20, 23; Schlage, p. 15; KSUF, pp. 51-52.

31. KSUF, pp. 50, 54-56.

32. v. Beust, p. 34; Generalmajor a.D. Kaus Uebe, Reaktionen und Haltung (Benehmen) der russichen Flugseugbesatzungen im Gefecht (A questionnaire on the combat reactions and behavior of Russian air crews, dated 1 Feb. 1950, hereinafter cited as RHRFG), p. 5.

33. v. Beust, pp. 34-35; Jaehne, p. 22; Schlage, p. 16; Wilke, pp. 20-22; ELUH, Part II, pp. 1-2.

34. Huffmann, pp. 5-7, 28-32, 44-45; Frankewitz, p. 10.

35. Jaehne, p. 22; Gottschling, p. 18.

36. Schlage, p. 16; Wilke, p. 23; KSUF, p. 52.

37. Brunner, p. 1; Jaehne, p. 23; Kath, pp. 7-8; Meyer, p. 6; contribution by Major a. D. G. Rall, pp. 10-11; v. Riesen, pp. 9, 12; ELUH, Part III, p. 1; Generalleutnant a. D. Hermann Plocher, Die russische Luftwaffe waehrend der Operation Zitadelle 1943 (the Russian Air Force during Operation Citadel, hereinafter cited as RLOZ), pp. 3-5.

38. v. Beust, pp. 36-39.

39. Huffmann, Part II, pp. 7, 32, 45.

40. Kath, p. 6.

41. v. Beust, p. 36; ELUH, Part III, pp. 1-2; K. O. Hoffmann, "Entstehung, Einsatz und Erfolg der Sowjetluftmacht" /"The formation, commitment and success of Soviet air power"/, (hereinafter cited as Hoffmann), published in Nos. 6-8 of Luftwaffenring, 1956, No. 8, n. place, n. pub., pp. 5-6; KSUF, pp. 41, 46-47; "SU Nachtjagd" /"Russian night fighters"/, special edition of Einzelnachrichten des Ic-Dienstes Ost der Luftwaffe, No. 10, Luftwaffenfuehrungsstab Ic, No. 3769/44 geh., (hereinafter cited as SUN), pp. 3-4.

42. Brunner, p. 2; Meyer, p. 6; Pabst Diary, pp. 59, 67; v. Riesen, Part II, p. 9; Schlage, pp. 18, 20; ELUH, Part III, p. 1; Einsatzerfahrungen im Osten (Russland) Winter 1941/1942 (combat experience in Russia, winter of 1941-42, an extract from the war diary of the 54th Fighter Wing, hereinafter cited as EOW), p. 4.

43. Brunner, p. 2; Kath, p. 11; Meyer, p. 6; Rall, p. 11.

44. v. Beust, p. 38; Brunner, p. 1; Jaehne, p. 23; Kath, pp. 9, 11; Schlage, pp. 17-18; ELUH, Part III, p. 2; EOW, p. 2.

45. Rall, pp. 11-12, 14.

46. Meyer, p. 7.

47. Meyer, p. 7; Rall, pp. 15-16; ELUH, Part III, pp. 2-4; EOW, p. 2.

48. Rall, pp. 12-13, 15-16.

49. Frankewitz, p. 11; Kath, pp. 8, 10; Pabst Diary, pp. 59, 63; Hans-Ulrich Rudel, Trotzdem /Published in English under the title Stuka Pilot, Euphorion Books (Dublin, 1952)/ Duerer Verlag (Buenos Aires, 1949), (hereinafter cited as Rudel), pp. 68-69; ELUH, Part III, p. 1.

50. v. Riesen, pp. 9-11.

51. v. Beust, pp. 36, 39; Rall, pp. 13-14.

52. Brunner, pp. 2-6.

53. Pabst Diary, pp. 42, 54, 56, 59, 67-68, 70, 72-73, 81.

54. Meyer, pp. 8-10.

55. Rall, pp. 14, 16.

56. Jaehne, p. 23; Wilke, p. 26; Russische Jagdverteidigung Juli 1943 und spaeter ueber den russischen Schwarzmeerhaefen, Bericht des I. Fliegerkorps (Russian fighter defense of Black Sea ports, July 1943 - a report of 1st Air Corps), p. 1.

57. Wilke, pp. 26-29.

58. Schlage, pp. 17, 19.

59. Contribution by Generalmajor a. D. Fritz Morzik, pp. 3-5; Hoffmann, No. 8, p. 6; v. Rohden, pp. 81-84; Streit, pp. 75, 140-42.

60. Brunner, pp. 7-10.

61. v. Beust, p. 39; Morzik, p. 4; ELUH, Part III, p. 8; SUN, pp. 5-10, 13.

62. Kath, pp. 7-8, 10, 12; Pickert, p. 1; ELUH, Part III, pp. 4-5; EOW, p. 4; RLOZ, p. 3; Die russische Luftwaffe im Sueden der Ostfront, die gegen den Kubanbrueckenkopf und die Krim vom 24. 6. bis 15. 11. 1943 zum Einsatz kam, Bericht des 1. Fliegerkorps (Russian Air Force operations over the Kuban Bridgehead and the Crimea, 24 June to 5 Nov. 1943 - a report of 1st Air Corps, hereinafter cited as RLSKK), p. 3.

63. Colonel Kupfer, Verhalten russischer Jagdflieger (Behavior of Russian fighter pilots), copy of a lecture given on 10 Sept. 1943, p. 1.

64. Rall, p. 16.

65. Frankewitz, p. 11; Huffmann, Part II, pp. 8-9; Jaehne, p. 23; Rall, p. 12; ELUH, Part III, pp. 5, 7.

66. Schlage, p. 18; ELUH, Part I, pp. 14-15.

67. Brunner, p. 1; Kath, pp. 7, 10-12; Rall, pp. 11, 15, 17; Schlage, pp. 20-21; ELUH, Part III, p. 4; Hoffmann, No. 8, p. 5; SUN, p. 11.

68. Jaehne, pp. 20, 24-25; Morzik, p. 5; Meyer, p. 5; Pickert, p. 3; Schlage, pp. 25, 27-28; Stoll-Berberich, pp. 6-7; Deichmann, pp. 3-4; RLOZ, p. 6; "Schlachtfliegertruppe" /"ground-attack aviation"/, in SU Fliegertruppe, ObdL Luftwaffenfuehrungsstab Ic, Ende 1943 (hereinafter cited as SFT), p. 4.

69. v. Beust, p. 40.

70. Frankewitz, pp. 11-12; Huffmann, Part II, pp. 9, 45-47.

71. Schlage, p. 22; Wilke, p. 34; KSUF, pp. 42, 47; SFT, pp. 5-7, 24.

72. Huffmann, Part II, pp. 19, 46; Jaehne, p. 25; Pickert, pp. 2-3; Schlage, p. 25; Stoll-Berberich, pp. 6-7.

73. Meyer, p. 6.

74. Huffmann, Part II, pp. 10-14; Jaehne, p. 24; Contribution by Colonel a. D. I. Pelsmueller, Part II, p. 2; Pickert, p. 2; Schlage, pp. 22, 25-27; Stoll-Berberich, p. 6; ELUH, Part II, pp. 2-7; Wilke, p. 37; <u>SFT</u>, pp. 23-24, 43.

75. Huffmann, Part II, p. 15; Kath, p. 8; Meyer, p. 4; Schlage, pp. 24-25; Stoll-Berberich, p. 7; ELUH, Part II, pp. 3-6; Wilke, p. 34; <u>SFT</u>, pp. 26-32, 36, 39-40.

76. Huffmann, Part II, pp. 10-18, 33-34, 39, 48; Pelsmueller, Part II, pp. 2-9; Franke, p. 2.

77. Jaehne, p. 15; Morzik, p. 6; Pickert, pp. 2-3; Schlage, p. 26; Stoll-Berberich, p. 7; RLSKK, pp. 2-3; Berichte des II. Flakkorps vom 21.6.1941 bis 28.3.1942 ueber die russische Luftwaffe (Reports of 2d Air Corps concerning the Russian Air Force, 21 June 41-28 March 42, hereinafter cited as BFRL), pp. 29-31.

78. <u>ZFME</u>, pp. 4, 15-19; <u>SFT</u>, pp. 36-37.

79. Huffmann, Part II, p. 39; Morzik, p. 6; Schlage, p. 23; Stoll-Berberich, p. 6; Wilke, pp. 34-35; BFRL, p. 31; <u>Rudel</u>, pp. 88-89, 95, 121-22.

80. v. Beust, p. 42; Huffmann, Part II, p. 14; Wilke, p. 35.

81. Huffmann, Part II, p. 15; Jaehne, p. 25; Schlage, pp. 24-25; Wilke, p. 36.

82. Huffmann, Part II, pp. 16-17; Morzik, p. 6; ELUH, Part II, pp. 6-7; <u>SFT</u>, pp. 37-39.

83. Meyer, pp. 4-5; Pickert, p. 3; Schlage, pp. 14, 24, 26-27; Kupfer, p. 1; <u>SFT</u>, pp. 9, 15-16, 18-22, 39-40.

84. Schlage, p. 14.

85. Brunner, p. 19; v. Cossart, p. 18; Jaehne, p. 26; Kath, pp. 11-12; Morzik, p. 5; Wilke, pp. 41-42; ELUH, Part III, pp. 12-13; Deichmann, pp. 4-5; EOW, p. 6; <u>Hoffmann</u>, in No. 8, pp. 4, 6; <u>KSUF</u>, pp. 61-62.

86. Jaehne, p. 26.

87. v. Beust, p. 42.

88. Huffmann, Part II, pp. 26, 36, 48-49; H. Neitzel, Sicherung der rueckwaertigen Verbindungen in Russland (Rear area security in Russia, hereinafter cited as SRVR), n. d., n. place, n. pub., p. 44.

89. KSUF, pp. 41-42, 48-49, 61-64, 66-70.

90. Brunner, p. 19, Huffmann, Part II, p. 26, Schalke, p. 2; Contribution by Generalingenieur a.D. O. R. Thomsen, p. 10; RHRFG, pp. 4-5; Generalleutnant a. D. Hermann Plocher, Taktische Erfahrungen im Kampf gegen russische Jaeger und Kampfflieger (tactical lessons from combat against Russian fighters and bombers, hereinafter cited as TEKRJ), Part I, p. 11.

91. v. Beust, p. 42; Huffmann, Part II, p. 19; Kath, pp. 9-10; ELUH: Part I, pp. 12-13, Part II, pp. 8-13; Part III, p. 13; KSUF, pp. 48-49, 64.

92. Huffmann, Part II, p. 25; Kath, p. 8; Contribution by Lieutenant Colonel H. Mahlke, p. 5; Morzik, pp. 7-8; Pickert, p. 4; v. Riesen, Part I, p. 6; v. Riesen, Part II, pp. 7-9; ELUH, Part II, pp. 9-13; EOW, p. 6; TEKRJ, Part I, pp. 11-15.

93. Huffmann, Part II, pp. 19-25, 34.

94. Huffmann, Part II, pp. 23-24; Pickert, p. 4; Schlage, p. 2; RLSKK, p. 2.

95. Morzik, pp. 7-9.

96. Brunner, p. 17; Huffmann, Part II, p. 23; Mahlke, p. 4; contribution by Major a.D. B. von Maubeuge, p. 1; Pickert, p. 4; BFRL, p. 30; Rudel, pp. 62, 88-89.

97. Pabst Diary, pp. 45, 48, 51, 58-59, 62-63, 69, 73-74, 76, 80.

98. Brunner, p. 17; Wilke, p. 40; RLOZ, pp. 2, 4; SRVR, pp. 44-52; Rudel, pp. 101, 104.

99. v. Cossart, pp. 17-18; Kath, pp. 11-12; v. Riesen, Part I, p. 6; v. Riesen, Part II, pp. 7-9.

100. Huffmann, Part II, p. 34; Mahlke, p. 7; Pickert, pp. 2-3; ELUH, Part III, pp. 7-9; Wilke, p. 35.

101. v. Beust, p. 41.

102. ZFME, pp. 30-32.

103. Brunner, pp. 18-19; Huffmann, Part II, pp. 34-35; Mahlke, pp. 5-6; Morzik, pp. 7-8; Pickert p. 5; v. Riesen, Part II, p. 9; Thomsen, p. 10; ELUH, Part III, pp. 10-11; Wilke, p. 35; SRVR, pp. 44-52; v. Rohden, p. 95; Rudel, p. 96.

104. Kath, p. 10.

105. Frankewitz, p. 14; ELUH, Part III, p. 7; Wilke, pp. 35, 41.

106. Brunner, p. 17; Wilke, p. 41; EOW, p. 6; KSUF, p. 64.

107. Brunner, p. 18; Pickert, p. 3; Thomsen, p. 10.

108. Pickert, p. 6; KSUF, pp. 65-66, 107.

109. Wilke, p. 24; KSUF, pp. 34, 37, 78-79; Feindnachrichtenblatt No. 19, ObdL, Luftwaffenfuehrungsstab Ic, No. 5860/42 geh. (Luftwaffe High Command Intelligence bulletin, hereinafter cited as FNB), p. 3.

110. v. Cossart, p. 15; Frankewitz, p. 11; Huffmann, Part II, pp. 29-30, 44-45; Pickert, p. 6; General der Flieger a. D. Veit Fischer, Versorgung russischer Banden auf dem Luftweg (Air supply of Russian partisan units), pp. 2-5; SRVR, pp. 5-7.

111. Jaehne, p. 21; Wilke, pp. 18, 42.

112. KSUF, pp. 18, 32.

113. Jaehne, pp. 23, 25; Wilke, pp. 42, 43.

114. KSUF, pp. 24, 35, 36.

115. Jaehne, pp. 26-27; Rall, p. 17; Wilke, p. 43; KSUF, pp. 32, 57.

116. KSUF, pp. 18, 34-35.

117. Gottschling, pp. 8-15; Schlage, p. 18; ELUH, Part I, pp. 15-16; FNB, p. 3.

118. Gottschling, p. 16; Jaehne, p. 21.

119. Gottschling, p. 13; Schlage, p. 29; Hoffmann, in No. 8, pp. 6-7; SUN, p. 12.

120. Schlage, p. 13; FNB, p. 4; KSUF, pp. 51, 58, 80-87, 96.

121. BFRL, p. 30; "Luftlandetruppen" /"airborne troops"/, in SU Fliegertruppe, Luftwaffenfuehrungsstab Ic/ Fremde Luftwaffen Ost, No. 39896/43 geh., (hereinafter cited as SUFL), p. 16.

122. KSUF, pp. 99-103; Hoffmann, in No. 6, p. 5; FNB, p. 4; SUFL, pp. 7, 17, 21, 23, 25, 58, 69-70.

123. This section is based on: Jaehne; Bericht des Wehrwirtschafts- und Ruestungsamtes beim OKW ueber die wehrwirtschaftliche Lage der UdSSR Anfang 1942 (An Armed Forces High Command report on the Russian military economy in early 1942); Colonel (engineer) Schwenke in einer Zusammenstellung der auslaendischen Flugzeugproduktion von Juni 1942 (Compilation of foreign aircraft production figures, June 1942, by Colonel Schwenke); KSUF; UdSSR-Ausbringungs- und Einfuhrprogramm 1941 und 1942 fuer Jagdflugzeuge, in Anlage zu OKL Ic/Fr. Lw. Ost 1403/45 g. Kdos. und der Chef des Generalstabes der Luftwaffe vom 8.7.1945 (Russian production and import programs for fighters, 1941 and 1942); SU Flugzeugbestand, Flugzeugausbringung, Flugzeugverluste, ObdL Luftwaffenfuehrungsstab Ic, April 1945 (Russian aircraft strength figures, production figures, losses).

124. KSUF, pp. 107-110.

125. Jaehne, p. 27.

126. Kath, pp. 7-8; Rall, p. 17; Hoffmann, in No. 8, p. 1; FNB, p. 4.

127. Impact, No. 7, Oct. 1943.

Chapter 4

1. This section is based on: Contributions by Major a.D. Richard Brunner, Generalleutnant a.D. Gerhard Feyerabend, Generalleutnant a.D. Bruno Frankewitz, Generalleutnant a.D. Helmuth Huffmann, Major a.D. Heinz-Joachim Jaehne, Captain a.D. Otto Kath, Generalmajor a.D. Fritz Morzik, General der Flakartillerie a.D. Wolfgang Pickert, Lieutenant Colonel a.D. Douglas Pitcairn (General Staff), Captain a.D. Volker Reschke, Lieutenant Colonel a.D. Horst von Riesen (General Staff), Major a.D. Hans-Egon Schlage, Captain a.D. Dr. Karl-Heinz Wilke, General der Flieger a.D. Paul Deichmann; Generalmajor a.D. Klaus Uebe, Der taktische Einsatz der russischen Luftwaffe zur Unterstuetzung des Heeres (The employment of the Russian Air Force in ground-support missions, hereinafter cited as ELUH); Kapitaen zur See a.D. Wilhelm Moessel, Einsatz der russischen Luftwaffe ueber See. Lehren und Folgerungen (Over-water employment of the Russian Air Force. Lessons and Conclusions, hereinafter cited as ERLUS); Vizeadmiral L. Buerkner, Sowjetische Seefliegeroperationen im 2. Weltkrieg einschliesslich Heeresfliegeroperationen zur Unterstuetzung von Marineunternehmungen (Russian Navy and Army air force operations in World War II in support of Russian naval operations, hereinafter cited as SSHUM); Die russische Luftwaffe im Jahre 1944, auszug aus einem Bericht eines Schlachtfiegers vom Nordabschnitt der Ostfront (extract from the report of a ground-attack pilot in the northern sector on the Russian Air Force in 1944, hereinafter cited as BSNO); Einzelnachrichten des Ic-Dienstes Ost der Luftwaffe Nos. 10 - 38, OKL Fuehrungsstab Ic, Fremde Luftwaffen Ost (Luftwaffe High Command Intelligence bulletins, hereinafter cited as FLO); Bewertung der Kampfmoral der SU-Fliegertruppe, Bemerkung zum Luftkrieg Ost No. 1/45, Fremde Luftwaffen Ost (Luftwaffe High Command appraisal of Russian Air Force combat morale, hereinafter cited as BKSUF); Luftlageberichte Ost vom 1.1.1944 - 1.2.1945, OKL Fuehrungsstab Ic, Fremde Luftwaffen Ost (Luftwaffe High Command air situation reports from 1 Jan 1944 - 1 Feb 1945, hereinafter cited as LLBO); Russische Luftkriegfuehrung, Auszug aus einer Studie der 8. Abteilung/ Gen. St. Chef d. Lw. vom 15.12.1944 (extract from a study by Branch 8 of the Luftwaffe General

1. (cont'd)
Staff on Russian air warfare, 15 Dec 1944, hereinafter cited as RLKF); Die Luftverteidigungskraefte in Russland, Sept 1944, OKL Fuehrungsstab Ic, Fremde Luftwaffen Ost, (Luftwaffe High Command Intelligence report on Russian air defense, Sept 1944, hereinafter cited as LVKR); Die russische Luftwaffe im Finnenbusen und in der oestl. Ostsee, Stand Anfang Maerz 1944, Marinekommando Ostsee Geh, Kdos. No. 400/44 Chefsache, Anl. 5 (a secret German Navy report on the Russian Air Force in the Gulf of Finland and the Eastern Baltic as of March 1944, hereinafter cited as RLFOO); Aufmarsch der russischen Fliegertruppe, Stand 25. 4. 1945 (Skizze), (Order of Battle of Russian Air Force, 25 April 1945, hereinafter cited as ARF); SU Flugzeugbestand, Flugzeugausbringung, Flugzeugverluste, ObdL Luftwaffen-fuehrungsstab Ic, April 1945 (Russian aircraft strength figures, production figures, losses, hereinafter cited as SUFF); Bemerkungen zur feindlichen Luftruestung No. 1/45, SU Flugzeugverluste, OKL Fuehrungsstab Ic, Fremde Luftwaffen Ost (Luftwaffe Intelligence report of Russian aircraft losses, hereinafter cited as SUFV); K. O. Hoffmann, "Entstehung, Einsatz und Erfolg der Sowjetluftmacht" /"The formation, commitment and success of Soviet air power"/, (hereinafter cited as Hoffmann), published in Nos. 6-8 of Luftwaffenring, 1956, n. place, n. pub.; Ingenieur R. Lusar, "Die Sowjetunion auf dem Wege zur Luftmacht" /"The Soviet Union on the road to air power"/, in Militaerpolitisches Forum, Vol. 12 (Munich, 1953), (hereinafter cited as Lusar); Generalleutnant a. D. Herbert J. Rieckhoff, "Geheimnisse um die Luftwaffe der Sowjetunion" /"Secrets surrounding the Soviet air force"/, in Flugwehr und- Technik (Arme et Technique de l'Air), Huber & Co., Frauenfeld, Switzerland, No. 8, Aug. 1948 (hereinafter cited as Rieckhoff); Hans-Ulrich Rudel, Trotzdem /published in English under the title, Stuka Pilot, Euphorion Books (Dublin, 1952)/, Duerer Verlag (Buenos Aires, 1949), (hereinafter cited as Rudel); General der Infanterie a. D. Kurt von Tippelskirch, Geschichte des zweiten Weltkriegs /"History of World War II"/, Athenaeum Verlag (Bonn, 1951), (hereinafter cited as Tippelskirch).

2. Brunner, pp. 11, 14, 17; Kath, p. 12; Morzik, p. 1; Pickert, p. 7; Pitcairn, pp. 5, 9; v. Riesen, I, pp. 6-7; v. Riesen, II, pp. 13-14; Schlage, pp. 34-35; Wilke, pp. 7, 9; Deichmann, p. 4; ELUH, I, pp. 2, 5-7, 9-15; LLBO, 1 Oct 1944, pp. 1-3; BKSUF, pp. 1, 3.

3. Reschke, pp. 1-2, 18-23.

4. Jaehne, pp. 28-29, 32.

5. Huffmann, III, pp. 4-6, 12-17, 24-27, 30-32; Frankewitz, p. 19; Tippelskirch, pp. 429, 613.

6. Feyerabend, p. 9.

7. SSHUM, pp. 2, 5-7; ERLUS, pp. 6-7, 10-17, 21-23; BKSUF, p. 3; FLO, No. 28, pp. 1, 6.

8. Brunner, p. 13; Schlage (Annex), pp. 8-13; Rudel, p. 169; LVKR, p. 2; BSNO, pp. 4-5.

9. Pitcairn, p. 8; Schlage, pp. 44-45; Wilke, p. 19; Rieckhoff, p. 184; RLKF, pp. 2-3; LLBO, 1 Oct 1944, p. 3.

10. Hoffmann, I, p. 4; FLO, No. 11, p. 13.

11. Schlage, p. 42; Hoffmann, I, p. 4; LLBO, 1 Jan 1944, p. 3; RLFOO, p. 1; SUFFF.

12. Schlage, pp. 46-47; Wilke, pp. 10, 30; LLBO, 1 Oct 1944, pp. 4-9; ARF, 25 April 1945.

13. Reschke, pp. 2-3, 8-9; Schlage, pp. 48-49; Wilke, pp. 31, 33, 39-41; Lusar, p. 32; RLFOO, p. 2; SUFFF; SUFV, p. 3.

14. Reschke, p. 25.

15. This section is based on: Contributions by Huffmann, Jaehne, Reschke, Schlage, Wilke; ERLUS, ELUH, FLO, Nos. 11, 22, 28, 38; Aufklaerungstaetigkeit der SU-Fliegertruppe im Monat September 1944 (Skizze), (Russian air reconnaissance activities in Sept 1944 (sketch), hereinafter cited as ASUF); "Verbaende im Fronteinsatz" in SU Fliegertruppe, Stand Mitte September 1944 (Russian Air Force units committed at the Front, mid-September 1944, hereinafter cited as VFE); LLBO, 1 Jan 1944 - 1 Feb 1945.

16. Jaehne, p. 29; Reschke, p. 3; Schlage, pp. 54-55; Wilke, pp. 23-24; FLO, No. 22 (I) pp. 3-5, No. 38, pp. 3, 23-24; ASUF; LLBO, 1 July 1944, pp. 1, 3, 1 Sept 1944, p. 1, 1 Oct 1944, p. 2, 1 Nov 1944, pp. 2, 7, 1 Jan 1945, p. 1.

17. Schlage, pp. 54-55; FLO, No. 38, pp. 6, 26.

18. FLO, No. 22 (I), pp. 6-11, No. 38, pp. 4-5; VFE, pp. 126-28.

19. Reschke, p. 3; Schlage, pp. 50-54; Wilke, pp. 20, 23; FLO, No. 38, pp. 6-13, 18-22.

20. Reschke, p. 10; FLO, No. 38, pp. 3, 17; LLBO, 1 Sept 1944, p. 1, 1 Oct 1944, p. 2, 1 Nov 1944, p. 2.

21. Reschke, pp. 11, 21, 23; Wilke, pp. 20-22; ELUH, II, pp. 1-2; FLO, No. 11, I, pp. 1-5, No. 38, pp. 3, 13-17, 22-25; LLBO, 1 July 1944, p. 1, 1 Sept 44, p. 1, 1 Jan 45, p. 1.

22. Reschke, p. 21.

23. Wilke, p. 22.

24. FLO, No. 38, p. 22.

25. Huffmann, III, pp. 40-42.

26. ERLUS, pp. 5-6, 14-15, 18; FLO, No. 28, pp. 4, 6-7, 16.

27. Schlage, pp. 52-54; Wilke, p. 23; FLO, No. 11, I, pp. 3-4; FLO, No. 22, I, pp. 11-16, No. 38, pp. 3-4, No. 28, pp. 6-7.

28. This section is based on: Contributions by Major a. D. A. Blasig; Brunner, Huffmann, Jaehne, Kath, Major a. D. B. von Maubeuge, Pitcairn, Reschke, v. Riesen, Schlage, Wilke; ELUH; BSNO; Die russische Luftwaffe, Auszug aus einer Arbeit der 8. Abteilung der Luftwaffe vom 15.1.45 (extract from a study of Branch 8 of the Luftwaffe General Staff on the Russian Air Force, 15 Jan 1945, hereinafter cited as DRL); FLO, Nos. 10, 11 (II), 16, 25 (I), 28 (I), 38; VFE; Kampffuehrung der Fernkampffliegertruppe, OKL, Ic, Fremde Luftwaffen Ost, 18 Feb 1945 (Luftwaffe High Command Intelligence report on combat command of long-range bomber forces, hereinafter cited as KFFT); SU-Fliegerausbildung

28. (cont'd)
(Russian air training, hereinafter cited as SUF); Ausbildung der Jagdflieger (fighter-pilot training, hereinafter cited as AJ); BKSUF; Jaegereinsatz im Osten, 8 Jan 1945, Luftflottenkommando 6 (fighter commitment in the East, a report of Sixth Air Fleet, hereinafter cited as JIO); LLBO, 1 Jan 1945 and 1 Feb 1945; Rudel; Bericht eines Staffelfuehrers ueber Luftkaempfe am 11 Feb 1945 in Ostpreussen, in Jaegerblatt, Nos. 7 & 8, n. place, n. pub. (report of a squadron leader on dog fights on 11 Feb 1945 in East Prussia, hereinafter cited as BSFL).

29. Brunner, pp. 11, 14, 17; Jaehne, p. 29; Pitcairn, pp. 6, 8; Reschke, pp. 4-6; v. Riesen, I, p. 6; Wilke, p. 33; ELUH, III, p. 1; BSNO, pp. 1-2; FLO, No. 25, I, pp. 3-4, 15.

30. Wilke, p. 33.

31. Reschke, pp. 14-17.

32. Schlage, pp. 56, 58, 64-68.

33. JIO, pp. 3-4, 8.

34. Huffmann, p. 43.

35. Schlage, p. 57; FLO, No. 25, I, pp. 5-14; VFE, pp. 12-27, 66-90; LLBO, 1 March 1944, p. 10, 1 April 1944, Annex: Flugzeugbestand (aircraft strength), 1 Sept 1944, pp. 9-10, 1 Jan 1945, p. 7.

36. FLO, No. 10, pp. 2-4.

37. Brunner, p. 12; Blasig, pp. 3-4; Rudel, p. 126; Huffmann, III, pp. 26, 42.

38. Pitcairn, p. 8; Schlage, pp. 56, 62, 64, 66; BSNO, pp. 2-3; BKSUF, p. 1.

39. Jaehne, p. 29; Kath, p. 12; Pitcairn, pp. 5-6; Reschke, pp. 4-5; Schlage, pp. 56, 66; Wilke, pp. 17-18, 31; ELUH, III, p. 7; FLO, No. 25, I, pp. 5-6.

40. Blasig, p. 3; Pitcairn, p. 6; Reschke, pp. 5, 15; Schlage, pp. 59, 65.

41. ELUH, III, pp. 1-4.

42. Blasig, p. 2; Huffmann, III, p. 26; Jaehne, p. 29; Pitcairn, p. 6; Reschke, pp. 4, 18; Schlage, p. 67; ELUH, I, p. 8; BKSUF, p. 2.

43. Kath, p. 13.

44. BSFL, pp. 1-2.

45. Brunner, pp. 11-12; v. Riesen, I, p. 7; LLBO, 1 April 1944, pp. 3-4, 8.

46. v. Riesen, I, p. 8.

47. Reschke, p. 4; BSNO, pp. 2-3.

48. Rudel, pp. 114, 127, 149-50, 115-59, 169, 185, 190, 193-95, 250-51.

49. Reschke, pp. 4, 11-15, 17; Schlage, pp. 56, 58-62, 67; Wilke, pp. 17-18, 30-33; BKSUF, p. 1; LLBO, 1 Mar 1944, p. 3, 1 July 1944, p. 1, 1 Oct 1944, p. 2, 1 Nov 1944, p. 2.

50. v. Reschke, p. 13.

51. Ibid., pp. 20-21.

52. Brunner, pp. 12-13.

53. Ibid., pp. 14-16.

54. v. Maubeuge, p. 1; v. Riesen, I, p. 7; FLO, No. 16, pp. 1-3; FLO, No. 10, p. 5, KFFT, pp. 5-6; LLBO, 1 April 1944, p. 5, 1 May 1944, p. 3, 1 June 1944, p. 3.

55. Huffmann, III, pp. 30, 43; Pitcairn, p. 7; Reschke, pp. 15-16, 22; Schlage, pp. 56-57, 63; ELUH, III, p. 4; FLO, No. 38, p. 7; LLBO, 1 March 1944, p. 5.

56. Huffmann, III, pp. 16, 26, 30, 43; Reschke, pp. 6, 16-17, 22; Schlage, p. 57; Wilke, p. 13; ELUH, III, pp. 5-6; LLBO, 1 April 1944, p. 9, 1 May 1944, pp. 3, 7, 1 June 1944, p. 3, 1 July 1944, p. 1, 1 Aug 1944, p. 1, 1 Sept 1944, p. 1, 1 Oct 1944, p. 2, 1 Nov 1944, pp. 7-8, 1 Dec 1944, p. 1, 1 Jan 1945, p. 1, 1 Feb 1945, p. 1.

57. FLO, No. 28, pp. 7-10.

58. Huffmann, III, p. 43; Schlage, pp. 57-58, 65; Rudel, p. 185.

59. Pitcairn, p. 8; Reschke, p. 14; Schlage, pp. 63-64, 66; ELUH, I, p. 3, III, pp. 4-5; BSNO, p. 4; DRL, p. 1; FLO, No. 10, p. 11; LLBO, 1 Feb 1944, p. 8, 1 Mar 1944, p. 10, 1 April 1944, pp. 12-13, 1 Nov 1944, pp. 7-8; BKSUF, p. 2.

60. This section is based on: Contributions by Blasig, Frankewitz, Huffmann, Jaehne, Pickert, Pitcairn, Reschke, v. Riesen, Schlage, Wilke; ELUH; General der Infanterie a.D. Hans von Greiffenberg, Taktik russischer Tiefflieger bei Bekaempfung von Erdzielen (tactics of Russian ground-attack aircraft, hereinafter cited as TRTBE); RLKF; Kampffuehrung der Schlachtflieger, OKL, Ic, Fremde Luftwaffen Ost, 19 Feb 1945 (Luftwaffe High Command Intelligence report on combat command of ground-attack aircraft, hereinafter cited as KSF); FLO, No. 11, V, No. 20, II, No. 28, I, No. 38; OKL, Fuehrungsstab Ic, SU Schlachtfliegertruppe, OKL No. 239 (Luftwaffe High Command Intelligence report No. 239, Russian ground-attack forces, hereinafter cited as SUSFT); VFE; BKSUF; LLBO, 1 Jan 1944 - 1 Feb 1945; Rudel.

61. Jaehne, p. 30; Pickert, p. 7; Pitcairn, p. 9; Reschke, pp. 7-8, 17-18, 23; v. Riesen, II, p. 14; Schlage, p. 69; Wilke, p. 38; RLKF, p. 4; LLBO, 1 March 1944, pp. 1, 5, 1 April 1944, pp. 3-4, 1 May 1944, p. 7, 1 June 1944, p. 2, 1 Sept 1944, p. 1, 1 Dec 1944, p. 1, 1 Jan 1945, p. 1.

62. Huffmann, pp. 27, 45, 49.

63. Schlage, p. 69; SUSFG, pp. 7-9; VFE, pp. 12-16, 28-32, 96-106; LLBO, 1 April 1944 (annex, Flugzeufbestand), 1 May 1944, p. 7, 1 Nov 1944, p. 8, 1 Jan 1945, p. 7.

64. Huffmann, p. 46; Reschke, p. 7; Schlage, pp. 71-72; ELUH, I, pp. 8-9; BKSUF, p. 2.

65. Reschke, pp. 7-8; Schlage, p. 71; ELUH, II, p. 4; RLKF, p. 4; KSF, pp. 2-4; SUSFT, pp. 21-23, 31.

66. Huffmann, III, pp. 14-25; Pitcairn, pp. 9-10; Reschke, pp. 7, 10; Wilke, pp. 36-37; ELUH, I, p. 9; ELUH, II, pp. 2-8; TRTBE, pp. 2-4; FLO, No. 20, II, pp. 1-2; KSF, pp. 3, 5.

67. Frankewitz, p. 16; Huffmann, III, pp. 5, 7-11, 16, 24-25, 29-30, 46; TRTBE, pp. 2-4.

68. Reschke, pp. 15, 21; Schlage, p. 70; Wilke, pp. 33-34; ELUH, II, p. 8; LLBO, 1 Sept 1944, p. 1; LLBO, 1 Nov 1944, pp. 7-8.

69. Konteradmiral a. D. Otto Schulz, in a letter to the author; FLO, No. 28, I, pp. 10-11.

70. Blasig, p. 4; Reschke, pp. 10, 16, 18-19; Schlage, p. 70; Wilke, pp. 35, 38-39; ELUH, II, p. 8; TRTBE, p. 4.

71. Huffmann, III, p. 47; Schlage, p. 70; Wilke, p. 35; KSF, p. 3; LLBO, 1 April 1944, p. 5.

72. Reschke, p. 23; Schlage, p. 70; Wilke, p. 36.

73. Huffmann, III, p. 17; Reschke, p. 22; Wilke, p. 38; ELUH, II, pp. 6-7; FLO, No. 38, pp. 22-25; KSF, p. 4.

74. Reschke, p. 8; Schlage, p. 71; FLO, No. 20, II, pp. 3-8; KSF, pp. 1-2; SUSFT, pp. 11-18; Ausruestung der IL-2 mit 3.7-cm Kanone (equipping the IL-2 with 3.7 cm canons, hereinafter cited as AIL-2), pp. 10-12.

75. This section is based on: Contributions by Blasig, Brunner, Major a. D. H. Franke, Frankewitz, Huffmann, Jaehne, Mahlke, Pickert, Pitcairn, Reschke, v. Riesen, Colonel a. D. H. Schalke (General Staff), Schlage, Schulz, Wilke, Deichmann; ELUH; ERLUS; SSHUM; Hoffmann; LVKR; VFE; BKSUF; KFFT; RLKF; Einsaetze der SU-Kampffliegertruppe im Monat September 1944 (Skizze), (commitment of Russian bomber forces, Sept 1944, (sketch) hereinafter cited as ESUKT);

75. (cont'd)
FLO, Nos. 16, 11, 28 (I, II, III); LLBO, 1 Jan 1944 - 1 Feb 1945; Ic Feindnachrichten No. 1, Auffrischungsstab Ost, 29 Feb 1944 (an Intelligence report on enemy information, Refitting Staff, East, hereinafter cited as FNAO); Rudel.

76. Brunner, p. 17; Jaehne, p. 30; Mahlke, pp. 3-4; Reschke, pp. 9, 12, 18, 21; Schlage, pp. 72-73; Wilke, pp. 18, 39-42; ELUH, II, p. 9; Hoffmann, III, p. 2; LVKR, p. 1; KFFT, pp. 1-2; FLO, 11, III, p. 6; RLKF, pp. 2-5; LLBO, 1 Jan 1944, p. 6, 1 Feb 1944, pp. 2, 5-6, 1 March 1944, pp. 1, 7, 1 April 1944, p. 3, 1 June 1944, p. 2, 1 July 1944, p. 1, 1 Aug 1944, p. 1, 1 Sept. 1944, p. 1, 1 Oct 1944, pp. 1-2, 1 Nov 1944, pp. 1-2, 5, 1 Dec 1944, p. 1, 1 Jan 1945, pp. 1-2, 5, 1 Feb 1945, p. 1.

77. Schlage, p. 73; Hoffmann, III, pp. 2-3; LVKR, p. 1; KFFT, p. 1; VFE, pp. 12-16, 33-39, 107-25; FNAO, pp. 203; LLBO, 1 March 1944, p. 10, 1 April 1944, p. 7 (Annex Flugzeugbestand), 1 May 1944, p. 5, 1 June 1944, p. 6, 1 Aug 1944, p. 6, 1 Sept 1944, p. 7, 1 Oct 1944, p. 7, 1 Nov 1944, p. 6, 1 Jan 1945, pp. 1, 7, 1 Feb 1945, p. 4.

78. Brunner, p. 19; SSHUM, p. 6; Mahlke, p. 4; Reschke, p. 20; Schlage, p. 47; BKSUF, p. 3; LLBO, 1 March 1944, p. 8.

79. Reschke, p. 9; ELUH, III, pp. 8-9; KFFT, p. 3; FLO, No. 16, pp. 1-2; LLBO, 1 Feb 1944, p. 7, 1 Oct 1944, p. 2.

80. Pitcairn, pp. 12-13; Reschke, pp. 9, 15, 17, 19; Wilke, p. 40; ELUH, II, pp. 9-12.

81. Franke, pp. 3-4; Huffmann, III, pp. 8-9, 12, 14-15, 25, 53-54; Reschke, p. 15; Konteradmiral a.D. Otto Schulz, in a letter to the author.

82. Schalke, p. 2; Schulz letter; ERLUS, pp. 7-8, 10-12, 16-17, 19; SSHUM, pp. 4, 6; FLO, No. 28, I, pp. 12-15, 18-23.

83. Brunner, p. 17; Jaehne, pp. 30-31; Pickert, pp. 7-8; Reschke, pp. 10, 12, 17-19; v. Riesen, II, pp. 13-14; Schlage, p. 47; Rudel, p. 202.

84. Brunner, p. 18; Pitcairn, pp. 10-11; Reschke, p. 7; ELUH, III, pp. 8-11; KFFT, pp. 3-4; LLBO: 1 April 1944, p. 4; 1 May 1944, p. 3.

85. Blasig, p. 4; Pickert, p. 7; Reschke, pp. 7, 10, 13, 21; Schlage, p. 73; Wilke, p. 41; KFFT, p. 4; ESUKT; LLBO: 1 April 1944, p. 4; 1 May 1944, p. 3; 1 June 1944, p. 3.

86. Mahlke, pp. 4-5; Schlage, p. 74; Deichmann, p. 5; FLO, 11, III, pp. 6-8; LLBO, 1 April 1944, p. 4, 1 June 1944, p. 3.

87. Pickert, p. 7; Deichmann, p. 5; FLO, No. 16, pp. 4-5; FLO, 11, III, pp. 6-8.

88. Wilke, p. 41; ERLUS, p. 19; FLO, 11, III, p. 5.

89. Reschke, pp. 8-9; Deichmann, p. 5; Hoffmann, III, p. 2; FLO, No. 16, pp. 7-8; KFFT, pp. 2-3; FLO, 11, III, p. 6; FNAO, pp. 8-10.

90. This section is based on: Contributions by Reschke, Wilke; General der Flieger a.D. Veit Fischer, Versorgung russischer Banden auf dem Luftwege (Air supply of Russian partisan units, hereinafter cited as VRBAL); KFFT; FLO, No. 11, IV; FLO, No. 16.

91. Reschke, p. 24; KFFT, p. 6; FLO, No. 16, pp. 1-2.

92. Reschke, pp. 16, 24; Wilke, p. 25.

93. Wilke, pp. 25-26; VRBAL, pp. 2-5; KFFT, p. 7; FLO, No. 11, IV, pp. 8-10.

94. This section is based on: Contributions by Brunner, Jaehne, Reschke, Schlage, Wilke; FLO, No. 25, I, No. 36; LLBO, 1 Jan 1944 - 1 Feb 1945; Russische Aushilfen und Findigkeiten, OKL Fuehrungsstab Ic, Fremde Luftwaffen Ost (Russian improvisations and ingenuity, an Intelligence bulletin of the Luftwaffe High Command, hereinafter cited as RA).

95. Brunner, pp. 15-16; Jaehne, p. 31; Reschke, pp. 12, 24; Schlage, p. 76; Wilke, p. 42; LLBO, 1 June 1944, p. 4, 1 Aug 1944, pp. 4, 7, 1 Nov 1944, p. 5, 1 Dec 1944, p. 5, 1 Feb 1945, pp. 4-5.

96. Reschke, pp. 12, 24; RA, pp. 8, 17; LLBO, 1 Aug 1944, p. 7.

97. Reschke, p. 24; FLO, No. 25, I, pp. 13-14, No. 36, pp. 15-18; RA, pp. 8-17.

98. Reschke, p. 5; Wilke, p. 43; FLO, No. 36, p. 19; LLBO, 1 March 1944, p. 10.

99. This section is based on: LVKR; FLO, Nos. 10, 38; SU-Luftnachrichtentruppe, Stand Mai 1944, Luftwaffenfuehrungsstab Ic, Fremde Luftwaffen Ost (a Luftwaffe Intelligence report on Russian air signal corps as of May 1944, hereinafter cited as SULNT); SUSFT; Dienstanweisung fuer die Organisation von Nachrichtenverbindungen bei den Fliegerverbaenden (OKL No. 122), (service regulations for the organization of signal communications by air force units, hereinafter cited as DONV).

100. SULNT, pp. 2-4.

101. SULNT, pp. 3-11, 13, 26-29; DONV, p. 7.

102. SUSFT, p. 33; FLO, No. 10, pp. 29-30, No. 38, pp. 19-20; DONV, pp. 2, 5, 32-33.

103. FLO, No. 10, p. 12; LVKR, p. 1.

104. SULNT, pp. 12-13, 29; DONV, p. 18.

105. This section is based on: "Ausbildungswesen," SU-Fliegertruppe, Luftwaffenfuehrungsstab Ic, Fremde Luftwaffen Ost (a Luftwaffe bulletin on Russian Air Force training, hereinafter cited as AUSW); SUF; AJ; SUSFT.

106. This section is based on: FLO, No. 11, IV; FLO, No. 14; "Luftlandetruppen" /"airborne troops"/, in SU Fliegertruppe, Luftwaffenfuehrungsstab Ic/Fremde Luftwaffen Ost (hereinafter cited as SUFL).

107. This section is based on: ERLUS; RA; Verlagerung von Flugzeugwerken, Auszug aus einem Protokoll des Jaegerstabes vom 19.5.44 (extract from the minutes of the Fighter Staff for 19 May 1944, concerning the displacement of aircraft

107. (cont'd)
factories); SUFFF; SU Flugzeugausbringung und Gesamtverluste im Dezember 1944 und im Maerz 1945 (sketches showing Russian production and total losses of aircraft for Dec 1944 and March 1945, hereinafter cited as SUFG); Die Luftruestungsindustrie der Sowjetunion, Stand September 1944, Luftflottenkommando 6, Fuehrungsabteilung I/Ic (an Intelligence report of Sixth Air Fleet on the status of the Russian air armament industry in September 1944, hereinafter cited as LSSS); "Ruestungswirtschaft" /"armament economy"/, in Der Frontsoldat erzaehlt, No. 7, 1952, n. place, n. pub.

108. ERLUS, p. 30; SUFFF, pp. 1-2; SUFG; LSSS, pp. 3-5, 7-8, 12-14.

109. This section is based on: Jaehne, Reschke; Schlage; FLO, No. 25, I; LLBO, 1 Jan 1944 - 1 Feb 1945; LSSS.

110. Jaehne, p. 31; Reschke, p. 16; FLO, No. 25, I, p. 16.

111. LLBO, 1 July 1944, p. 2, 1 Aug 1944, p. 1; 1 Sept 1944, p. 2.

112. Schlage, p. 77; Rudel, p. 172; LLBO, 1 Jan 1944, pp. 14-15; LSSS, pp. 8-9.

Appendix 1

LIST OF EQUIVALENT LUFTWAFFE AND USAF GENERAL OFFICER RANKS

Reichsmarschall des Grossdeutschen Reiches (Goering's rank: Reichs Marshal of the Pan-German Reich)	No equivalent
Generalfeldmarschall	General of the Air Force (Army)
Generaloberst	General
General der Flieger (der Flak, etc.)	Lieutenant General
Generalleutnant	Major General
Generalmajor	Brigadier General

The initials a. D. /ausser Dienst/ given between an officer's rank and his name indicate "retired" status.

Appendix 2

LIST OF GAF MONOGRAPH PROJECT STUDIES

I. Published

Study No.	Title
173	The German Air Force General Staff
175	The Russian Air Force in the Eyes of German Commanders
189	Historical Turning Points in the German Air Force War Effort

II. To be Published at a Later Date

Study No.	Title
150	The German Air Force in the Spanish War
151	The German Air Force in Poland
152	The German Air Force in France and the Low Countries (including Airlanding Operations in Belgium and the Netherlands)
153-155	The German Air Force versus Russia on the Eastern Front
156	The Battle of Britain
157	Operation Sea Lion
158-160	The German Air Force versus the Allies in the West
161	The German Air Force versus the Allies in the Mediterranean
162	The Battle of Crete

Study No.	Title
163 & 165	German Air Force Close Support and Air Interdiction Operations
164	German Air Force Air Defense Operations
166	German Air Force Counter Air Operations
167	German Air Force Airlift Operations
168	German Air Force Air-Sea Rescue Operations
169	Training in the German Air Force
170	Procurement in the German Air Force
171	Intelligence in the German Air Force
172	German Air Force Medicine
174	Command and Leadership in the German Air Force (Goering, Milch, Jeschonnek, Udet, Wever)
176	Russian Patterns of Reaction to the German Air Force
177	Russian Use of Airlift to Supply Partisan Forces
178	Problems of Fighting a Three-Front Air War
179	Problems of Waging a Day and Night Defensive Air War
180	The Problem of the Long-Range Night Intruder Bomber
181	The Problem of Air Superiority in the Battle with Allied Strategic Air Forces
182	Fighter-Bomber Operations in Situations of Air Inferiority

Study No.	Title
183	Analysis of Specialized Anglo-American Techniques
184	Effects of Allied Air Attacks on German Divisional and Army Organizations on the Battle Fronts
185	Effects of Allied Air Attacks on German Air Force Bases and Installations
186	The German Air Force System of Target Analysis
187	The German Air Force System of Weapons Selection
188	German Civil Air Defense
190	The Organization of the German Air Force High Command and Higher Echelon Headquarters within the German Air Force

www.ingramcontent.com/pod-product-compliance
Lightning Source LLC
Chambersburg PA
CBHW080721300426
44114CB00019B/2443